Strategic Public Relations Management

Strategic Public Relations Management features an applied approach to evidence-based, strategic public relations management. It emphasizes understanding audiences through research and demonstrates success through quantitative evaluation methods. This volume presents a scientific approach that helps future and current practitioners understand and communicate the value of public relations to others, using performance metrics to demonstrate return on investment.

New to the third edition:

- New examples on the effective use of digital communication and online research tools;
- Updated guidance on researching using digital tools and social media;
- New examples that provide a more accessible pathway to real-world application.

In addition to these new features, the book covers:

- Creating a framework for planning;
- Up-to-date research tools and how to develop a research plan;
- Gathering useful data for strategic guidance;
- Real-world examples that provide readers with realistic cases and situations;
- Applying theory to professional practice.

The book's accessibility will be welcomed by instructors and students with definitions of terms, a how-to approach, and a pragmatic consideration of research.

Erica Weintraub Austin is Vice Provost for Academic Affairs and Director of the Murrow Center for Media and Health Promotion Research at Washington State University.

Bruce E. Pinkleton is Professor and Director of Research and Graduate Studies in the Edward R. Murrow College of Communication at Washington State University.

Routledge Communication Series

Jennings Bryant/Dolf Zillmann, Series Editors

Selected titles include:

- Preiss et al: *Mass Media Effects Research: Advances Through Meta-Analysis*
- Gayle et al: *Classroom Communication and Instructional Processes: Advances Through Meta-Analysis*
- Allen et al: *Interpersonal Communication Research: Advances Through Meta-Analysis*
- Burrell et al: *Managing Interpersonal Communication: Advances Through Meta-Analysis*

Strategic Public Relations Management

Planning and Managing Effective Communication Programs

Third Edition

Erica Weintraub Austin
Bruce E. Pinkleton

Routledge
Taylor & Francis Group

NEW YORK AND LONDON

Third edition published 2015
by Routledge
711 Third Avenue, New York, NY 10017

and by Routledge
2 Park Square, Milton Park, Abingdon, Oxon, OX14 4RN

Routledge is an imprint of the Taylor & Francis Group, an informa business

First edition published by Routledge 2000
Second edition published by Routledge 2006

Library of Congress Cataloging in Publication Data
Austin, Erica Weintraub.
    Strategic public relations management: planning and managing
    effective communication programs/Erica Weintraub Austin,
    Bruce E. Pinkleton. — 3rd edition.
    Includes bibliographical references and index.
    1. Public relations—Management. I. Pinkleton, Bruce E. II. Title.
    HD59.A97 2015
    659.2—dc23
    2014023917

ISBN: 978–0–415–51768–3 (hbk)
ISBN: 978–0–415–51769–0 (pbk)
ISBN: 978–1–315–75483–3 (ebk)

Typeset in Times New Roman
by Florence Production Ltd, Stoodleigh, Devon, UK

Contents

Preface to
the Third Edition

We wrote the first edition of this book after attending a national Public Relations Society of America convention in Seattle. We had observed with some surprise that the sessions on measurement and evaluation attracted standing-room-only crowds, and many conversations in the hallways focused on the same issues. Managers seemed frustrated with the challenges of proving the value of public relations and developing credibility as counselors to upper management. Meanwhile, discussions about the need to prove results in the trade press had increased steadily. We were getting calls from organizations wanting research that never before had seen the need for it. We had alumni reporting back to us about how well their coursework in research and planning had prepared them for the so-called real world and how their training had positioned them advantageously in their organizations. Both experience and observation had taught us that research and strategic planning serve as powerful tools.

We continue to see a hunger for accessible research and strategic planning tools among professionals and students, partly because the tools keep evolving. As a result, just as strategic plans need updating every few years, we have realized we need to provide another update to our book. As authors and teachers, we wrote this volume to serve as our ideal resource for our own classes and then hoped others would find it useful, too. We have felt honored and gratified that many other teachers and practitioners also have put it to use successfully since publication of the first edition in 2001. We have appreciated the feedback and suggestions we have received from them.

This edition highlights how the field of evidence-based communication management continues to change. Digital communication and online research tools provide many new opportunities and challenges that innovative communication managers have put to work effectively. We have many new examples to share that can help others continue to advance the field.

The primary changes in this edition cover two main areas. First, we have updated the information on research methods to incorporate methods that make use of digital tools and social media. Second, because we believe in learning by seeing and doing, we have updated examples and added examples in spots that seemed to need more accessible pathways to real-world application.

We would like to thank those of you who have given this book a try and provided us with feedback. We encourage others to contact us as well so that we can continue to make the book as useful as possible. We also would like to express our deep appreciation to Michelle Kistler, who has checked our work, offered additional ideas and tracked down references and permissions for material we have reproduced. Finally, we owe a debt of gratitude to Brett Atwood and Rebecca Cooney who provided helpful feedback and suggestions regarding the digital-communication additions to the book, and to Davi Kallman who provided tremendous last-minute help with examples.

As before, we again want to extend our grateful thanks to the many individuals and organizations who have served as role models for us as we have worked to bridge applied and academic experiences. These have included our own teachers and mentors, colleagues in the academic and professional communities, our students and our alumni.

We also have appreciated the helpfulness and expertise of senior editor Linda Bathgate and assistant editor Chad Hollingsworth. We are grateful for the advice and support of Stan and Rodelle Weintraub, who have written many more books than we ever will and who make it look easy. Finally, we continue to owe a monstrous debt to our families for their unselfish support and incredible patience.

Erica Weintraub Austin
Bruce E. Pinkleton

The Need for Strategic Public Relations Management

Chapter Contents

- Surviving Amid Fierce Competition
- Strategic Versus Tactical Decision Making
- Defining Public Relations
- The Often Misunderstood Role of Public Relations
- Using Research to Enhance the Credibility of Public Relations
- Organization of the Book

Strategic public relations planning and research techniques have evolved into the most powerful tools available to public relations practitioners. Success requires practitioners to demonstrate in a measurable way how the results from public relations programs benefit the organizations they serve. Practitioners well prepared to use the tools available to them can enjoy bigger budgets, more autonomy in decision making, and greater support from management. On the other hand, managers who rely on an intuitive model of public relations based on their knowledge of media markets and a well-developed network of contacts have less credibility, enjoy less autonomy, receive lower priority, and suffer greater risk of cost cutting that threatens job security.

Surviving Amid Fierce Competition

The increasingly competitive business and social environment makes it critical for public relations managers to understand how to apply public relations planning, research, and program-evaluation practices that help ensure success and demonstrate accountability. Research-based public relations practices enable managers to solve complex problems, set and achieve or exceed goals and objectives, track the opinions and beliefs of key publics, and employ program strategies with confidence. Although the use of research in public relations management cannot guarantee program success, it allows practitioners to maximize their abilities and move beyond reactionary management to scientific management. An evidence-based and strategic management style can help control the ways a situation will develop and the outcomes practitioners achieve in those situations.

Consider the following scenarios in which communication professionals can use research-based planning to develop effective strategies for solving a problem and demonstrate program success.

Community Relations

You are the public affairs director for the largest employer in a community. The local media have been running stories about problems at the company, claiming management has lost sight of its unique role in the community. The board of directors wants a clear understanding of public perceptions of the company. It also wants to develop new programs that will better serve the community and improve community relations. You remain unconvinced the company needs to establish new programs more than it needs to support its existing programs. How do you determine the opinions and attitudes of community members toward the company? How do you measure community perceptions of existing programs, as well as community interest in new programs? How can you convince your board to embrace the most effective course of action?

Special Events Planning and Promotion

You are the manager of a performing arts coliseum. The coliseum has lost money on several events over the past 2 years and now is threatened by competition from a new community theater scheduled for construction in 2 years. The coliseum management and its board of directors sense they have lost touch with the community and are unsure how to address the situation. How can management determine community programming interests and begin to reorient itself to the needs and desires of community members without wasting valuable resources?

Political Campaign

You are the campaign manager for a state senatorial candidate. The mostly-rural district has 75,000 registered voters, many of whom work as farmers or in farming-related businesses and industries. The election is 9 months away, and the candidates already are engaged in a close contest. How do you track changes in voters' perceptions of your candidate as the election nears?

Nonprofit

You are a public relations practitioner at a small, nonprofit organization. Your new assignment is to rescue a local special event with a troubled history. The event, sponsored by the local chamber of commerce, is supposed to raise money for your organization while attracting visitors who patronize businesses in your community. The most recent event was a disaster, however, despite a strong media relations effort that included social media. Because of low attendance, the organization barely broke even on the event, and local businesses have lost interest in participating next year as sponsors. How do you find out what went wrong and make next year's event a success?

Development

You are a senior development officer at a major university. Development, also known as philan-thropic giving, has gained importance as state budgets have dwindled. Just as the university is making preparations for the largest development campaign in its history, students let their partying get out of hand after a big football win over their cross-state rivals. The fracas attracts national media attention. You worry the negative media attention will significantly hinder university development efforts. You need to understand the opinions and attitudes of key segments of the public to quickly develop and implement a plan that will allow you to respond in an effective manner. How do you determine the responses of donors and non-donors to news of the disturbance?

Public relations practitioners face problems like these on a regular basis. Small problems can help organizations deal with bigger ones when they arise. J. Wayne Leonard, the chief executive of Entergy, the power company serving the New Orleans area, said his company felt prepared for the unprecedented catastrophe of 2005's Hurricane Katrina because "we have the skills and planning to deal with catastrophe because we deal with it on a small scale all the time." Besides the company's efforts to restore power to 1.1 million customers, his management response included evacuation for his own employees, assurances that their jobs would be preserved, coordination with government officials, and making sure "front-line" employees were "em-powered to make common-sense decisions" (Feder, 2005, p. B2). Similarly, Lt. Sue Kerver of the Coast Guard explained that they coped effectively with the BP oil spill in 2010 because they had prepared and trained to implement a multifaceted plan and to adjust it based on how events evolve: "The last thing you want to do is create a crisis plan during a crisis," she said (Williamson, 2011, ¶ 2).

Preparation also can include learning from others, known in the business as *secondary research.* In other words, not all situations can be practiced and not all lessons need to be learned the hard way. John Deveny of Deveny Public Relations in New Orleans felt prepared to work with the Louisiana Office of Tourism when Katrina and the BP oil spill happened because he had spent time tracking others' experiences and results. In particular, he employed his analysis of Nashville's success following its own natural disaster in 2010 to respond to the BP oil spill aftermath. "You have to prepare a proactive and a reactive strategy."

Strategic Versus Tactical Decision Making

According to Dick Martin (2005), who served as executive vice president of public relations for AT&T until his retirement, successful public relations management requires acting as "an honest broker" who understands the concerns of internal and external stakeholders "and can synthesize them into a perspective the CEO can actually use." Martin went on to say, "it means making forecasts instead of compiling yesterday's clips, and backing up those predictions with plans for dealing with them" (p. 23). In other words, successful public relations management requires strategic research and strategic planning.

Research helps practitioners acquire accurate information quickly at a relatively low cost to aid them in sophisticated planning and problem solving every day. When practitioners respond to organizational problems and challenges by engaging in media relations campaigns, they typically respond tactically instead of strategically. Strategic decision making is goal directed and guided by an organization's larger purpose. According to Fred Nickols (2000), "strategy is the bridge between policy or high-order goals on the one hand and tactics or concrete actions on the other." Tactical decision making, on the other hand, focuses more on day-to-day actions and therefore tends to be more response oriented in nature. Tactical decision making can allow public relations programs and campaigns to drift aimlessly, lacking direction or purpose. Practitioners often use media clips as the basis for tactic-based program accountability, but the benefits of clip-based evaluation are limited. It is impossible, for example, for practitioners to determine message effects on targeted audiences' opinions, attitudes, or behavior using clips. Practitioners find their ability to solve organizations' problems through such a response also severely limited because no basis exists for determining the extent of a problem or evaluating the results of their programs.

Finally, organizational managers can become frustrated in their attempts to adapt to changing internal and external environments because practitioners have no basis for understanding and accomplishing the steps necessary to successfully address or accommodate stakeholders' opinions. The result is that practitioners' success may be limited. They typically end up in a defensive position with external and internal audiences, having little basis for effectively communicating the benefits of their campaigns and programs to organizational management.

When practitioners respond to problems and challenges strategically instead of tactically, they have a much greater likelihood of helping organizations meet their challenges, solve or avoid protracted problems, and adjust to the expectations of key stakeholders in mutually beneficial ways. Research and planning are not simple remedies for every organizational problem. No amount of research or planning, for example, can rescue an organization from the consequences of its own poor performance. Nevertheless, practitioners' use of research, planning, and evaluation contribute to an informed organizational decision-making process with a greater likelihood of success. When practitioners use these tools, their programs and campaigns can have clear goals that direct program implementation. Practitioners can use formative research to set initial measurement levels—called benchmarks—for goals and objectives and to determine campaign strategy. Practitioners using tactics purposefully and selectively can communicate the benefits of public relations campaigns and programs to organizational management more easily. Ultimately, practitioners have the opportunity to enjoy greater success at placing their organizations in stable, mutually beneficial relationships with key target-audience members when they engage in strategic planning and problem solving.

Defining Public Relations

The first step toward successful public relations management requires adopting a clear definition by which to live. This is a surprisingly difficult task. We will start with the official definition of public relations adopted by the Public Relations Society of American in February of 2012: "Public relations is a strategic communication process that builds mutually beneficial relationships between organizations and their publics."

In their widely adopted textbook, Broom and Sha (2013) similarly defined public relations as "the management function that establishes and maintains mutually beneficial relationships between an organization and the publics on whom its success or failure depends." These definitions, although simple on their face, actually suggest a complex set of processes. For public relations practitioners to operate as managers, for example, they cannot simply input the decisions made by others in an organization. They need to assert themselves as members of what is commonly called the *dominant coalition*, those members of an organization who have the authority to make decisions and set policy. In other words, they need to help lead organizations and not just provide communication services to them. As Arthur W. Page, widely considered a founder of corporate public relations management, famously said, "Public perception of an organization is determined 90% by what it does and 10% by what it says." Practitioners operating as service providers instead of as management consultants commonly find themselves limited to advocating organizational viewpoints. This prevents them from helping the organization build and maintain long-term relationships that ensure long-term organizational success, which requires some adjustment to public perceptions and needs. As Edward L. Bernays, often called the founder of modern public relations, cautioned, public relations should be considered a social science and must serve the public interest (Bernays, 1923).

Agencies think they do better at building long-term relationships than their clients do. A 2004 survey of about 600 public relations executives and about 87 corporate public relations executives, by the Counselors Academy and sponsored by *PR News,* found that agencies often believe they act strategically, but clients think agencies' actions display more of a tactical orientation ("PR Measurement," 2004). As Chapter 3 explains, tactics represent day-to-day tasks and may ignore how those tasks fit the priorities of an overall strategy. According to 73% of the clients surveyed, at least half of the services agencies provide should be strategic in nature. Less than 33% however, believe that PR agencies deliver that type of focus. Meanwhile, a full 87% of agencies agree their emphasis should tilt toward strategy, and 62% think they deliver on this priority. Both clients and agencies agreed that "more meaningful" measurement would improve their relationships, although they differed on other actions that should take priority.

The Often Misunderstood Role of Public Relations

Public relations practices encompass a broad range of activities that can lead to confusion about how public relations differs from marketing and advertising. The goals of each differ in important ways. *Advertising* typically focuses on selling products to consumers through controlled placement of paid media messages—a narrow and specific role. *Marketing*, including integrated marketing communications, often uses public relations techniques to sell products and services. The marketing role is broader than that of advertising but still focuses on consumers rather than on all the key publics of an organization. *Public relations*, on the other hand, strives to help organizations develop and preserve the variety of stakeholder relationships that ensure long-term success, and typically has broader goals than those of advertising or marketing. These stakeholders can include not only consumers but also government regulators, community members, shareholders, members of the media, employees, and others. Therefore, although advertising and marketing often employ public relations techniques, it is more appropriate for organizational management to treat public relations as the umbrella under which other activities, including marketing and advertising, occur.

Many practitioners struggle with the fact that this is difficult to put into practice, and they often find their role misunderstood. A survey of members of the New York chapter of the Public Relations Society of America (PRSA), for example, found that 92% believed that most people do not understand what public relations is ("PR Pros," 1998). The experience of the Public Relations Society of America, which worked in 2011 to develop a consensus definition of public relations, shows that practitioners themselves often disagree on what public relations means. Their invitation to professionals to submit suggestions elicited 927 definitions. Relying on the top 20 words used in definitions, blog posts and online commentary, the task force then developed a set of three definitions. An online vote picked the winner, which replaced a vague definition that had been developed in 1982.

Partly because of the difficulties associated with defining the field, public relations also suffers from low credibility. In the New York survey, 93% of the professionals said they enjoyed their work, and 68% were proud of their field, but 67% believed the field did not have a good image and 65% believed they were not as respected as members of other professions. This image problem has been supported by a variety of other studies as well. For example, another credibility study undertaken by PRSA found the public relations specialist ranked almost at the bottom of a list of approximately 50 professions (Public Relations Society of America, 1999). A Gallup poll of 1008 adults in 2011 found advertising and public relations rated positively by 32% of the respondents, negatively by 37% and neutral by 29%. Although this placed public relations below the computer industry, restaurants, agriculture, movies, sports and utilities, it ranked ahead of airlines and education, attorneys, healthcare, oil and gas industries, and the federal government.

To improve their stature within organizations and among a broad range of publics, public relations professionals must take a planned, strategic approach to their programs and problem solving. When operating as subordinates instead of organizational leaders, practitioners implement decisions made by others instead of contributing to organizational decision making. In short, they work at a tactical level. In 2004, only 25% of agencies believed they were "very involved" in helping clients research, discuss, and decide the business goals relevant to their communication programs ("While Agencies," 2004). As leading experts continue to emphasize, communication specialists who operate as technicians cannot effectively solve organizational problems, build public consensus or position an organization on issues of strategic importance (e.g., Broom & Dozier, 1990; Broom & Sha, 2013; Dozier et al., 1995; Harrison, 2013; "Keys," 1998; "M&As," 1998; "Personal competency," 1998; "Reputation," 1994; Rockland, 2013).

Using Research to Enhance the Credibility of Public Relations

One reason communication specialists experience frustration and insufficient credibility appears to lie in how they conduct and apply research. According to Bruce Jeffries-Fox (Jeffries-Fox, 2004), much public relations research serves only as window dressing. The situation seems to have changed little since a national survey of 300 professionals in 1996 found that managers see themselves in a double bind (Pinkleton, Austin, & Dixon, 1999). Professionals reported clients and CEOs as enthusiastic about research but reluctant about providing the budget to pay for it. In that study, the more the managers performed a specific type of research, the less they valued it, and the more they valued a particular research method, the less they employed it. As shown in Table 1.1, practitioners relied most on measures of volume of media pickups and tracking of media coverage, which they found the least beneficial.

On the other hand, practitioners relied least on measures of changes in awareness, knowledge, attitudes, sales, and behavior, which they found the most valuable. The results also showed that the professionals almost uniformly embraced research as vital for proving that public relations programs are effective, but less than half agreed that research is accepted as an important part of public relations. A 1995 PRSA survey also found that 92% believed research was talked about more than used (Public Relations Society of America, 1995).

Table 1.1 Use and Value Of Research Measures Among Public Relations Practitioners

Research measure	Mean for use (rank)	Mean for perceived value (rank)
Advertising equivalency	3.71 (9)	3.37 (9)
Volume of media pickups	5.43 (2)	4.57 (8)
Favorable media treatment	5.35 (3)	4.96 (7)
Media coverage	5.47 (1)	5.19 (5)
Changes in awareness	4.95 (4)	5.64 (4)
Changes in knowledge	4.85 (5)	5.90 (2)
Changes in attitudes	4.74 (6)	5.77 (3)
Changes in sales	4.07 (8)	5.08 (6)
Changes in behavior	4.64 (7)	6.02 (1)

Note. All measures on 7-point scales, with 1 indicating less use or value and 7 indicating more use or value.

This pattern of results suggests that constraints prevent communication professionals from doing enough research, or at least enough of the type of research clients and senior executives find compelling. It comes as little surprise, then, that more than third of respondents to a survey in 2004 considered credibility of the profession a major issue for them ("2005 Challenge," 2005).

Measurement still ranks as a top concern, with annual measurement and research conferences drawing big crowds. An international survey of 520 public relations professions in 2009 by the Association for the Measurement and Evaluation of Communication and the Institute for Public Relations found that 88% of professionals consider measurement an integral part of the PR process, and most (77%) said they actually do it (Wright, Gaunt, Leggetter, Daniels, & Zerfass, 2009). Tables 1.2 and 1.3 illustrate the 2009 data on the perceived importance of various measurement tools and methods. The survey found no consensus, however, on what to measure or how to measure it.

A majority of practitioners continue to prioritize publicity placement in their budgeting (Cone & Feldman, 2004; "PR and Sales," 2005). According to Carole Cone, reporting on a *PR News*/Counselors Academy survey of 364 public relations executives (Cone & Feldman, 2004), budgeting challenges greatly damage accountability efforts. Cone asserted that stand-alone funding for public relations research rarely rose above $2,000, although some larger companies were beginning to set a higher standard. But if most proposed research focuses on tactical-level publicity instead of on more valuable research that demonstrates effects, why should clients devote more money to the enterprise? Todd Defren of Shift Communications ("PR and Sales," 2005) noted that public relations executives often have emphasized "wrong-headed thinking about how to measure PR success, such as buzz phrases like 'Share of Voice' or 'Ad Value Equivalency.' Everyone's trying to measure PR the way other people measure other marketing programs, and it's not working" (p. 3). Measuring the wrong things can make it look as if communication programs accomplish less than they really do. In addition, with online measurement techniques having become so easy to use, it can seem as if every company and organization are surveying everyone all the time about everything. This can try respondents' patience and compromise the value of research results. Measurement projects, like public

Table 1.2 Measurement Criteria and Ranking

Criterion	%	Position
Hit target media	20	1
On time, on budget	16	2
Measures of message output	16	2
Awareness/image	15	4
Client satisfaction	15	4
Achievement of goals	15	4
Other	3	7

(Wright, et al., 2009)

Table 1.3 Measurement Tools and Ranking

Tool	2009 (%)	Position	2004 (%)	Position
Clippings	17	1	n/a	
Internal reviews	10	2	10	5
Advertising value equivalency	10	3	17	1
Benchmarking	10	4	14	3
Media evaluation tools	9	5	15	2
Blog measures	8	6	n/a	
Dashboards	7	7	6	7
Traditional opinion survey	7	8	8	6
Online opinion surveys	6	9	n/a	
Reputation index	6	10	n/a	
Focus groups	5	11	12	4
League tables	3	12	4	8
Other	1	13	3	9

(Wright, et al., 2009)

relations efforts themselves, need to be done strategically. One exasperated practitioner and consumer responded with a blog entitled, "Infant who begins Babies 'R' Us customer satisfaction survey dies of old age" (Grimes, 2012, p. B1).

Despite the challenges, the field seems to have made some progress on measurement issues. Some have called the new millennium the *Neolithic Age* for public relations measurement, a time of tremendous change ("Measurement, " 2003). Experts assert measurement has become more mainstream and that agencies that effectively incorporate measurement into their proposals obtain bigger budgets overall. Increasingly, practitioners are focusing on the demonstration of appropriate communication outcomes ("PR Measurement," 2004; Wright, et al., 2009). This demonstration requires finding something simple that connects communication efforts to better business performance. The authors emphasized that this requires some creativity to go beyond standard return on investment (ROI) measures. "ROI is one of the most overused terms in the business," noted Barr, a founder of a PR measurement firm (p. 6).

Moving from a tactical approach to a strategic management style requires skillful use of research and planning techniques. Managers need to anticipate problems and opportunities instead of merely reacting to them. In addition, an increasingly crowded and complex media and social environment requires practitioners to design innovative programs they can prove will work.

Gaining autonomy and the support and confidence of clients and upper management requires several things. These include providing evidence to support the need for communication programs, reasons why proposed strategies will work, and evidence at the end of a program that the program has indeed worked. In short, strategic public relations management demands a set of abilities that require competence in planning principles, research methods, communication theories, and effective communication presentation skills. Jeffrey Ory of Deveney Communications (Miller, 2005) exhorts public relations professionals to become experts at explaining how effective public relations can be measured and, therefore, how public relations can be used effectively. More professionals appear to be mastering these skills: a 2012 report indicated that corporate budgeting for measurements efforts has risen, on average, to 9% of total public relations budgets. This was more than double the figure from two years before, a demonstration of increasing confidence from top-flight management in evidence-based public relations management. Even more telling, corporate spending on public relations overall was on the increase (USC Annenberg Strategic Communication and Public Relations Center, 2012).

Some communication experts such as Jeffries-Fox (2004) have stated that fear is one of the biggest constraints preventing managers from doing a better job of using research to guide strategic planning and demonstrate results. The purpose of this book is to allay those fears and replace them with skills and confidence. You do not have to be a statistical wizard to conduct and interpret meaningful research. In addition, when you do research strategically, you do not need to fear what the results will show. Evidence-based planning tends to produce good results. Even poor results for one program, however, can point the way to more effective future planning when research is sensitive enough to demonstrate not just *whether* a program has an effect but also *how*. "It's not a question of pass or fail," according to *PR News* ("Measurement," 2003).

Organization of the Book

The organization of this book is designed to provide communication managers with the range of tools required for the development, communication, and evaluation of effective programs. The toolkit includes basics of the strategic planning process, a general overview plus a range of specific guidelines for managers to use when hiring or performing their own research, theoretical perspectives that can help managers interpret research and develop effective strategies and tactics, and guidelines for the presentation of research findings and program plans.

Part I of this book presents a framework for planning that managers can apply to guide decision making. Chapter 2 addresses mission statement development, problem statement creation, and situation analysis, all of which form the basis for program development. Chapter 3 introduces the elements of the strategic planning process, which include goals, objectives, strategies, and tactics. Chapter 4 focuses on how to determine research needs and develop a research plan to gather information that will help practitioners plan their program.

Part II addresses when and how to do research for public relations planning and evaluation. Chapter 5 covers basic issues to consider when developing research plans. Chapter 6 provides the basics of sampling using terms and concepts accessible to those uninitiated in social science methods. Chapter 7 introduces the range of informal methods available to the communication manager, whereas Chapter 8 provides some detail about how to conduct focus groups. Chapter 9 introduces the range of formal methods commonly used in communication research, and Chapter 10 covers the nuances of survey research specifically. Chapter 11 focuses on how to construct questionnaires that provide trustworthy and useful information, and Chapter 12 discusses how to collect and analyze questionnaire data.

Part III explains how communication theory can assist the manager in strategic planning. Chapter 13 introduces public relations and communication theory and demonstrates its relevance to daily practice. Chapter 14 covers the range of theories available to help managers develop effective program strategies, and Chapter 15 boils down decades of research into a set of principles and applications for practical use.

Part IV discusses how to present a persuasive case for public relations programming, with Chapter 16 explaining the elements of a public relations proposal and providing a set of writing and presentation tips.

Experts in public relations seem to agree that public relations practitioners have the most success when they operate from a research-based, strategic management style. This book is designed not only to help novices through the strategic-planning process but also to provide the depth required for an experienced professional looking for a concise reference. It is intended for use at either the undergraduate or graduate level and has been written to be accessible to those on a self-guided tour. The goal of this book is to provide professionals and advanced public relations practitioners with the information they need to engage in strategic public relations management. Communication specialists who apply the skills explained in this book should secure a place for public relations and communication management at the leadership level in organizational decision making.

PART I

Framework
for Planning

2

Where the Strategic Manager Begins
Taking Stock

Chapter Contents

- Management by Objectives
- The Accountable Manager
- The Mission Statement
- Mission Versus Vision and Values
- The Problem (or Opportunity) Statement
- The Situation Analysis
- Sources of Information
- Final Thoughts

For communication practitioners trained more as writers than as social scientists, the bottom-line-oriented environment presents a major challenge. Organizations want cost-effective results. Many public relations practitioners argue that the cultivation of relationships is a fuzzy business, difficult to document with numbers. The result: public relations positions become vulnerable to organizational cost cutting and restructuring.

The best insurance against cost cutters and the best way to gain credibility and mobility in management is to adopt what Broom and Dozier (1990) called the *scientific management* approach. This approach does not discount the importance of creativity and communication skills, but it does put them into an *effects-oriented* context. Say a hospital plans to open a new wing in preparation for increased business. For a hospital, this is a touchy subject: it does not want to appear greedy by taking advantage of people's bad news and emergencies. Moreover, the promotion budget probably is limited because many hospitals are struggling to keep up with increasing medical costs and decreasing insurance reimbursements. Hospitals also do not want to appear wasteful, particularly if financed publicly. How can the hospital increase business without causing offense and without spending too much or appearing unseemly?

In what Nager and Allen (1984) called *traditional public relations*, the communication manager would come up with creative ideas for communication vehicles such as brochures and advertisements according to the budget and staffing available and would begin with questions. Should we use two-color or four-color? Glossy or matte? In the current digital landscape the questions might address how often to update Web pages and social media vehicles. The manager's decision making would focus on what looks best, sounds best, and works within the budget.

The scientific manager, in contrast, would begin with a different set of questions. Why do we need this new wing? At whom are we targeting this campaign? How much increased traffic do we need, and how much is realistic to expect? What will motivate people to take advantage of this new service? How will this change benefit them? The bottom line is: What goals should we set for this campaign?

The effects emphasis is *goal oriented*, lending itself to the bottom-line perspective of most organizations. Once you know what you must accomplish, you can focus your efforts more efficiently and to greater effect. You can embrace accountability with confidence. The two major components of the scientific management approach are planning and research.

Management by Objectives

The most common planning tool used by communication managers is known as *management by objectives* (MBO). MBO is an effects-oriented process for developing goal-oriented campaign recipes. A well-developed plan is a lot like an easy-to-follow recipe and, just as having skilled personnel in your kitchen engenders confidence that you can achieve the intended end result, personnel with relevant skills will promote confidence that you will cook up a successful campaign. To succeed, just like writing a recipe, however, MBO requires that you make strategic decisions about what you want to serve (a meal or just a dessert), how many you want to serve (your definition of bottom-line success), whom you expect for dinner (your publics), and when they will arrive (your deadline). You can adjust the ingredients according to your budget. Not every recipe for chocolate cake needs Belgian chocolate and not every campaign will need glossy, four-color print materials and high-end multimedia production. But just as you would not leave flour out of a bread recipe, the MBO approach can help you identify which campaign ingredients cannot be compromised. Moreover, the MBO approach can provide the hard evidence and persuasive reasoning you will need to convince your key decision makers that the campaign ingredients you identify as essential really are essential. In short, the MBO approach gives the communication manager credibility, flexibility, and control.

The MBO approach sounds easy but frequently confuses managers because practitioners often have an incomplete understanding of the elements that go into MBO. If you have ever wondered what the difference is between a goal and an objective, you have a lot of company. Definitions of goals and objectives rarely are provided, even in public relations textbooks. This chapter makes those distinctions clear.

The Accountable Manager

Let's begin by comparing the communication manager's role in traditional and scientific management approaches. As discussed by Nager and Allen (1984), the bottom line of communication programs differs fundamentally. Traditional practitioners do lots of communication activities, but they may have a piecemeal perspective on what they do. They may produce newsletters, social media, news releases, and an occasional special event, for example, without giving much thought to how each communication piece serves a specific and an overall purpose. MBO practitioners, in contrast, have strategic goals they plan to accomplish. Their perspective is more holistic. As a result, everything MBO managers do has a clear, effects-oriented purpose. Because they organize their activities according to a results perspective, they can show the need and the effectiveness of each effort more readily than traditional practitioners can. Each newsletter, social media tactic, news release, and special event serves a clear purpose that contributes to a larger framework.

The MBO manager, or scientific manager, focuses on six activities, as summarized by Ehling (1985):

1 *Conceptualization.* A leader must hold the big picture and be able to identify and organize the smaller elements to fit that larger picture. The goal is to identify specific tasks and responsibilities that need to be fulfilled to maintain mutually beneficial relationships between an organization and the public on which its success depends, such as budgeting, goal setting, strategic planning, organizing, administering, and evaluating (notice that these elements constitute tasks 2 through 6).

2 *Monitoring.* Monitoring means research. The scientific manager will do much issue tracking to stay ahead of emerging trends and on top of potential crises. The goal is to anticipate and evaluate opportunities and challenges that arise out of the organization's interactions and relationships with other organizations and society.

3 *Planning.* The manager must be able to build the recipes that will guide the organization through the opportunities and challenges identified in the monitoring process. The goal is to ensure the achievement of measurable results that fulfill needs identified in the monitoring process.

4 *Organization and coordination.* The manager must make effective use of available resources. These include budget and personnel within the organization as well as opportunities for cooperative partnerships with other organizations that can help to achieve mutually beneficial results. The goal is the effective and efficient implementation of strategies for the communication programs developed in the planning process.

5 *Administration.* The manager must fulfill the promises made in the planning process. The manager will supervise the programs to activate and adjust communication programs. Nothing ever goes exactly according to plan because resources and the environment continue to change; thus, the manager must maintain motivating, creative leadership throughout the implementation of each program. The goal is the fulfillment of communication program goals on budget and on deadline.

6 *Evaluation.* The scientific manager remains accountable. Every communication activity must have a clear purpose and an anticipated result. The manager must show results and an ability to use program successes and failures as part of the monitoring process to develop even more effective future programs. The goal is the accountability, credibility, and guidance to make future communication programs even more successful.

Table 2.1 MBO Roles and the 4-Step PR Planning Processes

MBO roles	4-step PR planning process	Goal
Conceptualization	Defining the PR problem	To identify needed tasks and responsibilities.
Monitoring	Defining the PR problem	To anticipate and evaluate relevant opportunities and challenges.
Planning	Planning and programming	To ensure achievement of relevant, measurable results.
Organization and coordination	Planning and programming	To implement strategies effectively and efficiently.
Administration	Taking action and communicating	To fulfill program goals on budget and on deadline.
Evaluation	Evaluating the program	Demonstrate accountability, earn credibility and obtain guidance for future success.

As shown in Table 2.1, the MBO process parallels the four-step public relations process familiar to many practitioners (Broom & Sha, 2013).

> *Step 1 is defining the public relations problem.* The definitional process helps the manager identify the effects campaigns need to accomplish. This encompasses Roles 1 and 2.
> *Step 2 is planning and programming.* At this point the manager develops the campaign recipe in detail. This encompasses Roles 3 and 4.
> *Step 3 is taking action and communicating,* or implementing the program, which encompasses Role 5.
> *Step 4 evaluating the program,* in which the manager identifies program successes and failures for accountability and future use. This encompasses Role 6.

With the manager's roles and the planning process identified, we turn to the products the manager will use and produce at each stage. These are the key elements the manager must develop. They include (a) a mission statement, (b) a problem statement, (c) situation analysis, (d) goals, (e) objectives, (f) strategies, and (g) tactics.

The Mission Statement

We can think of these elements as a pyramid (Figure 2.1), for which the mission statement forms the base. Everything we do must show clear relevance to the organization's mission. A *mission statement* is the statement of philosophy and purpose for an organization. Every organization should have one, and thus your first step as a manager is to obtain a copy, or, if one does not exist, to help your organization develop one. Mission statements can take a lot of time and effort to develop and can stretch for pages. The communication manager needs some sort of summary, however, to guide the daily activities of everyone connected with the

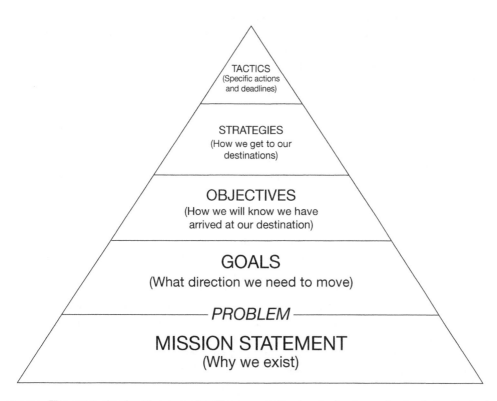

FIG. 2.1. The strategic planning pyramid. The organization's mission forms the basis for strategic planning. Decisions at each level of the pyramid depend on the decisions made on the underlying levels.

organization. Everyone associated with an organization should have a clear idea of why the organization exists—beyond "to make money"—something along the lines of an abstract or point summary.

The Robert Mondavi Winery (PR Reporter, 1998), for example, developed a one-line vision statement reflecting the mission of the organization to appear in every voicemail message from the CEO, in all statements to analysts, in most official statements, and at the beginning of most formal presentations to employees. The statement, "We will be the preeminent fine wine producer in the world," drove all strategic planning. Development of the deceptively simple statement required input from all employees to make sure that they would buy into it. The senior management drafted a statement and met with 6 to 10 groups of 15 to 20 employees to discuss and evaluate the statement. A second draft, based on employee comments, was tested the same way, resulting in the final version. Although the winery has since been sold after Mondavi acknowledged that "We have lost our image" by straying from the vision (Goldfarb, 2008, ¶ 18), the new management has stayed close to that carefully developed vision with an updated statement that embraces the origins of the company balanced with the realities of increased competition in the wine industry: "to produce wines from the Napa Valley that would stand in the company of the world's finest" (Robert Mondavi Winery, 2013, ¶ 1).

The mission statement should identify the products the organization produces, the services it provides, and the types of relationships it strives to cultivate. A regional charter airline such as Private Jet Services Group in New Hampshire focuses on delivering "aviation services that enable our clients to focus on what matters most to them. We strive to add value to our client's travel plans by offering a consultancy-based approach to the global aviation marketplace" (Private Jet Services Group, 2013, ¶ 1), reflecting its specialist status. A discount passenger airline such as Spirit Airlines focuses instead on "offering ultra low base fares with a range of optional services for a fee, allowing customers the freedom to choose only the extras they value" (Spirit Airlines, Inc., 2013, ¶ 1). Singapore Airlines, with a global focus, is "dedicated to providing air transportation services of the highest quality and to maximising returns for the benefit of its shareholders and employees" (Singapore Airlines, 2013, ¶ 3). Southwest Airlines, previously known for its emphasis on "low fares, lots of flights, and the friendliest service in the sky," (Southwest Airlines, 2005) has more recently de-emphasized the low-fares commitment to focus on customer service, promising to provide "dedication to the highest quality of Customer Service delivered with a sense of warmth, friendliness, individual pride, and Company Spirit" (Southwest Airlines Co., 2013, "Mission," ¶ 1). DHL, meanwhile, delivers packages and not people, yet its mission statement does not specifically identify what service DHL provides. DHL's mission, as stated in 2013, is to "simplify the lives of our customers," to "make our customers, employees and investors more successful," to "make a positive contribution to the world," and to "always demonstrate respect when achieving our results" (DHL, 2013, ¶ 2).

Organizations that appear somewhat similar may have missions that differ in important ways. Religion, for example, can infuse faith-based hospitals with a variety of emphases that best suit their clientele and communities. The mission of Kingsbrook Jewish Medical Center in Brooklyn (2013) is "to partner with our culturally diverse communities to provide a continuum of outstanding health care services to individuals and families through a caring and trustworthy staff" (¶ 1). Meanwhile, Florida Hospital (2013), run by the Seventh Day Adventist Church, states that its mission is "extending the healing ministry of Christ" and that through their caregivers, they hope that "His healing touch will be felt by all those who come to us for care" (¶ 1). The mission statement of Tsehootsooi Medical Center (2013) in Ft. Defiance, AZ, reflects its Navajo history and commitment to the Navajo culture, aiming "To provide superior and compassionate healthcare to our community by raising the level of health, Hózhó, and quality of life" (¶ 1).

Differences in mission can present difficult challenges for communication managers when organizations merge for financial or other reasons. A particularly dramatic situation can arise in communities such as Springfield and Eugene, Oregon, which have very different community norms but now share a Roman Catholic hospital. A diverse community might expect a hospital to provide whatever services the community members desire, but the teachings of the Catholic church preclude services that conflict with its values regarding family planning.

Mission Versus Vision and Values

Whereas the *mission statement* sets out a strategic focus for accomplishing a long-term outcome, the *vision* conveys this long-term ideal. Organizations frequently develop a vision statement as a short abbreviation of the mission suitable for publication on websites, business cards, and stationery. Sidebar 2.1 illustrates some effective vision statements. The *vision statement* includes the following purposes:

- shares the organization's values and intended contribution to society;
- fosters a sense of community and purpose within the organization in order to challenge members of the organization to work together toward a long-term aim;
- articulates how the organization should look in the future, presenting the ideal, or an ambitious, long-term goal.

Sidebar 2.1
Effective Vision Statements*

An organization called Top Nonprofits (Top Nonprofits, 2012) analyzed vision statements of 100 well-regarded nonprofit organizations and discovered that effective vision statements tended to be short (an average of 15 words, and as few as 3). For example:

- Oxfam: A just world without poverty
- Feeding America: A hunger-free America
- Human Rights Campaign: Equality for everyone
- Habitat for Humanity: A world where everyone has a decent place to live
- Oceana seeks to make our oceans as rich, healthy and abundant as they once were
- San Diego Zoo: To become a world leader at connecting people to wildlife and conservation
- In Touch Ministries: Proclaiming the Gospel of Jesus Christ to people in every country of the world
- NPR, with its network of independent member stations, is America's pre-eminent news institution
- Teach for America: One day, all children in this nation will have the opportunity to attain an excellent education

---

*Adapted with permission from Top Nonprofits.com

Some organizations also articulate a set of values intended to help support their mission. Citrus Memorial Hospital (2013) in Inverness, Florida, for example, encourages employees to embrace ten organizational values—compassion, respect, integrity, creativity, teamwork, knowledge, commitment, accountability, trust and humor in support of their mission "to improve the health and quality of life of the people and communities we serve" (¶ 5). The Atlanta VA Medical Center (United States Department of Veterans Affairs, 2012), meanwhile, has a more specific focus on being "veteran-centric" (¶ 9), committing to a different set of core values that include prioritizing veterans by exhorting its employees to include advocacy for veterans and their beneficiaries among employees' core values, which also include integrity, commitment, respect and excellence. Medical City Hospital (2011) in Dallas, Texas, has distinguished among its mission, vision, and values as shown below (p. 20).

Displaying the mission or vision statement prominently on internal and external communication pieces ensures that everyone with whom the organization has a relationship will

---

Medical City Hospital

Mission: Above all else, we are committed to the care and improvement of human life. In recognition of this commitment, we will strive to deliver high quality, cost-effective healthcare in the communities we serve.

Vision Statement: We are committed to excellence and innovation and inspiring other organizations to join in our passion.

Statement of Values:

- We recognize and affirm the unique and intrinsic worth of each individual.
- We treat all those we serve with compassion and kindness.
- We act with absolute honesty, integrity and fairness in the way we conduct our business and the way we live our lives.
- We trust our colleagues as valuable members of our healthcare team and pledge to treat one another with loyalty, respect and dignity.

---

have a clear understanding of what the company has on its list of priorities. Unfortunately, many companies fail to do this. Because the mission, vision and values statements provide the organization's justification for existence and underpinnings for a desired operational culture, communication managers can effectively substantiate their importance as a department and as individual staff members by showing how communication programs enhance the organization's mission, support the vision and communicate its values. Using the mission statement in particular, communication managers can show how the communication department's activities are central to the organization's success. When public relations is viewed as a partner, not as a subordinate, public relations departments become much less vulnerable to the budget axe.

The Problem (or Opportunity) Statement

Because public relations is the construction and maintenance of mutually beneficial relationships, the mission statement provides the guidelines for all strategic planning and monitoring. In particular, it enables the manager to produce the *problem statement*. To do so, the manager must address two key questions: How do you know a problem when you see one, and what is a problem statement?

A *problem* occurs when the organization encounters something in its environment or in its relationships with key publics that threatens its ability to fulfill its mission. The hospital, for example, may have encountered new insurance rules regarding maternity hospitalization that cut in half the number of days patients may stay following a healthy birth that is free of complications. The average stay in 1996 had shrunk from 2 weeks to 1 week to 3 days to 2 days to about 1 day, finally prompting legislation to require a 48-hour minimum stay in most states. In addition to the potential threat to maternal and infant health, the increasingly empty beds in the maternity ward could threaten the hospital's ability to maintain a healthy bottom line. More changes to health care laws and insurance practices, along with competition for elective services such as maternity care, continue to present challenges to hospital management. This information alone does not give the communication manager anything substantive to guide planning, however. "We need to make more money" provides no clues to identify which ways of making money are appropriate for the hospital, nor does it provide any reason why key publics inside and outside the organization should feel motivated to care whether the hospital makes money or, particularly in rural areas, remains viable. The manager needs to know the *philosophy and purpose* of the organization—its values and mission—to guide planning and to build mutually beneficial relationships.

So, what is the mission of a hospital and how would a reduction in insurance coverage for a service such as maternity care threaten this mission? Some hospitals take a broad focus, providing high-quality care for the community, and some hospitals serve communities that have higher birth rates or more uninsured individuals. Some hospitals also have a research-related mission or a teaching-related mission, as shown in Sidebar 2.2. Some have quite specialized missions that might make the changes in maternity policies irrelevant. These statements help the communication manager identify publics and activities that are appropriate.

SIDEBAR 2.2
Hospital Mission Statements

A mission statement should identify the products the organization produces, the services it provides, and the types of relationships it strives to cultivate. Note that statements differ according to the type and size of community served, the affiliation of the hospital, and the emphasis of the hospital on training, community outreach, or a specialized type of medicine.

University/Teaching

Stanford Hospital and Clinics
(Stanford University Medical Center, 2011)

The mission of Stanford Hospital and Clinics is to care, to educate and to discover. Our vision is healing humanity through science and compassion, one patient at a time (p. 4).

New York University Langone Medical Center (n.d.)

We are committed to making world-class contributions that place service to human health at the center of an academic culture devoted to excellence in research, patient care, and education (¶ 1).

Urban Community/Teaching

Detroit Receiving Hospital (2013)

Detroit Receiving Hospital (DRH) is the best place for patients to receive health care, physicians to practice medicine and employees to work. DRH fosters teaching, learning and innovation and ensures every patient, visitor and employee is treated with dignity, respect and compassion (¶ 7).

Saint Joseph Hospital, Denver, Colorado
(Exempla Saint Joseph Hospital, 2013)

To foster healing and health for the people and communities we serve (¶ 1).

Regional/Suburban

Medina General Hospital, Medina, Ohio
(Cleveland Clinic, 2013)

To provide better care of the sick, investigation into their problems, and further education of those who serve (¶ 1).

Jefferson Healthcare Hospital, Port Townsend, Washington
(Jefferson Healthcare, 2013)

Our primary mission is to provide access to quality health care services for everyone in our community (¶ 3).

St. Elizabeth's Hospital, Belleville, Illinois
(Hospital Sisters Health System, n.d.)

To reveal and embody Christ's healing love for all people through our high quality Fanciscan health care ministry (¶ 1).

Rural Community/Regional

East Adams Rural Hospital
(Adams County Public Hospital District #2, 2012)

Achieving excellence through exceptional quality to serve the health care needs of District residents and travelers. (¶ 2).

Ashland Health Center, Ashland, Kansas (n.d.)

Entrusted with peoples' lives, we are committed to provide, enhance, and preserve the health care of our community with compassion, dignity, and excellence (¶ 1).

Specialist

Mary Free Bed Hospital & Rehabilitation Center,
Grand Rapids, Michigan (2012)

Restoring hope and freedom through rehabilitation (¶ 7).

Rady Children's Hospital, San Diego,
California (2013)

To restore, sustain and enhance the health and developmental potential of children through excellence in care, education, research and advocacy (¶ 6).

Woman's Hospital, Baton Rouge,
Louisiana (n.d.)

To improve the health of women and infants (¶ 1).

If the mission statement represents the organization's foundational guiding document for all of its operations, the *problem statement* becomes the communication manager's foundational document to guide a communication campaign. The problem statement summarizes the key elements of the issue or opportunity and how it relates to the organization's ability to fulfill its mission. The problem statement is concise and specific, much like the lead of a news story. According to Kendall (1996), it should be 18 to 25 words, phrased in a simple subject-verb-object construction. In some cases, the problem statement may be more appropriately considered an opportunity statement. Armed with no information other than the problem (or opportunity) statement, a manager should be able to at least rough out some ideas for a successful campaign.

The problem statement comprises six elements (Figure 2.2):

1   *What* is the problem, issue, or opportunity? The problem may be one of reputation, of financial difficulty, of declining membership, of impending legislation, and so on.
2   *Where* is this problem occurring? This may represent an internal problem, a regional issue, a national issue, or even an international issue.

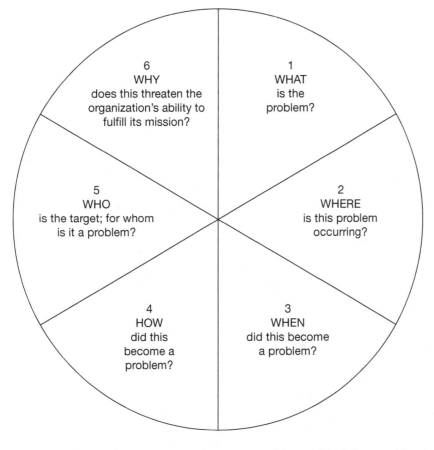

FIG. 2.2. Elements of the problem statement. A statement of the public relations problem is incomplete unless it includes all six of the elements portrayed.

3   *When* did this become a problem? Perhaps this issue always has been a problem, or perhaps this problem is getting better or worse or is cyclical.

4   *How* did this become a problem? Your problem may have developed because of a lack of awareness, poor product quality, or ineffective customer or member relations.

5   For *whom* is it a problem? Your problem most likely does not affect everyone in the world but instead involves certain key publics with whom your organization's relationship is threatened.

6   *Why* should the organization care about this problem? In other words, why does this threaten the organization's ability to fulfill its mission? Many organizations neglect to answer the "so what" question. If your problem has no easily identifiable "why," you probably will find it difficult to get key decision makers in your organization to buy into the need for your campaign.

Your problem statement, in short, provides the justification and the framework for your campaign, all in one or two sentences. Your goal, as discussed in Chapter 3, will be to negate the problem (or maximize the opportunity).

The Situation Analysis

Frequently, the communication manager receives a request to develop a campaign based on an initial issue statement that contains few of the elements necessary for a complete problem definition. To develop a complete problem statement usually requires formative research to flesh out the details. These details are known as the *situation analysis*.

The situation analysis is a detailed explanation of the opportunities and challenges (sometimes called *opportunities and threats*) that exist within the organization and in its environment. Sometimes the analysis of opportunities and challenges is called *SWOT analysis*, for Strengths, Weaknesses, Opportunities, and Threats. Referring to "threats" can seem defensive, however, whereas referring to challenges communicates more confidence. Both approaches emphasize the need for the manager to find out as much as possible about the problem, the relevant publics, and the environment.

A situation analysis usually begins with the problem statement, followed by a discussion of the history of the problem and how it conflicts with the organization's mission. The situation analysis then includes a discussion of the relevant publics as well as a discussion of opportunities that should help solve the problem and challenges that could pose barriers. Assumptions must be made clear, and all assertions must be backed up with evidence: data, theory, management and communication principles, expert sources, and other relevant information. The situation analysis represents everything you have been able to find out about the problem. It shows your familiarity with the organization, its publics, the environment, and the problem. It also helps you identify what additional information you may need to design a successful campaign.

The situation analysis makes it possible for the communication team to develop hypotheses, or hunches, about possible causes and solutions for your problem. You may conclude from your analysis that a problem initially presented as poor communication more likely stems from an informed lack of public support for a company's vision. On the other hand, research might reveal that an apparent lack of support stems from the noisy complaints of a small minority, with the majority unaware of the issue but ready to mobilize on the organization's behalf. These discoveries will affect the type of communication program an organization designs.

The situation analysis can spark creative problem solving by helping practitioners to organize seemingly disparate bits of information or to identify seemingly unrelated organizations that share similar concerns. The Arkansas Rice Depot, for example, a food bank based in Little Rock, identified a serious problem among disadvantaged schoolchildren: a school nurse had raised the concern that even if children received free school breakfasts and lunches, they often suffered hunger over weekends and holidays. The food bank and the school had operated independently, but they realized they needed to join forces. To make sure their food got to the children, the food bank began sending food home in the children's school backpacks. America's Second Harvest adopted the idea and the program has spread to affiliates nationwide.

Sources of Information

The development of a situation analysis requires a thorough understanding of the issue or problem, the client organization, the environment, and the relevant publics. Original research often is necessary, such as surveys and focus groups, but Internet and library research along with an examination of organizational records also can provide important information. The communication manager's ability to solve a problem depends on available resources (e.g., time and funding), available expertise, political realities, and the reasons for the problem. The manager's challenge, therefore, is to gather as much background information as possible, as quickly as possible, to determine the scope of the problem as well as the challenges and opportunities that will affect problem solving. Forces for and against change exist both within an organization and outside in the political and social environment. Along with the internal and external factors, the practitioner may find Hubbell's Helpful Questions useful, developed from the lessons of Ned Hubbell, former director of Project Outreach, Michigan Education Association, as a set of questions to ask before beginning to plan (Sidebar 2.3).

Internal Factors

Often, an organization attributes its problems to outside forces (the media are a favorite target for blame), but the communication manager must begin to understand the problem by developing an understanding of the organization itself. Important types of information include the organization's mission, its decision-making and operating structure, its evolution and history, and its culture. Sources of information include the following:

- Written documents such as mission/vision/values statements, charters, and bylaws
- Biographical statements of key members of the organization
- Descriptions of products and services
- Records regarding budgets, expenditures, and staffing levels
- Records regarding business policies and procedures
- Published documents such as annual reports and newsletters
- Specific records related to the problem, such as memos
- Records regarding organizational calendars of events
- Decision makers and other staff knowledgeable about the issue
- Existing surveys or other research of internal publics
- Websites, social media, and records related to Web use.

Sidebar 2.3

Hubbell's Helpful Questions (or 30-something questions you should ask before planning)*

I.   Organizational History

    A.   Why was the organization established?

    B.   When was the organization established?

    C.   Were there any problems to overcome in the development of the organization?

    D.   Have there been any major changes in organizational direction or policy?

    E.   What is the organization's status in the community?

II.   Organizational Structure

    A.   Is there an organizational chart available?

    B.   What is the total number of staff?

    C.   How are responsibilities divided?

    D.   What functions are handled in each department or section?

    E.   What importance does the organization attribute to each function and why?

III.   Organizational Philosophy/Mission/Goals

    A.   What is the purpose of the organization?

    B.   What is the stated mission of the organization?

    C.   Is there a dominant organizational philosophy?

    D.   Does the organization have any set goals?

IV.   Organizational Policies of Operation

    A.   Who constitutes the board of directors? How was the board selected?

    B.   Does the organization have any advisory panels or committees?

    C.   Who determines how the organization operates?

    D.   Who must be consulted before decisions are made? Why?

    E.   What government regulations (if any) impact the organization?

    F.   What mistakes has the organization made in the past? What have these mistakes taught the organization?

    G.   What is the agency's operational budget?

V.   Competitive Posture

    A.   Where does the agency rank in the industry?

    B.   Where does the agency rank in the community?

    C.   What is the agency's reputation?

    D.   Who does the agency compete with?

    E.   Does the agency have any opponents? If so, who?

    F.   Does the agency have any allies? If so, who?

    G.   Are there important neutral parties to be considered?

    H.   What additional factors are impacting competitive posture?

VI. Situation Analysis (Trends)

    A.   What are the perceived key changes taking place outside of the organization?

    B.   What are the perceived key changes taking place within the organization?

    C.   What issues are emerging in the industry? How will these impact the agency?

    D.   Are there broad social trends impacting the agency?

    E.   Are there any developing innovations within the industry that may impact the agency? Is the agency working on any innovations?

    F.   Are agency funding sources secure?

---

* Reprinted with Permission

External Factors

Sources of information outside the organization can provide an understanding of opportunities and challenges that the organization needs to anticipate or that it has encountered in the past. Regulations enacted by the Food and Drug Administration to protect the safety of the nation's blood supply, for example, have made it more difficult for prospective blood donors to qualify. People no longer can give blood, for example, if they have had a headache during the past week or if they lived in England for three months between 1980 and 1996. Blood banks have had to find a way to maintain sufficient reserves under increasingly tight restrictions (Manning, 2003).

Important types of external information include publics who come in contact with the organization, information networks linking individuals inside and outside the organization, portrayals of the organization by key individuals and the media, and information about political, social, economic, and environmental issues that can affect the organization's ability to control an issue. Sources of information include the following:

- Consumer and trade publications in which the organization or the issue is mentioned
- Publications in which competing organizations or their issue positions are mentioned
- Records of broadcast news coverage of the organization or the issue
- Records of Internet sites relevant to the organization or issue
- Individuals and organizations that favor or criticize the organization or its stance on an issue (sometimes an organization has lists of key contacts, friends, or critics)
- Individuals at key media outlets and *bloggers* who cover the organization or the issue
- Calendars of events for the community and other relevant regions
- Existing surveys of relevant publics from national, regional, or specialized sources
- Lists of relevant government agencies and key contacts that deal with the organization and relevant issues
- Records of relevant government regulations that are pending, current, and repealed.

Final Thoughts

Once communication managers have reviewed existing background information, they can assess the situation more effectively. The exercise of drafting the problem statement can reveal information gaps that require further investigation. Only when all of the elements of a problem statement can be written with specifics can the manager determine appropriate strategy.

This means that a significant part of program planning depends on research. The manager's confidence in the effectiveness of a program plan and the manager's ability to demonstrate accountability to a client increases with each bit of relevant information obtained. Public relations programs exist in an environment filled with uncertainty and variables that managers simply cannot control. The better the manager's understanding of all elements of the situation, the more control—or at least predictability—the manager will have over the result of a *communication* program.

Elements of the Campaign

Pre-campaign research positions communication managers to revise the problem statement and situation analysis to guide effective campaign design. Keep in mind that change is constant, thus all planning documents must respond to changes in resources, context, and available information. The manager will revise a problem statement if research demonstrates the initial problem diagnosis overstates, understates, or misstates the problem. Similarly, managers can revise the situation analysis as the situation changes. It follows that the campaign plan, too, may require adjustment occasionally. Campaign plans based on thorough pre-campaign research, however, will rarely need a major change.

Goals

The campaign plan includes at least four levels of information, all presented in writing. The first is the *goal*. A goal is a conceptual statement of what you plan to achieve. The goal is essentially a set of declared intentions that together negate the problem. For example, if research has traced the problem for an organization to a lack of awareness, the goal will focus on increasing awareness. If the problem stems from a lack of credibility, the goal will focus on increasing credibility. If the problem arises from a lack of volunteer involvement, a series of goals may focus on recruiting new volunteers, increasing involvement among existing volunteers, and increasing opportunities for volunteer activity. Managers can provide clients with long-term or short-term goals, depending on the context of a program or campaign.

A goal statement includes the following elements:

1   *The word* "to." This signals to the reader that an action statement will follow. It also demonstrates a results orientation. Both of these characteristics make goals easy for busy clients and CEOs to understand quickly.

2   *An active verb.* This demonstrates that a proposed communication plan will have specific effects. The verb should reflect an effect rather than an action. In other words, the goal should not promise to do something, such as disseminate newsletters; instead, it should promise to accomplish a result, such as improving customer loyalty. Appropriate verbs include increase, decrease, and maintain. Occasionally, others are appropriate, such as initiate or eliminate (Table 3.1).

3   *A conceptual, quantifiable statement of the desired outcome.* This specifies what will be changed and by how much. The focus may be on outcomes such as knowledge, beliefs, opinions, behaviors, sales figures, membership figures, or donation levels. This signals the reader how the manager plans to measure success. As a result, this outcome must be quantifiable in some way. For example, levels of employee satisfaction may be quantified in terms of a combination of sick time, complaints, longevity, work quality, and self-reported opinions. Each proposed measure on its own may not adequately represent employee satisfaction, but as a group they seem appropriate. Each proposed measure will become the focus of a stated objective of the campaign. Increasing levels of employee satisfaction, therefore, can be the focus of a goal statement. Each goal should focus on only one outcome. A program designed to change several outcomes should state each outcome as a separate goal.

4   *Identification of relevant target publics.* The client should not only see at a glance what is going to change but also know among whom it will change. A single communication campaign cannot promise to improve a company's reputation among every individual in the world; the manager must offer some parameters. This will guide the development of strategy, which will differ depending on the target public.

For example, DSM Nutritional Products and Carmichael Lynch Spong, in partnership with the National Center for Creative Aging (NCCA), created a Silver Anvil Award–winning campaign, called *Beautiful Minds*, to promote a nutritional supplement that supports brain health. The Silver Anvil Award is given annually by the Public Relations Society of America (PRSA) to honor communication programs that incorporate sound research, planning, execution, and evaluation (Sidebar 3.1). The overall goal for the *Beautiful Minds* campaign included, "to educate and empower consumers surrounding the four dimensions of brain health: nutrition, physical health, mental health and social well-being" (PRSA 2012a, p. 1).

Table 3.1 Active Verbs Appropriate for Goals and Objectives

Address	Evaluate	Protect
Administer	Examine	Raise
Analyze	Expand	Reassure
Approve	Finish	Recommend
Arrange	Gain	Record
Assign	Generate	Recruit
Attain	Govern	Rectify
Authorize	Group	Reduce
Build	Guide	Regain
Calculate	Hire	Release
Catalog	Identify	Remove
Communicate	Improve	Request
Complete	Increase	Require
Conceive	Index	Research
Conduct	Implement	Reshape
Confine	Inform	Retain
Contract	Initiate	Review
Control	Institute	Revise
Convince	Interview	Schedule
Coordinate	Investigate	Secure
Correct	Justify	Select
Create	Keep	Sort
Decide	Locate	Start
Decrease	Maintain	Stimulate
Delegate	Make	Straighten
Demonstrate	Moderate	Strengthen
Design	Motivate	Submit
Develop	Negotiate	Summarize
Diminish	Notify	Supervise
Direct	Obtain	Supply
Disapprove	Organize	Systematize
Distribute	Outline	Tabulate
Document	Overcome	Teach
Draft	Persuade	Tell
Earn	Plan	Trace
Educate	Position	Track
Employ	Prepare	Train
Enhance	Present	Verify
Enlarge	Preside	Write
Enlist	Provide	
Establish	Publish	

Sidebar 3.1

Campaign Excellence: A Survey of Silver Anvil Award Winners Compares Current PR Practice with Planning, Campaign Theory

---

Each year, thousands of organizations across the United States develop and implement PR campaigns. Some of these campaigns fail. Some are modestly successful, and some achieve smashing success.

Each year, some 650 of these campaigns are submitted for consideration for a Silver Anvil Award, PRSA's recognition of the very best in strategic PR planning and implementation. Of these, about 45 will be awarded the profession's highest recognition. What makes these campaigns so outstanding? Are there common characteristics among Silver Anvil Award-winning campaigns? And can they be identified, interpreted and used to help professionals produce better campaigns for their companies and clients?

These are the questions that a 2002 study of Silver Anvil Award–winning campaigns from 2000 and 2001 sought to answer. This study, which I conducted with Courtney C. Bosworth, Ph.D., assistant professor of advertising and public relations at Florida International University, compares current PR practices in the profession with PR planning and campaign theory. Adding to the study are the observations of some of the profession's leading practitioners—people who judge Silver Anvil entries and, as a result, see the best and worst in PR programming today. The results are revealing. Although every campaign has practical constraints and technical flaws, campaigns with certain characteristics—notably thorough research and benchmarking, clear objectives, research-based strategies, and documented results—have a good chance of rising to the highest level of campaign excellence. This study of Silver Anvil winners reveals the most common campaign-planning practices of this elite group, as well as shortcomings even great campaigns share that the profession should address in the future.

The Study

The purpose of the study was to determine if there are any common characteristics of effective PR campaigns. A content analysis of all aspects of PR campaigns was conducted, looking at primary and secondary research methods used, objectives set, communications tactics implemented, and output and outcome evaluation methods reported. In all, some 121 variables typically present in PR campaigns were assessed, used key words and phrases appearing in the two-page summaries of the campaigns.

A random sample of 33 campaigns was analyzed in depth out of winning entries. The campaigns were distributed among the 15 Silver Anvil categories, and among subcategories that included business products, business services, government, associations/nonprofit organizations, and partnerships.

Budgets: Myths vs. Realities

There's no question that big-budget programs are well represented among Silver Anvil–winning campaigns. But, according to Lew Carter, managing director for affiliate relations worldwide for Manning, Selvage & Lee, what counts is not the size of the budget, but the way it is used. When asked what distinguishes a great campaign from a typical one, he says, "innovative strategies and the efficient use of budget."

The analysis of winning campaigns bears this out. The largest number of winning entries (29%) are not in the highest budget category studied. They are in the $100,000–$199,000 budget range—a healthy expenditure but not overly large, especially since most of these campaigns spanned large geographic regions and used innovative tactics to stretch their dollars. The second-highest category is programs of $500,000 and above (25%—these tended to be national or global in scope), while programs in the $300,000–$399,000 category rank third (12%).

Research: Critical to Building Strategy

The judges say that too many campaigns lack solid research. "I've seen campaigns that seem to contradict the research," says Jennifer Acord, regional manager for public relations and media events for Avon Products Inc. "The best campaigns use research to develop the objectives, create the strategy and provide clear benchmarks for evaluation."

Mitch Head, APR, Fellow PRSA, managing director for Golin/Harris Atlanta and former chair of the Silver Anvil Committee, has also noticed the lack of research.

"Everyone does tactics well," he says. "To me, a great campaign is one that has a great nugget of research that leads to a great strategic approach."

What types of research do award-winning campaigns depend on? Top campaigns depend on primary research techniques that involve personal contact with target audiences. Interviews with, and observations of, key audiences are the most popular form of primary research (65% of campaigns used this technique), while telephone surveys rank second (57%), focus groups rank third (38%), and impersonal mail surveys a distant fourth (12%). Internet surveys are used in only 6% of campaigns. Fax surveys are definitely out of favor—no campaign reported using this technique.

With secondary research, literature searches (44%) and competitive analysis (42%) rank as the most frequently used techniques. Used with less frequency are archival research (25%), syndicated databases (24%), organizational research (24%), media audits (22%) and sales and market share data (22%). General online research is used in 19% of campaigns.

When it comes to examining audiences, half of the winning campaigns use demographic profiles. Psychographic profiles are used by 33%, while only 13% report using geographic profiles.

Experimental research is done with less frequency. Messages are tested in 37% of winning campaigns, while specific communications vehicles are tested in 18% of campaigns, media testing occurs in 13% of campaigns and products are tested in 6% of campaigns.

Benchmarking: Key to Proving Results

In order to attribute an outcome to the PR campaign, the campaign must be benchmarked. However, after studying the type of benchmarking research typically done prior to the launch of a campaign, even some of the top campaigns came up short.

"The thing that distinguishes the great campaigns is that they 'move the needle'—and are able to clearly show that it is public relations that did the heavy lifting," says Christopher K. Veronda, APR, manager of communications and public affairs for Eastman Kodak Company and a longtime Silver Anvil judge.

Only 45% of campaigns benchmark awareness prior to launch. This is significant because 79% of the campaigns seek to increase awareness, meaning 34% of the campaigns seeking to increase awareness fail to establish their starting point. Other types of benchmark research done include benchmarking perceptions (41% benchmarked perceptions, while 63% of campaigns sought to change perceptions), attitudes (40% benchmarked/12% sought to change) and opinions (27% benchmarked/28% sought to change).

Objectives: What Are We Trying to Do?

The most important aspect of a campaign is the objective, says Gerard F. Corbett, APR, Fellow PRSA, chairman of PRSA's 2003 Honors and Awards Committee and vice president of Hitachi America, Ltd. "You need to identify where you want to be at the end of the day and what needs to be accomplished when all is said and done," he says.

Four out of five Silver Anvil campaigns studied sought to change behavior. And yet, in order to change behavior, a hierarchy of effects must occur that involves the creation of awareness, informing and educating audiences, changing opinions (persuading) and changing attitudes.

The campaigns studied did not systematically set multiple objectives to reflect the process of behavior change. Although 82% had behavior-based objectives and 79% had awareness- and visibility-based objectives, only 28% had opinion-based objectives and only 12% had attitude-based objectives. Practitioners might consider working backward— identifying the behavior objective for the campaign, and then thinking through the attitude-change, opinion-change and awareness-change objectives necessary to produce the behavior.

How Well Are Objectives Written?

Judges agree that poorly written objectives are one of the top reasons campaigns are eliminated from Silver Anvil competition. Among the ones that win, however, what does the study find?

Winning campaigns still reveal gaps that should be addressed by the profession. While 96% show a clear tie to the organization's mission and goals and 75% specify the nature of the desired change, only 43% specify the time frame for the change and only 35% specify the amount of change sought. In order for objectives to be adequately expressed and, ultimately, an outcome to be measured, all four elements must be present.

"Many losing Silver Anvil entries did not have the kind of objectives that can later be measured and evaluated," says Catherine Pacheco, APR, president of Pacheco Rodriguez Public Relations. "Once we read the first half of the entry and find this wanting, we know the last half will be worse. After all, how can you possibly measure the success of a campaign if you do not clearly specify what you are out to achieve?"

Measuring Results

While the results are the most important aspect of a good campaign, judges say that too often entries will only demonstrate the number of clips, meetings held, and the like, instead of evaluating the impact of the program and actions taken by relevant audiences.

It is accepted in the profession today that assessing bottom-line results, or outcomes, is more important than assessing campaign activities, or outputs. The study shows a wide variety of both types of evaluation taking place.

Top output evaluation methods include documentation of messages placed in the media (73% of campaigns), documentation of participation in events or activities (62%), documentation of the number of campaign events implemented (52%) and documentation of content of messages placed (50%). "I see thinly veiled attempts (in losing entries) to gauge the success of a campaign solely based on the number of news clips that are generated," Pacheco. "If it's one of several markers, that's great, but to call a campaign a best practice, it better contain other measurements of success than just clips."

In the more important arena of outcome evaluation, 87% of campaigns document behavior change. However, only 24% document attitude change and only 18% document opinion change—both necessary precursors of behavior change, unless a latent desire to behave in the desired direction already exists in the target audiences. This suggests that the profession should pay closer attention to evaluating opinion and attitude change after a campaign is implemented, in order to more fully understand if the behavior was produced as the result of communication effects or some other factor.

To do so is a struggle, however, when companies or clients, satisfied with the results of a campaign, will not offer additional funds for follow-up research. Practitioners should be prepared to argue that such research will add to the company's knowledge base and, in the long run, pay off with more efficient use of dollars in future campaigns.

Interestingly, 75% of campaigns document that the audience received the intended message and 67% document that the audience understood the message, but only 12% document that the audience retained the message. This suggests more attention should be given to documenting the long-term effects of communication efforts on the intended audiences.

The X Factor: Does It Exist?

Asked whether there is an "X" factor that sets excellent campaigns apart from those that are merely good, solid ones, the overwhelming response from Silver Anvil judges is yes. But that factor, they say, ranges from daring creative approaches to solid implementation.

"What distinguishes a great campaign is a genuinely creative approach to a worthy challenge that is executed flawlessly and yields significant, measurable results," says Pat Pollino, APR, Fellow PRSA, and vice president for marketing and communication for Mercer Management Consulting, Inc. "To borrow an analogy from pro football, anyone can diagram a power sweep, but it takes a team like Vince Lombardi's Green Bay Packers to pull it off successfully."

A dramatic or daring approach sets outstanding campaigns apart, says Head. Dreaming up something creative is "hard to do in this day and age, when everything seems to have already been done," he says.

Corbett agrees and further defines the X factor that winning campaigns share.

"The great campaigns are those that are strategic in nature, have a well-defined goal, are very targeted and have results that stand out like a crystal in the sun," says Corbett. "I believe that there is an X factor, although it is difficult to discern at first glance. It is the chemistry that makes the program gel. It could be an out-of-the-box idea; it could be the people involved or the manner in which the campaign was implemented. Or it could be many factors woven together like a resilient fabric."

Veronda doesn't believe there is an X factor. "It's solid implementation of the four-step process," he says. "Some of our critics would say you should just look at results, but to show it was public relations that moved the needle, you had to do the upfront research and establish the benchmarks."

The best public relations does not impress the reader as merely public relations, but approaches the business problem of the organization, says Clarke Caywood, Ph.D., graduate professor of integrated marketing communications at Northwestern University. "It uses the richness of the field to solve problems and create new opportunities to increase revenues or reduce costs and contribute to the triple bottom line of social, environmental and financial security of the organization, its employees, investors and other stakeholders," he says. But bottom-line result, he says, is the X factor. "I'd like to know how behavior was changed. For example, did sales increase? Was there greater turnout at an event? What I want to know is how the PR program made a difference for the organization."

Final Thoughts on Campaign Planning

The bottom line for campaign planning? Focus on those aspects of campaign planning that will help you achieve your goal: do good, solid research that benchmarks your starting point; use that research to build your strategy; set complete objectives that specify type, amount, and time frame for change; and document your outcomes. Sprinkle in a heavy dose of creativity, both in problem-solving and tactical execution, and efficient use of funding, and you are well on your way to producing an outstanding PR campaign.

Catherine B. Ahles, APR, Fellow PRSA, is associate professor of advertising and public relations at Florida International University. She spent 27 years in nonprofit and governmental public relations, where she conducted large-scale public information and ballot proposal initiatives, and she has won two Silver Anvils for such campaigns. Ahles can be reached at ahlesc@fiu.edu.

From "A Survey of Silver Anvil Award Winners Compares Current PR Practice With Planning, Campaign Theory," *Public Relations Strategist*, by C. B. Ahles, 2003 (Summer). Reprinted with permission.

Objectives

Although this goal is not directly *measurable*, it is *quantifiable*. In other words, they cannot count "education" and "empowerment" which is an idea, but they can count something that represents that idea, such as the number of people who visit their website for information. They also can measure levels of awareness among their target public of consumers aged 45–64 and key influencers such as health and medical professionals.

Nager and Allen (1984) wrote that it helps to think of a goal as a *directional statement*, such as planning to "go north." You cannot ever "arrive" at "north," because north is an idea, a concept. It is relative to where you are now, or where you used to be, or where you will be some other time. So you have to supply some context if you want to turn the direction into some sort of destination so that you will be able to say, "I have arrived!" You can go north from someplace, and you can go to specific places located in a northerly direction, but to know you have done it right, you need to give yourself some checkpoints. You need to know where you are starting out—known in communication campaigns as the *baseline*—and you need to know where you want to end up—known as the *objective*.

If the goal has promised to "improve employee morale," the manager will have created a directional statement but will not yet have any concrete destinations to guide campaign planning and provide accountability. You never will arrive at "improving morale." You can, however, find things to measure that will represent improvements in morale, just as you can find cities that represent north. These things that you measure—your destinations—will serve as your objectives.

In the *Beautiful Minds* promotion of *life's DHA*, the outcomes for the goal included education and empowerment. The manager cannot count either of these outcomes. To quantify these ideas, such as empowerment, DSM, Carmichael Lynch Spong and the NCCA might count the number of people who voted in a contest, and the number of people who shared information with others on social media. To quantify education, you might count the number of people who visited the website and who took a quiz about brain health.

An objective, then, is a measurable destination that represents the achievement of a campaign goal. Much confusion exists regarding objectives, most likely because several types of objectives exist. Many communication managers, for example, write conceptual statements (goals) and call them objectives. A true objective, however, is specific and measurable, stating not what the campaign will do, but rather what a campaign will accomplish. Three types of objectives exist.

Global objectives focus on general program outcomes. They summarize the overall effect of a campaign. For example, a global objective might be to obtain the necessary legislative support to enable a company to proceed with a planned expansion. Although concrete—the expansion either proceeds or does not—the objective does not specify the details that have to be in place for the expansion to take place. For example, the company needs to have enough sympathetic legislators win election or re-election in the next election. In addition, someone has to write and introduce the legislation. Advocacy groups with alternative views need to be persuaded or countered. These process-oriented or task-oriented outcomes are known as *intermediate objectives*. Finally, the campaign may state *terminal objectives*, which provide specific measurable or observable results to the campaign, measured by behaviors or actions, such as at least 60 senators voting for the passage of a particular bill in order to overcome a filibuster.

An objective must include the following elements:

1   *The word "to."* This signals that a promise of accountability follows.
2   *An active verb.* As before, this indicates that something specific will happen as a result of the communication program (Table 3.2 as well as Table 3.1).
3   *The "criterion outcome" or measurable destination.* This puts the focus on a concrete "operationalization" of the idea presented in a goal. This outcome must be measurable or reliably observable. Each objective focuses on a single criterion outcome, which means that several objectives may correspond to quantify a single goal statement. The wording of the criterion outcome must make clear what measurement technique is required for accountability. For example, an objective promising "to increase self-reported confidence in the institution" by a certain amount requires a survey; an objective pledging "to increase the number of participants in professional development seminars by 20%" requires an attendance record.
4   *The relevant target public.* Some objectives, such as those focused on raising awareness, may not be relevant to all target publics in a campaign. Therefore, to avoid overpromising, specify which objectives relate to which publics.
5   *The amount of change expected.* This critical piece of information distinguishes the objective from the goal by providing concrete verification of goal attainment. This can take the form of a number or a percentage. The amount of designated change must be ambitious enough to require real improvement but also be realistically attainable. Stating too high a level can impress a client in a pitch meeting but can make a competent

Table 3.2 Active Verbs Appropriate for Objectives

Administer	Enlist	Raise
Approve	Establish	Record
Assign	Finish	Recruit
Attain	Gain	Reduce
Authorize	Generate	Regain
Catalog	Hire	Request
Complete	Implement	Retain
Conduct	Improve	Schedule
Create	Increase	Secure
Decrease	Institute	Select
Develop	Interview	Start
Distribute	Make	Submit
Draft	Obtain	Locate
Earn	Present	Tabulate
Employ	Provide	
Enlarge	Publish	

Note. You can insert a number after each verb to indicate a specific, measurable amount of change.

campaign look like a failure. Understating the level can lead a client to think the campaign will be a sham and not worth the investment. As a result, objectives are difficult to write. However effective the campaign strategies may be, the objectives ultimately determine whether a campaign is a success or a failure.

How much change is necessary or realistic can be determined only through research and still may require the best judgment of the communication manager. In addition, objectives sometimes may require negotiation, particularly when they are set on the basis of political judgments or intuition instead of on the basis of research. Sometimes clients impose minimum levels of change, and sometimes these levels are not realistic. The Washington state legislature, for example, determined one year that all state universities had to improve student retention and graduation rates by specified amounts (Retention Council Report, n.d.; Washington State Higher Education Coordinating Board, 1997). The universities knew they would not be able to achieve the amounts. Ironically, the ability to achieve some of the stated objectives, such as decreasing time until graduation, would be compromised by increases in enrollment and retention, which were the focus of other objectives. The university administrators knew that many students drop out or change institutions because they are struggling, thus keeping them from leaving would probably hurt overall time-to-graduation rates. The universities' challenge, as a result, was to make their best effort to achieve the stated objectives while acquiring evidence to convince the legislators that alternative objectives would be more appropriate. Although the universities had to sacrifice some state funding because they failed to meet the original objectives, they were successful in guiding the legislature to more reasonable objectives during the next legislative session.

6   *A target date or deadline.* This seals the promise of accountability and is an essential element of the objective.

Note how concrete and specific the objective is. Many managers find objectives uncomfortable because they represent a clear promise. Objectives state in no uncertain terms what will be accomplished and by when. The obvious danger is promising too much. The manager, however, has only two viable alternatives: make promises that can be kept or make no promises. Because promises provide accountability, they make or break your reputation. To make no promises in a bottom-line-oriented environment keeps public relations marginalized and powerless. As a result, the only choice for the successful communication manager is to make promises that can be kept. The only way to do this—to determine realistic objectives—is through research. The promoters of *life's DHA* (PRSA, 2012a) were able to set objectives and develop strategy based on a combination of proprietary, primary and secondary research about the public's interest and concerns about brain health. The proprietary research included the development of a "brain health index" that ranked the nation's brain health on 21 indicators. The primary research included an experiment in which health people "with memory complaints" who took 900 mg of algal DHA capsules for six months demonstrated significant improvements in memory six months later. The secondary research included survey findings about Baby Boomers' memory concerns from the Mayo Clinic, the *New York Times* and MetLife. More sample outcomes appear in Table 3.3.

Objectives Drive Evaluation

Every objective, if written properly, necessitates some form of evaluation and dictates the form the evaluation should take. In the case of the *Beautiful Minds life's DHA* campaign (PRSA 2012a), some of the objectives included the following:

- To increase awareness by at least 2% from 2010 to 2011 for *life's DHA*
- To drive at least 20,000 visitors to the website as a primary source for brain health information.

Sharp-eyed readers may notice these objectives omit a few key elements the writers apparently thought were implied by other information in the campaign summary, such as the target audience (45–64 year olds) and the deadline's date (it appears in the first objective but not in the second). It is best to write objectives that can be understood without additional context. Nevertheless, *life's DHA* and Carmichael Lynch Spong (PRSA, 2012a) make it clear that their evaluation of the campaign would require survey findings and website analytics data. They were able to demonstrate a 14.3% increase in *life's DHA* brand awareness among members of their target audience from 2010 to 2011, exceeding the promised metrics for objective number one. In response to objective number two, they calculated that 42,000 individuals visited beautiful minds.com during the measurement period, with 65% of those visits traceable to referring websites, which further indicated that these organizations considered the beautifulminds.com website credible as a resource. They also documented 18,000 takers of their online Brain Health Quiz and 24,000 interactions with the interactive *Brain Health Index.*

Table 3.3 Examples of Communication Program Outcomes

Goal:	To create a personality for the Veloster brand to attract younger buyers to Hyundai.
Objective:	To secure a positive tone from 80% of all media coverage, demonstrating media's acceptance of the vehicle and its concept during Sept-Dec 2011.
Result:	Positive coverage demonstrated among 88% of tracked media stories (PRSA, 2012b).
Goal:	To build awareness for Chase Sapphire among "working affluent" San Franciscans as the ultimate card for all things culinary.
Objective:	To increase awareness for Chase Sapphire to 60% among affluent target in San Francisco within six months.
Result:	Awareness for Chase Sapphire increased 9% from baseline, to 62%, and applications from San Franciscans increased by 12% (PRSA, 2012c).
Goal:	To enable IBM and its clients to engage with local communities on volunteer projects on a large scale, while expressing IBM's brand and values to the world.
Objective:	To conduct service projects during the year-long campaign in the majority of the 170 countries in which IBM operates.
Result:	More than 5,000 projects in 120 countries helped 10 million people (PRSA, 2012d).
Goal:	To increase the understanding and usage of the IRS Free File program among young adults filing on their own for the first time, lower-income filers and adults close to retirement age.
Objective:	To assist the IRS by April 15, 2011 in achieving the mandate that 80% of all tax returns are e-filed by 2012.
Result:	The IRS exceeded its 80% filing rate goal for individual returns filed by April of 2011 and increased the use of the Free File program by 45% over the previous year (PRSA, 2012e).

from 2012 Silver Anvil Award Winners

The Importance of Coordinating Objectives with Evaluation

The objective should signal the appropriate form of evaluation. As an example of coordinating objectives with evaluation, the American Medical Women's Association (AMWA) and Fleishman Hillard, Inc., (PRSA, 1998) teamed up to increase awareness, diagnosis, and treatment of thyroid disease. The campaign took place in response to figures indicating that more than half of the estimated 13 million Americans with thyroid disease, most of whom are women, remain undiagnosed. Untreated, thyroid disease can cause cholesterol problems, osteoporosis, and infertility. Meanwhile, a simple blood test can detect the disease, and treatment is straightforward. As a result, AMWA and Fleishman Hillard's stated objective was to increase the number of women being tested for thyroid disease by at least 10% in the first 15 months of the campaign. This objective dictated that campaign success would depend on tracking figures of women tested for thyroid disease. The campaign documented an increase of more than 40% in the number of women tested. The campaign included other measures of success as well, such as the number of total prescriptions of thyroid treatment medication, which increased by 10% and indicated that more women were being treated for thyroid disease.

The campaign had several associated results as well (PRSA, 1998). More than 6,600 individuals were screened during local market-screening events, at a rate of more than 300 people per hour. AMWA and Fleishman Hillard achieved exposure to more than 100 million people with media coverage that included national coverage on television shows such as *Good Morning America*, CNN, Fox, and MSNBC; national coverage in print venues such as the Associated Press, *USA Today*, *The Washington Post*, and several magazines; and local print and broadcast coverage in various markets. A television public service announcement was broadcast 3,800 times, reaching an estimated 128 million viewers. A radio public service announcement reached an estimated 40 million listeners. The campaign also brought the issue to the attention of Congress through invited testimony and visits to four key Congressional members' home districts. These achievements, however striking, would not in themselves demonstrate campaign success as promised. If the stated objective promises behavior change in the form of increased blood tests, success must be measured in those terms.

It may seem unfair that a campaign might achieve results but still seem like a failure if the ultimate objective is not met. This makes it especially useful to include intermediate and terminal objectives along with global objectives for a campaign. In the case of the thyroid disorder campaign, an appropriate global objective would be to track treatment of thyroid disease and the incidences of related osteoporosis, cholesterol problems, and birth defects, which the campaign managers documented. An appropriate terminal objective would be to increase testing, which the campaign planners documented. Appropriate intermediate objectives would include media impressions, congressional hearings, and local screening successes, which they also documented. Even if the ultimate campaign objectives had not been met, the campaign managers would be able to show that progress had been made and that future efforts might have more striking results. Indeed, the success of the thyroid campaign led to a campaign expansion that attracted the collaboration of additional health organizations.

Strategies

Apparent success depends on how objectives are stated. Actual success depends on the competent use of appropriate *strategy*. If the goal represents the direction we plan to go and the objective represents destinations at which we plan to arrive, then strategies represent how we plan to get there. A *strategy* is a statement of the communication themes or vehicles that will be used to accomplish a specific objective. It represents an overall plan of action that will tie together each action taken to implement the campaign. The communication manager constructs strategies based on the following elements:

1   *Available data.* This includes the situation analysis and all the research that has gone into creating it. It also includes the manager's knowledge from previous experience with an organization and with communication campaigns. In the case of the thyroid campaign, available data included research by Fleishman Hillard with consumers, health care professionals, media, managed care organizers, professional societies, and consumer groups. It found that only 30% of women had been tested for thyroid disease

prior to the campaign, that nearly 90% of people did not know that thyroid problems could do things such as elevate cholesterol levels, and that although half of all women experienced three or more symptoms associated with a thyroid disorder 75% of them did not discuss the symptoms with a doctor (PRSA, 1998).

2   *Communication and public relations principles.* This includes knowledge of the public relations function and its parameters. Fleishman Hillard knew it could help by boosting public awareness, bringing the issue to the attention of Congress, and promoting testing among individuals at risk (women). It had expertise in all of these areas of promotion.

3   *Communication and persuasion theories.* The body of knowledge in the social sciences can provide you with the ability to make hypotheses, or likely informed guesses, about the types of strategies that will accomplish the stated objective and be relevant to a situation. Social science theories are essentially explanations of how and why things happen the way they do. In short, theories can tell you how people are likely to react to your campaign and why.

In the case of the thyroid campaign (PRSA, 1998), Fleishman Hillard realized the problem was a lack of awareness instead of active resistance to testing. People demonstrated they did not know much about the importance of the thyroid gland, its effects, or how easy it was to diagnose and treat thyroid problems. As a result, Fleishman Hillard knew it needed to build knowledge. It also knew from persuasion theories that people are more likely to take action if they understand the relevance of an issue and if they can see that taking action is both easy and effective. As a result, Fleishman Hillard developed three related strategies:

1   Build consumer knowledge, particularly among women, about the thyroid gland's function and effect on the body.

2   Humanize thyroid disease by demonstrating its effect on quality of life and risks to long-term health.

3   Demonstrate the ease and simplicity of a sensitive thyroid stimulating hormone (TSH) test to detect thyroid dysfunction.

Tactics

These strategies, of course, are ideas for guidance instead of a list of actions to implement. They are, in fact, counterparts to goals, which are ideas about campaign results. The communication campaign, therefore, also must include an action counterpart to the objective. These are called *tactics* and are the tasks that must be accomplished to achieve a stated objective. The tactics are the specifics of your recipe. They are, essentially, job assignments. Tactics include the following:

- The task
- Parties responsible for completing the task
- Deadline for completion of the task

Tactics include the development of specific communication vehicles, such as public service announcements, logos, brochures, training materials, and special events. For Fleishman Hillard, the tactics included development of an engaging theme, identification of a celebrity spokesperson (an Olympic gold medalist who had suffered with undiagnosed thyroid problems for 3 years), development of high-profile events that attract both national and local media coverage, implementation of special events such as a VIP breakfast to bring the spokesperson and physicians together with key members of Congress, a free TSH testing event on Capitol Hill, and more (PRSA, 1998). Each stated tactic related to a specific strategy that was designed to achieve a stated objective, which demonstrated the accomplishment of a stated goal.

Climbing Toward the Goal: The Strategic Planning Ladder

As the thyroid campaign illustrates, the campaign plan becomes a tightly organized set of specific tasks that put carefully selected strategies into action to accomplish stated objectives representing organizational goals that enable an organization to achieve its mission. To make sure all elements of the campaign plan are necessary and appropriate, it helps to think of the progression of specificity as a ladder (Figure 3.1 and Figure 3.2). When going up the ladder, such as considering the appropriateness of a tactic, ask "Why are we doing this?" In other words, does every action have a stated purpose?

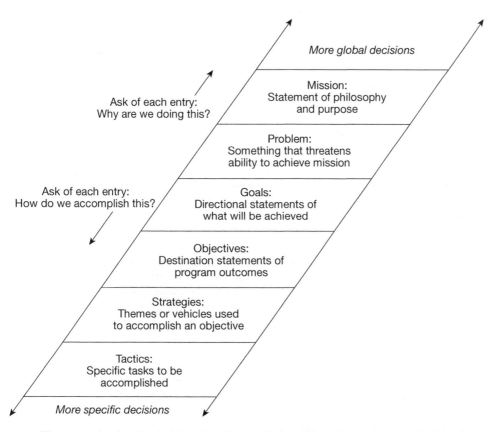

FIG. 3.1. The strategic planning ladder. How the mission, problem statements, goals, objectives, strategies, and tactics relate to one another.

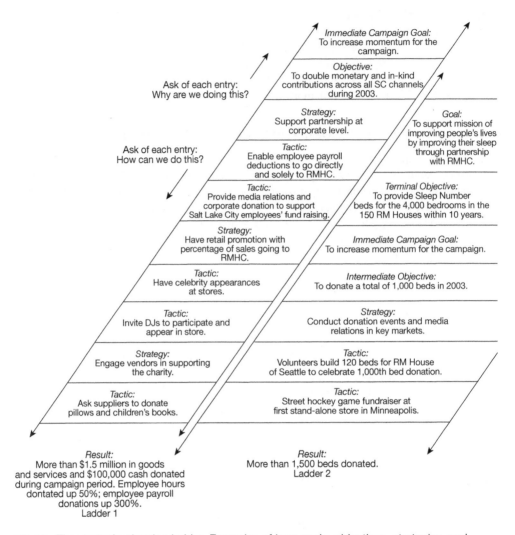

FIG. 3.2. The strategic planning ladder. Examples of how goals, objectives, strategies, and tactics relate to one another as demonstrated by the "Catching ZZZs for Charity" campaign implemented by Select Comfort and Carmichael Lynch Spong in 2003. A communication program may have a number of interrelated "ladders." RM, Ronald McDonald; RMHC, Ronald McDonald House Charities; SC, Select Comfort.

The answer to the why question for a tactic should be a strategy. The answer for a strategy should be an objective. The answer for an objective should be a goal, and the answer for a goal should be the problem, to which the answer is the mission. For example:

Why do we need to produce a website?
–   Because we need to provide information to potential applicants to spark their interest and gain their confidence.

Why do we need an informational campaign?
–   Because we need to increase applications from this target public by 30%

Why do we need to increase applications?
–   Because we want to increase representation from this target public in our program.

Why do we want to increase their representation?
–   Because our organization strives to serve the entire community, and they have not been represented in the same proportion in which they exist in the community.

In reverse, going down the ladder, the manager should ask "How will we accomplish this?" To solve a problem requires a goal statement. To achieve the goal requires objectives. To meet the objectives requires a strategy, and each strategy requires tactics to put it into action. For example:

How can we increase representation of the target public in our program?
–   We can increase the number of applications by the next deadline date.

How can we increase the applications?
–   We can develop an information campaign targeting interested community members from the target group.

How can we implement the campaign?
–   Among other things, we can build a website.

Initiating the Planning Process

The communication program plan represents the culmination of much research, analysis, and expertise. Sometimes it can be difficult to determine where to begin the planning process. Client representatives may have nonspecific or conflicting ideas, and communication personnel may have varying interests in and interpretations of the issue as well. As a result, it can be useful to begin the planning process with an old-fashioned brainstorming session. Several brainstorming techniques exist. One especially effective strategy is called *story boarding*.

Storyboarding, originally developed by the Walt Disney Corp. to design *Steamboat Willie*, is a highly visible, highly interactive way of gathering and sorting ideas. *Story boarding* refers to the process of creating the story that will guide strategic planning. In effect, it is a way to approach the process of analyzing the situation and identifying the strengths and opportunities that will inform decision making. Besides helping participants work through a problem, the technique provides a mechanism for tracking the decision-making process so others can see how collaborators arrived at a final decision. This gives confidence to participants who can be reminded of the factors that produced a decision, and it adds credibility to the decisions made because they are based on clearly presented evidence.

Managers can use storyboards for four purposes:

1   *Planning* is used to outline the steps required to reach a specific result, such as preparing for a special event.
2   *Idea* is used to develop a concept or a theme for a specific purpose.
3   *Communication* is used to determine who needs to know something, what they need to know, and how best to interact with them.

4   *Organization* is used to determine who will take responsibility for designated tasks, and how to work together as departments, individuals, or organizations to accomplish a plan.

Storyboarding uses a facilitated creative thinking process to guide brainstorming. The process includes three stages of idea generation, critical review, and consensus building to create a shared vision of a plan. It is a little like a focus group, requiring a facilitator to guide discussion and encourage freedom of thought. During the idea-generation stage, participants offer ideas for issues, such as the who, what, where, when, why, and how of a problem; the identification of important target publics, opportunities, and constraints for a campaign; and the creation of campaign themes. Each idea is noted on an index card, which gets pinned or taped onto walls or tackable surfaces. During critical review, the group sifts through ideas to organize, refine, and prioritize them. Finally, during consensus building, the participants try to arrive at an agreement for the plan, idea, communication strategy, or organization. The rules for the creative thinking process include the following:

- The more ideas, the better
- No criticism
- Hitchhiking is good (triggering ideas from others' ideas)
- Spelling does not count
- Handwriting does not count
- One idea per card
- Yell out each idea during brainstorming.

This technique helped the state of Washington develop a campaign focused on alcohol abuse prevention that required the cooperation of a wide spectrum of individuals from organizations with various agendas and perspectives. Representatives from the relevant state agency, the Governor's budgeting office, the state liquor control board, the public schools, higher education, and other organizations all gathered to determine how to focus the campaign and how to assign responsibilities (CF2GS, 1995). Beginning from the agency's stated goal, to "teach that alcohol is a drug," participants shared their personal experience, knowledge of research, and awareness of practical constraints such as how to ensure the cooperation of important stakeholders. The discussion gradually identified an agreed-upon target group: parents of children younger than the usual age of first experimentation. From there, the group developed an action plan for developing benchmark and formative research, which led to development of campaign materials.

The research for the campaign included a statewide survey of parents with children between the ages of 3 and 10 that would serve as a benchmark for later evaluation and would provide useful information for media relations activities. It also included a series of focus groups used to test the proposed message strategies (see Chapter 8).

The goal of the campaign was to educate parents of young children about talking to their kids about alcohol at an early age. A process goal was to equip parents with the knowledge and awareness that they can be the most significant source of help in influencing their children's attitudes and behavior toward responsible drinking habits. Objectives included distributing 100,000 informational brochures to parents over a 2-year period, increasing awareness of an "alcohol is a drug" message among Washington parents by 10% each year over a 2-year period, securing statewide media commitments to run $250,000 of pro bono advertising in support of the campaign each year, increasing by 10% the number of Washington parents who rank alcohol use by kids as a "serious problem," and increasing by 10% the awareness of "the harmful effects of alcohol use by children."

The strategy for the campaign included the development of a multiyear, multimedia statewide campaign focusing on increasing parents' knowledge that alcohol is a drug and that they can be the most powerful deterrent and source of help to their children regarding potential alcohol use. The strategy also included: securing cooperative funding sources to sustain the campaign for 2 years; to maintain high visibility through the use of public relations and media relations activities throughout the campaign; and to coordinate all campaign activities at state, county, and local levels to ensure a successful launch.

The five primary tactics for the campaign included: implementing the statewide surveys; developing three distinctly different conceptual treatments of the "alcohol is a drug" theme; obtaining commitments from magazines, newspapers, newsletters, television stations, and radio stations; developing a poster and a parent guide; and securing co-op partners.

The campaign achieved its objectives, distributing 103,265 informational brochures to parents over a 2-year period, increasing awareness from 53% to 62% (an increase of 17%), and securing more than $250,000 of pro bono advertising in support of the campaign. The campaign did not greatly increase the percentage of Washington parents who were "extremely concerned" about alcohol use by kids and considered it a "serious problem," which already was at 45% and averaged 5.8 on a 7-point scale. The number of parents who mentioned alcohol as the "most used drug" by children increased by 13%, rising from 46% to 52% among parents who recalled the campaign. The post-campaign survey demonstrated that 72% of parents saw or heard one of the public service advertisements produced for the campaign.

Final Thoughts

The Washington state campaign embodied all of the essential elements of scientific program planning, from the development of the situation analysis at the beginning of the campaign to the demonstration of accountability at the end of the campaign. The use of careful research and a clear plan ensured that every campaign tactic fulfilled a necessary strategy and that every strategy responded to a desired objective. Every objective realized a relevant goal, and the goals took aim at the problem of underage drinking. The clarity of the MBO process makes it easy for an outside observer to understand the purpose of the campaign, the reasons for actions taken in pursuit of campaign goals, and the results achieved at campaign's end. The MBO technique cannot guarantee success for the practitioner, but the focus it provides will make success a more likely outcome. Because of its overt emphasis on accountability, the MBO technique also makes an achievement impossible to dismiss.

4

Determining Research Needs

Developing the Research Plan

Now you know that you need to develop an effective communication plan and that to do this you need to develop strategies that will achieve stated objectives. To arrive at this plan, a communication manager needs to apply what Lloyd Kirban, at that time executive vice president and director of research for Burson–Marsteller in New York (Broom & Dozier, 1990, p. 21), called "informed creativity." The role of research is to focus brainstorming, confirm or disconfirm hunches, and help fine-tune your strategies (Sidebar 4.1).

Sidebar 4.1

Confessions of a Silver Anvil Judge

The Silver Anvil is the most prestigious award a public relations professional can win. But it doesn't come easy.

This year, I had the privilege of serving as a judge for the PRSA Silver Anvil awards. As a marketing strategist and researcher with more than 25 years in the business, I have judged numerous competitions.

The Silver Anvil award selection process is as good as or better than any other professional awards program. And the winning entries were all worthy of the awards bestowed upon them.

What concerns me, however, is the quality of the entries that did not win Silver Anvils. In some cases, they were so far off in conveying a strong program that one might conclude that many industry professionals need to revisit what constitutes a successful public relations program.

The entry criteria for the Silver Anvils is very specific, requiring documentation in four major areas: research, planning, execution and results. To win an award, an agency must demonstrate that its entry delivered in all four areas.

Where is research?

Many agencies failed to quantify their entry's contribution to each of the four areas. Research was clearly the area with the most room for improvement. Several submissions stretched the definition and in the process devalued the role that research can play in defining the goals and target audience of a public relations program.

For example, many entries seemed to support the notion that research consists of talking to a few editors about their perception of a company and its products. Other submissions relied heavily on what a top executive said was important to the progress of the product or company. While media soundings and senior executive interviews can be important factors in determining the parameters of a public relations effort, they do not begin to go far enough in terms of research.

A strategic public relations program will address the audience that is relevant to the public relations campaign. Many campaigns have multiple audiences, including end users, employees, members, investors, suppliers, and government officials. Research, when properly utilized, will define the target audience of the campaign and help set priorities.

It will often delineate the existing perceptions, needs and opinions of the program's target audience. Research initiatives should link this understanding to the marketing and brand situation of the product or company. In the process, it should provide a benchmark from which to judge the impact of the public relations program.

What are the goals?

Not every research effort has to be extensive or expensive. We have developed a number of quick and relatively inexpensive research tools to use when resources are limited. They include qualitative samples, in-house research panels and sophisticated analysis of existing data.

The planning stage is the second area addressed on the entry form. Here, the most frequent problem was that the choice of goals and objectives was not justified against the clients' business goals. A public relations program should be developed to support the broader needs of the client, with emphasis on corporate reputation and brand building.

The program goals should be articulated in a manner that enables the client to easily evaluate the effectiveness of the program. Many of the entries did not provide any way to quantify progress made towards the program's objectives, making it impossible to evaluate whether or not the program achieved its goals.

The classic example is a statement indicating that a program was designed to "establish the company as a leader." Again, the lack of documentation leads one to question the relevance of a program based upon poorly articulated goals and objectives.

Where's the support?

The third area addressed on the Silver Anvil entry form is the execution of the public relations program. This was where the real fun began.

Copies of press kits, videotapes, audiotapes, and collateral of all kinds filled submissions binders to the brim. The problem for many entries, however, was the lack of information regarding how promotional material supported the program's key messages.

Material generated by the creative team often demonstrated a complete disconnection between the creative and strategic elements of a program. The material looked slick but failed to convey key messages to the target audience. Lavish creative efforts on behalf of a low-budget campaign points to a lack of planning and poor execution on the part of the staff responsible for the program. It may be hard to imagine, but it is possible to overspend on production!

The final area on the Silver Anvil entry form is program results.

Stating that top management "liked the program" hardly constitutes results befitting a Silver Anvil award winner. To most professionals, letters received from the sales force or customers are also insufficient to be considered for an award.

What Is Success?

After opening several submissions that included clip reports as proof of a program's impact, I was forced to wonder how some public relations professionals are measuring success. Clips are an indicator of interest on the part of the media, not necessarily of influence on the purchasing behavior or attitudes of the public.

To be considered a successful public relations program, there must be evidence that the goals and objectives of a program have been met. For instance, if the stated goal of a program is to raise brand awareness, the public relations agency needs to provide documentation demonstrating that the goal was achieved. A brand awareness survey conducted before and after the public relations campaign would clearly illustrate whether the brand experienced increased consumer recognition or not.

Some other examples of quantifiable objectives are a 5% increase in sales, 10,000 new hits a month at the company website or one million dollars donated to a nonprofit organization.

Not every public relations program is well suited to the Silver Anvil awards. Entries are intended to represent the best a public relations program has to offer in a given year. Submissions that are clearly lacking in one of the four entry criteria devalue not only the awards, but also the public relations industry itself.

Programs that win Silver Anvils almost always demonstrate a tight linkage between the goals of the business and the program results. Failing to do that, other efforts will remain nothing more than submissions.

From "Confessions of a Silver Anvil Judge," by L. Chiagouris, 1998 (Winter), *Public Relations Strategist*, 74, pp. 29–31. Permission granted by *Public Relations Strategist*, a quarterly publication of the Public Relations Society of America.

The Role of Research

Because the strategic manager is goal oriented, the decision to conduct research depends on its relevance to program goals and an organization's mission. In other words, research should be goal oriented, like the program plan itself. "Doing research" may seem intimidating to those without a social science background, but research spans a range of activities, many of which managers do instinctively. What does it mean to do research, and what are the goals of research? Research is systematic listening used in an attempt to reduce uncertainty. The goal of research is to gain maximum control of the things that can be controlled and maximum understanding of the things that cannot be controlled.

Examine a simple model of the communication process and consider what elements we can control and what elements we cannot control. This varies with the context in which a manager works, but communication research has demonstrated that, overall, managers have the most control over the *source* and the least control over the *receiver*. With the use of paid advertising, the manager can control the source, the message, and the channel. Public relations messages, however, often must travel through *gatekeepers,* or people between the original source and the ultimate message recipient. These include editors, reporters, bloggers, and opinion leaders, among others. As a result, you may have control over who your initial source will be, such as the CEO of a corporation, and you can agree with your source on a message, but you can lose control quickly as the message goes through gatekeepers and evolves over the Internet. Your best hope for control, therefore, is to gain a thorough understanding of everything that might affect the dissemination, evolution, and interpretation of your key messages.

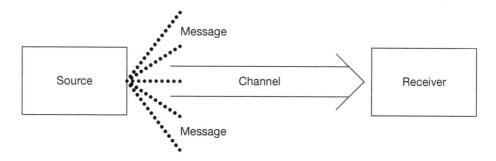

FIG. 4.1. A simplified model of communication.

The Benefits of Research

Research offers benefits that can help the strategic manager develop the understanding necessary to design and maintain successful communication programs. First, research can help the manager make sense of the increasing fragmentation of audiences in global, multimedia communication environments. Research can probe attitudes, identify opinion leaders, and help determine appropriate timing for actions and messages.

Second, research can help keep top-level management from losing touch with important stakeholders from which they may become insulated. According to the homophily principle (Rogers & Kincaid, 1981), people tend to exchange ideas most frequently among those who share similar characteristics, such as beliefs, values, education, and social status. Without extra effort, therefore, management can lose touch with non-management employees, as well as with other stakeholders. *Homophily* refers to the degree to which pairs of individuals who interact share similarities, which tend to help them understand each other and value each other's perspectives. Because effective public relations focuses on relationship building, it is important for stakeholders who depend on each other to understand and respect each other; two-way communication is essential for effective public relations. One survey found that 24% of unionized companies that used attitude surveys to gather information from employees suffered strikes, whereas 48% of those who had not done opinion research suffered strikes. Among all companies surveyed, 64% of those that suffered strikes had not performed survey research in the past year. Monsanto, for example, discovered through a benchmarking survey of employees that the employees were suffering from information overload. In response, the company consolidated 22 newsletters into one, and made more use of e-mail, less use of video and audio media, and more use of face-to-face communication. The company also adopted an open-communication policy that fostered trust on the premise that trust increases productivity. The company found in a more recent survey that 80% of employees felt they were getting good information, exceeding the program's objective of at least 50%.

Third, research can help confirm whether complaints about an organization are widespread beliefs or represent the impressions of a vocal minority that holds little credibility with key stakeholders. It also can prevent organizations from wasting effort on nonexistent issues. For example, the American Dairy Association (ADA) discovered that it did not need to do a multimillion dollar campaign to dissuade Americans from thinking cheese is an unsuitable lunch food because of its fat content. A survey of 1,002 respondents demonstrated that cheese already was the most common food chosen for lunch, that the top reason for choosing it was its taste, and that eating nutritiously was the second highest priority (after taking a break) at lunchtime (American Dairy Association, 1999). Because "low in fat" was one of the top two factors cited by respondents as making a meal nutritious, the ADA could safely conclude that fat in cheese was not preventing people from putting it into their lunch boxes. In fact, because no cheese–fat–lunch connection seemed to exist in public opinion, implementing a campaign acknowledging the connection could have created a problem where none previously had existed.

Fourth, research can guide strategy so that funds and efforts are spent wisely. Research can reduce the cost of a campaign and, as a result, can enhance the credibility of the communication professionals with top management. An organization may find that a paid-media campaign, in addition to being expensive, is less effective than a social media presence. Editors commonly grouse that they receive many shotgun style news releases that go straight into the garbage because the releases do not show immediate relevance to their readers or viewers.

Fifth, research can help prevent unintended effects. A firm called Successful Marketing Strategies found out the hard way, when a "tease and deliver" promotional strategy for a high-tech product backfired (Settles, 1989). The promotion for the product, which was designed to save data from accidental destruction, included a mailing to trade publication editors, in a plain brown envelope, which featured a note that read, "Who's been shooting [name of publication] readers?" A decal of a bullet hole appeared on the outside of the envelope, which was hand addressed to 50 editors and reporters without any return address. A second mailing, 2 days later, was stamped "CASE FILE 7734" and had a card that read, "Who's been shooting [name of publication] readers in the foot?" The answer, inside the fold-out card, was that they were shooting themselves in the foot by not having the product to protect their data. Had the firm done advance research of the target public, it would have learned that several editors had received bona fide threats in the past, which made them sensitive to this sort of mailing.

Had the firm done pretesting, it might have caught the typo on the first mailing (leaving out "in the foot") that increased the perception of real threat. It also might have discovered that editors receiving the anonymous mailing might call in the FBI or the Postal Service to investigate, which happened. Fortunately, the company managed to assuage the nerves of most editors through individual follow-up contacts and ended up with a lot of attention for the product. The firm learned, however, that public relations professionals need to consider the perspective of the people who will receive their messages to make sure messages will be received as intended. As Settles (1989) wrote, "Success in public relations comes from the ability to incorporate the lessons learned from past mistakes into bold future steps" (p. 39). To the extent the manager can make mistakes in the pretesting stage, fewer lessons will have to be learned the hard way.

Sixth, research can provide facts on which objectives for accountability can be based. Baseline or benchmark data on consumer attitudes or behavior, for example, are necessary to demonstrate change after a campaign is finished. NewsEdge Corp. demonstrated that a campaign to address high employee turnover following a merger of three competing companies reduced turnover to 6% from 40%, earning the company a Platinum PR Honorable Mention from *PR News*.

Specific Research Functions

As a manager, you will consider three types of research in planning: formative research, program research, and summative (or evaluation) research. Formative research provides data and perspective to guide campaign creation. Program research guides the implementation of the program to ensure that strategies have the intended effects instead of unintended, counter-productive effects. Summative research provides data to evaluate the success of a communication program based on the achievement of stated objectives. More specifically, research can help strategic planning in six key areas:

1   *Problem identification.* First, research can show whether a problem suspected to exist truly does exist. It also can help identify where the problem is, when the problem occurs, when it developed, or if it has not yet developed and could be prevented. For example, when Enron collapsed, other utility companies realized this could affect their own ability to survive. Kansas City-based Aquila therefore hired Edelman Public Relations to maintain its credibility with the public while it pursued a restructuring project. They identified two key target publics and developed messages appropriate for each.

They emphasized the maintenance of open communication and balanced the current bad news with information about long-term strategies for recovery. They avoided a variety of disastrous outcomes, such as a widespread equity sell-off, and the stock price began to rise again from its low point in 2003. The chair of the company won re-election at the company's annual meeting with 95% of the vote.

2   *Problem effects or implications.* Research can demonstrate how big a problem is, as well as for whom it poses difficulties. The National Heart, Lung, and Blood Institute, for example, discovered that in 2000 only 34% of women knew that heart disease is the biggest killer of women, with eight times more women dying from heart disease than from breast cancer. This convinced them to target women with an awareness campaign that increased awareness by 12% in 1 year.

3   *Strategic direction.* Research can suggest ways to communicate effectively about a problem and actions to solve the problem. When Burson-Marstellar had 3 months to convince California voters to defeat a proposition that would have eliminated the collection of racial data by public agencies, they had to move quickly and find a way to compete with the main event scheduled for that particular election day: a recall vote on the governor. The agency quickly gathered existing information related to a previous, similar initiative to analyze voter demographics, attitudes, profiles, exit polls, and media coverage. They also monitored current media coverage and messages distributed by the opposition. They held focus groups with grassroots representatives and formed a steering committee to ensure support and tight organization for the campaign. They learned that constituents responded strongly to a message that asserted that the initiative was "bad medicine" because the lack of racial ethnic data would compromise health care, public safety, and education programs. With a $200,000 budget, modest for a statewide political campaign, the drive convinced 64% of voters to oppose the proposition, when 3 months before only 29% had opposed it and 50% had supported it. One key to their success: 20% had been unaware of the measure, which meant the campaign could frame the issue as "bad medicine" before this target group formed other opinions that would have to be changed (Table 4.1).

4   *Strategy testing.* Research methods as diverse as focus groups and surveys can be used to test creative strategies to make sure they work as anticipated. Some companies now monitor their reputation through the use of chat rooms, mail lists, and news groups. On behalf of Cingular Wireless, Ketchum Public Relations designed a campaign to encourage teens to avoid dangerous distractions (such as talking on their cell phone) while driving ("Cingular Wireless Announces," 2005). They screened a video for 230 teens to ensure their receptiveness to the message, which needed to "be funny/make

Table 4.1 How Opposition to California Proposition 54 Grew

	July	*August*	*September*	*October*	*Election Day*
Oppose	29	35	40	49	64
Support	50	46	40	35	36
Undecided	21	19	20	16	—

Note: Reprinted with permission from the Public Relations Society of America based on field polling data and information from the California Secretary of State's office (PRSA, 2004a).

me laugh, be honest, be clear so I get the message, don't try too hard to be cool, say/ show something important, do not talk down to me, and use people my own age in your communications." They also showed the video to their safety partners and to dozens of teachers. Once re-edited in response to the feedback from each group, the video and associated lesson materials received an enthusiastic response from teachers, with 99% saying they would use it again. By 2005, 12 states had distributed the program to all driver education teachers statewide, exceeding the originally stated objective of 5 states.

5 *Tracking during implementation.* For a communication program to have an effect, the message must be distributed and received. In addition, activities need to take place as planned, and few things happen exactly the way a manager intended. For example, the Washington State Department of Ecology and PRR, Inc., wanted to improve air quality by convincing drivers to avoid long periods of idling while dropping off or picking up children at school. They made sure campaign materials actually reached faculty and staff at targeted schools on time, and then verified that the material was received by parents by keeping track of pledge cards that parents returned. Along the way, they discovered that they needed to hire temporary staff to help prepare materials after well-meaning sponsors missed their deadlines. They also discovered that they needed extra staff to help collect idling data in locations where volunteer data collectors (high school students) could not complete the task. If they had not tracked the process carefully, these unexpected crises could have ruined the campaign and made an evaluation impossible.

6 *Evaluation of results.* Research can provide accountability to help communication practitioners prove program impact by demonstrating program results that confirm success. In the Washington State Department of Ecology's "Dare to Care About the Air" campaign, they documented that idling times decreased by 112% during the implementation period, far exceeding the objective of 50%. They also documented a 66.8% participation rate, which exceeded the stated objective of 50%.

Elements of a Research Plan

Research plans, like communication plans, are vital to the success of communication programs. Because they too are goal oriented, they help keep strategic planning on track, on time, and within budget. A research plan includes an explanation of research needs; research goals; research objectives; hypotheses or hunches; and research questions to guide data collection and analysis, help propose research strategies, and prompt a discussion of how to use the results. Your organization may develop its own template for a research plan, but one model that includes all of the important elements appears in Table 4.2.

Determining Research Needs

To develop a research plan, you must determine your research needs. Your initial situation analysis can help you do this. What do you know about the problem, the situation, your opportunities, and your constraints? What do you need to know?

For everything you think you know, test whether you have evidence to confirm that your information is correct. You can use many types of evidence, ranging from experts' observations

Table 4.2 Elements of the Research Plan

Title Page
(include client's name, agency name, date, and title)

I.   Research Needs

- Problem statement
- Situation analysis
  - the issue (problem statement)
  - what was known about the client and the issue
  - history
  - reporting lines for budget and policies
  - internal and external opportunities and challenges
  - assumptions (things we think we knew but have not verified)
  - information needs (questions)

length: ranges considerably, often 2 to 8 pages

II. Research Goals (What are you trying to find out?)

- Formal statements of research goals
- Further explanation of each goal, as needed

length: usually 1 page or less

III. Research Objectives (How will you find out, and by when?)

- Formal statements of objectives

length: usually 1 page or less

IV. Hypotheses (Hunches or evidence-based expectations)

- Anticipated answers to questions
- Reasoning for answer anticipated

length: usually 1 to 2 pages

V. Research Strategies

- Explanation of proposed methodology, sampling approach
  - reasons for choices based on time, budget expertise, and need for precision
  - advantages and limitations of each choice against alternatives
- Operationalization of concepts (How will ideas be measured?)
  - wording of questions
  - relevance of questions to hypotheses
- Procedures for data analysis

length: usually 2 to 4 pages

VI. Expected Uses of the Results

- What will be done with the information gained (Market segmentation, theme development, strategy development)

length: usually 1 page or less

---

to survey or sales data. The more scientific your data, the more convincing it will be and the more it can be trusted. More specifically, you can consider the following as evidence:

1 Public relations principles, laws, and professional guidelines can provide guidance for procedural and ethical issues.
2 Communication and persuasion theories are scientifically tested ideas about how and why things happen the way they do. Theories do not provide hard and fast rules about how things work. The way social science works, a theory cannot be proven right; it only can be proven wrong.
3 Expert observations can provide some validation, particularly at the brainstorming stage, but they are not as unimpeachable as hard data from surveys, sales, spreadsheets, or experiments. Quotes from individuals with high credibility and relevance to the situation are most useful.
4 Quantitative data can include survey data, sales figures, content analysis, experimental results, budget histories, formal tracking of Internet traffic and data from websites, customer service calls, and so on.
5 Qualitative data can include focus groups, interviews, field observations, informal tracking communication among stakeholders, and so on. These also are most useful at the brainstorming stage.

You may find that some of your ideas about the problem are based on assumptions instead of hard evidence. If possible, test the veracity of these assumptions. For example, service organizations frequently assume that poor attendance, low subscriptions, or low registrations reflect a poor reputation that requires improvement. Upon further research, however, organizations may find that their problems stem from low awareness instead of from negative attitudes, requiring a communication program different from what a reputation management program would entail.

Determining and Understanding Target Publics

You want to know as much as possible about key stakeholders, often referred to as target publics. First you need to identify and prioritize them. This process is called *segmentation*. Then you need to understand more deeply their interests, their needs, their concerns, their beliefs, and their behaviors.

Your *target publics* are subcategories of your *stakeholders*. Stakeholders are those who should care and be involved or those who can be affected by or who can affect your program. Because public relations focuses on the development and maintenance of mutually beneficial relationships, ask yourself who benefits from your organization's activities, directly and indirectly, and on whom does your organization depend to achieve stated goals, both in the short term and in the long term. Who belongs in your problem statement? You can segment publics by various characteristics. These include the following:

1 *Demographics.* These include common census-type categories, such as age, gender, race or ethnicity, education level, occupation, family size, marital status, income, geographic location, political party, and religion.

2   *Psychographics.* These include personality and attitudinal characteristics, including values, beliefs, and lifestyle. These characteristics can help you identify who holds hopes, fears, and interests that most help or hinder your communication and organizational goals.

3   *Sociographics.* A wide variety of categories can be called sociographics, but they tend to focus on behaviors and characteristics common to an easily identified group of people. Broom and Dozier (1990) summarized several sociographic categories of value to communication professionals, including the following:

- *Covert power.* This represents an attempt to discover who holds indirect power over persons who may more directly affect your program's success. For example, an administrative assistant holds a great deal of covert power over a busy executive who relies on the assistant to screen calls and help prioritize schedules. Family members also hold covert power over many business decisions and certainly over purchasing decisions. Marketers refer to the power of children in sales as the *nag factor*.
- *Position.* This represents an attempt to identify occupations or leadership positions that make individuals important stakeholders and depends greatly on the context in which you work. For example, lobbyists, journalists, legislators, union representatives, PTA officers, and teachers all can act as opinion leaders with wide-ranging effects in certain situations.
- *Reputation.* Sometimes people who influence others' opinions and behaviors cannot be categorized neatly into occupations or positions but can be identified by other stakeholders. For example, particular older peers may influence the extent to which younger schoolchildren embrace a recycling or health-promotion campaign. People in a community may identify individuals who have credibility over a zoning issue by virtue of their social ties or community activism.
- *Organizational membership.* It is important to identify who is a member of competing or complementary organizations that can be of assistance to your program directly or indirectly. When the Seattle Sheraton wanted to gain the business of corporate executives, for example, it determined on which organizations the executives served as board members. Targeting its community service activities to these organizations helped the Sheraton cement ties with these important decision makers.
- *Role in decision process.* Decisions often are made in incremental steps by a combination of individuals and committees. Gaining support at each step can require different strategies.

4   *Behaviors.* Purchasing patterns and attendance histories can provide useful information about who is using your organization's services, who might use them, who has rejected them, and so on.

5   *Communication behaviors.* These include latent (inactive but relevant) and active publics. You need to determine levels of awareness and the extent to which individuals care or do not care about your organization and its activities. These characteristics are likely to affect how they react to information about your organization. Grunig and Hunt (1984) suggested three measures to determine activity:

- *Problem recognition.* This represents the extent to which publics sense that a problem exists. If they see no problem, they will not be "active" or interested in the issue. Their level of recognition will affect the extent to which they seek to process information related to the issue.
- *Constraint recognition.* This represents the degree to which individuals believe they have the ability to affect an issue or situation. They may see constraints, or impediments, that limit their ability to change a situation or participate in an activity. If they do not feel they can participate or make a difference, they will be less likely to make an effort to think extensively about the issue.
- *Level of involvement.* This represents the degree to which individuals feel a connection between a situation or issue and themselves. The more they believe an issue can affect them, the more likely they are to take an active interest. Less involved individuals take a more passive approach.

Grunig and Hunt (1984) proposed four types of publics: (a) those active on all relevant issues, (b) those apathetic on all relevant issues, (c) those active on issues only if they involve most people in a relevant population, and (d) those active only on a single issue. As a follow up ("Grunig's Paradigm," 1998), Grunig suggested that stakeholders can be divided into three segments, depending on their level of "excitement" or interest in an issue. The groups include:

- *Long-haul types*, deeply interested in a topic and its ramifications
- *Special interest types*, concerned only about certain elements of a topic, such as how a newly proposed school building will affect their property taxes
- *Hot-button types*, interested only in elements that spark emotional debate, such as gun control.

Determining Program Outcomes

You need to identify what your program outcomes will be, as well as whether you need to evaluate *intermediate outcomes* along with *ultimate outcomes*. Motivating some sort of behavioral outcome helps public relations demonstrate bottom-line value. Often, however, a number of intermediate steps are required before you can achieve that final outcome. For example, a campaign to promote donations for the hungry could find it difficult to gain people's attention, particularly if the campaign takes place at a time other than the winter holiday season, when donation activity tends to be high. Holding a special event that attracts a potentially interested public could attract their attention while encouraging them to bring a donation (even a single can of food). Once present at the event, they can be encouraged to make additional donations or to become a member of the sponsoring organization. Attendance would be an intermediate behavior, can donations would be a second intermediate behavior, and memberships would be the ultimate behavior.

Testing Communication Channels

You need to know as much as possible about the potential channels of communication available for your public relations program. Some channels will be more expensive, or more time consuming, or more efficient, or frequently must assume that target publics are not interested or at best are easily distracted by competing messages and priorities. This may vary depending on your market and the publics with whom you wish to communicate. The National Cancer Institute (1999) developed a helpful chart of mass media channel characteristics that can serve as a general guide.

To choose effective communication vehicles, you need to assess the following:

1   *Credibility.* This refers to the extent to which the target publics trust the source of your messages, believe the source is unbiased, and believe the source is competent or expert in the topic under discussion.

2   *Reach and exposure frequency.* Is it easy for the target publics to gain access to information via this channel? How much exposure can you achieve?

3   *Efficiency.* You need to consider relative cost (in advertising called *cost per thousands*) against relative benefits. Costs include production and distribution costs in terms of monetary investments and time and staff requirements. To what extent can you reach target audiences versus other audiences less critical to your program?

4   *Control.* You need to determine to what extent the content and distribution of the message can be managed and to what extent control is important for the communication program. In crisis situations, companies often buy advertising to get their messages out without any filters. In other cases, a lack of control is preferred because of the increased credibility for a message that appears as editorial copy instead of as a purchased advertisement.

5   *Flexibility.* This refers to the extent to which the target publics can gain access to the message in a way convenient to them. The Internet, for example, provides users with the flexibility to review as much information as they wish whenever they wish, as opposed to having to wait to learn about a topic until the 11:00 news.

6   *Context.* This refers to the environment in which a message is presented, such as in the middle of a sports or entertainment program, during the news, or on the ceiling of a subway train.

You want to be able to predict how a message will be received by those you want to receive it. To do this you need to know how your target public feels about your organization and possible information sources and how their attitudes relate to specific message strategies you might employ. Keep in mind that you need to be able to anticipate the extent to which unintended recipients may have access to your message and how their reactions may affect your program goals.

You do not want to have to pull costly advertising, as did the Ad Council and Connect for Kids, a child advocacy initiative of the Benton Foundation, when humor in their ad campaign disparaged other child advocates. The copy in the ad called school board members "boogerheads," attracting nationwide protests from school boards and superintendents for being disrespectful in a campaign that was intended to promote respect ("Humor Backfires," 1999).

Testing the Message

The Center for Substance Abuse Prevention developed a helpful guide for avoiding problems in message development ("Avoiding Common Errors," 1990). They recommend checking to make sure messages are *clear, accurate, and relevant. Clarity* means checking whether the target public might interpret a message in a way other than, especially opposite to, what was intended. Mixed messages may appear to include contradictions. Pretesting can help the message designer avoid confusion.

Accuracy means making sure factual statements are correct and based on solid, verifiable evidence. Taking information out of context can change its meaning so that it no longer can be considered accurate. Unfortunately, many professed facts spread over the Internet without the benefit of fact checkers and editors, and they sometimes end up in print in credible media. Be careful to verify information independently such that the original source can be traced and checked. Secondhand information should not be considered real information. According to Kogan Page, Ltd., creators of a Corporate Communication Handbook ("Culling Lessons," 1998), the lack of accurate information is one of the three most important characteristics of a crisis. Supplying accurate information, therefore, can be one of the most effective tools for defusing a crisis.

Relevance means making sure the intended receivers will pay attention to the message. Messages must appeal to their values and interests and communicate in a language they use and understand. Porter Novelli, for example, found that calling obesity a *disease* instead of a *condition* made overweight individuals more receptive to messages about an anti-obesity drug. Attempts to use current slang and dialects can backfire and require careful pretesting.

Testing the Information Sources

When testing a message, it is imperative to test the credibility of the source. Research can guide you as you consider who should serve as information sources for your program messages. Sources must be *credible, expert and relevant*, and—you hope—interesting. To the social scientist credible includes various elements, but in general it simply means that people will find the source trustworthy. Public relations issues often boil down to a lack of trust. Expertise means the person seems knowledgeable about the topic. Relevant means that the target public will relate well to the person. Teenagers, for example, often would rather hear from another teenager than from an authority figure. In a crisis, even if the public relations officer is knowledgeable about company policies and plans, and even if the officer has a credible reputation among journalists, the most relevant source still is the CEO because the CEO is the person in charge.

One way of testing credibility is to have the moderator of a focus group, a semi-structured group interview, ask what participants would think of a message if the sponsor were a commercial advertiser, or a religious organization of some type, or the government, or a local chamber of commerce. A clear, accurate, and relevant message from a source perceived as untruthful, biased, or incompetent can backfire. As Chapter 15 explains, credibility is one of the most important requirements for effective communication and, when necessary, for persuasion.

Developing a Research Strategy

A myriad of approaches is available for tackling a problem and developing a complete situation analysis. The approaches explained here each offer a slightly different emphasis; depending on the context, one or a combination of these techniques may be most appropriate.

It has been said that asking "Why is this happening?" five times in a series will reveal the cause of a problem, which initially may be obscured. This technique, called the *Five Whys*, is especially useful when a problem is difficult to understand or particularly unusual. For example, when a large piece of the Jefferson Monument in Washington, D.C., fell off, threatening the safety of visitors and creating a public relations worry, the Five Whys traced the problem as follows:

The observation was that acid rain appeared to be eroding the monument, causing it to crumble. This suggested that a shelter might need to be built to protect it, which would be an expensive and potentially unattractive solution. But why was the erosion also evident on the inside of the monument, where rain would not be a factor?

> *Why? # 1* This erosion was traced to the strong soap used to clean the monument daily, combined with jet fumes from nearby Reagan National Airport. Why was it necessary to do so much more cleaning than at other monuments in the area?
>
> *Why? #2* It was pigeon droppings that required the extra cleaning. Why were pigeon droppings such a problem at this location?
>
> *Why? #3* An infestation of spiders that pigeons find especially tasty had occurred. Why was there an infestation of spiders?
>
> *Why? #4* Spiders were finding a bounty of midge eggs to eat, which they loved. Why were there midge eggs?
>
> *Why? #5* Midges live in the reeds in the backwaters of the Potomac River, which runs near the monument. At sunset, they swim and mate and lay their eggs, but they can get distracted by bright lights, which they love.

The solution was to turn on the lights near the monument 1 hour later. It was inexpensive, effective, and not unattractive (Geistfeld, 1995).

Whichever strategy you use while researching an issue, this example nicely illustrates a tactic useful for delving into the heart of a problem. Some specific types of research strategies include the following:

1   *Communications audit.* According to Kendall (1996), an audit examines, describes, and evaluates the status of a designated program. A communications audit examines the vehicles through which messages are sent and received from stakeholders. The audit requires:

   - Identifying the relevant internal and external publics
   - Collecting data from designated publics, using methods such as interviews, focus groups, and surveys to determine their use of communication vehicles, as well as their impression of the vehicles and of the organization
   - Analyzing current programs, personnel, and materials used for communication
   - Examining trends, opportunities, and challenges relevant to the organization.

   The audit, which can focus on the communication department or on the organization as a whole, culminates in recommendations for action. Just as financial audits occur regularly, communication audits also should take place on a regular basis. Because audits are broad based they can help address specific problems but they also can help guide more global, long-term planning.

2   *Social responsibility audit.* This is a more specific form of the communications audit. Kendall (1996) recommended a social responsibility audit as an examination of an

organization's performance related to corporate citizenship. As described by Kendall, the social responsibility audit focuses on factors that affect the organization, rather than on publics and communication activities. The social responsibility audit involves the following tasks:

- Identifying issues that have social or civic implications
- Ranking the issues based on when the issue will affect the organization, the extent to which its effects will be direct or indirect, and the significance of the issue to the organization
- Examining which departments can affect or will be affected by the issues
- Developing possible responses.

3   *Reputation audit* ("Can Value," 1996). Reputation is so important that it may be helpful to quantify. A reputation audit can provide a situation analysis focused on reputation. The audit involves the following:

- An identity analysis, which is essentially a communications audit
- An image analysis, to determine how the organization is perceived by key constituencies via surveys
- A coherence analysis, to compare the desired identity with the perceived identity.

4   *Gap research.* Sometimes called *perception gap* or *need* research, the gap method uses a series of four questions to ask target publics to perform their own diagnosis of an organization's strengths and weaknesses ("Gap Research," 1994). The questions include the following:

- On a scale (such as 1–9), how would you rate us on . . . ?
- Why did you give that rating? (This could evolve into the Five Whys.)
- Knowing the organization as you do, how good could we get if we really tried (on the same scale as used for question 1)?
- What would we have to do to get there?

The gap method is a way to perform focused brainstorming with a variety of stakeholders. Sometimes this makes a more sophisticated analysis unnecessary.

5   *Environmental scanning.* This phrase can mean different things in different fields of specialty, but in communication management it generally refers to systematically monitoring the communication environment for trends, competitors' positioning, potential opportunities and potential threats to organizational success. These opportunities and threats can take the form of scientific, technological, economic, political and social events. By identifying trends and anticipating change, the organization can position itself as a leader and avoid crisis situations. In some cases, environmental scanning simply helps an organization to understand the culture of a market niche or geographic area by identifying accepted norms for behavior and communication. For example, with new technologies shifting so quickly in popularity, organizations must anticipate how their key stakeholders like to gather information. Will a trend such as using mobile phones to scan bar codes simply fade, will it remain popular only with segments of the market who do not represent your core consumer, or does your company need to get ahead of this next emerging trend?

6   *Co-orientation research.* This is a perspective especially appropriate to public relations problems because of its focus on relationships. According to co-orientation theory, successful communication depends on accurate perceptions from all parties involved, with ultimate success defined as consensus (Figure 4.2). In the case of a controversy, an organization can ask the following questions:

- What does the organization think about X?
- What does the organization think the public thinks about X?
- What does the public think the organization thinks about X?
- What does the public think about X?

By asking these four questions, the communication manager can determine the extent to which the problem is one of true disagreement or one of perceived agreement or disagreement. Co-orientation, as a result, is a good way to diagnose the potential for miscommunication that can hurt attempts at building consensus and damage an organization's reputation. Broom and Dozier (1990) asserted that the most common

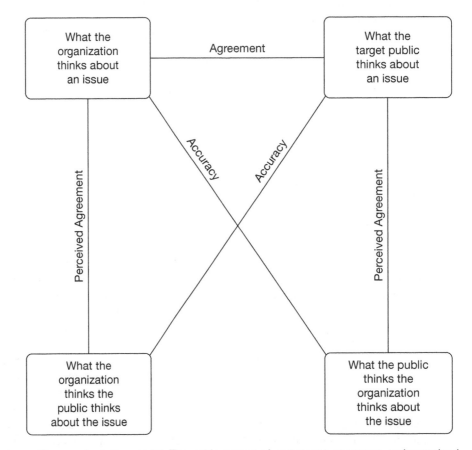

FIG. 4.2. The co-orientation model. The achievement of agreement, accuracy, and perceived agreement constitute consensus, which is the ideal outcome for public relations.

public relations audit involves establishing an organization's view on an issue, determining the target public's view on the issue, and determining the distance between the two views. This type of audit, however, does not account for the extent to which these views may be based on misperceptions of the other party's views or intentions. The co-orientation model accounts for both actual disagreement and perceived disagreement, which makes it a more powerful strategic planning tool. Co-orientation analysis determines actual agreement, perceived agreement, and accuracy. True consensus cannot occur until both parties agree and know they agree.

Developing a Realistic Research Proposal

It may appear that an organization can perform unlimited types of research endlessly. Clearly, organizations cannot afford the time and expense involved in such extensive research. As a result, the development of a research plan also requires an examination of constraints and priorities that can guide the type and extent of research pursued. The manager needs to prioritize research needs and appropriate research methods because the ideal research will never take place. Some mysteries will remain unsolved, and good research often raises additional, new questions (recall the Five Whys). The manager can rely on four issues to develop realistic parameters for the research plan:

1   *Time.* When are the results needed to develop the final communication plan by the required deadline? If the organization faces an immediate crisis, lengthy research cannot occur. If the organization's focus turns to long-term planning, more time can be devoted to research.

2   *Budget.* How much money and staff time can be devoted to research? Some types of research, such as face-to-face surveys, are expensive. You do not want to spend too much of your program budget on research and have too little left for implementation of the campaign itself. As a result, a common guideline for research spending suggests devoting 8% to 10% of a total program budget for research. A survey of 620 senior-level communication professionals in 2011 indicated that the field may finally be approaching this level of investment in evidence-based practice. The survey found that measurement and evaluation budgets had, on average, increased from 4% to 9% compared to the previous two years (USC Annenberg Strategic Communication and Public Relations Center, 2012). This represented a striking increase from 2004, when a survey of 1,026 professionals suggested that only 3% of communication budgets were dedicated to research, a decrease of 2% from the previous two years (Harris T. L. and Impulse Research, 2004). The survey leaders indicated that an appreciation for social media analytics probably had driven the most recent increase in research budgets. The danger in this otherwise good news is that much emphasis continues to go towards media exposure and corporate reputation, rather than on more sophisticated, outcome-oriented research. Professionals find that it can help to bundle relevant research costs in with the cost of a product such as the production of a website.

3   *Levels of expertise available.* Consider who will collect the data and how knowledgeable they are about data collection and analysis procedures. If data collection cannot be farmed out to an independent research firm, make sure the project does not require specialized expertise. As Chapters 6, 11, and 12 discuss, a variety of details

related to sampling, question design, and analysis can affect the veracity and credibility of research results. Do only what can be done well.

4   *Need for precision and depth (how research will be used).* Sometimes sophisticated research is overkill, but other times more refined information is required. For example, an election on a controversial issue can hinge on the details. Be ready to explain how research will be applied to strategic development and why the level of research proposed is necessary for program success. Public relations managers commonly report that clients want research but do not want to pay for it. Some resolve the issue by embedding research in the cost of campaign activities instead of categorizing it as a separate budget item. Research does not necessarily have to cost a lot, but the program manager needs to provide convincing reasons for performing desired research that will require an investment of resources such as time or money. This is where it is helpful to include hypotheses, or hunches, regarding what results you expect to find. The ability to explain how the results will direct strategy and how they will affect the likely outcome of the program can help convince the recalcitrant client.

Final Thoughts

A carefully conceived research plan will lay a strong foundation for program planning. Clear research goals and well-considered research strategies that correspond to the needs and constraints of the situation at hand give the manager the best chance of success in the later stages of program planning. The following chapters provide more background on the strengths and weaknesses of various research methods and sampling techniques. Managers can refer to these as they consider how to make choices that will not cost too much or take too long to implement but that will guide the effective selection of target publics, program outcomes, communication channels, and message strategies.

PART II

Gathering Useful Data for Strategic Guidance

5

Understanding Audiences

Research and Data-Collection Considerations

Chapter Contents

- Applications of Research
- Before Starting the Research Process
- Formal and Informal Approaches to Public Relations Research
- Informal Research Concerns
- Research Issues to Consider
- Steps to Research Project Design
- Final Thoughts

Measuring the success of public relations campaigns continues to generate interest, Internet chatter, invitations to what seems like endless evaluation seminars, and even controversy among professionals. Some practitioners suggest public relations evaluation is an art while others argue it is a science and still others propose it is both. Terms such as "metrics" and "return on investment" now are common parts of public relations' discussions as practitioners seek to assure supervisors and clients their spending on public relations campaigns is a worthwhile investment that will maximize impact and reap appropriate dividends. Meanwhile, practitioners' ability to fully evaluate public relations campaigns is complicated and hindered by limited resources including organizational and client resistance to costs, a lack of practitioner training and the increasing breadth of practices that are part of evolving public relations' practices.

Historically, public relations practitioners relied on strong media relations skills and key media placements to succeed in public relations. Public relations campaigns were based on practitioner hunches, knowledge of the market, and simple common sense. Practitioners used savvy media relations skills and well-honed campaign tactics to generate media attention for publicity-seeking organizations. Often, campaign evaluations were based on tactical campaign outputs (e.g., holding special events, distributing news releases, scheduling media interviews) resulting in media placements. Practitioners relied on thick binders filled with media clippings, inflated audience-exposure measures, and questionable cost-per-impressions numbers to demonstrate the value of public relations to clients and organizational executives.

Tracking media placements still has relevance to our field and many practitioners use services provided by Cision, BurrellesLuce or even Google Alerts which makes this a simple, inexpensive process for many applications. Even so, several organizational and environmental changes have required practitioners to increase their sophistication when it comes to campaign evaluation. An inconsistent and sluggish economy generally has required greater justification of financial resource expenditures from practitioners who must operate in increasingly competitive markets. Add to this the tidal wave of change in digital communication practices and increasing costs of doing business, and the result is greater client and organizational attention to public relations programs and a greater demand for evidence-based validation that public relations programs have achieved desired outcomes. The result is that practitioners who enjoyed past success based solely on their practical understanding of local media markets, a well-developed network of contacts, and strong media relations skills are struggling to survive in an era of greater organizational expectations and accountability.

In early 2013, David Geddes, chair of the Institute for Public Relations, wrote in a blog: "The time has come when we, as public relations practitioners and researchers, must develop industry-wide measurement standards" (¶ 4). Geddes cited the "market-driven imperative to measure campaign success" and suggested those in the profession

> need to create a toolkit of consistent, reliable, and comparable metrics that would allow practitioners to work more efficiently to . . . document how public relations contributes to building organizational value. In the specific case of social media, a lack of consensus about measurement standards has led to client trepidation.
>
> (Geddes, 2013, ¶ 3)

His declaration followed by nearly a year the formation of the Coalition for Public Relations Research Standards by the Council of Public Relations Firms, the Global Alliance for Public Relations and Communication Management, the International Association of Measurement and Evaluation and the Public Relations Society of America. The stated purpose of the coalition was "to create a broad platform of standards and best practices for public relations research, measurement and evaluation" (Siebert & Ovaitt, 2012, ¶ 1). Whether or not this effort leads to standardized measurement efforts, research indicates organizational budgets allocated to measurement and evaluation have increased (GAP VII, 2011) and practitioners who enjoyed past success using unproven and unreliable methods of campaign evaluation find themselves struggling to gain organizational resources and maintain organizational support in an era of greater program accountability (Pinkleton et al., 1999; "What Trends," 1997).

Even though practitioners' reliance on research has increased, not every successful campaign requires original research. Often, research requires a substantial financial investment and clients may be unwilling to budget for these expenses, preferring to put all of their financial resources into campaign implementation. In these instances, organizations may evaluate their campaigns based on their existing understanding of markets and their assessments of key audience responses to a campaign.

Some situations may require only the tracking of public responses to media placements, for example, or votes on political initiatives. In addition, some public relations efforts are so limited in scope they simply do not require or receive the resources necessary to conduct even small-scale research. In these situations, both practitioners and the organizations with which they are working may be satisfied with subjective interpretations of outcomes that appear to result from public relations programs.

Unfortunately, practitioners who make campaign recommendations without research are typically limited to arguing that, perhaps based on their years in the business, they know a situation and can recommend a solution. With little concrete evidence to support these claims, they may have difficulty generating organizational support for their recommendations when others from different backgrounds propose different options.

Research reveals the perceptions, interests, and opinions of targeted audience members, produces evidence used to select from among competing solutions, and provides a benchmark from which to evaluate campaign success. Research also allows campaign planning and evaluation based on facts rather than on intuition, rule of thumb, or past practices. Practitioners find research particularly useful as the costs and importance of a campaign increase or as the certainty concerning an issue or public decreases.

In practice, each research setting is unique, and research decisions are often affected by several constraints, the greatest of which typically are time and budgetary limitations. The result is that no single "best" research method exists. Instead, the best research method is the one that most completely meets managers' information needs within the constraints of a given project. Given the often-confusing decisions that accompany many research projects, the purpose of this chapter is to discuss the practical issues that practitioners should consider before they make final decisions concerning a research project. These issues include questions asked and answered before starting a research project; various constraints that affect research method choices; an overview of formal and informal research techniques; the steps taken in a typical research-planning process; and some issues to consider when dealing with research firms, in-house departments, or consultants.

Applications of Research

Managers can use research throughout the campaign planning, implementation, and evaluation phases, as shown in Figure 5.1. The ways public relations professionals use research, however, change as the program evolves and typically depend on a manager's campaign needs. Practitioners may use pre-campaign, or formative, surveys, for example, to better understand and help segment audiences. Similarly, campaign managers may employ focus groups to help them explore changes in people's opinions regarding a key issue or to help them refine message strategies as part of the campaign-monitoring process.

Campaign planners often use research to provide initial benchmarks against which they can measure post-campaign accomplishments. Initially, practitioners may rely on survey research to provide measurements of the awareness, attitudes, and behaviors of targeted audiences. Once practitioners have concluded a campaign, they commonly conduct additional research and compare their post-campaign results with their pre-campaign findings. In many cases, post-campaign research really is between-campaign research because practitioners use it as a platform from which to launch another campaign. In an ideal world, public relations professionals' use of research results in fact-based evidence of a campaign's accomplishments (or failures) and may serve as the basis for requesting additional organizational resources or creating new campaign initiatives.

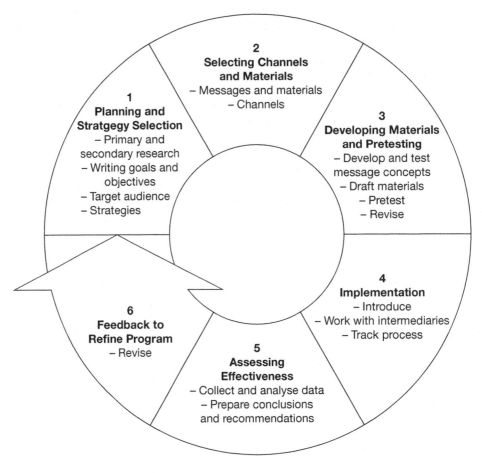

FIG. 5.1. Stages of communication. Strategic planning of communication programs is an ongoing process in which previous experience informs the planning of new programs and the refinement of old programs. Developed by the Center for Substance Abuse Prevention for the planning of alcohol and other drug communication programs.

This use of research to measure campaign effectiveness following a communication program helps practitioners achieve credibility with clients and/or organizational managers. Organizations are looking for a concrete return on what they perceive as an investment of limited resources in public relations. In today's highly competitive organizational environments, practitioner intuition and understanding rarely provide an acceptable basis from which to plan a communications campaign. Practitioner voices are drowned out by competing voices in an organization when their experience and intuition are pitted against quantitative research data. Managers who have access to such data have a strong credibility advantage over their intuition-reliant peers when it comes to influencing organizational decision making, developing communication strategies, and receiving organizational resources.

Practitioners can also use research to help management monitor changes in internal or external environments. It is too easy for organizational managers to become insulated from key publics in their busy and chaotic world. The rigorous demands of their schedule often leave decision makers unaware of the critically important attitudes and opinions of consumers, community members, employees, government leaders, and other key groups. In this case, public relations research can be used as what Peter Drucker called an organizational "hearing aid" ("Reflections," 1998) to keep management in touch with the attitudes and opinions of those individuals on which organizational success or failure depends.

Organizational managers also may use research to keep in touch with their competition. The current public relations environment is extremely competitive. An increasing number of organizations are battling for the fragmented attention of target audience members. Savvy public relations practitioners and their clients make it a priority to understand the strategies and tactics of their competition to increase their own chances of success. Research can provide insight into various interest areas, such as an analysis of the features and appeals used by competitors in their messages and of audience responses to those messages.

Finally, practitioners can use research to generate publicity for organizations and clients. In most cases, organizations produce legitimate research with newsworthy results that benefit the sponsor of a project. In other cases, however, organizations manipulate participants' responses and purposefully misinterpret research results to attract as much media attention as possible. The result is that the media, and ultimately the public, may be misled by unscrupulous research firms or practitioners who engage in unethical practices in an attempt to make a media splash. Serious research scientists and public relations practitioners must use care when conducting research for publicity purposes. Journalists increasingly are skeptical about projects sponsored by organizations with a vested interest in the results. Despite these concerns, the potential uses of research in public relations are nearly endless; practitioners can rely on research results to inform nearly every aspect of the public relations process.

Before Starting the Research Process

Before starting a research project, campaign planners must consider some basic issues that often are important to the successful completion of a project. Initially, it is important for practitioners to determine what they need to learn from a project with as much specificity as possible. Even exploratory projects need to have a clear purpose. Although this may appear obvious, a surprisingly small number of research projects start with well-defined objectives. Instead, project managers commonly have such a vague sense of purpose that it is nearly useless. Organizations that want to use research to "better understand the market" or "see what people think of us" probably are wasting their time and money.

Keep in mind that research projects are an expensive investment intended to provide an anticipated return. The company that engages in a poorly conceived research project and receives a relatively small benefit as a result will pay just as much for its research as the company that uses a well-designed project with specific objectives and benefits accordingly. Although determining informational needs and project objectives can be time consuming and challenging, it is the first important step in the successful completion of a research project and helps provide the best return on an organizational investment.

Practitioners need to ask several questions when considering a new research project, as shown in Figure 5.2. The first is, "What do we already know about the subject of our research?" Answering this question is intended to help narrow the scope and focus of a project. Once a project is started, several potential topics and questions typically compete for limited project

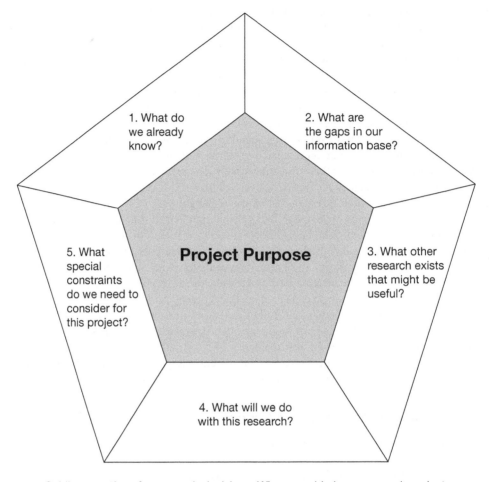

FIG. 5.2. Guiding questions for research decisions. When considering a research project, managers should ask these five questions. All decision making should focus on the purpose of the project to prevent unnecessary or useless research.

resources. Unfortunately, research managers typically eliminate a number of potentially important questions and even whole topics as time and budgetary realities force unrealistic expectations into real-world constraints. When research managers must make difficult decisions about what to keep and what to discard in a research project, it is critical that they have an understanding of their current knowledge base.

The next question is, "What are the gaps in our information base?" The answer to this question provides concrete direction to organizational managers as they consider research topics and potential methods. Managers need to avoid approaching a research project as a single study and instead approach a project as part of an ongoing program of research concerning a topic or topics of importance to their organization. In reality, no single study can answer all the questions managers have concerning a topic, particularly given the increasingly complex and competitive environment in which many organizations exist. In fact, research studies often raise new questions. When practitioners view single studies as part of a larger, ongoing program of organizational research, the result is more likely to provide a valuable contribution to an organization's base of knowledge concerning key audiences and issues.

The third question project managers must ask is, "What other research currently exists that might be useful?" An organization typically has an array of research available that it can use to inform its decision-making processes. Various syndicated research exists, for example, that provides useful information about target audiences' product and service usage, lifestyle, media usage, and other important characteristics. Similarly, a variety of Census Bureau data are available online and this high-quality, detailed information may be quite useful for organizations. Professional associations often conduct research that benefits association members. This research, although fairly broad in scope, can provide useful background information from which to begin a new project. Additionally, trade or academic publications often report research results concerning topics of potential interest to practitioners.

Researchers also may be able to reuse previously collected data as part of a new research project. This practice, called *secondary data analysis*, is a way to recycle data. It occurs when researchers use a set of data for a purpose different from its original use. Once researchers collect and analyze a data set, they often catalog it and set it aside. In other instances, educational institutions, foundations, and other organizations conduct large, multipurpose surveys and release the results to the public. In either case, practitioners may re-analyze these data for their own purposes if the data are available for use. If an organization is interested in interpreting changes in public opinion during an election year, for example, it may gain access to polling data during or after an election. In this case, the organization is bound by the methods and questions researchers used in the original study; however, the data still may be useful, and they may cost little or nothing to access. Any of these resources, and various additional ones, may provide information that has a significant bearing on a research project in the planning stages.

The fourth question project managers should ask is, "What will we do with this research?" Practitioners often initiate research projects as part of a problem-solving process. Research is most useful in this process when managers know how they will use the results as part of the problem-solving process. Unfortunately, it is not uncommon for organizations to complete major studies and, after a short time, set the results aside and never look at them again. In reality, conducting a study does nothing for an organization by itself. Research findings only are useful when skillful managers use them as part of the planning and problem-solving process.

The fifth question managers need to ask is, "What special constraints do we need to consider for this project?" As discussed in Chapter 4, project decisions depend on the time available to conduct the research, budgetary limitations, the expertise available to conduct the research, and the extent to which managers require precision and depth from a research project among other considerations. In addition, some special situations can arise that make it advisable to consult a research specialist. Practitioners may have trouble collecting information about specific issues, for example, or may have trouble collecting information from hard-to-reach audiences. In some instances, people may be unwilling to discuss their private behavior with intrusive researchers. In other cases, practitioners may find it too difficult to locate sample members. Is it possible to find a random sample of pregnant women, for example, and is such a sample really necessary for the successful completion of a research project? What if you want to survey urban residents, 25 to 34 years old, who use public transportation? In each of these cases, experts typically can develop customized research methods and sample-selection strategies to provide practitioners with information concerning specific issues and hard-to-reach populations. Practitioners spend their money wisely when they use knowledgeable professionals who have access to relevant information and appropriate facilities to help them solve difficult data-collection issues.

By answering these questions, practitioners will gain a better understanding of the purpose of a research project and the conditions required to make it successful. They also will be able to use research results to give a project the direction necessary to make it a worthwhile investment with an anticipated and valuable return.

Formal and Informal Approaches to Public Relations Research

At its most basic level, research simply is collecting information. Practitioners can use any number of methods to gather information, each with its own strengths and weaknesses. The most basic designation researchers typically make concerning research methods is formal versus informal—researchers also call these *casual*—approaches to data collection. Rather than fitting neatly into one of these categories, however, research methods generally fit along a continuum. As Figure 5.3 shows, the continuum ranges from nonscientific, casual research methods on one end to fully formal, scientific research methods on the other end. Just because a research method is casual does not mean it has no benefit or practical application. Instead, casual research methods simply fail to meet the standards required of formal, scientific research. In addition, scientific research is not automatically better than casual research. Scientific research may not be necessary or even useful to address some research questions.

A quick look at some informal research methods makes it clear why researchers consider them nonscientific. One of the most common forms of public relations research, for example, involves practitioners' use of clip tracking to monitor media coverage of an organization or issue. Through clip tracking, a practitioner can examine the messages targeted audiences may receive, attempt to gain a rudimentary understanding of public opinion concerning an organization or issue, and even determine the need for potential responses to media coverage, if necessary.

As digital communication platforms have evolved, it's possible to monitor citizens' responses to issues—typically called Internet chatter—in a variety of formats including real-time-web applications. Citizens' reactions on Twitter, for example, are easy to follow to get a

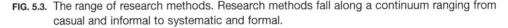

Informal Research	Middle Ground (More formal but not fully formal)	Formal Research
Variable process Unrepresentative sample Examples: 　　Personal contacts 　　Clip files	Partially systematic process Purposefully selected sample Includes originally formal research with flaws compromising integrity Examples: 　　Surveys with small, unrepresentative samples 　　Focus groups	Systematic process Fully representative sample Examples: 　　Surveys 　　Experiments

FIG. 5.3. The range of research methods. Research methods fall along a continuum ranging from casual and informal to systematic and formal.

quick sense of public opinion in response to an emerging issue or event. Unfortunately, a study by the Pew Research Center indicates only 13% of adults use Twitter and they tend to be younger and more liberal than the general population. As a result, citizens' responses to issues posted on Twitter do not reliably reflect public opinion and may be quite different from the reaction of adults nationwide (Mitchell & Hitlin, 2013).

A network of personal contacts is another common form of casual research. When practitioners want to get a sense of public opinion on an issue or event, for example, they may simply call several acquaintances with relevant expertise and ask them for their opinions. Practitioners can use such information as the basis for organizational decision making, even though it is not scientific. Other types of casual research include analyses of field reports from organizational sources such as salespeople or recruiters.

In each instance, information collected by these methods may provide an organization with potentially useful information from which to make decisions about key issues or events, so what is it about this information that makes it casual and nonscientific? For one thing, the informal research methods typically rely on information gathered from a sample that is not representative. When researchers collect data, they normally collect information from a sample, or subset, of the population. When a sample is *representative*, it has the same distribution of characteristics as the population it is supposed to represent. Because of this, the opinions collected from a representative sample generally represent the opinions or behaviors that exist in a population. Thus, a sample of registered voters in Michigan, for example, theoretically represents the attitudes and behaviors of all registered voters in the state. Although researchers never draw a perfectly representative sample, some samples—based on probability sampling methods (discussed in Chapter 6)—have a greater likelihood of producing representative results than other samples. When practitioners contact just a few people to ask their opinions, participant's opinions are unlikely to represent the range of opinions that exist in a target audience consisting of thousands or even millions of people. When practitioners use informal research methods, they typically collect information from a sample that is not representative.

A second characteristic of informal research methods is that practitioners collect information in a manner that lacks a systematic process. When practitioners contact personal acquaintances to ask their opinions, for example, they are unlikely to use a standard set of questions with predetermined response categories for each person. Such a process would defeat the purpose of the research by not allowing practitioners to take advantage of the different areas of expertise and experience of each of their contacts. As a result, this research does not benefit from a formal process or set of procedures that practitioners can use to collect information in a precise, reliable manner.

As an additional note, practitioners cannot accurately know or understand public opinion based solely on media or portrayals or Internet chatter as already noted. There are times, for example, when information and portrayals in the media have an obvious and direct effect on public attitudes or behavior. In a now-classic example, Tickle-Me Elmo became a Christmas-season sellout after Tyco's public relations agency arranged appearances on the *Rosie O'Donnell* and *Today* shows. In this instance, Tyco's managers actually canceled advertising for the toy as stores ran out of the product and skirmishes broke out between parents trying to get their hands on this must-have toy (Fitzgerald, 1996). The promotional efforts concerning the toy were so successful that Tickle Me Elmo made *Time* magazine's list of "All-*TIME* 100 Greatest Toys" and Tyco released a 10th anniversary toy called Tickle Me Elmo TMX in 2006 (Terapeak, 2006).

In other instances, however, media portrayals have little or no effect on attitudes or behavior. In fact, most media are full of persuasive messages warning people not to do some things such as smoking or drinking to excess and encouraging them to do other things such as eating more healthy foods or getting more exercise. Although some people heed these messages, many others simply ignore them. As these examples demonstrate, practitioners' observations and assumptions about public opinion based on media placements are risky and necessarily informal.

In the middle of the casual–formal research continuum are various methods that typically require a more formal process than purely casual methods but still do not fulfill the requirements of formal, scientific research. The most commonly used research method in this category is focus grouping. A *focus group* (discussed in detail in Chapter 8) is a directed group discussion typically consisting of 6–12 people. Participants usually share similarities with respect to key characteristics such as age, gender, product usage, political party affiliation, or any other characteristics deemed important by a project's sponsor. The discussion is led by a moderator who asks questions and probes participants' responses. The process is recorded and transcribed, and research professionals and their clients attempt to gain key insights and draw meaning out of the participants' comments.

Even after all this effort, researchers still understand that focus group research is not formal research because of the size of the sample and the lack of systematic research procedures. A study must have an appropriate sample size (discussed in Chapter 6) to qualify as formal research. Even the largest focus group is too small to meet the sample size required of formal research. In addition, under the best circumstances, scientific research follows a formal set of procedures that researchers apply equally to everyone in a study. When researchers conduct focus groups they typically do not apply the same procedures equally to every participant. In some cases, for example, a moderator may wish to ask certain participants follow-up questions based on their initial question responses, which is a strength of focus groups. Other participants may be reluctant to speak up or may hesitate to express their true opinions. In these situations, focus groups do not follow a standard procedure closely enough to qualify as formal, scientific research.

Other research methods that fall between formal and informal research include surveys that suffer from methodological limitations such as the use of nonrandom sampling methods. When mall-intercept surveys are conducted, for example, members of an interview team typically position themselves at key locations throughout a mall and interview willing shoppers. The shoppers who participate in the survey make up what is called a *convenience* or *incidental* sample because survey team members select them solely on the basis of accessibility. Convenience sampling, however, is a nonprobability, nonrandom sampling method. Even though standing in a mall and talking to shoppers as they happen by appears to rely on a random-selection process, this sampling procedure falls short of the requirements of probability sampling. When researchers use truly random sampling methods, every person in a population has an equal chance of being included in the sample. In a mall intercept, even when researchers use a carefully constructed questionnaire that contains specific response categories, the sampling procedures still render the project's results potentially unrepresentative because they are not random. This leaves the project short of the standards necessary to qualify as formal, scientific research.

Informal Research Concerns

When researchers label a method *casual* or *informal*, it does not mean that the method is without benefit. In reality, practitioners use informal research methods on a regular basis and successfully apply their findings to many different public relations problems and campaigns. It is important to note, however, that managers' use of such research comes with risk. Practitioners who use focus groups, for example, must be careful in their interpretation and application of study results. It is easy to misinterpret focus group results because no matter how many focus groups researchers conduct, the results potentially suffer from significant flaws. Because focus group results provide no numerical measurement, for example, researchers may find it difficult to understand and interpret participants' ideas and comments. Ultimately, two practitioners who view the same focus group may interpret the results very differently, and it is quite possible that both interpretations may be correct in some respects and incorrect in other respects.

More importantly, the results of focus groups and other informal research methods have little scientific generalizability, or projectability. As already noted, researchers typically collect information from a sample of population members rather than from all population members. When researchers use formal research methods, they typically select a sample using probability sampling methods. Probability sampling methods have a greater likelihood of accurately reflecting the wide variety of attitudes and behaviors that exist in most populations because each member of the population has an equal chance of being included in the sample.

The result is that practitioners can generalize or project research results from a probability-based sample to all members of a population with relative confidence. Practitioners have no basis for such projection when they use informal research methods because the sample typically does not accurately represent the population from which it was drawn. When researchers use informal research methods, they have no scientific basis for projecting research results from a sample to a population because not everyone in the population is represented in the sample.

Other problems with nonscientific research methods involve selective observations and ego involvement, both of which contribute to research results that are subjective instead of objective (Baxter & Babbie, 2004). When research findings are objective, they are an unbiased reflection of the attitudes and behaviors of study participants, regardless of the personal views of researchers or project sponsors. Nevertheless, selective observation may occur when researchers purposefully interpret focus group results so that they match the ego needs of a client. When this happens, research results are worse than meaningless, they are wrong. These results will misdirect the decisions of organizational managers who are counting on accurate research to inform their decision-making process. Both formal and informal research methods can suffer from selective observations and the ego involvement of researchers, but these concerns are greater when researchers use informal research methods rather than formal research methods.

The potential problems with informal research were exemplified by the experiences of Milwaukee-based Marquette University when it decided to change the name of its sports teams to the "Gold" based in part on the results of focus groups. The university nicknamed its teams the Warriors from 1954 until 1994. In 1994, Marquette dropped the name in response to concerns it was offensive to American Indians and adopted the name Golden Eagles. Additional research conducted later by the university revealed its fans generally were unenthusiastic about the new nickname, and the issue built to a climax in May 2004 when a member of its board of trustees offered the university a $1 million gift, which would be matched by another anonymous trustee, if it would return to its Warriors nickname (Business Journal of Milwaukee, 2005).

Although university administrators refused to return to the Warriors nickname, they eventually settled on the Gold as a new moniker, a name that originally emerged in some focus groups conducted by the university in 1993 (Siegel & Norris, 2005). Unfortunately, students, alumni, and news media responded quite negatively to the name, resulting in campus protests and an avalanche of unwanted media attention. Marquette returned to its Golden Eagles nickname, based on the results of a voting process that included students, alumni, and faculty and staff.

Why did a relatively simple decision result in so much rancor when Marquette staff members followed a process that is fairly standard among organizations? There likely is more than one reason but it is apparent that the conclusions of the focus group did not accurately reflect the opinions of university stakeholders. Although focus group participants apparently liked the Gold as a nickname, the results of the research lacked external validity or projectability from the research sample to the larger population of university publics. This situation points out the problems practitioners face when they rely on informal research. Informal research findings misled university administrators who made an unpopular decision, as a result.

When conducted properly, however, scientific research methods are more likely to result in accurate observations that are high in projectability by following a formal process and well-conceived research design to its logical conclusion. As Nachmias and Nachmias (1981) noted, scientific research methods differ from other methods of acquiring knowledge based on their assumptions. At a philosophical level, the assumptions of science include, for example, that nature is orderly and regular, that it is possible to know nature, that nothing is self-evident, and that knowledge is derived from experience. At an applied level, scientific research methods are built on a system of explicit rules and procedures that, when correctly applied, have a high likelihood of producing accurate, reliable results. These research methods are by no means perfect, and social scientists regularly work to develop new research methods and to improve existing ones. The result is that formal research methodology has slowly grown in sophistication, as scientists exchange ideas and information.

The scientific research methods available to practitioners include experiments, content analyses, and surveys, which are perhaps the most common type of formal research practitioners use (2005 Challenge, 2005). In addition, practitioners may use a variety of public and private databases and syndicated research resources that rely on scientific research methods. Newcomers to research methods should not be intimidated by the lofty goals and sometimes confusing terminology used in scientific research. Just as math expertise is not required to use a calculator, a scientific background is not required to understand formal research methods.

Instead, practitioners should learn the strengths, weaknesses, and assumptions of each research method so that they clearly understand the advantages and limitations of the information they are using for strategic planning and evaluation. Research methods appropriate for some projects may be inappropriate for other projects. Substantial risks are associated with the misuse of research methods that provide unreliable or misleading information, which may result in negative consequences for organizations.

Research Issues to Consider

Any time researchers collect information for campaign planning and evaluation, they must consider several issues that affect the quality of the information they collect because they directly affect the degree to which research results can achieve representativeness and objectivity.

In some cases, strategic planners should not trust research results as the basis for major decisions because they contain limitations and weaknesses. In other cases, researchers understand potential problems and can negate them through the use of selected research and sampling methods. Ideally, practitioners' trust in research results is appropriate to the level of accuracy, precision, reliability, and validity of a research method and the results it produces (Baxter & Babbie, 2004).

The first of these areas, *accuracy*, concerns whether a research method produces error-free data. Although practitioners may establish a minimum degree of accuracy for every research method, they do not always require highly accurate research results in applied research settings. In some cases, a general understanding of the attitudes, opinions, and behaviors of targeted audience members is enough, and a research method that provides that kind of information, such as a focus group, is appropriate. When managers demand a high degree of accuracy, however, they use scientific research methods and probability sampling methods to provide relatively error-free results. In fact, when researchers use probability sampling procedures in survey research, they can calculate the range of error for participants' responses. Although no study is without some degree of error, when researchers use scientific methods, rely on an appropriate formula to calculate sample size, and use probability-based sampling methods, they are able to evaluate the accuracy of research results with relative confidence.

Research managers also must consider the *precision* of research findings that result from the use of different research methods. When research findings are precise, they are exact. Consider the difference between asking a friend what the weather is like outside and using a thermometer to determine the temperature. In the first instance, our friend may say it is "warm" or "hot" outside. In the second instance, a thermometer may indicate it is 98°F. Both answers are informative and useful, however, one answer is more precise than the other. Although researchers generally desire precise research findings over imprecise research findings, at times precision may be less important to practitioners, especially if it comes with a high cost. Some research methods produce results that generally lack precision. Because focus groups are essentially a group discussion, for example, it is nearly impossible to measure the results exactly within the context of the discussion.

A focus group may provide impressions, ideas, or general group agreement or disagreement, but these results will be broad and interpretive to an extent. When practitioners require precision, they will more likely turn to a survey questionnaire that contains specific questions and numerical response categories to record the attitudes and opinions of respondents. This is not to suggest, however, that practitioners find focus groups or other less-precise research methods useless. When researchers are exploring people's attitudes and opinions, for example, a highly precise questionnaire is likely to hurt their ability to gather useful information. At this point in the research process, practitioners typically are more interested in exploring people's attitudes and opinions rather than in precisely measuring them. As an additional note, do not confuse precision with accuracy. It may be more precise to learn it is 98°F outside rather than it is "hot," but both answers are wrong if it is snowing.

Research methods that produce accurate and precise results also should produce reliable results. Strictly speaking, *reliability* is repeatability. If researchers make repeated measurements of sample members' attitudes, opinions, or behaviors, the results should be similar each time. When researchers use informal research methods, a lack of reliability often arises as a concern. If you call some of your friends to solicit their advice on an issue, the results are likely to vary considerably depending on the people you contact. This means the research method is not reliable. The same reliability concerns are true of informal research methods including mall intercept-surveys and focus groups. When research managers use scientific research methods to collect data, however, the results generally are highly reliable. As an additional note, research methods that are reliable are not necessarily accurate. A scale that consistently weighs people 5 lbs lighter than their actual weight—we all should have such a scale—is high in reliability but not accuracy (Baxter & Babbie, 2004).

Finally, practitioners must consider the *validity* of results produced using various research methods. At a basic level, valid research results are legitimate or genuine. An IQ test is a valid measure of intelligence, for example, if it genuinely measures the intellectual abilities of the individual taking the test. Social scientists have divided *validity* into numerous components in an attempt to reflect all of the nuances of the term and their implications for data collection. Although it is important for research professionals to understand validity concerns in all of their manifestations (and readers can learn more in any good research methods textbook), we purposefully simplify this discussion to selectively consider applied aspects of validity in keeping with the purposes of this text and the patience of our readers. Kerlinger (1973) suggested two broad categories of validity: external and internal.

In general, *external validity* refers to the representativeness, or generalizability, of research results. When researchers conduct a study, they draw a sample, or subset, of people from a population as potential participants. When they draw a sample, researchers must be certain it accurately represents the population. In many instances, only a few hundred people will actually complete a survey, and research professionals will use the responses of a few hundred participants to make inferences about the entire population, which may consist of millions of people. When research results are representative, researchers can accurately take sample responses and project them onto the entire population. Researchers use probability sampling methods, which require random-selection procedures, to ensure that everyone in a population has an equal chance of being included in a sample. If the sample accurately reflects the population and researchers use a scientific research method, the results of a study will be high in external validity and researchers will be able to generalize study results from a sample to the population with confidence.

In terms of practical implications, informal research methods generally lack external validity, which commonly causes problems in public relations. When researchers use focus groups, for example, they do not use probability sampling methods or choose a sample size large enough to produce results that are high in external validity. In fact, a lack of generalizability is one of the reasons researchers consider these methods informal. Researchers must use fully formal, scientific research methods, including probability-based sampling, to achieve a high degree of external validity.

Kerlinger (1973) illustrated *internal validity* with the simple question, "Are we measuring what we think we're measuring?" If, for example, we want to measure people's voting habits but instead ask for their opinions about how important it is to vote, we have not measured their behavior and the measure potentially lacks internal validity. Many methods exist for identifying internal validity.

One of the simplest methods of determining validity is called *face validity*. When researchers check for face validity, they examine a research measure to determine whether it appears to assess what they want it to measure in an obvious way. This form of validity relies on researchers' judgments and is not scientific. For years, market researchers measured brand awareness, for example, when they ultimately wanted to evaluate the effect of an advertising campaign on consumer purchase behavior. Measuring top-of-the-mind awareness is fine but its link to sales is tenuous and using it as an indicator of campaign success raises issues regarding the face validity of the measures.

Content validity refers to the comprehensive nature of research measures. Questions high in content validity most fully represent, or capture, the idea they are supposed to measure. When examining consumers' media-use habits, for example, a set of questions measuring only newspaper reading and television viewing lacks content validity. In this case, consumers are likely to use a variety of media, including digital media, not included in the questionnaire. A lack of content validity leaves a project seriously flawed by compromising its relevance.

A final type of validity that may be especially relevant to public relations campaigns, *predictive* or *criterion validity*, concerns the soundness of a research measure when tested against an external standard. In applied research, predictive validity most commonly concerns the ability of a research measure to predict actual performance. When a driving test has predictive validity, for example, it should predict actual driving performance. People who perform well on a driving test should be able to drive a car safely. If they drive poorly despite performing well on the test, the test lacks predictive validity. Predictive validity is critical when organizations use research to understand and predict the behavior of targeted audience members based on research results. In public relations campaigns, practitioners often measure awareness and knowledge presuming they lead to behavior. These measures often lack predictive validity, however, making the research findings an incomplete or incorrect basis from which to develop campaign strategy and predict campaign outcomes.

Steps to Research Project Design

Once managers have considered accuracy, precision, reliability, and validity as they relate to the research project at hand, they can turn to the actual design of the project. Despite the uniqueness of every research project, it helps to follow a series of steps in a more-or-less sequential order to guide the design and implementation of a project, as shown in Figure 5.4. The research plan discussed in Chapter 4 largely corresponds to the steps followed to implement the project itself. The research-design process briefly discussed here contributes to an orderly decision-making process that maximizes the benefits of a study and the information outcomes it provides. It also can help minimize study costs and the risks associated with obtaining poor quality data.

1   *Identify or clearly define the research problem*. When research projects lack a well-defined purpose, they produce results that, although interesting, have little benefit. Clients often approach research firms or consultants with a relatively vague understanding of what they need to learn, with the expectation that the focus of the project will emerge and they will know what they want when they see it. Even exploratory research projects should have clear direction.

2   *Review the literature*. This refers to checking existing sources of knowledge for useful information. At one time, managers found it difficult to get accurate, reliable market research. As organizations have increased in sophistication, their reliance on research has grown and the supply of existing research available to any organization has greatly increased. Various academic research publications, trade publications, syndicated market research, and databases can prove useful when practitioners develop a project. These resources can help practitioners define targeted audiences; provide insight into

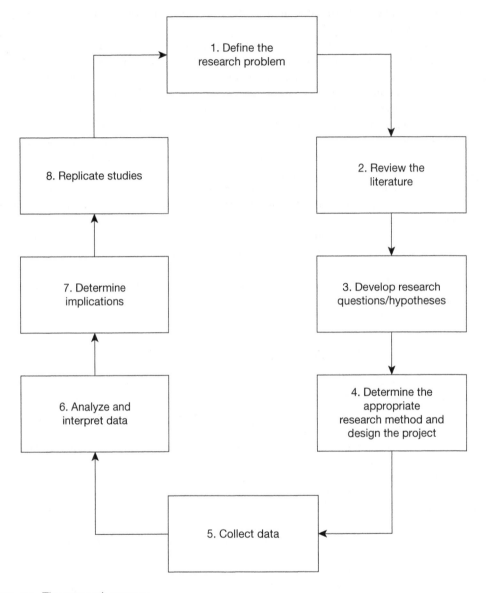

FIG. 5.4. The research process.

audience opinions, attitudes, and behavior; and answer secondary questions related to a primary research project.

3   *Develop research questions or hypotheses.* After examining existing sources of research information, managers can develop hypotheses or research questions. Essentially, hypotheses and research questions help researchers understand their study and the outcomes it is supposed to produce. In this way, they become part of the problem-identification process and give researchers specific outcomes to look for as they engage

in a research project. In academic research, hypotheses (and research questions to a lesser extent) typically drive the research process and provide expectations about variable relationships and other important research findings. In applied research settings, researchers commonly use research questions instead of hypotheses. Practitioners can use both hypotheses and research questions in applied research settings, however, to help determine the project purpose and to help inform the research-design process.

4   *Determine the appropriate research method and design the project.* Several methods exist for collecting information, and in this book we address the most common methods. Whether practitioners do a research project on their own, deal with an in-house research department, or contract with an outside research firm, they must understand the strengths and weaknesses of different research methods to make informed decisions and to gather useful and affordable information. Practitioners who stick to research methods because of familiarity, or who blindly follow the advice of others without understanding the strengths and limitations of different research methods, risk disappointment and, worse, can make decisions based on inaccurate results.

5   *Collect data.* Implementation of the study follows research-method selection and study design. In applied settings, informal research designs commonly require a less systematic application of data collection procedures than formal research methods because of their purposes, which may involve exploration or idea generation. Formal research methods, conversely, require researchers to carefully follow research procedures to ensure that they systematically measure participants' attitudes and behaviors producing unbiased results that are high in validity.

6   *Analyze and interpret data.* Data analysis and interpretation vary depending on the research method used and the nature of the data. Qualitative data, such as comments provided by focus group participants, typically require broad, subjective interpretations. Quantitative data, conversely—which might result from participants' answers to survey questions containing numerical response categories, for example—require statistical analysis and generally should produce objective results and interpretations. In either case, meaningful data analysis and interpretation are the natural outcomes of a well-designed, properly conducted research project.

7   *Determine implications.* After completion of a study, campaign strategists, planners, and others must carefully examine the results for their practical implications. What do these results suggest in terms of strategy or tactics? How should an organization attempt to frame an issue for members of a critical audience? What public affairs programs are likely to have the greatest audience impact according to study results? What media do these audience members regularly use? How do these results help improve understanding or, more important, motivate behavioral change? It is a waste of time and money to conduct a study and, after brief consideration, simply put the results on a shelf where they gather dust.

8   *Replicate studies.* As research projects provide answers to the questions they were designed to answer, they also raise new, important questions. These new questions typically are the genesis for additional research, and as organizational managers address these new issues in a systematic process, they move forward in terms of their understanding and ability to solve problems. This makes it critical for managers to make studies replicable, meaning reproducible, so that results build on each other.

Final Thoughts

Public relations programs increasingly rely on research-based planning and evaluation. The benefits of research—to illuminate the perceptions, interests, and opinions of targeted audiences; to produce evidence used to select from among competing solutions; and to provide a benchmark from which to evaluate campaign success—often far outweigh the costs of research. Some managers have the luxury of hiring out research projects to specialists, whereas others need to implement research projects on their own. Either way, a personal investment in learning about these sometimes complex topics can lead to increased credibility and autonomy for the communication manager. The following chapters provide a basic grounding in the most important aspects of applied public relations research.

Making Research Decisions
Sampling

Chapter Contents

- Sampling Basics
- Generalizing From a Sample to a Population
- Sampling Methods
- Nonprobability Sampling Methods
- Probability Sampling Methods
- How Big Should a Sample Be?
- Calculating the Appropriate Sample Size
- Sample Size Formula
- Error Calculations
- Issues and Assumptions
- Final Thoughts

Sampling is a powerful tool and a critical part of communication-campaign research because it has a direct relationship to the generalizability of research results. Practitioners use sampling in partnership with the research methods they select to collect critical information that helps them solve complex problems, monitor their internal and external environments, and engage in sophisticated campaign planning and evaluation. When done properly, sampling helps practitioners get accurate information quickly at a relatively low cost. It provides them with a cost-effective way to collect information from a relatively small number of target audience members, called a *sample*, and draw conclusions about an entire target audience. These processes are based on principles of statistical sampling and inference.

Although it sounds complex, sampling really is simple. If we want to know whether our spaghetti sauce needs more garlic, we usually taste a small sample. We do not need to eat all of the sauce to determine whether we need more garlic (and by the way, the sauce almost always needs more garlic). Researchers sample people in the same way. We do not need to contact all members of a target audience to understand their opinions, attitudes, and behaviors. Instead, practitioners can learn this information from a properly selected sample of target audience members, with a high degree of confidence they will produce accurate results. The purpose of this chapter is to explain basic aspects of sampling including both probability and nonprobability sampling methods and sample size calculations, in a simple, easy-to-understand manner. For the math phobic, we use only a small amount of math in this chapter. Instead of manipulating numbers, we want readers to develop a conceptual understanding of the principles of sampling and statistical inference.

Sampling Basics

Even though sampling methods are relatively easy to understand and use, understanding a few basic terms and concepts makes it easier to understand sampling practices. While these definitions are not terribly interesting, they make it a lot easier to understand principles of sampling and inference.

At a basic level, readers should understand the difference between a population and a sample. A *population* or *universe* consists of all the members of a group or an entire collection of objects. In public relations, a population most commonly refers to all the people in a target audience or public. When researchers conduct a *census*, they collect information from all members of a population to measure their attitudes, opinions, behaviors, and other characteristics. These measurements, called *parameters*, are the true values of what a population's members think and do; this means that parameters are a characteristic or property of a population. In theory, parameters contain no error because they are the result of information collected from every population member. Often, parameters are expressed in summary form. If a census reveals that 59% of voters in King County, Washington, support a property tax initiative, for example, this characteristic is a parameter of the population of all voters in King County.

Research professionals and social scientists often find it difficult or impossible to conduct a census because they are expensive and time consuming. More important, a census usually is unnecessary. By collecting information from a carefully selected subset, or *sample*, of population members, researchers can draw conclusions about the entire population, normally with a high degree of accuracy. This is why sampling is such a powerful part of communication campaign research.

A *sample* is a subset of a population or universe. When researchers conduct a survey using a sample, they use the resulting data to produce sample statistics. *Sample statistics* describe the characteristics of the sample in the same way that population parameters describe the characteristics of a population. Statistics result from the observed scores of sample members instead of from the true scores of all population members, and they necessarily contain some error because of this. The amount of error contained in sample statistics, however, usually is small enough that researchers can estimate, or infer, the attitudes, behaviors, and other characteristics of a population's members from sample statistics, often with a high degree of confidence.

If you find all of this confusing, read this section again slowly and it will become clearer, although no more exciting (perhaps take two aspirin first). This topic and chapter improve in terms of their ease of understanding, but it is important for readers to have a basic understanding of sampling terminology and concepts before we discuss other aspects of sampling. It also becomes clearer as we move into discussions of sample representation, sampling techniques, and sample size calculations.

Generalizing From a Sample to a Population

Researchers normally collect data to make generalizations. During a state gubernatorial election in Michigan, for example, a political campaign manager may survey a sample of registered voters to determine the opinions of all registered voters in the state. In this case, the campaign manager wants to generalize the results of the survey from a relatively small sample (perhaps consisting of no more than several hundred people) to all registered voters in the state. This process of generalization, when researchers draw conclusions about a population based on information collected from a sample, is called *inference*. Researchers generalize findings from samples to populations on a regular basis. How can researchers generalize in this way and have confidence they are right? The answer is that if a sample accurately represents the population from which it is drawn, this allows investigators to make valid inferences about the population based on sample statistics.

An often-used example from the annals of survey research helps make the point. In 1920, editors of the *Literary Digest* conducted a poll to see whether they could predict the winner of the presidential election between Warren Harding and James Cox. Editors gathered names and addresses from telephone directories and automobile registration lists and sent postcards to people in six states. Based on the postcards they received, the *Literacy Digest* correctly predicted Harding would win the election. *Literacy Digest* editors repeated this same general process over the next several elections and correctly predicted presidential election winners in 1920, 1924, 1928, and 1932.

In 1936, *Literacy Digest* editors again conducted a poll to predict the winner of the presidential election. This project was their most ambitious yet. This time, they sent ballots to 10 million people whose names they drew from telephone directories and automobile registration lists, as before. More than 2 million ballots were returned. Based on the results of their survey, the editors predicted that Republican challenger Alfred Landon would receive 57% of the popular vote in a stunning upset over Democratic incumbent Franklin Roosevelt. Roosevelt was reelected, however, by the largest margin in history to date. He received approximately 61% of the popular vote and captured 523 electoral votes to Landon's 8. What went wrong?

Simply put, the sample did not represent the population. *Literary Digest* editors drew the sample from telephone directories and automobile registration lists, both of which were biased to upper income groups. At that time, less than 40% of American households had telephones and only 55% of Americans owned automobiles. The omission of the poor from the sample was particularly significant because they voted overwhelmingly for Roosevelt, whereas the wealthy voted primarily for Landon (Freedman, Pisani, & Purves, 1978). Not only did the sample not represent the population, but the survey method and low response rate (24%) contributed to biased results.

This often-used example illustrates a key point about the importance of sample representativeness. The results of research based on unrepresentative samples do not allow researchers to validly generalize, or project, research results to population members. It is unwise for investigators to make inferences about a population based on information gathered from a sample when the sample does not adequately represent a population. It is a simple, but important, concept to understand.

In fact, George Gallup (of Gallup poll notoriety) understood the concept well. In July 1936, he predicted in print that the *Literary Digest* poll would project Landon as the landslide winner and that the poll would be incorrect. He made these predictions months before the *Literacy Digest* poll took place. He also predicted that Roosevelt would win reelection and perhaps receive as much as 54% of the popular vote. Gallup's predictions were correct, even though his numbers concerning the election were imperfect. How could Gallup be sure of his predictions? The primary basis of his explanation was that the *Literary Digest* reached only middle- and upper-class individuals who were much more likely to vote Republican. In other words, he understood that the *Literacy Digest* sample did not represent the population (Converse, 1987).

As an additional note, for those who believe a larger sample is better, here is evidence to the contrary. When researchers use *nonprobability* sampling methods, sample size has no scientifically verifiable effect on the representativeness of a sample. Sample size makes no difference because the sample simply does not represent the population. A large, unrepresentative sample is as unrepresentative as a small, unrepresentative sample. In fact, had editors used a probability sampling method along with an appropriate survey method, a sample size of less than 1% of the more than 2 million voters who responded to the *Digest* poll almost certainly would have produced a highly accurate prediction for both the *Literary Digest* editors and George Gallup.

Sampling Methods

Sampling is the means by which researchers select people or elements in a population to represent the entire population. Researchers use a *sampling frame*—a list of the members of a population—to produce a sample, using one of several methods to determine who will be included in the sample. Each person or object in the sample is a *sampling element* or *unit*. When practitioners study target audience members, the sampling frame typically consists of a list of members of a target audience, whereas the sampling unit is an individual person. All the sampling units together compose the sample. If a nonprofit organization wants to examine the perceptions and opinions of its donors, for example, the sampling frame might be a mailing list of donors' names and addresses, whereas the sampling unit would be the individual names and addresses selected from the list as part of the sample. When researchers generate a sample, they select sampling units from the sampling frame.

When researchers draw a sample, their goal is to accurately represent a population. This allows them to make inferences about the population based on information they collect from the sample. There are two types of samples: *probability* and *nonprobability*. Researchers select probability samples in a *random* way so that each member of a population has an equal chance, or probability, of being included in a sample. When researchers draw a nonprobability sample, an individual's chance of being included in a sample is not known. There is no way to determine the probability that any population member will be included in the sample because a *non-random* selection process is used. Some population members may have no chance of being included in a sample, whereas other population members may have multiple chances of being included in a sample.

When researchers select probability, or random, samples, they normally can make accurate inferences about the population under study based on information from the sample. That is, probability samples tend to produce results highly generalizable from a sample to a population. When researchers select samples in any way other than probability-based, random sampling, they cannot be sure a sample accurately represents a population. In this case, they have no basis for validly making inferences about a population from the sample. Even though a nonprobability sample may perfectly represent a population, investigators cannot scientifically determine its representativeness. For this reason, the results of research based on nonprobability samples are low in generalizability (external validity).

Why use nonprobability sampling if the research results it produces are not representative? In some cases, researchers use a nonprobability sample because it is quick and easy to generate. At other times, the cost of generating a probability-based sample may be too high, so researchers use a less-expensive, nonprobability sample instead. While the use of a nonprobability sample is not automatically a problem, it does present a significant limitation in the valid application of research results to campaign planning and evaluation. Research managers often use nonprobability samples in exploratory research or other small-scale studies, perhaps as a precursor to a major study. In addition, some commonly used research methods, such as focus groups or mall-intercept surveys, rely exclusively on nonprobability sampling.

The lack of generalizability should serve as a warning to communication campaign managers. Do not assume research results based on nonprobability samples are accurate. When practitioners want to explore a problem or potential solution in an informal fashion, get input on an idea, or obtain limited feedback from members of a target audience, a nonprobability sample normally is an acceptable choice. As editors of the *Literary Digest* discovered, however, nonprobability samples have limitations and should not serve as the sole basis by which practitioners seek to understand audiences and develop programs. In other words, nonprobability methods have value for problem exploration and informal campaign planning but provide an insufficient basis for formal planning and campaign evaluation.

Nonprobability Sampling Methods

Several methods exist for generating nonprobability samples. No matter how random the selection process appears in each nonprobability-based sampling method, researchers do not select sample members in a probability-based manner. This means population members have an unequal chance of being selected as part of a sample when investigators use these sampling methods. The most common types of nonprobability sampling are incidental (also called *convenience*) sampling, quota sampling, dimensional sampling, purposive (judgmental) sampling, volunteer sampling, and snowball sampling.

Incidental, or Convenience, Sampling

Researchers select incidental, or convenience, samples by using whoever is convenient as a sample element. A public opinion survey in which interviewers stop and survey those who walk by and are willing to participate constitutes such a sample. Mall intercepts generally rely on convenience samples because their sample consists of shoppers who happen to walk by and are willing to complete a questionnaire. Like all nonprobability samples, incidental samples typically do not provide accurate estimates of the attributes of a target population. There simply is no way for researchers to determine the degree to which research results from a convenience sample are representative of a population. Like all nonprobability sampling methods, incidental samples are most appropriate when research is exploratory, precise statistics concerning a population are not required, or the target population is impossible to accurately define or locate (Johnson & Reynolds, 2005).

Quota Sampling

Researchers tend to use this sampling method to learn more about subgroups that exist in a population. As a result, they draw their sample so it contains the same proportion (or quota) of subgroups. Investigators fill the quotas non-randomly, typically using sample members who are convenient to fill subgroup quotas. In practice, research staff members typically base quotas on a small number of population characteristics such as respondents' age, sex, education level, type of employment, or race or ethnicity. An interviewer conducting a survey on a college campus, for example, might be assigned to interview a certain number of freshmen, sophomores, juniors, and seniors. The interviewer might select the sample non-randomly by standing in front of the university library and asking people to complete a survey. Interviewers would stop surveying members of individual population subgroups as they filled each quota.

Dimensional Sampling

This method is similar to quota sampling in that researchers select study participants non-randomly according to predetermined quotas, but project managers extend sample quotas to include a variety of population attributes. Generally, interviewers ensure that they include a minimum number of individuals for various combinations of criteria. Extending the college survey example, interviewers might non-randomly select participants to meet additional criteria, or dimensions. Interviewers might have to interview a minimum number of males and females, traditional and nontraditional students, or married and unmarried students, for example, in addition to the class quota. Interviewers could use a seemingly endless number of potential attributes to develop a sample.

No matter how many attributes researchers use when selecting members of a sample, they select both quota and dimensional sample members using nonprobability selection methods. The result is that researchers cannot determine whether their participants fully represent the similarities and differences that exist among subgroups in the population. Ultimately, there is no scientific way to determine whether a nonprobability sample is representative and no scientific evidence to suggest quota sampling is more representative than other nonprobability sampling methods. Researchers correct the nonprobability selection weakness of quota sampling and dimensional sampling when they use *stratified* sampling, which we address under *Probability Sampling Methods*.

Purposive Sampling

In purposive, or *judgmental*, sampling, researchers select sample members because they meet the special needs of the study based on the interviewer's judgment. A researcher's goal when using purposive sampling typically is to examine a specially selected population that is unusually diverse or particularly limited in some way, rather than to study a larger, more uniform population (Johnson & Reynolds, 2005). If a product manufacturer wants to open a new plant in another country, for example, company management needs to learn the concerns of local business, government, and labor leaders. In this case, the sample is relatively small and diverse, and interviewers may simply select sample members using their own discretion to determine which respondents fit into the sample and are "typical" or "representative." This creates situations in which sample-selection decisions may vary widely among interviewers. Even if the definition of the population is reasonably clear, the procedures researchers use when drawing a sample may vary greatly among interviewers, limiting the comparability of sample members (Warwick & Lininger, 1975). While studies using purposive sampling may provide useful results, their nonrandom-selection procedures limit the generalizability of their findings, as is the case with all nonprobability sampling methods.

Volunteer Sampling

When media organizations ask viewers to call in or text their opinions, they are using a volunteer, or self-selected, sample. Instant phone-in or text-message polls have become a common way for media outlets to determine and report so-called public opinion, for example, in an attempt to attract and keep the interests of viewers and listeners. This tool is more effective as marketing than as research. There are numerous potential sources of bias when research is based on a volunteer sample. First, sample representation is hindered because only the people who are exposed to the survey have an opportunity to participate. All other potential respondents are unaware of the poll. Second, those who feel strongly about the topic of a poll may view the survey as an opportunity to vote for their viewpoint. Such individuals may respond more than once and/or encourage other like-minded individuals to respond in the same way. As a result, volunteer samples typically are not representative and research results based on volunteer samples are highly untrustworthy. Organizations using volunteer samples should use them strictly for their entertainment value, not their scientific value.

Snowball Sampling

When researchers use snowball sampling, they collect data from a limited number of population members and then ask these individuals to identify other members of the population who might be willing to participate in the study. The sample continues to grow as new research participants direct interviewers to additional sample prospects. The sample snowballs, starting from a small number of people and growing larger as each new participant suggests other potential participants.

Researchers may have no choice but to have to rely on snowball sampling when they can locate only a few members of a population. If a social welfare organization wants to learn about the particular difficulties of migrant workers, for example, it might start by interviewing those migrant workers it could locate. After each interview is concluded, interviewers can ask participants to identify other workers who might be willing to participate in the study. Interviewers hope the sample will grow to a desirable size through this process. Research results based on such a sample, however, have little or no generalizability, no matter how large the sample grows. A snowball sample relies on nonrandom methods of selection and there is no way to scientifically determine the degree to which results based on snowball samples represent a population because of this. Nevertheless, the snowball method may be the only way to locate members of hard-to-reach populations such as those who want their status to remain anonymous. As with all projects based on nonprobability samples, managers need to interpret and generalize research findings resulting from snowball samples carefully.

Probability Sampling Methods

Researchers generate probability samples using a random-selection process so each member of a population has an equal chance, or probability, of being included in a sample. The use of probability sampling normally allows investigators to make accurate inferences about a population based on information collected from a sample. Even so, investigators' conclusions about a population are not perfectly accurate even when they use probability sampling. Researchers calculate estimates of the population parameter within a range of possible values at a specific level of probability (you'll understand this better after reading the chapter). Research findings resulting from probability-based samples normally are highly representative and possess a high degree of generalizability, or external validity. The most common type of probability sample is simple random sampling. Common variations of simple random sampling include systematic sampling, stratified sampling, and cluster sampling.

Simple Random Sampling

Researchers must ensure each member of a population has an equal chance of inclusion in a sample and select each sample element independently to produce a random sample. Simple random sampling is the most basic method of random sampling, and investigators use it to ensure the sample they produce is representative of the population to the greatest extent possible. Although true representation never is guaranteed unless researchers conduct a census, the use of a random-selection process significantly reduces the chances of subgroup over-representation or underrepresentation, which helps eliminate sample bias. Researchers then can estimate, or infer, population parameters based on sample statistics. Although these inferences are not perfect—they have some error—investigators use statistical procedures to understand this error as noted previously.

From a practical standpoint, the primary requirement for simple random sampling is for researchers to clearly and unambiguously identify each member of a population through the use of a comprehensive sampling frame. This allows the direct, independent, and random selection of sample elements, typically through a list which contains each element or potential participant (Warwick & Lininger, 1975). To generate a simple random sample by hand, research staff members might number each element on the list sequentially, for example, and select the sample by using a table of random numbers or a computer program that produced random numbers. Each number selected by researchers would correspond with a member of the sampling frame.

Technology has simplified this process greatly. If leaders of the Public Relations Society of America (PRSA) wanted to survey their membership to determine members' level of satisfaction with PRSA services, for example, a project manager could use a computer to generate a list of randomly selected members from the PRSA directory. If properly conducted, this random process would produce a probability sample of PRSA members who have a high likelihood of accurately representing the attitudes and opinions of all PRSA members.

Systematic Random Sampling

Researchers use an unbiased system to select sample members from a list when they use systematic random sampling. This system allows them to generate a probability-based sample that normally is highly representative of the population it represents, without some of the inconveniences that can occur with simple random sampling. Depending on the sample-generation procedures involved, those who use simple random sampling can find the sample-generation process tedious, especially when a population is large and computer generation of the sample is not available. When researchers use systematic random sampling, they develop an uncomplicated system using the total sample size and the size of the population to help them draw a probability-based sample relatively easily.

First, research team members determine the final number of completed interviews they need for a study. As shown in Figure 6.1, researchers often need to generate a total sample several times larger than their targeted number of completed interviews because of the number of sample elements who are difficult to contact or who refuse to participate in a survey. Once researchers determine the total sample size, they determine a *sampling interval* by dividing the number of elements in the sampling frame (this is the total population) by the desired total sample size. The result is a number (*n*) researchers use to generate a sample by selecting every *nth* element from a sampling frame. Researchers must select the first sample element randomly from the frame to produce a probability sample, so they randomly select the first element from within the sampling interval. They complete the sample-selection process by selecting every *nth* element from the sampling frame and the result is a systematic random sample.

An example helps to clarify systematic random sampling. If corporate personnel managers want to survey their classified staff as part of a program to improve employee relations, their first step is to determine the final number of completed interviews they want for the study. We discuss sample size calculations later in this chapter, but for this example, let's say that after some careful thinking and a little fun with math, administrators determine they want a total of approximately 400 completed interviews from the approximately 6,000 employees who work as full- or part-time classified staff.

After some additional calculations (explained in Chapter 12), researchers determine an original total sample size of 850 classified staff members would produce about 400 completed surveys from participants, as shown in Figure 6.1. The projects' directors decide to use a list of classified staff members as a sampling frame because it contains the names and addresses of all classified staff members and has no duplicate listings. They divide the sampling frame (6,000) by the original sample size (850) to determine the sampling interval (approximately 7). Project managers must select the first sample element randomly, so they use a table of random numbers to produce the first number between 1 and 7. If project managers drew the number 5, they would draw the sample by selecting the fifth name on the list and selecting every seventh name after that. Thus, researchers would draw name 5, name 12, name 19, name 26, and so on. By using the sampling interval, researchers produce a systematic random sample.

Systematic random samples and simple random samples are not exactly the same; however, systematic samples closely approximate simple random samples to produce a probability sample that normally is highly representative. In terms of bias, the greatest danger researchers face when using systematic sampling is periodicity. *Periodicity* refers to bias that occurs when a sampling list has a repetition of a population characteristic that coincides with a sampling interval. If this occurs, the sample elements selected are not generalizable to the population they are supposed to represent. Researchers should be careful to inspect population lists before sampling to make sure there are no obvious signs of periodicity. When researchers are careful, the potential for bias in systematic sampling normally is small. Ultimately, researchers use systematic random sampling more than simple random sampling because of its usefulness in complex sampling situations (Sudman, 1976).

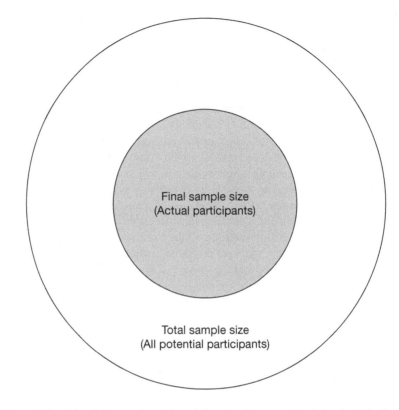

FIG. 6.1. The relationship of the number of participants who complete interviews to the total sample size. Communication managers need to generate a total original sample that is several times larger than required for their final sample because of the number of people who cannot be contacted or refuse to participate in a survey.

Stratified Sampling

Researchers divide a population into different subgroups, or *strata*, when they engage in stratified sampling, similar to quota sampling. The key difference between the methods is that investigators use a random, probability-based method to select sample elements when they engage in stratified sampling, whereas they use a nonrandom, nonprobability-based method to select sample elements when they engage in quota sampling. Researchers have two primary reasons for stratification: to control the representativeness of the sample and to use different probability-based selection procedures in different strata (Warwick & Lininger, 1975). Researchers also may use stratified sampling when they primarily are interested in the key similarities and differences among members of strata, such as high-income consumers, when the prior information they have for individual strata is different, or when they want to improve sampling efficiency and help control sampling costs (Sudman, 1976).

Researchers use two types of stratified sampling: proportional and disproportional. When they use *proportional* sampling, project managers draw sample members from each stratum in proportion to their existence in the population. The resulting sample proportionally represents individual strata as they exist in a population. Researchers use *disproportionate* sampling to help ensure that the overall sample accurately produces results that represent the opinions, attitudes, and behaviors of a significant stratum within the population. Project managers may use disproportionate sampling when strata are too small to be accurately represented in a sample selected through other means. This may be necessary, for example, when researchers' use of other probability sampling methods would underrepresent the opinions, attitudes, and behaviors of minority members of a population. In this case, research staff may find it necessary to weight the data to obtain unbiased estimates of the total population. When researchers use either proportional or disproportional stratified sampling to their advantage, they can produce highly representative, probability-based samples.

Cluster Sampling

Researchers select sample elements using groups rather than individuals when they use cluster sampling. The sample frame consists of clusters rather than individuals, and each cluster serves as a sample element. The clusters researchers use for sampling commonly are preexisting natural groups or administrative groups of the population. These may include geographical designations such as neighborhoods, cities, counties, or zip code areas, for example, or other common groupings such as universities, hospitals, or schools.

Researchers often use cluster sampling to make data collection more efficient (Sudman, 1976). If an urban school district wanted to learn about the attitudes and experiences of its students, it could send interviewers to meet one on one with individually selected student sample members. This process, however, would be expensive and increase the time needed to complete the project. If researchers used schools as sample clusters and randomly selected from among them, the project would require less time and travel, which would increase the efficiency of data collection.

Investigators also use cluster sampling when a comprehensive list of sample elements is not available. If an organization wanted to sample city residents as part of a community relations program, project managers would likely have trouble locating a complete list of all community residents, and the process would be costly and time consuming. If researchers wanted to use cluster sampling, they could create a sampling frame by using city blocks as clusters. After research staff identified and labeled each block, they could randomly select an appropriate number of blocks. Next, researchers would randomly sample dwelling units within each block. Finally, interviewers would randomly sample people living in each dwelling unit and collect data. Researchers call this sampling process *multistage sampling* because sampling takes place in different stages; they select city blocks in stage one, followed by dwelling units in stage two and individual people in stage three.

Researchers' primary concern when using cluster sampling is the potential for increased error relative to other probability-based sampling methods. When investigators use cluster sampling, standard error may increase if sample members' attitudes, behaviors, and other characteristics generally are the same, or homogeneous, within each cluster. In this instance, samples selected from within homogeneous clusters will not reflect the diversity of attitudes and behaviors existing in the larger population. Project managers can help counter this problem by selecting a high number of small clusters and selecting a relatively low number of sample elements from within each cluster (Johnson & Reynolds, 2005).

Cluster samples, along with systematic and stratified samples, are acceptable alternatives to simple random sampling. In each case, population elements have an equal chance of being included in a sample. Ultimately, researchers' choice of a sampling method often depends on the time and money available for a project, the population being sampled, the subject under investigation, and the availability of a comprehensive list of target population members.

How Big Should a Sample Be?

One of the first questions clients, managers, and others involved in a research project typically ask is "What is the best sample size for a project?" Unfortunately, as is the case so often in life and particularly in survey research, the answer is a firm "it depends." In fact, the methods researchers use to determine the appropriate sample size for a study can be relatively complicated and even controversial. Research professionals often use different formulas to calculate sample size—in some cases based on different assumptions about population characteristics—and may suggest conflicting sample sizes as a result. Several common misperceptions exist concerning sample size calculations including the following:

– *Myth 1: Bigger samples are better.* The *Literary Digest* case demonstrates the fallacy concerning bigger sample sizes. When researchers use probability sampling methods, a mathematically calculated sample size based on an appropriate formula nearly always produces trustworthy results with known ranges of error. Researchers can use simple math to verify this information. When researchers use nonprobability sampling methods, there is no scientific way to determine how well a sample represents a population or how much error survey results contain. Remember, a large unrepresentative sample is no more representative than a small unrepresentative sample. In addition, a representative sample that is unnecessarily large is a waste of resources. A sample's size should be the result of a researcher's purposeful decision-making process, not a number that researchers stumble upon as they try to generate the largest sample possible.

– *Myth 2: As a rule of thumb, researchers should sample a fixed percentage of a population to produce an acceptable sample size.* It is not uncommon for those uninitiated in survey research methods to suggest using a fixed percentage of the population to determine sample size. If researchers sampled 10% of a 50,000-person population, for example, they would generate a sample of 5,000 participants. Once again, probability-based sampling methods allow the use of mathematical formulas to calculate sample sizes that normally produce highly trustworthy results with known ranges of error. Arbitrarily sampling a certain percentage of the population is unnecessary and results in an arbitrary sample size. Such a practice is as illogical as if you ate a certain percentage of the food in your refrigerator because you were hungry. Just as the amount of food you eat should be based on your body's needs (with notable exceptions for ice cream and chocolate in any form), so should a study's sample size be based on the requirements of a research project instead of on an arbitrary percentage of a population.

– *Myth 3: Researchers should base sample sizes on industry standards or "typical" sample sizes used in other research projects.* In reality, there is little that is standard about a research project. Although researchers may use familiar formulas to determine the sample size for a study, they should not use these formulas without careful consideration. A project's unique needs, the individual characteristics of a population and its resulting sample, and other issues greatly affect sampling decisions. Researchers serve the needs of clients and organizations best when they make thoughtful sample-size decisions, based on the unique requirements of individual research projects.

Having said all of this, we must engage in a small amount of backpedaling. Many communication students (and some campaign practitioners for that matter) have varying degrees of math phobia and short attention spans when it comes to highly technical or theoretical information. With this in mind, we use simple sample-size calculation formulas and avoid math when possible. In short, we take some shortcuts in some instances. If you find these basic concepts and formulas easy to understand, or if you will be involved in research on a regular basis, you should read more about additional aspects of sampling and sample-size calculations so you are fully informed.

For the math-challenged among us, we offer our encouragement. Read the next section slowly, draw pictures of the concepts if it helps you understand them, and try the math out yourself. Put in a little effort and you should emerge with a clear understanding of the topic. To explain sample-size calculations, first we provide a conceptual understanding of sample-calculation concepts and processes. Then, we do some basic sample-size calculations, based on the concepts we have explained. Finally, we calculate the amount of error that exists in survey data once researchers have completed a survey.

Calculating the Appropriate Sample Size

Anyone can determine with precision the optimal size for a sample, provided they understand a few key concepts based on probability theory and a bell-shaped curve. These concepts include sample distribution and standard deviation, confidence level, confidence interval, and variance. Once you grasp these concepts, it is easy to understand the basis for sample-size calculations; the rest is simply a matter of applying the formulas.

Sample Distribution and Standard Deviation

Sample distribution and standard deviation are the first and, in some ways, most complex concepts to understand. A *sample distribution* is a grouping or arrangement of a characteristic that researchers measure for each sample member, and it reflects the frequency with which researchers assign sample characteristics to each point on a measurement scale (Williams, 1992). Almost any characteristic that researchers can measure has a sampling distribution, but in survey research investigators typically study sample members' opinions, attitudes, behaviors, and related characteristics. If we were to chart a sampling distribution, the result would be shaped like a bell, provided the sampling distribution was normal. It would be tall in the middle where the average of the sampling distribution is located because most people would be near the average. There would be fewer people toward either edge, or tails, of the bell because fewer people would have characteristics or behaviors so far above or below the average.

If we were practitioners at a university health facility, for example, we might conduct a survey to better understand smoking behavior among students. We could ask a randomly selected student sample to fill out a questionnaire that contained attitudinal and behavioral questions,

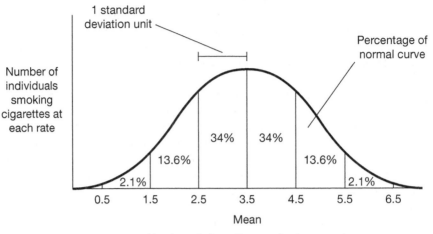

FIG. 6.2. Smoking distribution example. The number in each portion of the curve shows the percentage of the sample that corresponds to each segment. For example, 34% of this sample smokes between 2.5 and 3.5 cigarettes per week. The percentages added together equal more than 99% of a normal distribution. The segments of the curve are divided according to standard deviations from the mean.

including a question about the number of cigarettes participants had smoked in the previous 7 days. Participants' responses likely would vary greatly. Many students would have smoked no cigarettes in the previous 7 days, whereas other students would have smoked a high number of cigarettes. When we compute students' responses to our smoking question, we could use the information to generate a sample distribution. If our research revealed the average number of cigarettes smoked in the past week by participants was 3.5, this number would be placed under the middle of the curve at its tallest point and most participants would be near the average, or mean, in the large part of the bell-shaped distribution. Our sample's smoking distribution would get smaller at its tails because fewer participants would smoke in numbers that were far above or below average. Figure 6.2 contains a normally distributed, bell-shaped curve for the smoking example.

As we planned our campaign, we could make inferences about the population (all students at our university) based on the responses of our sample. Error occurs when researchers take measurements from a sample and use them to make inferences about a population because there are differences between a sample distribution and a population distribution.

We could not determine the exact average number of cigarettes smoked weekly by students at our university, for example, unless we conducted a census by interviewing every student. We did not conduct a census in this example and because of this, the responses of our sample would not exactly represent the true responses of the population. In our smoking survey, our sample mean for cigarettes smoked in the past 7 days might be 3.5, whereas the true value for the population might be 3.8. The difference between the opinions and behaviors of the sample and the opinions and behaviors of the population is *error*.

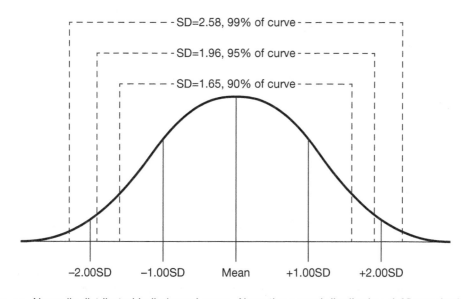

FIG. 6.3. Normally distributed bell-shaped curve. Along the normal distribution, 1.65 standard deviations (SD) measure 90% of the curve; 1.96 standard deviations measure 95% of the curve; and 2.58 standard deviations measure 99% of the curve.

As researchers, we must understand this error, so we use a tool to measure it called *standard deviation*. Standard deviation is a standardized measure of dispersion (or variation) around a mean. Basically, a standard deviation is a standardized unit of measurement that researchers use to measure distances from a sampling distribution's midpoint to its outer limits (don't get lost here). Think of standard deviation as a simple unit of measurement. Researchers use standard deviation to measure distance from the mean in a bell-shaped curve in the same way a carpenter uses inches to measure the length of a board, as Figure 6.3 shows.

Researchers use standard deviation for various purposes. If the publishers of a book survey 10 people and ask them to read and rate it using a scale of 0 to 10, for example, the text might receive an average rating of 5. If all 10 people who read the book actually rated the text as a 5, the average rating is perfectly accurate and there is no standard deviation. If 5 people rate the text as a 10, however, and 5 people rate the text as a 0, the mean rating still is 5. This time, however, the average rating is not very accurate. No one, in fact, actually gave the text a 5 rating. The standard deviation would be relatively large because there is a lot of dispersion among the scores.

Although the means are the same in each case, they actually are different and standard deviation helps us measure and understand this. Using our smoking survey example, if every participant in our smoking survey said they smoked 3.5 cigarettes in the past 7 days, our mean would be highly accurate and we would have no deviation from the mean. When we ask sample members about their smoking habits, however, we will undoubtedly receive different responses, and we can use the mean and standard deviation to help us understand these responses.

How do standard deviation and sample distribution help us when we calculate sample size? A standard deviation gives researchers a basis for estimating the probability of correspondence between the normally distributed, bell-shaped curve of a perfect population distribution and a probability-based sample distribution that always contains some error. Researchers call standard deviation measurements *standard* because they associate with, or measure, specific areas under a normal curve. One standard deviation measures about 68% of a normally distributed curve; two standard deviations measure a little more than 95% of a normally distributed curve; and three standard deviations measure more than 99% of a normally distributed curve. Research professionals use standard deviations to determine the confidence level associated with a sample, which we address next.

Confidence Level

A *confidence level* is the degree of certainty researchers can have when they draw inferences about a population based on data from a sample. Basically, it is the level of probability researchers have that they can accurately generalize a characteristic they find in a sample to every member of a population. In essence, the confidence level answers the question, "How confident are we that our sample is representative of the population?" A confidence level of 90% means researchers are 90% confident that the sample accurately represents the population. In the same way, a confidence level of 95% means researchers are 95% confident that the inferences they draw about the population from the sample are accurate.

This raises an important question: Are researchers really 90% or 95% confident about the representativeness of the sample, or are they simply guessing, perhaps based on their experience? In fact, researchers' claims of a confidence level are accurate because the confidence level is based on standard deviations. Remember, a standard deviation allows researchers to estimate probability between a normally distributed population curve and a less-than-perfect sampling distribution because standard deviation measurements associate with specific areas under the curve. A standard deviation of 1.65 measures 90% of a normally distributed curve, a standard deviation of 1.96 measures 95% of a normally distributed curve, and a standard deviation of 2.58 measures 99% of a normally distributed curve (remember these numbers because we will use them again shortly).

When researchers calculate sample size, they select standard deviations associated with specific areas under a normally distributed curve to provide the desired confidence level. When investigators use 1.65 in the sample-size formula, they calculate a sample size that provides a 90% confidence level; when they use 1.96 in the formula, they calculate a sample size that provides a 95% confidence level; when they use 2.58 in the formula, they calculate a sample size that provides a 99% confidence level.

Most often, researchers use 1.96 standard deviations to calculate sample size, resulting in a 95% confidence level. A confidence level of 95% means our sample statistics will more-or-less accurately represent the true parameter of a population 95% of the time. Here is another way to think about this: if we conducted a survey of the same population 100 times, our sample responses would be accurate in 95 of the 100 surveys we conducted. The 95% confidence level is a standard convention of social science, but researchers can use other confidence levels. In particular, if researchers desire an exceptionally high degree of confidence when making inferences about a population based on data from a sample, they may choose a higher confidence level. Rarely do researchers use a lower confidence level.

Confidence Interval

A *confidence interval* is a range or margin of error that researchers permit when making inferences from a sample to a population. As noted, the inferences researchers make about a population based on sample data are not completely accurate. Unless investigators conduct a census, the observed values they collect from a sample (statistics) will not provide completely accurate information concerning a population's true values (parameters).

The population parameter falls somewhere within the range of the confidence interval, although researchers never are exactly sure where the parameter is located unless they conduct a census. Normally, researchers describe the confidence interval as a positive-to-negative range, such as ±3% error or ±5% error. A confidence interval of ±3% has a total error margin of 6%, whereas a confidence interval of ±5% has a total error margin of 10%. If 57% of registered voters in California express support for a citizens' initiative in a survey with a ±5% confidence interval, for example, the true population value may be as high as 62% (+5%) or as low as 52% (−5%).

What is an acceptable confidence interval for survey results? As is often the case in survey research, the answer depends on various factors. Many applied communication and market research surveys have a ±5% confidence interval, but there is nothing critical about this range of error. Researchers commonly choose smaller confidence levels when they want to reduce the margin of error and increase the precision of the inferences they draw concerning a population. When media organizations poll the public to predict election outcomes, for example, they often use a smaller confidence interval, such as ±3%. Ultimately, researchers should make decisions about confidence intervals based on the necessities and challenges of individual research projects.

It may surprise you to learn that the confidence level and the confidence interval do not have to add to 100%. Those new to research often assume the confidence level and confidence interval must add to 100% because researchers often conduct surveys with a ±5% error at a 95% confidence level. It is incidental that these numbers add up to 100. Researchers commonly conduct surveys with a ±3% margin of error at a 95% confidence level, for example, or surveys with larger or smaller error margins. In addition, it is typical to use a 95% confidence level as a standard and only make adjustments to the confidence interval when calculating sample size. As noted previously, researchers should make decisions concerning confidence levels and confidence intervals based on the requirements of individual research projects.

Variance

Simply put, *variance* is dispersion. When researchers calculate sample size, it helps them to understand how the characteristic or variable they are examining is dispersed throughout a population. If we want to understand the use of public transportation in our community as a way to reduce traffic and pollution, for example, it would be useful to know the percentage of community members who actually use public transportation. In short, we want to know how public transportation use is dispersed throughout our community as a characteristic of the population.

For research purposes, it is useful to consider variance as a simple percentage. Community members who use public transportation, for example, fit into one category containing a certain percentage of the population. Community members who do not use public transportation do not belong in this category and make up the remaining percentage of the population. Together, the percentages add up to 100%. Researchers can examine the dispersion of most variables this way because a population can be divided into two categories on the basis of almost any characteristic. This includes, for example, students who snow ski and students who do not ski, community residents who ride bikes and residents who do not ride bikes, workers who are employed and workers who are unemployed, and people who drink coffee and people who do not.

Any time researchers examine a variable or characteristic, they want to know its dispersion within a population because they can use this information to help them calculate sample size. Population members who have a characteristic or variable fit into a single category, and researchers use this to distinguish them from the rest of the population. In the formula we examine shortly, the percentage of a population that belongs to a category is expressed as a decimal. The remaining percentage of the population (that does not belong to the category) also is expressed as a decimal and subtracted from 1. Together, these two numbers add to 1.0 or 100% of the population.

Readers with allergies to mathematical algorithms will be relieved to know that despite the importance of variance, researchers often use a predetermined, maximum variance percentage when they calculate sample size. They do this because researchers commonly examine multiple variables in a single survey, each with a different percentage of dispersion. Each variable would require a different sample size, which is impractical and unnecessary. Researchers address this problem by using the largest measure of variance available to calculate sample size because, at a minimum, it provides an acceptable measure of dispersion for all variables. To use the largest measure of variance, researchers use .5 (or 50%) as the percentage of a population that belongs to a category. Researchers also use .5 as the percentage for the rest of the population because $1 - .5 = .5$ and these percentages add up to 1.0, or 100%, of the population. Although it is not necessary for researchers to use .5 and $1 - .5$ in every sample-size calculation, this practice is regularly required by the necessities of a multifaceted research project, and so we use it in all of our sample-size calculations.

Sample Size Formula

Now that you understand standard deviation, confidence level, confidence interval, and variance, you are ready to calculate sample size. Researchers commonly use the following formula—or formulas that are similar but more complicated—to calculate sample size:

$$n = \left(\frac{cl}{ci}\right)^2 (v)(1-v)$$

where

   n (number) = the number of completed interviews or what we call the final sample size
   cl (confidence level) = the standard deviation associated with a specific area under a normal
      curve and corresponding to the desired confidence level (by definition, 90% confidence
      level = 1.65; 95% confidence level = 1.96; and 99% confidence level = 2.58)

ci (confidence interval) = the margin of error expressed as a decimal (±3% error would be expressed as .03; ±5% error would be expressed as .05; ±10% error would be expressed as .10)

v (variance) = the variance or distribution of a variable in a population, expressed as a percentage in decimal form. For our purposes, variance always will be .5. Note also that $1 - v$ always is .5 when v is .5, as we have recommended.

Here is a basic sample-size calculation using this formula. We calculate the sample size at a 95% confidence level and a ±5% margin of error, or confidence interval:

$$n = \left(\frac{1.96}{.05}\right)^2 (.5)(.5) = 384$$

Based on this formula, we need a final sample size of 384 people—or 384 completed interviews—to produce findings with a ±5% margin of error at a 95% confidence level.

What if we want less error (a smaller confidence interval), meaning more trust in our survey results? It is easy to adjust the formula to fit the demands of any research situation. In the following calculations, for example, we determine sample sizes based on different confidence levels. We calculate each sample size with a ±5% confidence interval, but with different confidence levels to show how different confidence levels affect sample size. To change confidence levels, we use standard deviations that correspond to different areas under a normally distributed, bell-shaped curve.

Recall that the standard deviation for a 90% confidence level is 1.65; the standard deviation for a 95% confidence level is 1.96, and the standard deviation for a 99% confidence level is 2.58. Notice that we increase sample size as we increase the confidence level. The only difference in each calculation is the level of confidence researchers have when they make inferences from a sample to a population. Here is the final sample size—or number of completed interviews—needed for a survey with a 90% confidence level and a ±5% margin of error:

$$n = \left(\frac{1.65}{.05}\right)^2 (.5)(.5) = 272$$

Here is the final sample size (number of completed interviews) for a survey with a 95% confidence level and a ±5% margin of error:

$$n = \left(\frac{1.96}{.05}\right)^2 (.5)(.5) = 384$$

Finally, here is the final sample size (number of completed interviews) for a survey with a 99% confidence level with a ±5% margin of error:

$$n = \left(\frac{2.58}{.05}\right)^2 (.5)(.5) = 666$$

How do changes in the margin of error, or confidence interval, affect final sample size (the completed number of interviews) researchers need? In the following calculations, we determine sample sizes with the same level of confidence but differing margins of error. Each sample size is calculated at a 95% confidence level. Here is the final sample size for a survey with a ±10% margin of error at a 95% confidence level:

$$n = \left(\frac{1.96}{.10}\right)^2 (.5)(.5) = 96$$

Here is the final sample size for a survey with a ±5% margin of error at a 95% confidence level:

$$n = \left(\frac{1.96}{.05}\right)^2 (.5)(.5) = 384$$

Finally, here is the final sample size for a survey with a ±3% margin of error at a 95% confidence level:

$$n = \left(\frac{1.96}{.03}\right)^2 (.5)(.5) = 1,067$$

In each case, we reduced the margin of error while maintaining a consistent level of confidence.

Error Calculations

The same information you learned to calculate sample size also will help you calculate the margin of error for a survey, once you have collected data. In most cases, the number of completed interviews—or what we call the final sample size—is not 384 or 1,060 completed interviews, even if this is researchers' target. Researchers aiming for a specific sample size typically collect additional interviews for various reasons. Research staff may have to throw out some interviews, for example, because of problems with data collection, such as a survey that is only partially complete. At other times, researchers may collect a larger sample size so they have a stronger basis from which to make sample subgroup comparisons. Regardless of the reason, researchers can use standard deviation, confidence level, and variance to calculate the margin of error that exists in a survey's results based on its final sample size. Here is the formula:

$$e = cl \sqrt{\frac{(v)(1-v)}{n}} (100)$$

where

   e (error) = the final margin of error for the completed survey based on sample size *cl* (confidence level) = the standard deviation associated with a specific area under a normal curve and corresponding to the desired confidence level (as before, 90% confidence level = 1.65; 95% confidence level = 1.96; and 99% confidence level = 2.58)

v (variance) = the variance or distribution of a variable in a population, expressed as a percentage in decimal form. As before, variance is .5 and 1 – *v* always is .5 as we have recommended

n (number) = the number of completed interviews or what we also call the final sample size.

Here is the margin of error for a survey in which the final sample size, or number of completed interviews, is 485. The calculation is made based on a 95% confidence level:

$$1.96\sqrt{\frac{(.5)(.5)}{485}}(100) = 4.45$$

In this example, the margin of error for this survey is ±4.45% based on 485 completed interviews.

How do changes in the confidence level affect the margin of error, or sampling interval, for survey results? In the following calculations, we determine margins of error for survey results using the same final sample size, or number of completed interviews, at different levels of confidence. We calculate each margin of error using a final sample size of 575. Here is the margin of error at a 90% confidence level:

$$1.65\sqrt{\frac{(.5)(.5)}{575}}(100) = 3.44$$

Here is the margin of error at a 95% confidence level:

$$1.96\sqrt{\frac{(.5)(.5)}{575}}(100) = 4.09$$

Here is the margin of error at a 99% confidence level:

$$2.58\sqrt{\frac{(.5)(.5)}{575}}(100) = 5.38$$

These calculations reveal the trade-off between confidence level and the margin of error, or confidence interval, for a survey. If researchers want to increase their level of confidence or certainty as they make inferences from sample data to a population, they must be willing to accept a larger range of error in their survey's results. If researchers desire a smaller range of error, they must be willing to accept a lower confidence level when they make inferences.

Issues and Assumptions

The formulas we have presented require various assumptions and raise some important issues. We have addressed many of these issues and assumptions in the preceding sections, but note that you may need to alter these formulas or disregard them completely, as the assumptions on which we have based these formulas change. One of the primary assumptions of all sample-size formulas, for example, concerns researchers' use of probability-based sampling methods. When researchers use nonprobability sampling, no sample-size formula will produce an accurate result because it is impossible for researchers to determine the representativeness of the sample.

One issue we have not yet addressed concerns the need to correct the formula according to a population's size. Researchers sometimes use sample-size formulas that contain something called *finite-population correction*. Finite-population correction is an adjustment factor that is part of a sample-size formula. Table 6.1 contains population-corrected final sample sizes for probability-based survey results with a ±5% margin of error at a 95% confidence level. The appropriate sample size for a population of 1 million people is 384, the same sample size we calculated for a survey with a 95% confidence level and a ±5% margin of error.

Is it necessary for researchers to correct for population size? Generally, most researchers have little need for population correction unless the size of the population is small and the

Table 6.1 Population-Corrected Sample Sizes

Population size (N)	Sample size (n)	Population size (N)	Sample size (n)	Population size (N)	Sample size (n)
5	5	650	242	2,500	333
10	10	700	248	3,000	341
15	15	750	254	3,500	346
20	19	800	260	4,000	351
25	24	850	265	4,500	354
50	44	900	269	5,000	357
75	63	950	274	6,000	361
100	80	1,000	278	7,000	364
150	108	1,100	285	8,000	367
200	132	1,200	291	9,000	368
250	152	1,300	297	10,000	370
300	169	1,400	302	15,000	375
350	183	1,500	306	20,000	377
400	196	1,600	310	25,000	378
450	207	1,700	313	50,000	381
500	217	1,800	317	75,000	382
550	226	1,900	320	100,000	383
600	234	2,000	322	275,000+	384

Note: Figures reported are for probability-based survey results with a ±5% margin of error at a 95% confidence level. Calculations are based on Cochran's (1977) formula for finite-population correction. Further information is available in Kish (1965). According to this formula, even populations more than 1 million require a sample size of 384.

sample is more than 5% of the total population (Czaja & Blair, 1996). In most sample surveys, population correction makes relatively little difference in sample-size calculations and researchers simply exclude a population-correction factor because it is unnecessary. In fact, in theory researchers could use the same sample size for a survey of registered voters in Chicago, a survey of registered voters in Illinois, or a survey of registered voters in the United States! Although there are important exceptions, once a population reaches a certain size, sample sizes generally remain consistent. For this reason, and to keep our sample calculations simple, the sample size formula we presented does not include population correction.

Final Thoughts

Sampling is a powerful tool that helps practitioners obtain accurate information at a reasonable cost. Researchers' selection of a proper sampling method is as important as their selection of a proper research method to the success of a study. Even the most carefully planned and executed study will produce untrustworthy results if research managers use an improper sampling method. Although sampling can be complex, it is in readers' own best interests to learn all they can about the sample-selection procedures used in a study. Few people would buy an automobile without first inspecting the vehicle they are purchasing, yet a surprising number of practitioners make research "purchases" without ever inspecting one of the most critical elements of their research project, the sampling procedures used in a study.

As demonstrated in this chapter, it is not necessary for practitioners to become sampling experts to understand many important issues related to sampling selection. It is necessary, however, for practitioners to understand basic distinctions in sampling methods and to work with researchers to ensure that the sample used in a study has the greatest chance of accurately representing the attitudes, opinions, and behaviors of the population from which it is drawn.

7

Making Research Decisions

Less-Formal Research Methods

Chapter Contents

- Monitoring the Web
- Professional Contacts, Experts and Opinion Leaders
- Advisory Committees or Boards
- Field Reports, Customer Contact
- Learning Community and Consumer Sentiment
- Databases
- Clip Counts and Media Tracking
- Real-Time Message Testing/Surveys
- In-Depth Interviews
- Panel Studies
- Final Thoughts

In a sense, research simply is listening and fact finding. While those in the field heatedly discuss issues related to campaign impact, return on investment, and campaign metrics, practitioners' use of systematic research and evaluation still lags behind the rhetoric (Broom & Sha, 2013). Nevertheless, such research often is critical to organizations as they monitor their internal and external environments, track public opinion concerning emerging issues, and address potential areas of conflict with target audience members before they become problems. Informal research methods often provide organizations with quick and inexpensive ways to listen to critical publics such as employees, community members, consumer groups, and government regulators. Despite these potential benefits, practitioners take a sizable risk when they use informal research methods as the sole basis for campaign planning and problem solving. Because these methods lack the rigors of scientific research, they have a much greater likelihood of producing unreliable, inaccurate results.

What makes a research method less formal or casual? As noted in Chapter 5, one of the reasons researchers consider a method less formal is its lack of a systematic process. When researchers use a casual process to collect information, the results typically lack objectivity. A second characteristic of less-formal research has to do with the samples practitioners use. In informal research, the sample may be too small or the responses of selected sample members may be too narrow to adequately reflect the views of everyone in a population. When research results are high in *generalizability*, researchers can project, or generalize, study results from a smaller sample to a larger population with confidence. The results of informal research typically lack generalizability.

This does not mean that informal research methods produce useless information. On the contrary, advances in digital communication have made listening to stakeholders easier and perhaps more important than ever for practitioners. It is important, however, for practitioners to understand the limitations of their information. Normally, less-formal research methods are useful for gaining a broad, nonscientific sense of what the public might be thinking or thinking about, exploring problems, and for pretesting campaign ideas and strategies. It is not advisable, however, for campaign managers to use them as the sole basis for program planning and evaluation. With this in mind, in this chapter we briefly present some of the casual methods most commonly used by communication campaign practitioners as they engage in the research and planning process.

We will begin by discussing recent developments in digital communication and move to more traditional means of less-formal research methods.

Monitoring the Web

The meteoric pace of digital technology has led to the creation of numerous accessible and scalable platforms supporting customer relations management, search engine optimization, trackable analytics, social media engagement and networking, online advertising, digital direct mail, content-based applications including collaborative content creation and content aggregation, and more. As a result, public relations practices have rapidly shifted from top-down, reactive programs to real-time efforts to monitor, measure, and modify digital-communication environments, engage audiences and manage relationships.

The benefits of social media and other digital-communication applications are obvious: they provide a way for public relations professionals to easily engage and dialog with consumers, stakeholders, bloggers and journalists. Rather than barraging targeted audiences with one-way marketing messages, practitioners can listen to audiences and, when appropriate, undertake meaningful, two-way conversations. In this environment, it is important for practitioners to use digital technology to understand audience members and to follow trends and Internet chatter concerning an organization and/or its products and services.

As with traditional media outlets, public relations professionals monitor, manage and report on all forms of digital media. This provides them with critical data they use to identify and understand audience behavior and to get a sense of public opinion as it exists among members of the public and stakeholders. All digital media tools are set up using a series of algorithms designed to track and measure the impact of user behavior and response. Social media tracking focuses on user preferences, sharing and frequency, for example, while Web statistics look at user paths including entry and exit points, browser use, visit length, page views and mobile access. Monitoring the digital-communication landscape helps practitioners stay ahead of the curve as crises emerge, gather useful information about their competitors, and get a sense of the public's reaction to specific public relations campaigns and programs. Armed with this information, practitioners can create and manage their programs on a real-time basis for maximum impact.

Like many companies, for example, Samsung makes use of real-time monitoring software to listen to audiences, get a sense of consumer sentiment, and adapt its marketing communication strategies and tactics accordingly. Soon after Apple announced the introduction of its newest iPhone, Samsung practitioners began following the reactions of consumers in social media. Members of the company's marketing team developed a new advertising campaign based on what they learned from their monitoring activities. As soon as Apple made its new iPhone available to consumers, Samsung unleashed its new marketing campaign satirizing some of the iPhone's features and gently poking fun at the consumers waiting in line to buy it. Samsung practitioners also monitored conversations about their own campaign, which consumers viewed more than 70 million times online (Abramovich, 2013).

Given the continuously changing digital-technology landscape, any attempt to catalog and describe the ways practitioners can engage in Web-based audience research will be outdated before its publication. The incredible upsurge in platforms and applications keeps practitioners rushing to understand and apply new technologies as quickly as they emerge. Even so, practitioners are using a plethora of tools to listen to and evaluate audiences, develop public relations campaign strategies, and tactically manage relationships. As a result, there are some important listening, Web optimization, and search concepts and tools that all public relations practitioners should understand.

In many cases these tools fall under the realm of less-formal research and evaluation. In terms of understanding public opinion, the results they produce are not necessarily high in scientific external validity, or generalizability, from the sample of users to a larger, inclusive population. Facebook users may provide an easy-to-generate research sample, for example, but Facebook users are different from non-users and do not accurately reflect public opinion (Hargittai, 2007). As a result, research results based on a Facebook sample may actually mislead practitioners and work against the successful implementation and evaluation of a broad-based public relations campaign.

In other instances, however, digital communication tools are highly accurate. Practitioners can use Google Analytics, for example, to evaluate the navigation behavior of all visitors to a website producing highly reliable data. Other Web-based tools provide similar levels of evaluation accuracy. The key to the successful application of online toolsets is to understand their strengths and limitations and also to understand targeted audiences.

Digital media platforms offer practitioners a number of important and potentially beneficial tools for listening to audiences and evaluating key aspects of public relations campaigns. Some of the most useful tools for managing the digital-communication landscape, such as SproutSocial, help organizations monitor and analyze what consumers are saying, engage in customer relationship management, conduct Web-publishing activities, generate user-behavior reports, and provide other forms of valuable data.

As an alternative, practitioners can use HootSuite—a dashboard with useful monitoring tools—to manage multiple accounts across Twitter, Facebook, WordPress and other digital-communication spaces. Media monitoring companies, which started as clipping services for traditional media, also offer blog and other forms of social media monitoring as part of their services. A good monitoring service should provide results in an easily usable format giving practitioners the ability to search, compare, edit and organize results while conducting analyses and generating reports.

Some listening and analytic tools are specific to individual platforms and provide users with the ability to locate a range of useful information and evaluate campaigns. FBsearch.us, for example, allows users to search Facebook for specific posts, photographs, pages, people, groups and other information. In addition, with Facebook Insights individuals can measure their page's performance, locate aggregated demographic data about their audience and monitor how individuals are discovering and reading posts. Practitioners can use Monitter to monitor Twitter for a set of keywords and to narrow the search to a particular geographic location while TweetReach allows practitioners to evaluate the influence of a Twitter campaign or hashtag.

Most digital-communication products are relatively inexpensive and many offer a zero-cost option with base-level access to features, free-trial periods, or other cost-management options. SocialMention, for example, is a free social media monitoring tool that aggregates user-generated content from across the Web. This information helps practitioners monitor a large number of social-media properties including Facebook, Twitter, YouTube, and Google. SocialMention also tracks blogs, blog comments, mainstream news, images, video, and audio, and includes a number of potentially important metrics such as reach (the number of unique authors referring to an organization or brand divided by the total number of mentions) and sentiment (the ratio of positive mentions to negative mentions). Practitioners can receive daily e-mail alerts concerning their brand, company, CEO, marketing campaign, a developing news story, or a competitor.

Digital direct mail providers such as Constant Contact or VerticalResponse contain tools to help practitioners distribute e-mails and e-newsletters to contact lists. Constant Contact allows practitioners to see the percentage of message recipients who opened a message and how long recipients spent reading digital materials. Practitioners also can learn which links generated the most click-throughs and track important metrics such as the number of recipients who like or share e-mails on Facebook, tweet about e-mails, or forward messages to friends. Data comparing multiple e-mails also are available and the analytic reports are easy to use and understand.

Finally, Google provides a number of effective tools practitioners can use to enhance and maximize their listening and tracking efforts. For example, iGoogle is a customizable dashboard with search functions. Practitioners can organize the page to provide search updates and other useful information according to their needs. As a basic search tool, Google Alerts allows practitioners to establish keyword searches for their company or product, a client's or competitor's brand, and almost any other relevant topic. Practitioners receive automatic notifications based on their keywords providing a useful form of monitoring.

Web analytics allow practitioners to measure and evaluate data so they can optimize web pages. Google Analytics is many practitioners' preferred tool for improving effectiveness, access, visibility and performance of a website. While other useful website analytic tools exist, including those for Word Press, Google Analytics has an array of thoughtful and intuitive tools that sets the standard for Web analytics. The number of useful evaluation functions are too numerous to mention, but Google Analytics is relatively easy to use and is an effective way for practitioners to track traffic to and through an organization's website. For example, Google Analytics allows practitioners to measure the number of new and returning visitors to a website, determine where they came from, check the keywords they searched, measure how long they stayed on a page, and note what links visitors clicked on during their visit. Figure 7.1 provides analytics for e-newsletters, called *ZZU News*, developed as part of a health-promotion campaign.

Google Analytics Metrics
Summary Stats (across all 6 issues)

	VOLUME 1	VOLUME 2	VOLUME 3	VOLUME 4
Total visitors	135 with 79% new visitors	563 with 86% new visitors	141 with 62% new visitors	137 with 52% new visitors
Total pageviews	471	1,326	490	632
Total unique pageviews	387	1,070	429	504
Average time spent on articles	00:01:01	00:00:46	00:00:46	00:01:20
Top 3 articles	• #258 Party Foul (35 pageviews) • #264 Quiz (31 pageviews) • #30 Quiz (25 pageviews)	• #665 Lambda Alpha Chi (423 pageviews) • #756 Keeping the 21-Run Fun (80 pageviews) • #754 Saving the Face (78 pageviews)	• #1112 Famous Greeks (29 pageviews) • #1146 Kappa Alpha Theta (27 pageviews) • #1000 Cooler Heads (22 pageviews)	• #1472 Caution: Sorority Women Crossing (37 pageviews) • #1499 Caution: Sorority Women Crossing (29 pageviews) • #1394 One Shot, Two Shot, Three Shot, Floor (27 pageviews)
Average # of articles read per visit	3.49	2.36	3.46	4.61
Average visit duration	00:02:31	00:01:02	00:01:53	00:04:49

Wordpress Google Analytics Comparison Notes...

- Volume 2 was particulary popular and well-read. The implication is that articles specifically tied to a Greek house and appear in all issues – is most popular.

- Volume 4 showed the longest time spent on each article + the highest average of articles viewed per visit. Volume 1 also yielded the best stats for average visit duration. The spikes on all accounts is an indication that those who follow ZZU News are spending more time reading – and looking through more articles during their visit.

- It should be noted that the best performing issues included prevention content where the lowest performing issues were in the general interest category

FIG. 7.1. Some of the analytics for e-newsletters, called *ZZU News*, sent to target-audience members as part of a health-promotion campaign. Column on far left lists comparison categories.

In addition, practitioners can use analytics to monitor how well their site's pages are working and provide developers with data to improve the overall user experience. Analytics allows practitioners to segregate Web visitors based on their behavior patterns while on a website and to examine micro conversions and macro conversions. *Micro conversions* reflect relationship-building activities within a website such as signing up for a newsletter or viewing a product-demonstration video. *Macro conversions* concern ultimate outcomes such as consumer sales or donations to nonprofit organizations.

Keep in mind, it is important for practitioners to understand targeted audiences as they venture into digital-communication monitoring, even as they use listening tools to learn more about audiences. Recently, for example, Twitter and Tumblr have grown rapidly in popularity among adolescents even as Facebook's most-recent expansion has come primarily from growth in users outside North America. Having a sense of who the key audience members are for an organization will help PR staff listen and plan much more effectively than chasing after the latest tools and technology that, while interesting, may have less relevance to their organizations.

Additionally, it may be useful to monitor the work of respected bloggers and others who serve as opinion leaders in digital communication to help you in this process. The work of public relations practitioner and blogger Adam Vincenzini, for example, is a great resource for public relations and digital-communication trends and served as the source for some of the information presented here (e.g., Vincenzini, 2012). There are a number of other expert bloggers who provide useful information to practitioners attempting to navigate the digital-communication environment.

Finally, at the risk of being redundant, here are two important reminders: First, digital communication is an ever-changing landscape. The key to successful Internet monitoring and brand engagement is to know and understand audiences and to use the appropriate tools and technologies to listen to and connect with them as they migrate to new Web-based spaces. Second, many monitoring activities do not provide a valid and reliable means of measuring public opinion. Research indicates individuals' use of social networking sites is not randomly distributed across a group of tech-savvy users (Hargittai, 2007). You may recall Twitter users are quite different from members of the general population, for example, and as a result, respond differently to events (Mitchell & Hitlin, 2013). Even so, listening tools and technologies provide a critical means of environmental monitoring with the added bonus of immediate response when warranted.

Professional Contacts, Experts and Opinion Leaders

Practitioners keep in regular contact with their peers, friends in related fields, and others who typically possess a wealth of useful experience and knowledge. These contacts may be especially valuable for practitioners when they are planning or implementing a new program for an organization. If an organization interested in holding a special event has never conducted one, for example, it makes sense for managers to talk to contacts who specialize in event planning and promotion to take advantage of their knowledge and experience. Veteran practitioners are likely to have a wealth of practical advice and their own set of contacts that can benefit someone new to the field. In some cases, managers may want to hire consultants or firms who specialize in certain areas of public relations, either for a single project or on a continuing basis.

Managers also may benefit by talking to recognized opinion leaders or those who are experts in a relevant field. This group may include members of state or local government, editors and reporters, leaders of special-interest groups, teachers and educational leaders, leaders of community groups, union leaders, or trade association managers, among others. Normally, the procedures used to collect information take the form of an informal, open-ended interview. Practitioners use the discussion to glean information and insights from a select group that is uniquely informed about a topic.

When using research from opinion leaders, practitioners should be careful. These people, because of their position, affiliations, and knowledge, do not necessarily reflect the understanding or opinions of the majority of citizens in a targeted audience. In this case, experts' opinions and insights are potentially useful and even important, but are not generalizable to a more-inclusive population.

In addition, their opinions will be shaped by the organizations for which they work. Some organizations such as unions, trade associations, and activist groups typically conduct research and make the results available for little or no cost. In many instances, such research provides valuable information and insights to practitioners and their organizations. In other cases, however, organizations may conduct research not to impartially learn the attitudes and opinions of the public, but to foster support for existing organizational positions and official viewpoints.

Pay particular attention to how organizations collect data. It is easy to create a research project that looks formal and scientific, when in fact it contains untrustworthy results because project managers used leading questions or a purposefully selected, skewed sample. When practitioners rely on research collected by a different organization (sometimes called secondary data analysis), it is important for them to learn as much as possible about the research method, including sample-selection procedures and the actual questionnaires or other instruments researchers used to collect data. This will ensure they are aware of the potential limitations of the information they are using. Even with potential limitations, such information may provide unique insights only possible through meeting with experts or opinion leaders or by examining the information they have at their disposal.

Advisory Committees or Boards

Advisory boards, standing committees, specially appointed panels, and similar bodies provide organizations with specific direction, help them plan and evaluate their programs and events, and help them identify and respond to feedback from the publics they serve. The nature and qualities of such groups differ widely according to their purposes. Public relations professionals often serve on the advisory board of local nonprofit organizations, for example, to help plan and direct their media relations efforts. Many local governmental bodies are advised by citizens' committees as they address community issues such as urban planning, public transportation, or local safety issues. Other advisory groups may consist of employees, consumers, or students. In fact, any group an organization is serving or anyone who may benefit an organization through expertise or ability may be qualified to serve in an advisory capacity.

Through their knowledge, experience, and insight, those who serve in an advisory capacity provide organizations with information critical for their successful operation. It is important for organizations to listen to advisory panel members and, when appropriate, work to incorporate their advice into their plans and actions. Members of advisory groups are quick to recognize when organizations are using them for appearances and when their advice has no effect on organizational behavior. In these cases, group members will potentially become a source of conflict rather than a useful source of information and advice.

When organizational managers blindly follow the advice and information provided by advisory groups, however, they also may experience problems. The accuracy and validity of the advice provided by such groups provides a limited point of reference for understanding public opinion; it cannot possibly represent the range of attitudes and opinions held by all members of a target audience. With this in mind, managers must use information gathered from such groups as counsel only. Gathering information from advisory boards does not serve as a substitute for the scientific approaches organizations use to determine the attitudes and behaviors of target audience members.

Field Reports, Customer Contact

Many organizations have field representatives including district agents, regional directors, or sales and service people. Often, these people have more direct contact with important target-audience members than anyone else in an organization. The activity reports routinely filed by some types of field representatives may be a useful source of information for an organization, especially if agents make note of customers' recurring questions and issues. It is important for supervisors to encourage their field agents to follow up on complaints and undertake related activities that help them monitor and evaluate an organization and its standing among members of target audiences.

Online retailer Bonobos, for example, started by selling its "better fitting" casual and dress pants to men. The company emphasized strong customer service, convenience, and technology to its patrons. By monitoring social media and listening to the feedback its customer-service representatives received from consumers, company executives identified a strong desire for superior-fitting shirts as well. The shirts are now the company's best-selling product line (Abramovich, 2013).

Management's desire to learn the truth is critical to the successful use of field reports or customer feedback as a beneficial source of information. Field reports—in fact, any formal or informal research method—will not be useful to an organization seeking to justify its actions. The information provided by those in the field is useful only when supervisors are willing to hear the truth from their representatives.

In addition, the information provided by field representatives has limitations. Representatives do not talk to a random sample of targeted audience members and their observations and suggestions are based on selective information. Input from the field, therefore, needs to be given appropriate weight, and organizational managers should use other forms of research to confirm or disconfirm this information when appropriate.

Learning Community and Consumer Sentiment

Community relations specialists may attend community forums or monitor social networking sites to learn about and better understand issues of concern to community members. When attending a meeting, practitioners should not conceal their presence but also should not be too vocal. Managers who attend meetings to learn the views of others run the risk of gaining a wrong sense of opinion if they involve themselves in the process because they may influence or alienate attendees. Instead, those who attend meetings should listen and consider the need for additional research as they help their organizations develop appropriate responses to emerging issues or other situations.

When monitoring social networking sites, practitioners should consider carefully how and when to respond to targeted audience members. While immediate, strategic responses to issues may be necessary and beneficial, the listening function will be inexorably altered when organizations respond prematurely. Citizens' backlash toward organizations providing poorly informed and inappropriate organizational responses often are quick and brutal in social media, resulting in substantial negative outcomes for the organization. When conducted properly, attending public meetings and monitoring relevant social media help practitioners monitor their internal or external environments, keep abreast of issues and opinions, and develop strategic responses to issues. When conducted poorly, these actions potentially will misinform practitioners, hindering their public relations efforts and creating additional problems.

In addition, it is in the best interest of organizational managers to listen carefully when individuals, whether local community members, consumers, members of activist groups, or others, go out of their way to communicate with them. Many people who have questions, concerns, or grievances never make the effort to communicate with an organization. They simply sever ties with the organization when possible, or maintain a frustrating relationship with an organization they dislike, perhaps expressing their frustrations in social media.

In an era of greater consumer sophistication and public activism, individuals and groups are increasingly likely to express their anger in negative comments and pages on social networking sites and potentially in ways that attract negative media attention. Depending on the situation and organizations involved, such expressions may evolve to include public protests, meetings with legislators or government regulators, demonstrations at shareholders' meetings, or other efforts designed to pressure organizational leaders to respond to issues and change their behavior.

Organizations can track social networking sites and all forms of consumer communication to learn about issues, gauge citizens' concern, and help determine when and how to best respond to these situations which can cause an organization serious harm. Since the early 1980s, for example, Proctor & Gamble has been the on-again, off-again target of untrue, vicious rumors that it is a proponent of Satanism (snopes.com, 2013). At the height of the crisis, the company handled more than 39,000 calls during a 3-month period (Cato, 1982). Not only were the calls a valuable source of information for Proctor & Gamble, they gave the company the opportunity to respond individually to consumers' concerns.

Digital communication technology makes communicating with publics and responding to their concerns a much easier and faster process today, along with making it easier for activist groups to target organizations. Reebok recently ended its endorsement deal with rapper Rick Ross over lyrics he performed in the song *U.O.E.N.O.* The controversial lyrics in Ross' song refer to having sex with a drugged woman after spiking her drink with MDMA, commonly known as Ecstasy or Molly.

The lyrics include these lines: "Put Molly all in her Champagne, she ain't even know it. I took her home and enjoyed that, she ain't even know it." While Reebok was attempting to increase its appeal to urban, hip-hop audiences with the sponsorship, activist groups, most notably UltraViolet, began using an online petition encouraging Reebok to end its sponsorship of Ross because his lyrics glorified rape. According to UltraViolet, the petition received 50,000 signatures during its first 24 hours in circulation. Other tactics included a protest at Reebok's Midtown Manhattan store, a Twitter campaign, a phone campaign, and ads on Facebook. When Reebok dropped Ross, UltraViolet thanked Reebok using a digital card that received 10,000 signatures in 40 minutes, according to its creator (Vega & McKinley, 2013).

Organizations routinely use social media, websites and toll-free telephone numbers to establish, maintain, and strengthen relationships with consumers. In 1981, for example, Butterball Turkey established a Turkey Talk Line—later expanded to include a website—to answer consumers' questions about all aspects of turkey preparation, ranging from thawing to cooking to carving. Staffed by professionally trained home economists and nutritionists, the line runs 24 hours a day in November and December. In 2012, more than 50 staff members responded to more than 100,000 questions during the 2-month period the Turkey Talk Line operated (Butterball.com, 2013).

Butterball's website offers a complete array of product-related information concerning food preparation, storage, and serving. The site encourages consumer engagement by allowing people who register to keep an electronic recipe box, for example, and by allowing visitors to sign up for an electronic *Turkey Lovers Newsletter*. The Turkey Talk Line and website serve as important reminders to consumers about Butterball's expertise in all aspects of turkey preparation and provide the company with important information about consumers' questions and interests.

As previously discussed, using a monitoring service or tools to track Internet chatter is a useful way for organizations to discover issues of consequence to important audiences and to help practitioners assess the need for organizational action concerning an issue or event. As with many informal methods of research, careful interpretation is necessary because the sample is not representative of the range of opinions and attitudes existing among all members of a target public. As a result, it may be wise for an organization to ignore a small number of complaints even if it results in some negative word of mouth from consumers in social media.

At the same time, however, organizations dismissive of negative comments, questions, and criticism as the off-base complaints of a few disgruntled people risk making a serious error in judgment. Initially, it is best to take all potential issues seriously, recognizing the few who speak often represent the opinions and attitudes of a much larger but silent group of individuals. In some cases, early warning signs produced through this type of informal information gathering indicate the clear need for a response or for additional research to further understand an issue.

Databases

There is an amazing array of smaller and not-so-small online databases available to practitioners. These provide access to a previously unimagined amount of information useful for identifying trends, engaging in customer relationship management and conducting digital communication campaigns. In public relations, relevant databases range from simple media directories, to massive amounts of aggregate data collected by social networking sites, to original research collected using both formal and informal methods conducted by foundations and government agencies. Practitioners can use databases to learn important information about major developments in fields as diverse as digital media, medicine, agriculture, education, and labor. In each of these cases, digital technology has made it possible for practitioners to gather and examine a wealth of information.

Online directories help practitioners find database resources. Some specialized databases contain proprietary research and are quite costly to access. When they use them, practitioners typically justify their costs based on the benefits they receive from having access to exclusive data that helps them identify trends and informs their decision making. The results of research conducted by governments, foundations, and educational organizations, by contrast, often are available online at little or no cost. Many times, this research makes use of formal research methods and is very high in quality.

The work of the Census Bureau deserves special attention in any discussion of database research. As a rule, this research is very high in quality, is available online, and contains some of the most abundant and beneficial sets of data available to practitioners. A visit to the government census website (www.census.gov) reveals a remarkable array of data with a variety of potential uses. Businesses, for example will find economic data collected by the Census Bureau useful for identifying local and national trends with important implications for new or expanding business opportunities, identifying retail store locations, designing and managing sales territories, and much more.

Demographic characteristics provided by the Bureau can help organizations uncover new opportunities for growth and develop targeted marketing campaigns. The economic data provided by the Census Bureau includes detailed statistical information about businesses including sales, inventory, revenue, expenses, and more. This information is available for specific industries by geographic region, for example, and provides practitioners with new ways to identify and understand important demographic trends and the behavior of stakeholders and members of other publics (Moran, 2013).

Clip Counts and Media Tracking

Typically, practitioners monitor their organization's or client's media placement to help track news coverage, evaluate communication campaigns, and sometimes erroneously, attempt to gauge public opinion based on media reports. In addition, services are available to monitor all types of media and digital-communication outlets and companies such as Cision or BurrellesLuce, for example, provide monitoring access to social networking sites, blogs, content-sharing sites and more. Media tracking and digital monitoring services can provide practitioners with a wide range of information useful for everything from engaging in customer relationship management to improving media relations.

For traditional media monitoring, for example, any organization in the news on a regular basis should have some way to track media coverage, the results of which practitioners organize and analyze. Although clip counts do not serve all purposes well—practitioners may mistakenly use clippings and similar placement measures to evaluate program impact (Broom & Sha, 2013)—they do help organizations understand and evaluate their media relations efforts. When practitioners desire greater accuracy, precision, and reliability in their analysis efforts, they need to conduct a formal content analysis (discussed in Chapter 9) of media clippings. Most organizational clip counts and other forms of media tracking fall far short of the demands of a formal content analysis but still serve useful purposes.

While differences exist in how services operate, practitioners typically provide monitoring services with search parameters including the organization's name, the name of its products or services, or even the names of its competitors and their products. As media monitoring services collect clips for their clients, they typically provide information about the source of the clip, such as the full text of the story, the headline, relevant photographs and graphics, and other important information. Practitioners then organize and analyze the clips. Figure 7.2 provides some examples of clip tracking and analysis provided by Cision.

Media monitoring typically has been an important aspect of campaign evaluation in public relations. Often, however, practitioners misuse publicity placements in an attempt to provide evidence of campaign impact. While this is an erroneous use of media monitoring results, media tracking does serve a useful purpose in public relations. When practitioners extend their tracking efforts to include social networking sites and other aspects of digital communication, it typically provides an essential listening function that helps practitioners engage in relationship management with stakeholders, customers and members of other publics as noted previously.

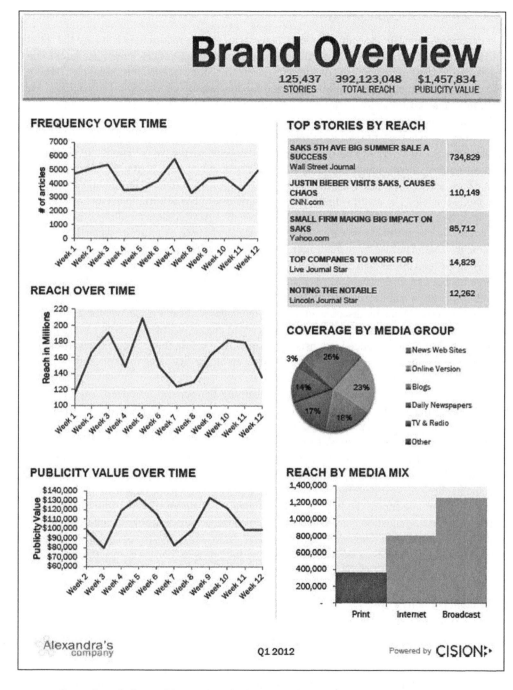

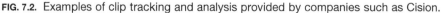

FIG. 7.2. Examples of clip tracking and analysis provided by companies such as Cision.

(Image courtesy of Cision)

Advertising Cost Equivalency

In an attempt to quantify the value of media placement, many practitioners compare the results of their publicity efforts with equivalent advertising costs. Practitioners sometimes refer to this as *advertising cost equivalency* or advertising value equivalency (AVE). It is relatively common, for example, to compare the column space and broadcast time generated by a campaign with the "equivalent" cost for advertising placement had the space been purchased. This method of evaluation allows practitioners to claim a dollar amount for the media coverage their campaign generates. In some cases, practitioners increase, or decrease, the value of publicity placements. In a marketing context, for example, practitioners may decrease the value of publicity placements recognizing that these commonly lack some of the benefits of advertising. That is, media placements lack a controlled message delivered to a specific audience and timed according to a planned schedule. The result is that managers sometimes give editorial placements less value than advertising placements because they cannot control their contents and placement.

Practitioners commonly argue publicity placements deserve a multiplier when determining placement value. The use of a multiplier inflates the results of advertising equivalencies by increasing the total circulation or audience for a placement. Three is a common multiplier among proponents but factors can range from 2.5 to 8 (Weiner & Bartholomew, 2006). Proponents of multipliers suggest public relations placements have a higher level of perceived credibility because consumers typically discount advertising messages as meaningless hyperbole. Unfortunately, the available research concerning the perceived credibility of advertising versus public relations messages has produced inconsistent results. As a result, there is no objective research to support this claim and practitioners may damage their credibility using multipliers haphazardly (Weiner & Bartholomew, 2006).

This issue raises a point of contention concerning the benefits of advertising versus the benefits of publicity, and it reveals some of the serious problems associated with claiming dollar amounts for publicity media placements. In reality, it is nearly impossible to compare advertising and publicity placements in terms of their relative value. How do you compare, for example, the value of a full-page print ad that appears in the middle of a publication with a front-page story that publicizes an organization's good works in a community? In terms of different publicity placements, how do you determine the value of a story on the front page with a story placed in the middle of a section? Or, how do you compare the value of clips in different media—a narrowly targeted publication that reaches an identified target audience, for example, with general media placement that reaches the public broadly? Also, how do you compare the value of different editorial contexts: a story that is positive, for example, versus a story that is negative or mixed? These issues, and related ones, present practitioners with difficult obstacles when determining the relative value of advertising versus publicity and when determining the value of different publicity clips.

Cost per Thousand

Another common method practitioners use to determine the value of publicity clips is based on the cost of reaching audience members. Advertisers, for example, commonly determine the most beneficial combination of media, programs, and schedules by evaluating and comparing the costs of different media and different media vehicles, as well as by considering the percentage of an audience that is part of a specific target audience for a campaign. One of the simplest means of comparing media costs is to compare the *cost per thousand* or CPM ("M" is the Roman numeral for 1,000) of different media. This figure tells media planners the cost of reaching 1,000 people in an audience. If a daily newspaper has 500,000 subscribers and charges $10,000 for running a full-page ad, for example, the cost per thousand is $20 (10,000 ÷ 500,000 × 1,000).

Cost Efficiency

To determine the relative cost efficiency of different media, media planners use the same general formula but reduce the total audience figures to include only those audience members who specifically are targeted as part of a campaign. Using the previous example, if the campaign primarily is directed at males 18 to 34 years old and 30% of the newspaper's audience fits into this category, the circulation figure can be reduced to 30% of the total audience, or 150,000. The resulting cost efficiency figure is approximately $67 (10,000 ÷ 150,000 × 1,000).

Cost per Impression

Practitioners can use these same formulas to measure the relative value of publicity clips. Sometimes practitioners refer to publicity clips as *publicity impressions*. They can calculate the *cost per impression* (CPI) of publicity clips after they have completed a campaign and compare the results with advertising campaign costs or other campaign costs. In public relations, the cost is any out-of-pocket expense associated with a campaign including, for example, the cost of a special event or the costs associated with holding a Internet media tour. Practitioners can calculate the cost efficiency of publicity impressions and use them to communicate value to their organizations or clients and also as a benchmark for achieving lower future impression costs (Van Camp, 2012).

CPM-type measures are difficult to use to compare the value of advertising versus publicity clips, however, primarily because CPM calculations are performed in the early stages of an advertising campaign and used for planning and forecasting, whereas a campaign must be over before practitioners can calculate final publicity impression costs because clips depend on media placement achieved during a campaign. More important, neither CPM nor CPI calculations measure message impact—they only measure message exposure. In fact, they are not even a true measure of message exposure but instead are a measure of the greatest potential message exposure. The exposure numbers they produce are useful in a relative sense but are likely to overestimate audience size.

Applications and Limitations of Clip and Tracking Research

Although practitioners can use any of these methods to quantitatively evaluate publicity clip placements and their use by practitioners is common, these methods are relatively unsophisticated and must not serve as the basis for determining message impact or campaign success. In most cases, formal research methods are necessary to evaluate a range of campaign outcomes from changes in the opinions and attitudes of target audience members to changes in individual behavior. This is not meant to suggest, however, that the use of clip files is not beneficial as a form of casual research. In fact, there are various potential improvements on standard clip counts and several valuable ways practitioners use such information.

The U.S. Army Corps of Engineers, for example, regulates the Missouri River, in part to protect the public from the potentially devastating effects of flooding. The Missouri River mainstream system is the largest reservoir system in the United States and in May 2011, heavy rains forced the Corp to release an unprecedented amount of water. The flooding broke every record along the Missouri River since the Corp began keeping detailed records in 1898. While the mainstream dams and levees in high-risk areas performed well under duress, the flooding displaced people, flooded farms and threatened entire communities.

To provide accurate and timely information to the public and media, the Corp formed the Missouri River Joint Information Center and dubbed the effort "Operation Mighty Mo" (PRSA, 2012g). As part of their efforts, team members conducted a variety of primary and secondary research. Among other things, research results revealed a lack of public understanding about the design and operation of the mainstream system and confusion concerning the emergency-response role of Corp. Other research revealed people distrusted the Corp and blamed it for the flooding. The Corp also discovered that citizens had been confused by past campaign efforts that relied on jargon-laden messages filled with acronyms and technical language.

The Corp's goals for its response efforts included gaining and maintaining public trust, communicating clearly to the public, educating the public, monitoring public perception and mitigating flood-related rumors to the extent possible. As the flooding peaked, members of the Corp addressed an average of 80 public and 30 media queries per day. Corp staff members dealt with all manner of media including the *New York Times, Washington Post, Wall Street Journal*, and CNN Online. Among other efforts, the Corp documented more than 900 media contacts, distributed 110 news releases, and held 91 call-in news conferences posting audio to the Web within two-hours of each conference.

Methods of campaign evaluation varied. Social media monitoring revealed the public relied on information provided by the Corp and Facebook views totaled more than 9.6 million by the middle of the event. In addition, the Corps' analysis of media clips indicated that 30% of the clips included clear delivery of the Corps' key messages. Surveys of media and stakeholders revealed the Corps successfully fulfilled information needs and by tracking rumors in the call center and in the media, and immediately correcting misinformation, Corp staff members were able to manage and largely mitigate rumors (PRSA, 2012g).

As another example, diabetes is a disease that receives a large amount of media coverage, yet many people fail to understand how to resist the disease. Media tracking revealed that, although reporters were covering diabetes as a disease, they largely were ignoring the link between insulin resistance and cardiovascular disease. To address this issue, the American Heart Association joined with Takeda Pharmaceuticals North America and Eli Lilly to produce an award-winning campaign to help people learn about insulin resistance, better understand the link between diabetes and cardiovascular disease, and help reduce their risk of developing cardiovascular disease.

The campaign included a major media relations effort designed to reach members of at-risk publics. Post-campaign media tracking indicated the program received extensive media coverage, including coverage in key media targeted to members of minority groups who were a specific focus of the campaign. More important, 15,000 people enrolled in a program to receive free educational materials, double the number campaign organizers set as an objective (PRSA 2004b).

It is important to reiterate a key point in the use and interpretation of media tracking and clip counts at this point. As a rule, this research reveals only the *media's use* of messages.

Of course, it provides information concerning a targeted audience's potential exposure to messages, but clip files and tracking studies by themselves reveal nothing about message *impact*. Sometimes the results of media placements are obvious and no additional understanding is necessary. In fact, in many cases agencies do not conduct formal campaign evaluations because an organization or client believes it easily can identify the impact of a particular campaign.

At other times, however, practitioners desire to learn more about a message's impact on an audience's level of knowledge, attitudes, or behavioral outcomes. When this is the case, clip files and analyses of media-message placement tell practitioners little about these outcomes. In addition, campaign planners who claim success based on media placements as revealed by clipping services and tracking studies may be overstating the impact of their campaigns. Although clipping services and media tracking may have some value, practitioners are unwise when they attempt to determine public opinion and gather similar information based on media-message placement.

Real-Time Message Testing/Surveys

Technological advances have made it easy and relatively inexpensive for researchers to collect information instantaneously through the use of handheld dials that participants use to select answers to survey questions or indicate positive or negative reactions to media messages. Researchers can use these systems, with trade names such as Perception Analyzer, to administer a survey question to a group of people such as focus group participants or trade show attendees, collect anonymous answers to the question immediately, and project participants' aggregated responses onto a screen. Once participants have had an opportunity to consider the result, a moderator can lead a group discussion about the responses and what they may or may not mean to participants.

In a twist on this process, researchers also can use these systems to collect participants' moment-by-moment, or real-time, responses to media including advertising, speeches, debates, and even entertainment programming. Managers and campaign planners then can use this information to help their organizations and clients develop more effective media messages and programming, for example, or determine key talking points for presentations and media interviews. This research tool, which we discuss in greater detail along with focus groups in Chapter 8, has the potential to provide researchers with highly valuable information. At the same time, practitioners must use information provided by these services carefully. Sample size and selection procedures normally will prevent researchers from obtaining a probability-based sample so, as is the case with almost all informal research methods, research results will lack a high degree of external validity or projectability.

In-Depth Interviews

In-depth interviewing, sometimes called *intensive interviewing* or simply *depth interviewing*, is an open-ended interview technique in which researchers encourage respondents to discuss an issue or problem, or answer a question, at length and in great detail. This interview process provides a wealth of detailed information and is particularly useful for exploring attitudes and behaviors in an engaged and extended format. In applied public relations settings, practitioners may use an interview technique similar to depth interviews to learn from opinion leaders or to conduct expert interviews as they engage in environmental monitoring or in the planning phase of a campaign.

Initially, an interview participant is given a question or asked to discuss a problem or topic. The remainder of the interview is generally dictated by the participant's responses or statements. Participants typically are free to explore the issue or question in any manner they desire, although an interviewer may have additional questions or topics to address as the interview progresses. Normally, the entire process allows an unstructured interview to unfold in which participants explore and explain their attitudes and opinions, motivations, values, experiences, emotions, and related information. The researcher encourages this probing interview process through active listening techniques, providing feedback as necessary or desired, and occasionally questioning participants regarding their responses. As rapport is established between an interviewer and a participant, the interview may produce deeper, more meaningful findings, even on topics that may be considered too sensitive to address through other research methods.

Most intensive interviews are customized for each participant. Although the level of structure varies, based on the purpose of the project and, sometimes, the ability of a participant to direct the interview, it is critical that researchers do not influence participants' thought processes. Interviewees must explore and elaborate on their thoughts and feelings as they naturally occur, rather than attempting to condition their responses to what they perceive the researcher wants to learn. A key strength of this research technique is that participants, not the researcher, drive the interview process (Wimmer & Dominick, 2014). When participants structure the interview, it increases the chances that the interview will produce unanticipated responses or reveal latent issues or other unusual, but potentially useful, information.

In-depth interviews typically last from about an hour up to several hours. A particularly long interview is likely to fatigue both the interviewer and the interviewee, and it may be necessary to schedule more than one session in some instances. Because of the time required to conduct an in-depth interview, it is particularly difficult to schedule interviews, especially with professionals. In addition, participants typically are paid for their time. Payments, which range from $100 to $1,000 or more, normally are higher than payments provided to focus group participants (Wimmer & Dominick, 2014).

In-depth interviews offer several benefits as a research method. Perhaps the most important advantages are the wealth of detailed information they typically provide and the occasional surprise discovery of unanticipated but potentially beneficial information. Wimmer and Dominick (2014) suggested that intensive interviews provide more accurate information concerning sensitive issues than traditional survey techniques because of the rapport that develops between an interviewer and an interviewee.

In terms of disadvantages, sampling issues are a particular concern for researchers conducting in-depth interviews. The time and intensity required to conduct an interview commonly results in the use of small, nonprobability-based samples. As a result, it typically is impossible to generalize the findings of such interviews from a sample to a population with a high degree of confidence. For this reason, researchers should confirm or disconfirm potentially important findings discovered during in-depth interviews using a research method and accompanying sample that provide higher degrees of validity and reliability. Difficulty scheduling interviews also contributes to study length and in-depth interviews may stretch over several weeks or even months (Wimmer & Dominick, 2014).

In addition, the unstructured nature of in-depth interviews leads to non-standard interview procedures and questions. This makes analysis and interpretation of study results challenging, and it raises additional concerns regarding the reliability and validity of study findings. Nonstandard interviews also may add to study length because of problems researchers encounter when attempting to analyze and interpret study results. As a final note, the unstructured interview process and length of time it takes to complete an interview result in a high potential for interviewer bias. As rapport develops between an interviewer and an interviewee and they obtain a basic level of comfort with one another, the researcher may inadvertently communicate information that influences participants' responses. Interviewers require a great deal of training to avoid this problem, which contributes to study cost and length. Despite these limitations, researchers can use in-depth interviews to successfully gather information not readily available using other research methods.

Panel Studies

Panel studies are a type of longitudinal study that permit researchers to collect data over time. Panel studies allow researchers to examine changes within individual sample members, typically by having the same participants complete questionnaires or participate in other forms of data collection over a specific length of time. This differs from surveys, which are *cross-sectional* in nature, meaning that they provide an immediate picture of participants' opinions and attitudes as they currently exist, but they provide little information about how participants formed those attitudes or how they might change. A strength of panel studies is their ability to provide researchers with information concerning how participants' attitudes and behaviors change as they mature or in response to specific situations.

Researchers might want to examine citizens' attitudes, information source use, and voting behavior concerning presidential elections, for example. They might survey the same group of people in late summer of an election year, immediately before the first televised presidential debate, immediately before the elections take place and even in the weeks following an election. Such a longitudinal study can reveal change among participants as they engage in political decision making over time rather than examining their attitudes and behaviors at a single point in time. The ability to examine change over time is a primary benefit of panel studies.

Today, some research organizations conduct sophisticated, large-scale consumer or other panel studies through online participation. These studies can be based on sizeable samples and provide organizations with a variety of useful information that has been nearly impossible for organizations to collect in the past. There are different types of panels that exist currently so generalizing to all panel studies is difficult. While some panel studies use probability-based samples, the vast majority of online panels rely on nonprobability-based sampling. Commonly, these are opt-in panel studies—often conducted in market research applications—in which individuals voluntarily choose to participate in surveys as a way to earn money or other rewards. While many in government, academic, and even market research have resisted online panel studies because of concerns over the accuracy of the results they provide, there has been a tremendous growth in the use of this method and its growth likely will continue.

In an attempt to provide study results more closely reflecting results from probability-based samples and reflective of population parameters, panel studies typically rely on quotas to match the demographic characteristics of study participants to the characteristics of population members. Organizers of a panel study might work to ensure their study participants reflect members of a population in terms of age, race or ethnicity, gender, education levels, income levels, political ideology, and more. In this way, panel-study results may be more likely to enjoy a high degree of generalizability. Unfortunately, some research results indicate panel-based studies have quite a bit more error than studies using probability-based samples (e.g., Yeager, et al., 2011) while other studies have produced results with more reasonable amounts of error (e.g., Ansolabehere & Schaffner, in press).

Practitioners considering conducting a panel study or purchasing information based on panel research should be careful, however. Although information that panels provide may be extremely useful, the samples that organizations use for most panel research projects are not representative because they are based on a nonrandom selection process, are too small to be representative, or both. As a result, the results of panel research may suffer from low external validity, or generalizability. This problem may be compounded by high rates of attrition, or mortality over time. That is, panel members may drop out of studies because they become busy or simply lose interest. When panel studies suffer from large-scale attrition, practitioners need to consider the results they produce with caution because they most likely lack representation. For these reasons, we treat panel studies as an informal research method and, despite the clear benefits and tremendous potential of the method, encourage practitioners to consider the results carefully.

Final Thoughts

It is important for readers to remember that informal research methods typically suffer from several limitations making them difficult to use with confidence. This, in fact, is the reason researchers consider them informal and casual. This does not mean practitioners should never use informal research methods. In fact, practitioners regularly use informal research methods, typically more frequently than they use formal research methods. Because of their limitations, however, practitioners must interpret and apply the results of informal research carefully and understand the limitations of the methods they are using. Considering the advice of selected members of a target audience, for example, makes sense in most situations, and such input can be invaluable when engaging in research and planning. At the same time, however, the prudent practitioner will consider this information for what it is—the opinions of a small number of people—instead of giving it the full weight of a scientifically conducted, formal opinion poll.

What does this mean for public relations practitioners? When possible, practitioners should use informal research to supplement formal research methods rather than to replace them. This provides practitioners with a variety of research results they can use to support the planning process. Unfortunately, practitioners may rely on informal research exclusively because of limited budgets and a lack of time. In these situations, it is wise to take every precaution in interpreting and using research results correctly. No research method is infallible, but managers should use special care when interpreting research results produced through informal methods.

8

Making Research Decisions
The Focus Group

Chapter Contents

- Characteristics of the Focus Group
- Advantages and Disadvantages of Focus Groups
- Selecting and Recruiting Participants
- The Focus Group Setting
- Staffing
- Characteristics of the Moderator
- Dealing with Difficult Group Members
- Protocol Design
- Message and Idea Testing
- New Options Made Possible by Technology
- Running the Group
- Analyzing the Results
- Final Thoughts

The focus group has long been a mainstay of public relations and marketing research, but it remains a controversial method for research and message testing. Practitioners often tell horror stories about focus groups that provided misleading information for a campaign that later failed. Nevertheless, the method has gained respect as a valid research tool, rather than a cheap and dirty alternative to so-called real research.

A recent proliferation of scholarly and how-to books and articles has made it possible for more practitioners to use the tool more effectively and wisely. Although focus groups still have limitations, careful application of the method can provide indispensable guidance available from no other tool. Keep in mind, however, that focus groups are designed to generate ideas, not evaluate them (Palshaw, 1990).

Characteristics of the Focus Group

A focus group is a semistructured, group interview analyzed using qualitative methods, which means researchers interpret responses instead of trying to count them. Focus groups explore the attitudes, opinions, behaviors, beliefs, and recommendations of carefully selected groups. Focused discussions, led by a moderator, usually include 6 to 12 participants and take place over 1 to 3 hours. Sessions attempt to define problems, gather reaction to proposed solutions to problems, and explore feelings and reasons behind differences that exist within the group or between the group and the organization.

Organizations typically use focus groups to obtain feedback during product or service development, to test messages for product or service introductions, to guide decisions about packaging design and promotional messages, to determine appropriate types of outlets and target publics for products or messages, to gauge public reaction to issue positions, and to explore opinions concerning company performance and community citizenship. Message testing explores participants' perceptions of the accuracy, clarity, and relevance of a message, as well as the credibility of the source.

More specialized uses of focus groups also exist. Focus groups can be used to gain a better understanding of groups whose perspectives are poorly understood by an organization. This can help an organization respond more effectively to the group's concerns. Focus groups also can help an organization explore its strengths and weaknesses relative to other organizations. In addition, focus groups can be used for brainstorming purposes, to develop strategies for solving a problem instead of simply testing strategies already under development. Focus groups can help an organization gain insight into complex behaviors and conditional opinions, for which survey questionnaires could provide conflicting or seemingly definite information. As a result, focus groups are often used as a supplement to survey research.

Group dynamics in a focus group can be used to reach consensus on an idea, such as the most credible source for a message or the best location for an event. Finally, focus groups can be used to pretest and refine survey instruments, particularly when likely responses to a question are unknown, such as the biggest barriers to a customer's use of a proposed product or service.

Instead of using questionnaires, researchers use protocols to guide focus group discussions. Protocols range from rough outlines to carefully constructed moderators' guides. Pre-session questionnaires can be used for screening. In addition, focus groups often use visual aids such as storyboards, mock-ups, or other sample materials for pretesting. Whereas surveys try to take a dispassionate, outsider's perspective to obtain the most objective information about a targeted population from a representative group, focus groups try to work more from inside the target group, exploring individuals' perspectives in depth to gain a deeper understanding of their decision-making processes. Surveys, in other words, try to avoid bias; focus groups try to explore and understand it.

Advantages and Disadvantages of Focus Groups

Focus groups should not be viewed as alternatives to survey research, as the two methods have different strengths and weaknesses. The focus group offers characteristics that give it a uniquely useful role in problem definition and message testing. Because focus groups are socially oriented, for example, they make it possible to uncover information about an issue that would not come out in individual interviews or in surveys. People initially may not recall using a product or service but may be reminded of a relevant situation as a result of another participant's observations during the focused discussion. In addition, the focused discussion makes it possible to probe positive or negative responses in depth. Because people can explain what they mean and moderators can probe for clarification, focus groups provide good face validity. In other words, managers can be confident that they are interpreting what people said in ways consistent with what they meant. This can be more difficult in a survey, for which individuals must check a box even if the question seems vague or the possible response categories do not reflect their views perfectly.

Focus groups also provide quick, relatively inexpensive results to guide a program that requires fast implementation. Although overnight survey services are available, they can be expensive and make it difficult to develop a tailored survey instrument that maximizes the relevance of findings obtained. Political campaigns, meanwhile, can use focus groups to try out possible responses to a competitor's political advertisement in time to air a response within a day or two.

Another advantage of focus groups is their flexibility. Literacy, for example, is not needed for a focus group whereas it is required for a written questionnaire. People without land-based telephones or with caller ID may never respond to a telephone survey but may participate in a focus group if recruited properly. In addition, focus groups can be held in different locations, even in a park. This makes it easier to recruit from populations that may be unable or unwilling to travel to a research facility.

As shown in Table 8.1, focus groups also have drawbacks that limit their usefulness and increase the risk of obtaining misleading information that can compromise communication program effectiveness. For example, although the group dynamics of a focus group make it possible for information to come out that might not be uncovered through individual interviews, group dynamics also make it more difficult to control the direction and tenor of discussions. A carefully trained moderator is essential to draw the full range of opinions out of focus group participants and to prevent individuals from dominating the group. Groups vary depending on the characteristics of the participants, the timing, and the environment, which makes their reliability questionable. They also can be difficult to assemble because individuals from targeted populations may be busy, resistant, or forgetful.

Because of these limitations, focus groups should never be used in confrontational situations, for statistical projections, if the unique dynamics of social interaction are unnecessary for

Table 8.1 Advantages and Disadvantages of Focus Groups

Advantages	*Disadvantages*
Socially oriented	Have less control than with interviews
Can probe responses	Tough to analyze in depth
Good face validity	Need carefully trained moderator
Low cost (compared to many other methods)	Groups vary
	Can be tough to assemble
Fast	Environment makes a big difference
Larger sample than for interviews	Cannot generalize/low projectability
No need for literacy	

information gathering, if confidentiality cannot be assured, or if procedures such as sampling or questioning are driven by client bias rather than by researcher design.

To summarize, focus groups can:

- Explore the roots of a problem
- Explore possible strategies for a campaign
- Gain the perspective of those you don't understand
- Provide insight into complex behaviors and conditional opinions
- Explore whether group dynamics lead to consensus on an idea
- Develop ideas for survey questions, pretest and refine survey instruments
- Concept test messages and strategies.

Focus groups should not be used:

- In confrontational situations
- To make statistical projections
- To perform program evaluation
- If interaction among participants is unnecessary
- If confidentiality cannot be assured
- If driven by client bias rather than researcher design.

The usefulness of a focused discussion depends on the willingness of participants to share their perspectives freely and honestly. As a result, focus groups must take place in a comfortable, nonthreatening environment. The composition of an appropriate setting requires attention to the makeup of the group itself, as well as the surroundings in which the discussion takes place. A poorly constructed environment can hamper discussion or make it difficult to ascertain true opinions. A focus group of parents, for example, may mask differences in perspective between mothers and fathers. Misleading information obtained from a restricted discussion can doom a campaign. As shown in Table 8.2, successful focus groups require planning ahead.

Table 8.2 Focus Group Planning Checklist

- Provide advance notice to participants
- Design and pretest discussion protocol
- Logistics
    - The setting
    - Materials for display or activities
    - Recording devices, including backup devices and power sources
    - Refreshments, including items needed for service and cleanup
    - Seating arrangements
    - Paperwork for participant consent, verification of incentives
- Moderator preparation
- Planning for analysis

Selecting and Recruiting Participants

People tend to feel most comfortable when they are with others like themselves. As a result, focus group participants usually are selected to be *homogeneous*, which means similar in certain characteristics. These characteristics depend on the issue explored by the group. For example, a discussion of a college's responsiveness to student financial aid issues could mix male and female students because they are likely to share similar problems regarding funding their education. On the other hand, a discussion of date rape is less productive if the group includes both men and women. Because women often are the victims of date rape, this may make both the men and the women uncomfortable talking about it in front of each other. As a result, separate focus groups can take place to separately explore the beliefs and feelings of men and women about date rape. Similarly, a discussion of workplace issues may need to probe the views of managerial personnel and secretarial personnel separately because employees may not feel comfortable speaking freely in front of their supervisors.

The most productive focus groups recruit participants who are similar but who do not already know each other. If they know each other, interpersonal dynamics such as power roles already have been established and can make open discussion and discovery more difficult. This becomes important in focused discussions that must mix participants with different perspectives, such as employees and supervisors, to explore the dynamics between them. This type of situation can work only if the participants feel they can be open with one another and only if the discussion can take place in a constructive, civil way. In other words, if participants need to include employees and supervisors, they should not include employees and their own supervisors.

Focus group participants often are recruited with respect to homogeneity in demographic characteristics such as age, income, educational level, product usage patterns, or group membership. Screening tests ascertain these characteristics to ensure that participants qualify for inclusion in the study. Such tests can be performed via telephone during recruitment or in the outer lobby on arrival. Several separate focus groups may be required to obtain reactions from different target publics.

Because the focus group method is qualitative not quantitative, it is not necessary to hold a certain number of focus groups to ensure a corresponding degree of reliability. Whereas a survey uses probability sampling to provide reliable results with a 95% level of confidence, focus groups are inherently biased by design. As a result, organizations typically rely on a combination of intuition, budgetary restrictions, and time constraints to determine the number of focus groups that will be held. If time and budget allow, focus groups should continue until all vital target publics have been represented or until the information obtained seems redundant; that is, little new information emerges from additional focus groups. In reality, however, organizations rarely have the time or budget to hold more than two to four focus groups.

Cost varies widely for focus groups. Hiring a professional firm to run a focus group can require $3,000 to $5,000, but organizations can run their own focus groups if they prepare carefully. The cost of using existing staff and volunteer participants can be as low as the cost of popcorn or pizza and soft drinks. Fees for professional moderators vary widely and depend on your region, the amount and type of responsibilities you require of the moderator, and the number of focus groups. Moderator fees can range from several hundred to several thousand dollars per focus group. Focus group participants are usually paid for their time. The going rate depends on the type of sample recruited. Researchers undertaking focus groups of children may rely on prizes or free products as compensation. Focus groups of adults usually pay around

$35 to $80 apiece. Recruitment of expert participants such as executives, physicians, or other professionals may require significantly greater payment.

It is necessary to recruit more participants than are actually needed for the group. In fact, researchers usually recruit twice the number needed to allow for no-shows and individuals who, for some reason, become ineligible. When recruiting from special populations, in particular, unforeseen circumstances can prevent attendance. People also tend to forget, so preparation requires a multistep process of recruitment, acknowledgment, and mail/e-mail and telephone reminders.

When time is tight, on-the-spot recruitment of focus group participants can take place in a shopping mall that has a market-research facility on the premises. Usually, however, focus group recruitment takes place 1 to 2 weeks before the session. Respondents can be recruited using different methods, but often they are contacted by telephone. Following the initial contact, recruits should receive a written confirmation of the invitation to participate that also serves as a reminder. Reminder phone calls the day or two before the session also helps to boost attendance. If possible, attendees should provide contact numbers and e-mail addresses upon recruitment so that they can be reached at home or at work.

The location of focus group facilities can help or hurt recruitment. The facility should be easy to find, such as in a shopping mall; be relatively close to participants' homes or work places; and have plenty of safe parking available. When recruiting parents, researchers may also find it necessary to provide child care. Proper facilities and staffing must be provided to gain the confidence of parents.

Timing can make a difference for focus group success. Most focus groups take place in the evening and avoid weekends or holidays. Other times, such as the lunch hour, may be appropriate for special cases. If two groups are planned for a single evening, the first typically begins at 6:00 p.m. and the second at 8:15 p.m.

The Focus Group Setting

Participants tend to speak more freely in an informal setting. Conference rooms are better than classrooms, circular seating is better than lecture-style seating, coffee tables are better than conference tables, and comfortable chairs or sofas are better than office or classroom chairs. Some organizations rent hotel suites for focus group discussions, whereas others use rooms specifically built for focus group research. Focus group facilities typically include a two-way mirror, behind which clients can sit to observe the discussion as it unfolds without disturbing the participants. This mirror looks like a window on the observers' side but looks like a mirror on the participants' side. Facilities also may include a buffet table or another area for refreshments because snacks and beverages tend to promote informality. Snacks need to be simple, however, so that the participants pay more attention to the discussion than to their food. Food can range from a complete meal, such as sandwiches, to a small snack, such as popcorn.

To aid analysis and for later review by the client, discussions are recorded unobtrusively on audiotape, videotape, or both. Participants are advised of all data collection and observation procedures. Taping and observation are never done in secret or without the participants' consent. Participants also must be informed if their anonymity may not be assured, such as by their appearance on videotape. Often, for the discussion, participants wear name tags but provide only their first names. Sometimes they go by pseudonyms for additional privacy protection. At no time should participants be identified by name in focus group transcripts or reports.

Staffing

Focus groups generally require a team effort. Besides staff for the planning and recruitment phases of the focus group, the interview itself usually requires several staff members. In addition to the moderator, who leads the discussion, the event requires at least one other staff member to serve as coordinator. The coordinator (or coordinators) welcome and screen participants; handle honoraria; guide participants to the refreshments and make sure refreshments are available; check and run equipment; bring extra batteries, duct tape, and other supplies; and interact with the client. In addition, the coordinator or another staff member takes prolific notes during the session. This is necessary because (a) transcription equipment can and does break down and human error with equipment does happen; (b) some people may speak too softly for their comments to register on an audio recording; (c) it may be difficult to identify the source of a comment, particularly if several participants speak at once; and (d) the note taker can provide

Table 8.3 Sample Focus Group Supplies Checklist

Documents list

No.	Document	Indicate quantity needed	Notes
1.	Consent Form	60	Participant keeps one copy and returns one copy to the moderator
2.	Focus group protocol and questions	2	For moderators
3.	Incentive sign-out sheet	2	Form includes name (in print), participant signature, staff signature, value of the incentive

Logistics list

No.	Items	Indicate quantity needed	Notes
1.	Recording device	2	Have extra for backup. Have extra power source (e.g. batteries)
2.	Demonstration materials	12	Projector, screen, portable whiteboards, etc.
3.	Background questionnaires	12 per group	If desired for participant screening
4.	Participant supplies as needed		May include instant-response technology, pencils, paper
5.	Focus group room prep	1	Instruction for placement of materials and seating arrangements
6.	Incentives		Anticipate security needs and procedures
7.	Staff	2	One moderator, one facilitator/note-taker
8.	Refreshments		Include checklist of ancillary supplies such as napkins, serving tools and clean-up supplies

an initial real-time analysis of themes emerging from the discussion. The note taker may develop the final report in collaboration with the moderator.

Table 8.3 provides a logistics checklist that can aid focus group set-up.

Characteristics of the Moderator

The focus group moderator is the key to an effective discussion. The moderator must be able to lead discussion, providing both structure and flexibility to keep the discussion on track but allow participants to pursue issues in depth. Because the moderator must be skilled in group dynamics, some people specialize in focus group leadership and can command an expert's salary to do so.

The moderator must display an air of authority while establishing an atmosphere of warmth and trust so that participants feel free to speak their minds. The moderator strives to keep the structure of the questioning strategy from becoming too obvious because that could detract from the informality that increases the likelihood of open discussion. In addition, the moderator must treat all participants with equal respect, staying neutral while encouraging all points of view. Moderators never offer their own personal opinions, and they must also avoid using words such as *excellent, great, wonderful*, or *right*, which signal approval of a particular point of view. The moderator must also be able to prevent any member of the group from dominating and must be able to draw out hesitant members.

Effective moderators memorize their topic outlines or protocols so that they can pay full attention to the unfolding dynamics of the group. An abbreviated checklist can help them keep on track. The best focus groups direct the discussion themselves to a great extent, instead of having their discussion directed by a highly structured questionnaire. As a result, moderators must be ready to make adjustments, including the sudden addition or deletion of questions by the client, who can convey messages to the moderator during the focus group by way of an ear microphone or notes. The moderator may need to modify a questioning strategy that fails with a particular group or pursue an unexpected discovery that, although unplanned, can provide useful information. Morgan and Krueger (1998) recommended the use of *5-second pause* and *probe* strategies to elicit more information from respondents (see also Krueger, 1994). The 5-second pause can prompt others to add their comments to one just made. The probe responds to an information-poor comment such as "I agree" with a rejoinder such as "Would you explain further?" or "Can you give an example of what you mean?"

Moderators have a sharp but subtle awareness of their own body language so that they can provide nonverbal encouragement without biasing responses. For example, leaning forward toward a participant can encourage the individual to go more deeply into a point, but too much head nodding gives the appearance of endorsement that can make another participant hesitant to express disagreement. Similarly, eye contact can provide encouragement to a member who seems withdrawn, whereas a lack of eye contact can help prevent another individual from dominating discussion by denying that individual the attention desired. Eye contact can seem aggressive to individuals who are shy or who come from cultural backgrounds in which direct eye contact is considered confrontational, which means that the moderator needs to understand and act sensitively toward cultural differences.

Even the moderator's dress can make a difference. Although a blue suit, white shirt, and tie can provide an air of authority, for example, it also can give the impression of formality and leadership that some may find offensive or threatening. The moderator needs to both lead the group and fit in with group. As a result, there may be times when the ethnic background, gender, and age of the moderator emerge as important characteristics. Participants often assume the moderator is an employee of the organization under discussion, which can hinder or bias responses. The moderator needs to do everything possible to communicate neutrality.

Dealing with Difficult Group Members

Moderators must anticipate the possibility of losing control of a group. Usually, dominant or disruptive participants can be managed using body language and occasional comments. For example, a moderator can hold up a hand as a stop sign to one participant and signal to another, "Let's hear from you now." A moderator also can suggest that participants answer a question one by one, going around the room, rather than allowing the most assertive respondents to speak out first every time. Seating charts, along with place cards on the table, can help moderators refer to people by name. If a group becomes too wild or argumentative, or if individuals become too antagonistic or disrespectful, a 5-minute break can help calm everyone down. In extreme cases, a particularly disruptive individual can be asked to leave during the break. The individual is thanked for participating and told that he or she was needed for the first part of the discussion but that the second part of the discussion will be different and not everyone will be needed. It is important to be firm but polite.

Protocol Design

The focus group protocol, or outline, is designed to provide a subtle structure to the discussion. Table 8.4 provides a summary of the characteristics of effective focus group questions. Unlike surveys, which rely primarily on closed-ended questions, focus group questions must be open ended. They include a combination of uncued questions and more specific, cued questions (probes) that can help spark responses if discussion lags. Uncued questions are ideal ("What impressions do you have of the XYZ organization currently?") because they give participants the most freedom to introduce new ideas. Cued questions provide more context or probe for more depth ("What about the news coverage of the incident bothered you the most?"). The protocol provides just enough structure to help the moderator stay on track. It also progresses from general questions to more focused questions so that participants have a chance to get comfortable before confronting the most difficult issues.

Closed-ended questions also can be useful if the focus group is being used to explore reasons for answers that might appear on a survey. Analysts, however, must be careful not to extrapolate from focus group participants' answers to closed-ended questions. Clients often appreciate both types of information but can be tempted to make more out of focus group "surveys" than is appropriate.

The subtleties of question construction can have a great effect on the type of discussion that takes place and the value of the information shared. Question phrasings need to avoid using *why* because that term can seem confrontational and can stifle open responses. Instead, questions should rely on *how* and *what* phrasing. For example, instead of asking respondents, "Why do you dislike this poster?" ask, "What did you dislike about this poster?" Questions also need to avoid dichotomous phrasing ("Did you enjoy the event?") because participants may answer the question literally or ambiguously ("Yes," or "Pretty much") without providing any context. "What do you remember about the event?" would be a better question in this context. Sometimes,

Table 8.4 Keys to Good Focus Group Questions

- Open ended
- Avoid "why" (confrontational language)
- Avoid yes/no questions (they do not invite discussion)
- Use cued and un-cued questions (probes)

however, a yes/no question can prod a reticent group into a simple answer that can be explored in depth through follow-up probes. Krueger (1994) also recommended opening with more positive questions and saving negative questions for later so that the overall tone of the group remains constructive, acknowledging both sides of an issue.

Two especially useful question strategies recommended by Krueger (1994) include *sentence completion* and *conceptual mapping*. Sentence completion questions can be introduced verbally by the moderator or handed out in writing. Participants are asked to complete sentences that request information on their motivations or feelings ("When I first heard about the change in policy I thought . . ."), often in writing, using notepads and pencils provided for the purpose. This enables the moderator to obtain the initial views of every member even if they change their minds during discussion or feel hesitant to speak out. Conceptual mapping asks participants to consider how an organization or product relates to other, similar organizations or products. For example, participants could be asked to "map" political candidates such that the most similar are closest together. The discussion then focuses on what characteristics each participant used to establish similarity, such as trustworthiness, conservatism, or experience. Conceptual mapping requires that participants have some prior impressions or knowledge on which to base their judgments.

According to Krueger (1994), the focus group protocol has five general sections of main questions, to which cued probes can be added to ensure discussion flows smoothly.

1 *The opening question.* This question functions as a warm-up or ice breaker and is intended to demonstrate to participants that they have characteristics in common with one another. It should be able to be answered quickly by the participants, requiring only 10 to 20 seconds from each. Krueger advised that these questions should be factual ("How many children do you have, and how old are they?") rather than attitude- or opinion-based ("What is your favorite flavor of ice cream?"). Questions need to avoid requiring disclosures of occupational status because that can create power differentials that hinder group dynamics.

2 *Introduction questions.* These questions set the agenda for the discussion by addressing the topic of interest in a general way ("What was your first impression of . . . ?" or "What comes to mind when you think about . . . ?"). These questions are designed to get participants talking about their experiences relevant to the issue but are not intended to provide much information for later analysis. During this period, participants should begin to feel comfortable talking about the topic with each other.

3 *Transition questions.* These questions begin to take participants into the topic more deeply so that they become aware of how others view the topic ("What events have you attended at the Coliseum this year?"). They provide a link between the introductory questions and the key questions that follow.

4   *Key questions*. These two to five questions form the heart of the focus group inquiry and directly address the issues of concern to the client. They can focus on message testing, conceptual mapping, idea generation, or whatever information is of interest to the client. These questions usually are written first, with the remaining questions built around them.

5   *Ending questions*. These questions bring closure to the discussion to make sure all viewpoints have been represented and to confirm the moderator's interpretation of the overall themes expressed. These can take the form of suggestions or recommendations for the client. Respondents are asked to reflect on the comments made throughout the session. These questions take the form of a final reaction ("All things considered . . ."), which often is asked of each member one by one; a summary confirmation, in which the moderator gives a 2- to 3-minute overview of the discussion followed by a request for verification ("Is this an adequate summary?"); and a final, standardized question ending the discussion following another overview of the study ("Have we missed anything?"). Krueger (1994) recommended leaving 10 minutes for responses to this question, especially if the focus group is early in a series. The answers to this question can give direction to future focused discussions. A sample focus group protocol is shown in Table 8.5.

Table 8.5 Progressing from the General to the More Specific in a Focus Group Protocol

An example for a Public Service Announcement shown to teenagers

Introduction Questions
Who has seen any of these ads before? Which ones are familiar to you?
- Which parts were most familiar?
- Who is this ad made for? How do you know?
- How do you think those people will react to the ads?
- How much were the characters in the ads like you?

Transition Questions
- What do you think of how the ad portrays smokers?
- What are your favorite and least favorite parts of the ad?
- What makes it likeable or dislikeable?

Key Questions
- What *meaning* do you take from this ad? In other words, what does the ad seem to be telling you?
- What would make this ad better?
- What if anything is confusing about this ad?
- How likely are you to visit the website promoted by this ad?

Ending Question
- Is there anything else you want the people who made these ads to know about them?

Those are all of our questions. Thank you for your help!

Message and Idea Testing

When using focus groups to try out campaign strategies, it is important to investigate a full range of possibilities and not just the one or two favorites of the client or agency. The manager does not want to limit the ability of the focus group to produce surprises or upset assumptions. Given the crowded marketplace of ideas that exists in the media and everyday environment, breaking through the morass presents communication programs with a challenging task. This challenge can tempt message producers to "push the envelope," going for the most shocking message or the most colorful message or the funniest message. As Chapters 14 and 15 explain, however, messages need to accomplish more than getting the target audience's attention. They also need to be perceived as relevant, memorable, motivating, accurate, and credible. Extremes may or may not be necessary to break through the clutter, and extremes may help or may backfire once people begin to pay attention to the message. As a result, it is useful to test strategies ranging from the tame to the outrageous. A simplified example of the key questions section for a concept testing protocol appears in Table 8.6.

Table 8.6 Key Questions for Concept Testing of e-Newsletters

- Please look at the e-newsletter shown on the screen. If this arrived in your e-mail, what would be you **likely** to click on to read more, and what would you be **unlikely** to click on to read more?

  o   Explore reasons

- Let's take a look at a few of the articles. *(Hand out printouts of articles).* How interesting are these articles, on a scale of 1 to 10, if 10 is most interesting?

  o   Explore reasons

- Overall, how would you rate this newsletter on a scale of 1 to 10, if 1 is the worst and 10 is the best?

  o   What leads you to give that rating?

  o   How good could it be if the people who made it really tried?

  o   What would they have to do to accomplish that?

- Who do you think produced this newsletter?

  o   To what extent would it make it more or less appealing if it were developed by
       [test desired sources for credibility]

  o   Explore reasons and suggestions

The messages tested for the "Talking to Your Kids About Alcohol" campaign, shown in Figures 8.1 through 8.3, provide such a range.

Managers must keep in mind that the target publics for messages may include gatekeepers as well as the ultimate audience. The Washington State Department of Alcohol and Substance Abuse (CF2GS, 1995), for example, wanted to run a media campaign exhorting parents of children between 3 and 10 years of age to talk with their children about alcohol. Because funds for paid placements were limited, they needed the cooperation of the Washington State Association of Broadcasters. As a result, they tested messages with parents and with broadcasters, who had different concerns. Because many broadcasters accept advertising for beer, they shied away from messages that seemed especially strident. They were supportive of the campaign, however, and ended up providing nearly $100,000 of free exposure for the final announcements during prime viewing hours.

FIG. 8.1. Rough of "Boy and TV" alcohol campaign advertisement. This image of a boy in front of a television was changed to a girl in print advertisements after feedback from focus group participants suggested that the image was too stereotypical. The image of the boy was still used for a television ad.

Image courtesy of the Division of Alcohol and Substance Abuse, Department of Social and Health Services, Washington State.

Make sure the most important message about alcohol comes from you.

Whether you know it or not, your children are already receiving powerful messages about alcohol.

Just by watching TV, they repeatedly see adults drinking to have fun. Drinking to relax. Even drinking to look attractive and be popular.

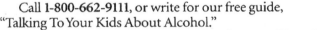

Parents can't control all the information young children receive about this drug. However, you can prepare them for the peer pressure and onslaught of pro-alcohol messages to come.

Call **1-800-662-9111**, or write for our free guide, "Talking To Your Kids About Alcohol."

And do it soon. Because they've already started listening.

Washington State Substance Abuse Coalition
Talking to Your Kids About Alcohol Brochure
12729 N.E. 20th, Suite 18, Bellevue, WA 98005

FIG. 8.2. Final version of boy and television advertisement. This image of a girl in front of a television was created in response to focus group comments.

FIG. 8.3. Rough of "Tea Party" alcohol campaign advertisement. The words "scotch and soda" in the headline accompanying this image of a girl having a tea party with her teddy bear was changed to "glass of wine" after focus group respondents suggested that the hard liquor phrase was too extreme. A second focus group reacted positively to the "glass of wine" version, and the revised image was accepted for use in television ads for the campaign.

Image courtesy of the Division of Alcohol and Substance Abuse, Department of Social and Health Services, Washington State.

New Options Made Possible by Technology

Focus group designers now can use hand-held response dials or keypads to gather information from participants. The use of these devices makes it possible to gather responses from every participant, even when some seem reticent about speaking their minds publicly. In addition, the electronic collection of data enables the moderator to display results from the group for discussion purposes. For example, after showing a series of five rough-cut video messages, the moderator can show the group how many participants chose each option as a "favorite" or "least favorite" choice. The moderator also can ask participants to indicate how believable each message seems and then display the results to explore what made the messages seem more or less credible.

Some systems enable researchers to explore real-time responses to messages on a second-by-second basis. Respondents dial a higher number when they like what they see or hear and dial a lower number when they do not like what they see or hear. As shown in Figure 8.4, the

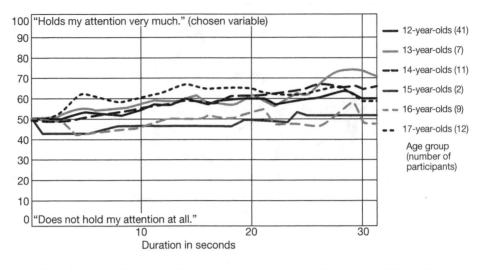

FIG. 8.4. Sample moment-by-moment youth responses to an anti-tobacco public service announcement.

Courtesy of The Murrow Center for Media and Health Promotion Research, Pullman, Washington

resulting graph can show where the message gained or lost audience support. Respondents can discuss the results or researchers can analyze the graph on their own. Although managers must carefully avoid the temptation to rely on the quantitative data produced by this technique, it can help to focus and motivate discussion among group members. Reticent adolescents quickly warmed up for an animated discussion in a project exploring their perceptions of anti-tobacco public service announcements, for example (Austin & Pinkleton, 2009) and unanimously praised the system.

Running the Group

The moderator begins by welcoming the participants, introducing the topic of discussion and purpose of the meeting very generally, and laying out the ground rules for discussion. The explanation of the study needs to be truthful but vague to avoid leading participants. The strategy of the focus group method, after all, is to let the group steer discussion to the extent possible. Ground rules usually cover the following points:

1 Participants should speak up so everyone can hear what they have to say.
2 Only one person should speak at a time to make sure comments are not missed.
3 Each person should say what they think and not what they think others want to hear. Honest responses are important, and respondents have been asked to participate because their true opinions are valued.
4 Negative comments are at least as useful as positive ones. ("If we thought we were doing a perfect job already, we would not be holding this focus group. We need to know how we can do things better.")
5 No right or wrong answers exist to the questions asked.

Moderators sometimes find it helpful to have participants jot down their answers to questions before opening a discussion. Participants also can be asked to deposit note cards into labeled boxes on the table so that the raw responses can be analyzed later and compared with opinions shared only during the discussion. This technique effectively reveals minority opinions.

Analyzing the Results

Analysis of qualitative data can range from an intuitive overview to rigorous scrutiny using methods accepted by scholars. A variety of computer programs for content analysis of qualitative data exist. In addition, technology for creating word clouds can help clients visualize the common themes discussed among focus group participants. In 2013, a variety of highly regarded and free online tools existed for creating word clouds, such as TagCloud, ImageChef, ABCya, Tagul, WordItOut, Tagxedo and TagCrowd. As shown in Figure 8.5, word cloud results can highlight things visually that come up frequently in comments, conversation, news articles or other text. One limitation, however, is that interpretation of results requires an understanding of context: a word may not appear frequently because it is assumed rather than because it does not matter. In Figure 8.5, for example, "cost," "time" and "quick" could have been perceived by participating parents as so fundamental to their concerns that they rarely mentioned those specific words.

Time pressure usually prevents the most detailed analysis of focus group data, but some scientific principles apply even to the most succinct report of results (Figure 8.5.). Krueger (1994) and others recommended the following principles:

1 *Be systematic.* Establish a procedure ahead of time that makes it possible to disconfirm assumptions and hypotheses. The procedure can be as simple as searching for themes and using at least two direct quotes to illustrate each point. Every interpretation needs to consider whether alternative explanations might provide an equally valid analysis.

2 *Be verifiable.* Another person should arrive at similar conclusions using similar methods. Keep in mind that focus groups can provide information that a client may find threatening or disheartening. To convince a determined or defensive client that a change in policy or strategy is necessary, the evidence must be compelling.

3 *Be focused.* Keep in mind the original reasons for holding the focus group and look for information that relates to those points. Focus groups that go on for 3 hours can produce transcripts with well more than 50 pages. Researchers must have a strategy ready to reduce the voluminous mass of data into meaningful chunks of information.

4 *Be practical.* Perform only the level of analysis that makes sense for the client and the situation. A complete transcript, for example, may not be necessary if the issues explored were fairly simple, and it may take time away from other planning activities during a tight implementation deadline.

5 *Be immediate.* During delays, the focus group observers' impressions may fade, compromising their ability to analyze the data. All observers must make notes during the focus group and immediately afterward to identify themes and direct quotes that seem important. These observations can be confirmed, fleshed out, and supplemented during later analysis but often provide the most valid and vivid conclusions.

FIG. 8.5. Sample Word Cloud from Tagul. This word cloud displays an analysis of transcripts from 6 focus groups conducted in 2012 with parents about nutrition websites (Austin & Pinkleton, 2012).

Final Thoughts

The focus group is probably the method most often employed by public relations professionals. It also is probably the method most often misused, which likely contributes to client and managerial skepticism of its value. The focus group offers tremendous benefits to the practitioner aiming to pretest strategies or understand communication processes in some depth. As long as the communication manager respects the limitations of the focus group, it can be an indispensable tool for responsive and effective communication program planning.

9

Making Research Decisions
Formal Research Methods

Chapter Contents

- A Brief Review of the Characteristics of Formal, Scientific Research
- Survey Research Overview
- Experiments
- Content Analysis
- Final Thoughts

Public relations practitioners need more sophisticated research methods as their informational needs evolve from simple fact finding and casual analysis to a more sophisticated understanding of the opinions, attitudes, and motivations of target audience members. In a perfect world, researchers follow a formal scientific process, use a representative sample of participants that produces results high in generalizability, and provides objective results instead of subjective results that reflect their own biases. Public relations practitioners use formal research to measure audiences' pre-campaign attitudes, opinions, and behaviors for benchmarking purposes, to understand and explain audience motivations and behaviors, to understand media message effectiveness and measure post-campaign effects, and to measure and describe important media characteristics. Ultimately, the results of such research help public relations practitioners and their organizations to successfully understand target audiences and measure campaign outcomes, increasing the likelihood of program success.

Even though all formal research methods could apply to some aspect of public relations, practitioners do not use all scientific research methods regularly. In addition, communication managers more commonly use informal research methods than formal research methods, despite the increase in sophistication, generalizability, known accuracy, and reliability that formal research methods can provide. As expectations for performance accountability continue to increase, however, communication managers must be prepared to adopt more formal methods to demonstrate program success. For this reason, this chapter introduces readers to a range of formal research methods including surveys, experiments, and content analyses. Detailed discussions of survey research methods and related topics follow in later chapters because surveys are the most commonly applied formal research method in public relations.

A Brief Review of the Characteristics of Formal, Scientific Research

Understanding research methods increases our knowledge of how to learn about the social world (Adler & Clark, 2011), including the world of our targeted audiences. The ways we learn about the world of our targeted audience members have benefits and limitations. Because Chapters 5 and 6 provide a detailed discussion of the characteristics of formal and informal research, we offer only a brief review here.

Public relations research can greatly increase the likelihood of program success, but poorly conducted research that misinforms campaign planners can have a strong, negative effect on program performance. In the same way, research conducted properly but misapplied to a public relations problem or campaign can have a negative effect on campaign effectiveness. This might be the case, for example, when a focus group (informal research) is used to gauge audience attitudes and opinions in the design phase of a campaign. If the results of the focus group are inaccurate, the campaign will fail to inform and motivate target-audience members. Most practitioners do not need to become formal research experts, but they do need to know and understand basic research issues to use research effectively and to commission research of quality, as Figure 9.1 demonstrates.

Generally, formal scientific research is *empirical* in nature (derived from the Greek word for "experience"), or concerned with the world that can be experienced and measured in a precise manner (Wimmer & Dominick, 2014). As a result, formal research methods produce results

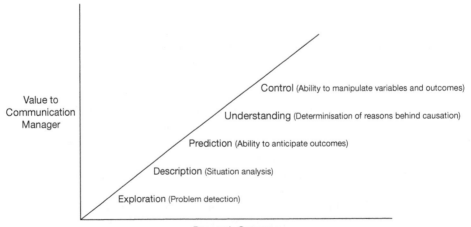

FIG. 9.1. The goals of science. Maximum control of a situation requires the ability to predict what will happen, understand why things happen, and control what will happen. At a lesser level, explorations of a problem and descriptions of constraints and opportunities also are useful outcomes of research and are prerequisites for strategic planning.

that are *objective* and values-free. This means the research results do not unduly reflect the biases of researchers or the attitudes and opinions of a few selected individuals but instead reflect events, facts, and behaviors as they exist or naturally occur in a population or group—typically these are members of a targeted audience in public relations.

Next, formal research methods require researchers to follow a systematic set of procedures providing for the uniform collection of data. This process helps ensure each participant in a study receives the same treatment and all participants express their answers to questions in the same manner. Scientific research results also rely on representative samples. When representative samples are not available, investigators must understand the limitations of samples to the greatest extent possible. When researchers use probability-based sampling methods and draw a sample of appropriate size (discussed in Chapter 6), they help ensure that the behaviors and attitudes of sample members reliably represent the range of behaviors and attitudes found in a population. In reality, no sample is perfectly representative; however, samples collected using probability methods are more trustworthy than other samples. This type of trustworthiness produces results high in *external validity* or projectability. That is, survey results can be projected from a sample to a population with a certain level of confidence (which we can calculate mathematically).

Finally, researchers should be able to reproduce the results of formal research projects. This is known as *replication*. If the results of a project are unique to a single study, we will conclude they may be biased, perhaps because of faulty sampling procedures or problems with the data-collection process. When study results are replicable, they provide accurate information for the population under study. Social scientists generally consider a research project formal to the extent it incorporates the characteristics of objectivity, systematic collection of data, representative samples, and replicable results into its design.

The following discussion of scientific research methods will introduce you to a range of possibilities available for research projects. We begin with a review of survey research, followed by a discussion of research designs for experiments, and media-based content analyses. Because of the wide application of survey research to public relations, more specific aspects of survey research design options are discussed in Chapter 10.

Survey Research Overview

Survey research is vital to organizations in a variety of different fields including all levels of government, political organizations, mass media corporations, educational institutions, entertainment conglomerates, and other product manufacturers and service providers. In public relations, practitioners use survey research to measure people's attitudes, beliefs, and behavior by asking them questions. Organizations commonly turn to survey research when they want to understand their target audience members' awareness, opinions, attitudes, knowledge, behavioral motivations, sources of information, and other information necessary for successful campaign implementation or evaluation.

Campaign managers may use research at all stages of the program planning, implementation, and evaluation process. Public relations practitioners most commonly use survey research in the planning and evaluation phases of a campaign. In the campaign planning phase, *pre-campaign* surveys help practitioners establish *benchmarks*—this is the pre-existing standard against which they will evaluate the success of a campaign—so they can set campaign goals. If one of the purposes of a campaign is to increase target-audience members' trust in an organization, for example, practitioners must establish current audience trust levels so they can set appropriate goals and objectives. In this way, pre-campaign research findings provide a point of reference—or benchmark—for campaign evaluation.

Practitioners use *post-campaign* research as part of the campaign evaluation process to help them determine whether a campaign has met its goals and related purposes. If the purpose of a campaign is to increase target-audience members' trust in an organization by 15%, a post-campaign survey provides a way for practitioners to determine whether the campaign has succeeded. Simply put, campaign outcomes are determined by comparing post-campaign research results with pre-campaign benchmarks.

Post-campaign research also can serve as *between-campaign* research. That is, many organizations simply transition from one or more existing campaigns to new campaigns without stopping to conduct new research at every point between campaigns. In these cases, post-campaign research may serve some pre-campaign research purposes when additional programs are in the planning or early implementation stages.

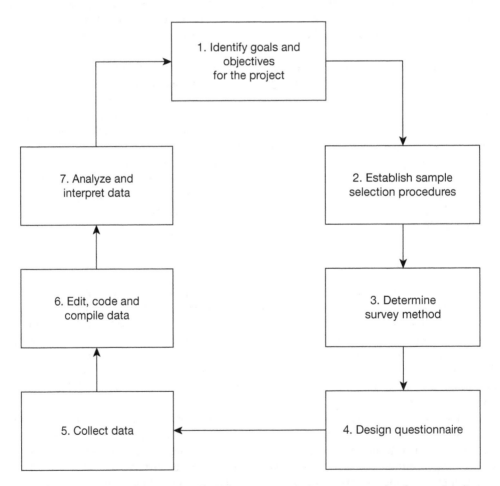

FIG. 9.2. The survey planning process. To help ensure project success, researchers generally follow these steps in a systematic manner when planning and implementing a survey.

Sometimes organizations conduct surveys and other forms of research during a campaign to provide intermediate campaign evaluations. This monitoring helps campaign managers determine whether a campaign is on course. In such a case, they use research results to monitor campaign progress and to make corrections in campaign strategies and tactics.

In addition, surveys generally fall into one of two broad categories: descriptive and analytical. Managers use *descriptive surveys* to document current circumstances and conditions and to generally describe what exists in a population. The Bureau of Labor Statics and the Census Bureau, for example, jointly conduct a monthly survey of about 60,000 households. This survey, called the "Current Population Survey," provides government policy makers and legislators with employment information as they plan and evaluate government programs. Similarly, political candidates, special interest groups, and media organizations regularly survey voters to determine their level of support for a particular candidate or policy initiative or to understand and predict election outcomes. Many applied public relations research projects are descriptive in nature.

Practitioners rely on *analytical surveys* to explain why certain circumstances, attitudes, and behaviors exist among members of a specific population. This type of survey research usually involves advanced forms of statistical analysis to test hypotheses concerning relationships among a group of variables under study. Academic researchers, for example, commonly study the relationship between exposure to negative political advertising and attitudes about politics and political participation. In many cases, surveys serve both descriptive and analytical purposes. In each instance, researchers follow formal procedures and use a systematic process to ensure that data collected are objective, reliable, and accurate.

Regardless of the purpose of a survey, most survey research projects generally follow the same planning process shown in Figure 9.2. Initially, researchers determine the objectives of the research project. Next, researchers design the study. During this phase of a survey they determine the population and sampling procedures they will use in the project, select a specific interview method, and design and pretest the survey instrument or questionnaire. Then, research-team members collect, edit, and code data. Finally, researchers analyze and interpret results.

Survey Planning

The most important aspect of survey planning involves identification of the purpose of a research project. This normally involves identifying a research problem and the potential hypotheses and/or research questions a project will address. Campaign practitioners often give this aspect of a research project relatively brief attention because they are busy and the purposes of many projects seem obvious. As discussed in Chapter 4, however, the most successful research projects are those with a high degree of direction. Surveys that lack direction often fail to live up to their potential as a planning or evaluation tool.

Survey Sampling

Sample selection procedures depend on survey objectives. As discussed in Chapter 6, sampling procedures range from convenient to complex. They also vary in terms of their trustworthiness. A scientific technique called *probability sampling*, when used correctly and in combination with a properly applied survey method, usually provides an accurate and reliable understanding of the characteristics of a population. For this reason, the use of proper sampling methods is one of the most critical aspects of any research project and an especially important characteristic of scientific survey research.

Determining the Data Collection Method

The primary means of collecting survey data include personal interviews, mail surveys, telephone surveys, and electronic surveys conducted via the Internet. In addition, researchers may combine methods to conduct a mixed-mode survey. Selecting a proper data collection method is critical to the success of a research project, and each method of data collection has its own strengths and weaknesses. No single best survey research method exists, but there typically is a best research method to use given the limitations and requirements of a research project.

The choices may seem overwhelming at first. If the purpose of a project is to interview managers working in digital communication startups, for example, telephone and personal interviewing probably are poor choices because these methods are likely to be inconvenient and managers will be too busy to participate. In addition, surveys sent via regular mail probably are a poor choice because these projects typically take longer to complete than projects using other survey methods. Completion times for mail surveys typically range from a few weeks to several weeks or more if multiple mailings are necessary. Given completion-time concerns and participants' schedules, an online survey may be the only viable option for data collection. Potential respondents can fill out online surveys relatively easily and at their convenience, which means this research method has more promise with this group of respondents. In addition, researchers can complete projects using this method fairly quickly and online surveys tend to cost less than surveys using other methods.

Research professionals must look at a variety of important issues when considering data-collection methods. Selecting an appropriate survey method is crucial to the successful completion of a research project. This topic is addressed in greater detail in Chapter 10.

Questionnaire Design

Proper questionnaire design contributes significantly to the trustworthiness of survey results. Good survey questions, when combined with appropriate data-collection methods, produce accurate responses. Poor survey questions or inappropriate data-collection methods produce untrustworthy results that can misinform public relations managers.

Poorly designed questionnaires often bias participants' responses. In this case, researchers are no longer measuring respondents' true attitudes, opinions, and behaviors, but instead are measuring manufactured participant responses they have created through a poorly designed questionnaire. Normally, practitioners cannot use these responses because they do not represent the true responses of research participants and are not projectable to members of target publics. A public relations campaign based on erroneous information is likely to fail. Erroneous information usually worsens situations in which practitioners use research as the basis for problem solving.

Several questionnaire characteristics that might seem minor can bias participants' responses, including question wording, question response categories, question order and even the layout of the questions and answers on a page or website (Dillman, Smyth, & Christian, 2009). In addition, when interviews are administered by another person either face to face or over the telephone, interviewers can bias survey results as they interact with participants. This topic is an important part of communication research, and Chapter 11 addresses questionnaire design issues in greater detail.

Data Collection

Data collection typically is the next step in the survey-research process, and in many respects it is the beginning of the final phase of a research project. By this point, the researcher often has made the most difficult project-related decisions. Practitioners' levels of involvement in data collection range from managing all aspects of data collection to leaving all aspects of data collection to a project manager or field-service provider. Although practitioners may leave projects in the hands of capable managers with relative confidence, it generally is in their best interest to monitor data collection for quality control. Occasionally, practitioners also need to make important decisions concerning data collection while it is taking place. When survey response rates appear unusually low or respondents do not understand a question, for example, practitioners should be involved in determining the best solution. As a result, Chapter 12 presents information to aid in decisions concerning data collection and analysis.

Editing and Coding

Editing and coding are the processes that research-team members use to translate the information collected in questionnaires into a form suitable for statistical analysis. Depending on the survey method, project managers may need to check questionnaires and eliminate or correct incomplete or unintelligible answers. Supervisors may need to edit questionnaires or computer entries during data collection to detect and correct errors. For example, they should pay careful attention to missing answers and inconsistencies that reveal a lack of uniformity among interviewers and introduce error into survey results.

Coding may be necessary when a questionnaire has open-ended responses or other data needing categorization. Trained supervisors working with a fixed set of rules typically conduct coding. Using these rules, research-team members typically place participants' responses into mutually exclusive and exhaustive categories to facilitate data analysis. This type of editing requires a high degree of consistency among researchers to generate reliable results. Software can help researchers with this analysis making the process quicker but also increasing the potential of missing important but subtle information in participants' open-ended responses.

In addition, coding may be necessary to help prepare data for analysis. Depending on the survey method used, it may be necessary to translate survey data into numerical form so that analysts can access and analyze the results. Researchers then analyze these data. Chapter 12 provides additional information concerning editing and coding participants' responses.

Analysis and Interpretation

Statistical analysis and interpretation are the next steps in survey research. Although a thorough discussion of statistical procedures is beyond the scope of this text, a brief review of common analytical techniques appears in Chapter 12.

Survey Critique

Survey research is a useful means of studying the attitudes, opinions and behaviors of targeted publics in public relations. Research team members often can complete surveys relatively quickly, which is a primary advantage of surveys. Cost may be an advantage, as well. The cost of most survey research is reasonable considering the amount of information practitioners receive. In addition, different methods of data collection provide for cost control through the selection and implementation of more- or less-expensive survey methods. The relatively low cost and ease of implementation make survey research attractive to communication managers.

Nevertheless, no research method is foolproof and survey research, which has suffered from lower rates of participation recently, has its limitations (Table 9.1). First, survey research cannot provide direct evidence of causation and researchers occasionally attempt to specify causes when research results do not support such conclusions. If a research project revealed that boating accidents increase as ice cream sales increase, for example, we might be tempted to conclude that ice cream causes boating accidents. Of course, this is untrue. Ice cream sales and boating accidents increase as the weather warms up and people enjoy boating and eating ice cream more often. Although this example is absurd, researchers need to take care to avoid drawing conclusions that are equally, if perhaps more subtly, absurd.

Other weaknesses of survey research are specific to data-collection methods. Personal interview surveys may be especially costly, for example, requiring the extensive training of field supervisors and interviewers among other expenses. Regular mail surveys typically take longer to complete than other survey methods because of the time required to deliver the questionnaires to a sample and receive responses back from participants. It is important to know the specific strengths and weaknesses associated with each method of data collection, and we discuss these in Chapter 10.

Other concerns associated with survey research apply in some way to all survey data collection methods. Sometimes respondents are inaccurate in the answers they provide, for example, whether in a direct interview or on a mailed questionnaire. Inaccurate responses introduce error into survey results. There are a variety of reasons for this problem. Sometimes, respondents simply do not remember information about themselves or their activities. They may simply make up a response rather than admit they do not know an answer. This also is a problem when respondents lack knowledge regarding the subject of a public affairs question, for example, but answer the question anyway.

Respondents also may provide incorrect answers in a misguided attempt to find favor with interviewers, and some survey questions include responses that are more socially desirable than alternative choices. In other instances, participants may simply choose to deceive researchers by providing incorrect answers to questions. Survey results concerning complex subjects may be further complicated by respondents who find it difficult to identify and explain their true feelings, especially using simple numerical scales. As a result, practitioners should consider the potential drawbacks to the successful completion of a survey before they start a research project.

Despite the weaknesses of survey research, its benefits outweigh its drawbacks for many research projects. Survey research is particularly useful for description and association, a necessity given the often exploratory and descriptive nature of many applied projects. In addition, a carefully prepared questionnaire contributes to results that are reliable and accurate.

Table 9.1 General Characteristics of Surveys

Selected benefits	Selected limitations
Can be relatively inexpensive (researchers can control costs using less-expensive methods)	Do not allow researchers to determine causation
Can have relatively quick project-completion time	Some survey methods are expensive
	Data collection may take a long time
Practitioners can implement surveys relatively easily	Sometimes survey results lack accuracy and reliability
Can provide information concerning a large number of variables	Participation rates have fallen
Useful for describing diverse populations	
Surveys can produce highly accurate, reliable results	

Electronic surveys, in particular, often enable researchers to collect a large amount of data from diverse populations within a short time at a reasonable cost. Given practitioners' information needs and the time and budget constraints placed on many research projects, survey research often is an excellent choice for public relations projects. This is why communication campaign managers use it so often.

Experiments

In essence, an *experiment* involves taking an action and observing the consequences of that action (Baxter & Babbie, 2004). In a sense, experiments are a natural part of public relations because in most cases, practitioners take action of one sort or another (researchers call this a treatment) and then gauge the effect of that action on a targeted audience members' attitudes or behavior. Although various study designs exist, an experiment generally requires at least one group of participants to receive a treatment (such as exposure to part of a public relations campaign). Researchers then can determine the effect of that treatment by comparing participants' before-treatment responses with their after-treatment responses, typically on a series of questions designed to measure their opinions or attitudes, for example (Broom & Dozier, 1990).

Practitioners can use experiments to make important contributions to campaigns because this method allows them to isolate campaign variables and control them. This high degree of control allows researchers to use experiments to systematically examine variables that may or may not influence target-audience members. If campaign planners want to determine adolescents' responses to potential prevention-campaign advertisements, for example, they might measure the attitudes and self-reported behavior of a relatively small group of adolescents (perhaps 40 or 50), expose them to the advertising stimuli, then measure their attitudes and projected behavior again. If no other variables were introduced in the process, the changes that took place from the first measurement to the second measurement would be due to the advertising.

Practitioners rarely use true experiments in applied settings. As illustrated in the previous health-campaign example, campaign managers are more likely to conduct a focus group and get participant feedback on different advertising executions (called *copytesting* in advertising) than to conduct an experiment. Yet, as already discussed, informal research methods such as focus groups normally produce results that are low in external validity and reliability. The result is that practitioners risk using incorrect research results as the basis for making important campaign decisions.

Controlled experiments, on the other hand, are the most powerful means of determining message effects because researchers can use them to determine causation. This is the primary benefit of experiments. From a scientific perspective, three conditions are necessary to determine causation. First, the cause (we'll call this variable A) must precede the effect (variable B) in time. Second, a change in the first variable (A) must produce a change in the second variable (B). This is called *concomitant variation*, and the idea is that a change in one variable is accompanied by a change in another variable. Third, researchers must control or eliminate all other possible causes of an effect in an experiment. This ensures the relationship between the variables is not caused by third variable (recall the previous example concerning ice cream and boating accidents; the researchers did not consider—or attempt to eliminate—the influence of other variables such as warmer weather in their study). By using experiments, researchers can examine and understand variable relationships under uncontaminated conditions. This allows them to develop greater insight into variable relationships, such as the effects of prevention-campaign advertising on young people.

Researchers use systematic procedures when they conduct experiments. Initially, they select the setting for the experiment. Next, they design or plan the project. In this phase researchers decide how to measure and manipulate variables, select a specific study design, and develop and pretest the materials they will use in the experiment. Finally, researchers collect, analyze, and interpret the data they collect.

Settings

The two main settings in which researchers conduct experiments include research laboratories or similar facilities used for research purposes and the field, which are the natural settings in which participants normally function. A laboratory setting is advantageous because it provides researchers with the ability to control almost all aspects of an experiment. By controlling outside influences, researchers can make exact determinations regarding the nature of the relationships among the variables they are studying. Generally, the more controlled and precise an experiment is, the less error that is present in research results. By controlling the conditions under which an experiment occurs, researchers can reduce the risk of contamination from unwanted sources.

The artificial nature of research laboratories has disadvantages, however. Isolated, tightly controlled research environments that exclude potential interference are different from most real-life situations. In measuring voters' responses to televised political advertisements, for example, it probably would be better to test voters at home (that is, "in the field") where they normally watch television. This environment is a natural setting likely to contain all the distractions and other influences people encounter when they watch television. In this environment, we most likely will measure participants' true and natural responses. Unfortunately, these distractions and other influences also are likely to contaminate our research results. This contamination makes the determination of causation nearly impossible.

When researchers pull people out of their natural settings and place them in controlled environments such as laboratories, participants also may react differently to the materials used in the experiment (televised political ads in this example) because this is not their normal viewing environment. Ultimately, the controlled artificiality of research settings tends to produce results higher in internal validity (because, for example, researchers can precisely measure the variables they intend to measure) but lower in external validity (because the artificiality of the research environment may reduce the generalizability of results from a sample to a population). Practitioners have to balance these advantages and disadvantages when choosing a study design.

Researchers conduct field experiments in the environment in which participants' behaviors naturally occur. In other words, the field is the environment in which participants live, work, and relax. The dynamics and interactions of small groups, for example, may be studied at places where small groups of people naturally congregate such as common meeting areas in college dormitories. Field experiments tend to have a higher degree of external validity because the real-life research settings are normal environments which encourage participants to respond naturally. The control available to researchers in field experiments, however, is rarely as tight as the control available in laboratory experiments because of the uncontrollable factors that exist in any natural environment. This may present challenges as researchers conduct studies and attempt to determine causation.

Terms and Concepts

Before we discuss specific designs, we should briefly examine (or reexamine in some cases) some important terms so you have a better understanding of research designs. The basic purpose of an experiment is to determine *causation*. In an applied public relations setting, practitioners typically are interested in determining the effects of a public relations campaign or program. When practitioners examine campaign effects, they are examining causation (these are the outcomes—or effects—caused by the campaign). What do campaigns typically influence in public relations? Most often, practitioners want to know how their campaign influenced the opinions, attitudes, and behaviors of target-audience members. Each of these are variables they want to examine. In its simplest sense, a *variable* is a phenomenon or event researchers can measure and manipulate (Wimmer & Dominick, 2014); variables such as attitudes change, or vary, within a population.

In the preceding example, the public relations campaign or program we are testing is the independent variable. The *independent variable* is the variable that researchers manipulate in an experiment to see if it produces change in the dependent variable. Changes in the *dependent variable* depend on, or are caused by, the independent variable. If we wanted to examine the effects of potential campaign messages on target-audience members, the messages are the independent variables. As independent variables, the campaign messages affect the dependent variables in the experiment, which are the opinions or attitudes of target-audience members toward our organization.

In addition, we might manipulate the independent variable (the content of the campaign message) to determine how to make it more effective. We might consider a humorous message versus a serious message, for example. In this case, variable manipulation is a critical aspect of study design. We must make sure our humorous and non-humorous messages are equal in terms of key message points and features so the only difference between the messages is the presence or absence of humor which we confirm through message testing. If all other message characteristics are equal, any differences in participants' responses to the messages would be due to the humor or lack of humor in the message. This controlled experiment allows us to test the effect of humor on participants' responses to our message and gives us a scientific basis for determining cause and effect.

Initially, you may notice researchers assign participants to a condition in experiments. A *condition* consists of all the people in an experiment who are treated the same way. In a source-credibility experiment, for example, some participants are exposed to a message delivered by a high-credibility spokesperson, whereas other participants are exposed to a message delivered by a low-credibility spokesperson. Each group member exposed to the same spokesperson in our example is part of the same condition.

Participants in the same condition are exposed to the same treatment. A *treatment* occurs when the participants in a condition are exposed to the same material, or *stimulus*, which contains the independent variable. Although it sounds confusing, it is really very simple. In the credibility experiment, the message from a high-credibility source is one stimulus, and each participant exposed to that stimulus receives the high-credibility treatment (these participants are in the same condition). In the same way, the message from a low-credibility source is a different stimulus. Participants exposed to the message from the low-credibility source receive the low-credibility treatment and are in the same condition.

Researchers typically place some participants in a condition in which they receive no treatment, or perhaps a meaningless treatment. These participants are in the *control group* or *control condition*. Because control-group members receive no meaningful treatment—in other words, they receive no independent-variable exposure—researchers can understand the effects of conducting the experiment on participants' attitudes or behavior (Baxter & Babbie, 2004). In medical research, for example, members of a treatment condition receive an actual drug, whereas the control-group members receive a placebo (commonly sugar pills). This allows researchers to determine the amount of patient improvement due to the new drug versus the amount of patient improvement caused by other factors, including participants' improved mental outlook that might result from the special medical attention they are receiving in the study.

Finally, researchers assign participants to either a treatment condition or a control condition in a random manner. When research team members use *random assignment*, each participant has an equal chance of being included in a condition. Random assignment helps to eliminate the potential influence of outside variables that may hinder the determination of causation. If researchers do not randomly assign participants to conditions, they cannot be sure participants in each condition are equal before exposure to study stimuli. When the participants in each condition are not equal, this is called *selectivity bias*. Random assignment helps ensure the outcomes researchers detect in an experiment are caused by exposure to stimuli and not by previously existing differences among participants.

Research Designs

Several ways exist to design a true experiment and, although a specific design may have advantages in certain circumstances, no single design is best. Instead, the best study design typically depends on researchers' hypotheses or research questions, the nature of the independent and dependent variables, the availability of participants, and the resources available for the project. The three designs social scientists use to conduct true experiments are the *pretest–posttest design with control group*, the *posttest-only design with control group*, and the *pretest–posttest design with additional control groups*, commonly referred to as the *Solomon four-group design* (Campbell & Stanley, 1963).

The pretest–posttest design with control group is a fundamental design of experimental research. Researchers use it often because it is applicable to a variety of different settings. When researchers use the pretest–posttest design with a control group, they randomly assign participants to treatment conditions or control groups and initially measure the dependent variable (this is the *pretest*) for each group. Research team members then apply an independent-variable manipulation to participants in the treatment condition, followed by further testing to determine independent-variable effects. The order of the research procedures, random assignment of participants to conditions, and use of a control group helps eliminate or avoid many of the potential problems that threaten to ruin the internal validity of the experiment. Although a detailed discussion of these problems (called *threats to validity*) is beyond the scope of this book, readers may be interested in reading Campbell and Stanley's (1963) short but important book *Experimental and Quasi-experimental Designs for Research*.

If we wanted to test the effectiveness of a prosocial advertisement designed to encourage young people to eat healthy foods, for example, we could randomly assign participants to one of two conditions: the advertisement condition and the control condition. Initially, we would pretest participants' attitudes by having them complete a questionnaire that measures their attitudes toward eating healthy foods. Following the pretest, we would expose participants in the treatment condition to the advertisement, whereas participants in the control condition might watch a brief clip of a cartoon containing no health-related information. Next, we would posttest participants' attitudes in both conditions using the same questions and scales we used in the pretest (Figure 9.3.).

Normally, participants' pretest attitudes toward healthy eating would be similar in both the treatment and the control conditions. If our advertisement was effective, the posttest scores of participants who viewed the prosocial advertisement would reflect some important changes. First, treatment group members would have more positive attitudes toward healthy eating than control group members. More important, the change in the attitudes of treatment group participants toward healthy eating would be greater than the change in the attitudes of control

R	O_1	X	O_2
R	O_3		O_4

FIG. 9.3. Pretest–Posttest Design with Control. Researchers randomly (R) assign participants to one of two conditions. All participants complete a pretest (O_1 and O_3). Only participants in the first condition receive stimulus exposure (X). All participants complete a posttest (O_2 and O_4).

Note: R = random assignment, O = measurement, and X = stimulus exposure

group participants. Because each condition was identical and only one condition received a treatment, any significant differences existing between participants at the end of the experiment likely would have been caused by the treatment.

As an additional note, if control group participants' attitudes changed in the same way attitudes of treatment-group members did, we would not be able to determine causation because our study would lack internal validity. In this case, we might have evidence of testing, for example, whereby all participants changed their posttest answers because they were sensitized to the issue of healthy eating as a result of taking the pretest.

A second design researchers commonly use when they conduct experiments is the posttest-only design with a control group. In this research design there is no pretest. Instead, research team members randomly assign subjects to treatment and control conditions. Members of the treatment group receive exposure to the stimuli containing the treatment, followed by a posttest of both groups. After they collect posttest scores, researchers statistically compare participants' dependent variable scores. Returning to our previous example, if a posttest examination of participants' scores revealed that members of the treatment condition had more positive attitudes toward healthy eating than members of the control condition, we could feel confident these differences were due to the prosocial advertisement (Figure 9.4).

R		X	O_1
R			O_2

FIG. 9.4. Posttest-Only Design with Control. Researchers randomly (R) assign participants to one of two conditions. Participants in the first condition receive stimulus exposure (X). All participants complete a posttest (O_1 and O_2). This design does not require a pretest.

Note: R = random assignment, O = measurement, and X = stimulus exposure

Pretesting, although an important part of experiments, is not required to conduct a true experiment (Campbell & Stanley, 1963). Instead, the random assignment of participants to conditions allows researchers to assume participants in each condition are equal at the beginning of the study. The random assignment of subjects to conditions controls for selectivity biases. This design is especially useful to researchers when pretesting is unavailable or inconvenient, or may somehow interfere with the experiment (Campbell & Stanley, 1963).

The Solomon four-group design is a complete combination of the first two designs. The Solomon design uses four conditions, in conjunction with random assignment, to help identify and control threats to validity, including the effects of taking a pretest on participants' posttest scores. Participants in the first condition receive a pretest, a treatment, and a posttest. Participants in the second condition receive a pretest and a posttest with no treatment. Those in the third condition receive no pretest, a treatment, and a posttest, whereas participants in the final condition receive only a single measurement, the equivalent of a posttest. Using our previous example, researchers measure participants' attitudes toward healthy eating and expose them to the prosocial advertisement in conditions one and three. In conditions two and four, however, participants receive no exposure to the treatment, only attitudinal measurement.

The Solomon four-group design is the most rigorous type of experiment, allowing researchers to separate and identify treatment effects independently of the effects of pretesting (Figure 9.5.). In other words, researchers can figure out specifically whether participants' posttest scores changed because they were influenced by taking a pretest, as opposed to whether the experimental treatment caused their posttest scores to change. The biggest drawbacks to the use of the four-group design are practical. Four groups are needed to properly execute the design, requiring a high number of participants and increased costs. As a result, researchers' use of this design is relatively rare.

R	O_1	X	O_2
R	O_3		O_4
R		X	O_5
R			O_6

FIG. 9.5. Solomon Four-Group Design. Researchers randomly assign participants to one of four conditions. Participants in the first two conditions complete a pretest (O_1 and O_3). Participants in the first and third conditions receive stimulus exposure. All participants complete a posttest (O_2, O_4, O_5, and O_6).

Note: R = random assignment, O = measurement, and X = stimulus exposure

Up to this point, the research designs we have discussed are completely randomized designs. This means they require researchers to randomly assign each participant to only one condition whether it is a control or a treatment condition. Researchers call this design *between-subjects* because they make determinations regarding treatment effects by finding differences between groups of participants, or subjects, based on their exposure to stimuli as part of a treatment condition.

We can compare a between-subjects design to a *within-subjects* design in which researchers use each participant in all conditions. Experts commonly call this type of design a *repeated-measures* design because researchers measure each participant two or more times as they expose individuals to different stimuli throughout the course of an experiment. In this design, each participant serves as his or her own control by providing a baseline measure, and any differences in measurement scores that researchers find between treatment conditions are based on measurements they take from the same set of participants (Keppel, 1991).

When researchers are concerned about having enough participants, they may opt to use a within-subjects design because it requires fewer participants. This design also provides an important way for researchers to learn how variables combine to influence attitudes and behavior. This type of design is called a *factorial* design, and it allows researchers to learn how independent variables interact. In our previous example concerning attitudes toward healthy eating, it may be that gender and perceived body image combine to influence participants' responses to our prosocial advertisement. Researchers can examine how these variables interact when they use a within-subjects design.

Project managers sometimes use other designs that are not fully experimental, often when they have limited options and decide that collecting some data is better than collecting no data at all. Researchers commonly consider these designs pre-experimental or quasi-experimental, and they include case studies and the one-group pretest–posttest design among other possibilities. Quasi-experimental studies suffer from design flaws because they lack control conditions or because researchers use nonrandom procedures to assign participants to different conditions in the study. As a result, these designs fail to protect studies from various threats to the validity of their results. Researchers use quasi-experimental designs for various purposes, including exploration, but these methods are not scientific and practitioners, therefore, should be careful when interpreting and applying study results.

It is often impossible or impractical to use probability sampling methods when recruiting research participants for experiments. Instead, researchers commonly select participants using incidental, or convenience, sampling methods (see Chapter 6). Because research participants may not be completely representative of a target audience or other population, the results of an experiment may lack external validity, or generalizability, from the sample to the population. In general, this is not as detrimental for explanatory research such as experiments as it is for descriptive research such as surveys. Social process and the patterns of causal relationships generally are stable across populations and, because of this, are more generalizable than individual characteristics (Baxter & Babbie, 2004). For this and other reasons, convenience sampling normally suffices in experiments when probability sampling is impossible or impractical, and researchers use random assignment to ensure participants' characteristics are equal, or balanced, in each condition.

As with any other research project, research team members should pretest variable manipulations (also called *treatments*), measurement questionnaires, and the procedures they will use in an experiment before they collect data. Pretesting allows researchers to correct any deficiencies in the procedures they will use for data collection and provides for a check of independent variable manipulations.

A manipulation check is particularly important in helping ensure the success of a study. A *manipulation check* is a procedure that helps researchers ascertain whether something they intend to happen in a study—in this case the independent variable manipulation or treatment— actually happened as they expected. In our previous example concerning prosocial advertising and healthy eating, we might intend for some participants to see a fear-based prosocial advertisement and other participants to see a humor-based prosocial advertisement. A manipulation check (in this case, we might simply ask participants to rate the amount of humor or fear in our messages using a standard scale) would help researchers determine the extent to which participants found the fear-based message frightening and the humorous message funny.

Finally, research team members must develop a procedure for telling participants what the purpose of the study is and how they will use the study's results. Research managers answer participants' questions at this time in a process called *debriefing*. Debriefing allows researchers to eliminate potential harms, however small, that may befall participants as a result of their involvement in a research project.

Bias in Data Collection, Analysis, and Interpretation

It is essential for researchers conducting experiments to collect, analyze, and interpret data carefully. Project managers must pay particular attention to the introduction of bias during data collection. Bias may come from several sources including the behavior of research team members. Any changes in participants' behavior due to something other than the variable manipulations—or treatments—which are part of the study ruin the validity of study findings. As a result, research team members work to control unintended influences during a study by using automated procedures and equipment, consistent testing processes and forms, a contained and controlled study environment, random assignment of participants to conditions and the like. Project managers also can minimize bias by using researchers who, along with participants, generally are unaware of the purpose of a study (called a *double-blind* experiment) or who have differing expectations regarding study outcomes.

Experiment Critique

When conducted properly, formal experiments allow researchers to isolate variables and establish causation (Table 9.2). This is a powerful benefit that only properly designed and executed experiments provide. In laboratory experiments, researchers have a high degree of control over the research environment, the selection and assignment of participants to conditions, independent variable manipulations, and dependent variable measurement. This high degree of control and isolation provides conditions free from the competing influences of normal activity and ideal for examining independent and dependent variable relationships (Wimmer & Dominick, 2014). Although field experiments do not allow as high a degree of control as laboratory experiments, they generally provide enough control for researchers to make determinations of causation when properly conducted.

Another benefit of experiments is their potential for replication. Because project managers typically provide detailed explanations concerning their scales and other aspects of their studies, it is common for social scientists to replicate research findings. Replication may take the form of an identical study or, more commonly, one that provides replication under slightly different conditions. The successful replication of studies that produce similar research findings contributes

Table 9.2 General Characteristics of Experiments

Selected benefits	*Selected limitations*
Allow researchers to determine causation (typically have a high degree of explanatory power)	Many research environments are artificial in social sciences (results may lack external validity)
Controlled research environments allow researchers to direct participants' assignment to conditions, independent-variable manipulations, and dependent-variable measurements	Sometimes challenging to develop appropriate stimuli and measure participants' dependent-variable responses
Can be relatively inexpensive	Potential for biased results
Good potential for replication	Can be difficult to conduct

to increased confidence in the validity and generalizability of research findings (Baxter & Babbie, 2004).

Finally, the cost of experiments can be comparatively low. Laboratory research, in particular, tends to be limited in scope, often requiring a relatively small number of participants and a comparatively short amount of time for data collection. These requirements often combine to provide a high degree of explanatory power at a reasonable cost.

There are two primary disadvantages of experiments: the artificiality of the research environment and the potential introduction of bias. Although isolation and control are necessary to determine causation, research environments may be so isolated and so controlled that they are completely unlike environments found in natural social settings. Here, the external validity, or generalizability, of research findings may be hindered. The artificiality of laboratory research settings presents a particular problem in applied campaign studies because it does not reflect the busy, competitive environment in which practitioners conduct most communication campaigns. In this instance, the generalizability of research findings from laboratory experiments to communication campaign settings may be limited.

A second disadvantage of experimental research is the potential for biased results. During an experiment there are a variety of possible sources of bias. When a study produces biased results, research outcomes are inaccurate and provide a flawed basis for campaign planning and execution.

Finally, experiments can be challenging to conduct. It is often difficult, for example, for researchers to measure complex human processes using a series of simple questions or other measures. It may be that participants have never considered the reasons for some of their attitudes and behaviors. As a result, they may find it difficult to identify and express their attitudes and other responses, especially given the typical limitations of self-report measurement scales. Sometimes, participants simply are unable to express their feelings, even if it involves answering just a few questions. Project managers also may find it difficult to find or create appropriate stimuli for experiments or to execute procedures with the care necessary to determine causation. In fact, it is possible to plan an experiment that is virtually impossible to conduct. Experiments, like all research methods, are useful only for specific situations, and campaign practitioners should carefully consider their limitations.

Content Analysis

Content analysis is a scientific research method used for describing communication content. Researchers typically use content analysis to develop objective, systematic, and quantitative descriptions of messages (Berelson, 1952). Many public relations practitioners work to place messages in the media—including digital communication outlets—on behalf of their organizations and clients. They continually monitor and track placement of these messages and traditionally have used clip counts—when they count, analyze, and categorize media placements—as a key basis for evaluating public relations' campaign success. When practitioners examine the attributes of different media placements such as the tone of media coverage or the balance of media portrayals, for example, they may use content analysis.

Content analyses are objective because their results are not based on the informal observations and biases of those conducting the study but instead rely on an objective classification system. They are systematic because researchers establish a set of procedures and follow a formal process when analyzing media content. Content analyses are quantitative because the results of the classification process produce numerical classifications of content that are subjected to appropriate statistical analyses. The result is a scientific (i.e., accurate and unbiased) description of the contents of communication messages.

If managers wanted to better understand the ways in which reporters portrayed their organization in local media, for example, a practitioner might decide to comb through a collection of media stories to determine the frequency of coverage, evaluate the general tone of the stories, and note recurring themes and major issues. This analysis would provide some useful information but likely would suffer from some significant weaknesses.

Alternatively, a practitioner could conduct a formal content analysis. In this case, the practitioner would determine the aspects of media coverage most important to the company and then categorize and quantitatively analyze the media content. The results and conclusions from such a study potentially would be more accurate than an informal evaluation. These results would provide managers with an unbiased assessment of the media coverage concerning the organization. Such findings could be part of a public relations audit and serve as the basis for future media relations efforts. The results also might serve as a benchmark if the company decided to undertake an effort to improve its media coverage.

Content analyses typically require steps similar to those used by project managers in survey research. In fact, a content analysis is a lot like a survey, except that researchers collect and analyze samples of messages instead of sampling people and their opinions. Initially, investigators identify a research problem and develop research questions or hypotheses. Next, they choose an appropriate sample of messages. Then, they determine the procedures and categories research team members will use when they code the content. Researchers must train those who code the data and they usually conduct a small pilot study (the equivalent of a pretest) to ensure the study is well designed. Content coding takes place once the pilot study proves successful, followed by data analysis and interpretation.

Research Problem and Question/Hypothesis Development

As with any other research project, investigators must clearly understand the purpose of their study, including potential problems they must address, in the first phase of a content analysis. This helps them design a useful study with realistic procedures. A good research design clearly integrates the procedures for sample selection, study execution and data analysis into a comprehensive plan, as discussed in Chapter 4. By implication, an investigator must understand the reason for the study, specify the evidence needed to test ideas or relationships, and know the methods of analysis they will use following data collection.

Researchers can use content analyses to study almost any form of communication, although they most often use it to address research questions or hypotheses concerning specific message attributes. This may include an analysis of messages over time (e.g., to track media coverage concerning an important issue) or an analysis of messages directed to different audiences (e.g., messages in blog posts versus messages in traditional media), for example.

Sometimes researchers erroneously use content analyses to make inferences about the effects of messages on receivers, such as the effects of violent television content on children's behavior. Content analyses conducted for this purpose are fatally flawed because they make several untenable assumptions concerning message exposure and message effects or causation. Ultimately, content analyses do not allow researchers to determine causation.

Sample Selection

Researchers must select the messages to analyze after they have determined research questions or hypotheses. First, they determine the body of messages, or population, from which they will draw the sample, just as the survey manager chooses a population of people to study. Through this process, also known as defining the *universe* or *sampling frame*, investigators might decide to examine blog entries concerning federal health care posted during the 3 months following passage of major health care legislation, for example. Just as with survey research, content analysts usually do not try to analyze all relevant messages (this would be a census). The sheer volume of potentially relevant messages normally makes some form of sampling necessary, especially given the time and monetary limitations accompanying most research projects. Researchers need to make sure the message population is comprehensive and logically consistent with the purposes and goals of their study.

In addition, content analyses may require some type of multistage sampling which involves sample selection procedures at two or more levels (Figure 9.6.). At the initial stage of sample selection, researchers might select specific media sources—daily newspapers published within 6 months of an election, for example—from among all possible content sources. At a second stage of sampling, researchers might choose specific newspaper dates to examine. At the third sampling stage, researchers might select specific pages within each newspaper and examine the stories on those pages. Additional stages of sampling may be necessary, as well. For example researchers may find it necessary to select specific stories from pages and even paragraphs with stories as additional sampling stages. See Chapter 6 for a discussion of sampling techniques.

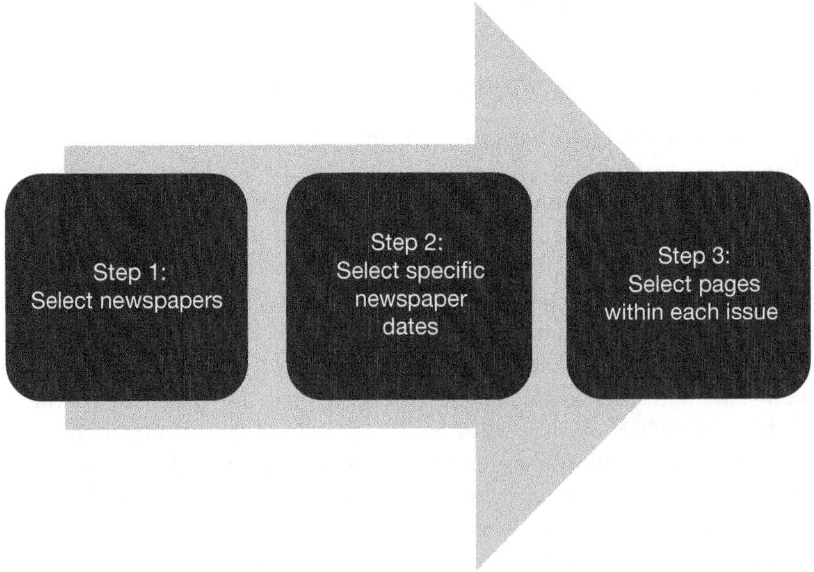

FIG. 9.6. Multistage sampling for an analysis of newspaper content.

Units of Analysis

Determining the unit of analysis and content categories is a critical part of any content-based study because researchers can analyze content in different forms. Each form of content they analyze is a *unit* for purposes of measurement and evaluation. A *unit of analysis* is a distinct piece of content, meaning this is the thing researchers actually count (Riffe, Lacy, & Fico, 1998). Units of analysis can include stories or articles, words or terms, themes, paragraphs, characters, and more. In a study designed to examine the media's portrayal of an organization, for example, the units of analysis may include positive, negative, or mixed stories about the corporation, specific aspects of the corporation's image mentioned in stories, mention of specific corporate programs in stories, names of competing organizations stories contain, and other relevant information. Researchers often find specification of the units of analysis challenging. This process typically requires research team members to define units of analysis, pretest their work, and then refine their definitions through trial and error as they analyze a sample of representative content. Normally, this procedure results in the modification and further refinement of unit descriptions.

Categories of Analysis

Next, researchers code and classify contents, placing each unit of analysis into the categories they have created for a study. Researchers may label a newspaper story as favorable or unfavorable in its portrayal of an organization, for example. Well-constructed categories are essential because they are the key to a successful study. Researchers who develop vaguely drawn or poorly articulated content categories will produce a study with inferior quality and limited usefulness. To be effective, content categories must be *mutually exclusive, exhaustive,* and *reliable.*

Categories are *mutually exclusive* when research team members can place a unit of analysis into only one category. If a unit simultaneously fits into more than one category, researchers must revise either or both categories. One means of avoiding problems related to exclusivity is to have category definitions that possess a high degree of specificity. When project managers use well-defined category units, research team members will have fewer questions regarding unit placement among categories.

Categories must be exhaustive in addition to being mutually exclusive. Categories that are *exhaustive* provide space for every existing content unit. It is necessary for project managers to expand content categories when researchers discover units not covered by existing categories. When only a few miscellaneous units are not covered by existing category systems, researchers typically use an "other" category.

Finally, the category system must be reliable. To be *reliable*, different coders need to agree on the placement of contents within categories. This is called *intercoder reliability*. Poorly defined content categories lack specificity and typically suffer from low intercoder reliability. Conversely, well-defined category systems help to increase intercoder reliability. The extensive pretesting of sample content helps researchers develop mutually exclusive, exhaustive, and reliable content categories.

Coding Content

Coding content involves the placement of units of analysis into content categories. This process generally is the most time-consuming aspect of content analysis, requiring researchers to train coders, develop a pilot study, and code the data. Reliability is critical in content analysis because content analyses are supposed to produce objective results and reliable measures help produce objective findings. The measures used in a study are reliable when repeated measurement of the same material produces the same results. Normally, a subset of data is coded by two coders working independently. Analysts can compare the results of each coder's work to determine the level of accuracy between the coders. This produces a test of intercoder reliability. Intercoder reliability can be calculated using one of several methods. Holsti (1969) reported a simple formula for calculating intercoder reliability:

$$\text{reliability} = \frac{M}{n1 + n2}$$

In this formula, *M* represents the number of coding decisions coders agreed upon, and each *n* refers to the total number of coding decisions made by the first and second coder, respectively. This formula has some limitations, but it is easy to use. Project managers may be interested in using other formulas if they need a more sophisticated measure of reliability. Researchers commonly use Scott's pi (Scott, 1955) or Cohen's kappa (Cohen, 1960) in this case because these reliability coefficients take into account chance agreement between coders and provide a more accurate estimate of reliability.

The thorough training of coders generally results in a more reliable analysis. It is helpful to have several training sessions in which coders work on sample data. Investigators compare the results among coders, discuss differences, and then repeat this process. When coders rely on detailed instruction sheets and participate in rigorous training efforts, studies normally enjoy higher intercoder reliability.

After a thorough training period, research team members conduct a pilot study to check intercoder reliability. As a result of the pilot study, researchers may need to revise study definitions and/or define category boundaries with greater specificity. This process continues until coders are comfortable with study materials and procedures and are able to maintain a high degree of reliability.

Finally, research-team members code content. They use standardized score sheets developed during training to help them collect data quickly and accurately. Researchers typically use statistics software to help them tabulate and analyze study results.

Content Analysis Critique

The objective and systematic nature of this research method often helps researchers produce content descriptions and analyses that are high in validity and reliability while avoiding the subjective interpretations of less rigorous methods of analyzing content. In addition, many content analyses are inexpensive and researchers can use them to examine content as it evolves over long periods of time. This gives researchers an important perspective not easily available from other research methods. Further, although most research methods typically pose little risk to participants, content analyses involve no risk because they don't use human participants. Together, these benefits make content analysis a potentially beneficial research method.

Despite its potential usefulness, however, organizational managers must use content analysis carefully because it is not an easy method to use correctly (Kerlinger, 1973). The primary problems associated with this research method are issues related to reliability, validity, and inference. The concept of reliability is of maximum importance in content analysis. A high degree of reliability may be particularly difficult to achieve when analyzing content. When researchers want to understand the appeal strategies used in alcoholic beverage advertising, for example, they may be interested specifically in the use of sex-based appeals. Does an ad containing a beach scene with bikini-clad women automatically constitute a sexual appeal? Can an ad contain a sexual appeal even if it shows no human models? If two people are just looking at one another but not physically touching can this be a sexual appeal? Ultimately, content analyses involve making judgment calls and these judgments typically create problems for coders and contribute to low levels of reliability in content studies.

In addition, validity in content analysis is directly connected to the design decisions and procedures researchers use when conducting a study. When sampling designs are incorrect—if categories are not mutually exclusive and exhaustive—or if reliability is low, the results of a content analysis are inaccurate and will possess a low degree of validity.

The final concern regarding the use of content analysis involves problems associated with inference. The strength of most content analyses is their ability to provide a precise description of communication content. Researchers sometimes are tempted, however, to use content studies to draw conclusions and make interpretations not supported by the research method. Most often, the problem comes when a company equates content analysis with public opinion analysis. Remember, public opinion resides in the perceptions of members of the public, not in the content of media messages. Message receivers from varied backgrounds, with varied cognitive skills and with varying levels of interest or motivation may interpret messages differently from the findings of an objective content analysis.

Final Thoughts

Formal research methods provide essential information for communication campaign managers. Because formal methods offer objectivity, systematic data collection, representative samples, and replicable designs, they typically provide trustworthy information. Only dependable information can help practitioners accurately describe situations and publics, predict the outcome of an election, or understand the reasons why public opinion seems to have turned against an organization, for example. Each formal method has strengths and weaknesses, meaning practitioners can use each method well or misuse each method badly. As a result, a good understanding of the benefits and limitations of each method can help managers conduct quality in-house research or knowledgeably purchase quality research services from a firm at a reasonable cost.

10

Making Research Decisions

Survey Research

Chapter Contents

- Mail Surveys
- Online Surveys Including Opt-In and Panel Surveys
- Telephone Surveys
- Personal Interview Surveys Including Mall Intercepts
- Final Thoughts

When researchers conduct a survey they collect information directly from members of a population. It usually involves interviews and questionnaires that participants fill out alone or with the assistance of an interviewer. Organizations' use of survey research has grown dramatically over the past several years. Today survey research is an indispensable part of organizations' attempts to monitor their internal and external environments; solve complex problems; understand the opinions, attitudes, and behaviors of key target-audience members; track public opinion; engage in sophisticated campaign planning and evaluation; and, in some cases, seek media attention for an organization or client.

What is responsible for the rapid increase in the use of survey research? Organizations have increasingly felt the need to understand the opinions, attitudes, and behavioral motivations of their key target audience members, including legislators and government regulators, community members, consumers, employees, and other important groups. In many cases, the environments in which organizations operate are more competitive than in the past; target audiences are more sophisticated and often given to greater activism. Stakeholders, members of single-issue activist groups, and others are more likely to use digital communication to challenge organizations and attempt to gain the attention and support of the media, other like-minded citizens, watchdog groups, and government regulators. In addition, survey research tools have become much more accessible to the public relations generalist due to online survey platforms developed by companies such as Qualtrics and SurveyMonkey.

Practitioners want to ensure a high level of performance for their programs and campaigns, particularly as the costs of a campaign increase or as organizational certainty about the success of a campaign decreases. In this case, survey research serves as a kind of insurance, providing critical information to practitioners as they plan and implement public relations programs. Valid, reliable information replaces practitioners' reliance on past practices, hunches, industry standards, or rules of thumb. In these circumstances, survey research is an invaluable part of program planning and problem solving.

Finally, organizational managers want to know how practitioners are using resources and the return on investment they provide to an organization. Traditionally, practitioners have relied on favorable media coverage, key story placements, media clip counts, and advertising value equivalency calculations to communicate the value of their work to managers and clients (e.g., Porter, 2009; Thieke, 2007; Watson, 2013). Clients and managers initially may be impressed when practitioners provide large clip counts, share of voice analyses, and low cost-per-impression numbers. They grow skeptical, however, when they begin to consider larger, more important questions about the effect of public relations activities on the attitudes and behaviors of key target-audience members (Ketchum Global Research & Analytics, 2014; Thieke, 2007). In this instance, survey research typically provides a more sophisticated means of tracking changes in the opinions, attitudes, and behaviors of target-audience members, and it is an indispensable tool for practitioners who desire to communicate the benefits of public relations activities to organizations and clients.

These are among the most critical issues practitioners face and are a large part of the reason practitioners' use of survey research has increased so rapidly. As noted in Chapter 9, surveys generally are descriptive or analytical in nature. Descriptive surveys characterize conditions and circumstances as they exist in a population, and analytical surveys attempt to explain why current conditions exist. In fact, many surveys serve both purposes, and this often meets practitioners' and organizations' needs for information. Surveys generally possess several advantages over other research methods.

Researchers primarily conduct surveys via regular mail, telephone, personal interviews, the Internet or a combination of these methods (called a multiple-mode survey). They can use these methods in a relatively straightforward manner or adapt methods to reach new audiences or to meet the demands of a particular research situation. In a typical survey, researchers initially set objectives for a study. Next, they design the study. When researchers design a study, they normally select a population and establish sampling procedures, select a survey method or methods, and design and pretest questionnaires. Next, members of a research team typically collect, edit, and code data. Finally, researchers analyze and interpret the results.

Because Chapter 9 presented the research planning process, this chapter focuses on some of the key advantages and disadvantages of each survey method. This discussion raises an important issue. Clients and organizations, often looking to make quick decisions, frequently want to identify the single best method for a survey. In reality, there is no single best method of survey research and many survey projects have shifted from the use of a single mode to collect data, such as a mail or telephone survey, to using multiple survey modes for data collection in the same study. The use of multiple modes helps compensate for the limitations of individual survey methods and also helps researchers meet the needs of sample members (Dillman, et al., 2009).

As a result, the best method or methods for a project depends on a number of project-specific factors. Beyond the informational requirements of a project, researchers must consider the population and sample, including the best way to contact sample members, the sampling methods available, the survey topic or topics, and the importance of reliability and validity. In addition, a project's budget and time frame often have a disproportionately large effect on survey-method selection.

Ultimately, researchers cannot answer questions concerning the best research method or methods without context. Beyond budget, some of the most critical aspects of study context relate to the best ways to reach participants and secure their participation (Dillman, et al., 2009). Given the differences between individual sample members and their preferred methods of contact, the potential advantages and disadvantages of each method do not apply equally, or even at all, to every survey situation. As a result, practitioners must consider their use of a survey method or methods carefully and in relation to the requirements and constraints of each project including potential participants.

Practitioners serve their own interest by understanding some of the key advantages and disadvantages associated with the use of one survey method over another, as well as other critical aspects of survey implementation such as the use of probability versus nonprobability sampling. This understanding allows them to make informed decisions regarding survey methods and makes them more sophisticated consumers of the research products they use and purchase.

The remainder of this chapter presents each of the primary survey research methods broadly, and includes information about the potential benefits and limitations of these methods. Understanding this information will help practitioners select the most appropriate research methods for a project, either alone or as part of a multiple-mode survey.

Mail Surveys

Traditional mail surveys are conducted by sending a questionnaire via regular mail to a sample of individuals. Participants fill out questionnaires and mail the surveys back to the researcher. A project manager may send a pre-notification card or letter to inform sample members of their inclusion in a survey, answer preliminary questions, and encourage their participation. A detailed cover letter accompanies the questionnaire to provide more information concerning the purpose of the survey and to again encourage sample members to participate by explaining why a response is important. Researchers typically include an incentive for participation—such as a small amount of money—and a stamped, addressed reply envelope to encourage respondents to complete their survey and mail it back.

Given the difficulties researchers face completing telephone surveys and the current challenges associated with probability-based surveys conducted via the Internet, mail-survey research is experiencing a small renaissance. Researchers often use mail surveys because of their low cost and ease of administration. If a mailing list is available (and it often is), it is relatively easy to use it as the source of a probability-based sample. Several challenges face researchers using mail survey research including the length of time it takes to complete a project and the low response rates mail surveys sometimes produce. Despite these concerns, the low cost and ease of administration of mail surveys are among the advantages that make them an attractive choice.

Mail Survey Considerations

There are many nuances that contribute to successful survey research, and this is especially true of mail surveys (Table 10.1). A mail survey is a self-administered questionnaire. This means

Table 10.1 Characteristics of Mail Surveys

Selected Benefits	*Selected Limitations*
Relatively Inexpensive	May suffer from low response rates
Reaches widely dispersed sample	(requires inducements and multiple
members easily	mailings to improve)
Mailing lists make it easy to generate	Data collection may take longer than
probability-based sample	other methods
May provide high degree of anonymity	No questionnaire flexibility; typically
(potentially useful for sensitive topics)	requires a shorter, self-explanatory
No interviewer bias	questionnaire
	Survey respondent may not be selected
	sample member
	Members of certain groups less likely to
	complete questionnaire

that participants fill out the survey on their own, without an interviewer's involvement. This requires research-team members to carefully write the cover letter and questionnaire to optimize the participation rate of sample members. Unfortunately, no matter how well a questionnaire and cover letter are written, this is not enough to ensure the success of a mail survey. Although this problem is not unique to mail surveys, the result of poorly written questionnaires and unclear cover letters is that many mail-survey projects suffer from low rates of response despite researchers' efforts to encourage participation. While there are many keys to a successful mail survey project, practitioners must pay special attention to the pre-notification card or letter, the cover letter and questionnaire, the sampling method, and monitor the response rate to help ensure a successful mail survey (Chapters 6, 11, and 12 contain more information about some of these important topics).

A well-written pre-notification card or letter and cover letter are critical to the success of a survey. They must introduce a survey to potential respondents who are busy and uninterested and motivate them to fill out the survey and return it immediately.

Beyond sending a prenotification card or letter to a potential participant, a cover letter usually is the only opportunity a researcher has to pique the interest of sample members, establish a minimal level of rapport, anticipate and answer key questions, and explain why a response is important. The difficulty of writing a good cover letter is increased because a long, dense letter that satisfactorily answers everyone's questions typically will discourage careful reading, or worse, will cause potential respondents to throw the questionnaire away.

The first paragraphs of a cover letter usually explain what the study is about and who is sponsoring the study, and are written to convince the reader the study is useful. Researchers typically use later paragraphs to convince readers their response is critical and to assure them of confidentiality. Given the importance of the cover letter to the success of a mail survey, researchers need to draft and pretest cover letters. Their goal is to write a letter that reflects a tone of appreciation and mutual respect to recipients, encouraging them to participate in a simple, straightforward manner (Dillman, et al., 2009).

Mail surveys also require researchers to use carefully written and pretested questionnaires. Mail questionnaires require careful writing and construction because they are self-administered and must be completely self-explanatory. Researchers must strive to produce an attractive questionnaire of reasonable length with plenty of white space and clear, simple instructions. The absence of an interviewer means there are no opportunities for interviewers to encourage survey response, help participants understand poorly written questions or instructions, or answer even basic participant questions (Dillman, 2000).

Although researchers can provide a toll-free telephone number, link, or e-mail address for such purposes, participants rarely use them. In fact, participants should not need to contact researchers to understand questions and instructions. Instead, the instructions and questions researchers use in mail surveys should be so clearly written that they are uniformly understood by all potential respondents. Poorly written questions decrease the accuracy, reliability and validity of survey results, and sample members who do not understand questions or instructions are unlikely to participate, resulting in low response rates and nonresponse bias. Pretesting is the best way to ensure that surveys are compelling and easy to answer.

Pretesting a questionnaire is essential to ensure readers understand survey instructions, questions, and response categories. When project managers pretest a questionnaire, individuals who are similar to sample members in terms of key sample characteristics—such as age, education level, experience, or other relevant qualities—actually complete the survey, making note of confusing or unclear questions and instructions. Researchers also note and discuss other aspects of questionnaire administration with pretest participants such as the length of time they needed to complete the survey and various features they liked or did not like about the questionnaire. There are many ways to pretest a questionnaire, and no method is singularly advantageous. It is important, however, for researchers to pretest all written material potential respondents will receive, preferably several times. Experience shows problems can sneak into even comprehensively tested questionnaires. Even so, researchers can identify and correct most survey problems through multiple pretests.

Even well-written and pretested mail surveys may suffer from low response rates, historically among the lowest response rates of the primary survey research methods. Although there are a variety of different formulas for determining survey participation, the response rate generally reflects the percentage of sample members who participate in a survey by completing a questionnaire (see Chapter 12). A low response rate raises numerous concerns including concerns of *nonresponse bias*. Nonresponse bias contributes to error in survey results because of differences between those who participate in a survey and those who do not, as noted previously. In addition, surveys with low rates of participation will be less likely to accurately represent the range of opinions, experiences and behaviors existing in a general population. Ultimately, when too many sample members choose not to participate in a survey, their lack of participation reduces the accuracy and external validity, or generalizability, of a study's results.

Well-designed surveys help increase participants' rate of response. Although each project is different, there are several elements to a successful project and a number of ways researchers work to increase mail survey response rates. Dillman and colleagues (2009) noted that integration and consistency among the individual elements of a mail survey are keys to increasing participation. These most commonly include the use of pre-notification and reminder cards or letters, as well as sending new cover letters and additional copies of the questionnaire to non-respondents. Initially, a pre-notification card or letter can be an effective way for research project managers to prepare respondents for survey participation, as Figure 10.1 demonstrates.

Typically, sample members receive this mailing a week or so before the questionnaire and cover letter are sent, and researchers use it to create understanding and even a small degree of

---

Please tell us what you think
about the media & elections.

We have randomly selected you to voluntarily participate in a short telephone survey. Soon, a trained student from the Murrow College of Communication at Washington State University will be contacting you in the evening by phone and asking to speak to a registered voter. Your responses will help Murrow College faculty and students to better understand important issues concerning the media and elections.

We are asking for your opinions only!

We are not calling for a political party or candidate.
We are not asking for donations
and we have nothing to sell.

WASHINGTON STATE
UNIVERSITY
World Class. Face to Face.

Thanks for your help!

FIG. 10.1. A sample pre-notification card sent in advance of a survey.

---

anticipation among sample respondents. Researchers mail the cover letter and questionnaire next. The cover letter and questionnaire typically are followed by a thank you card or letter. This mailing expresses thanks to those who have completed a questionnaire and serves as a reminder to those who have not. Typically, researchers send a new letter and questionnaire 2–4 weeks after the arrival of the initial questionnaire. Researchers sometimes send additional questionnaires to offer potential respondents as many opportunities as is reasonably possible to participate in the survey. These mailings typically result in very small participation increases (Table 10.2).

Research suggests follow-up mailings are an effective way to increase mail survey participation. In general, as sample members delay responding to a survey the likelihood that they will participate lowers significantly. Properly timed follow-up mailings provide additional encouragement to respond. Researchers can use other techniques to help increase mail survey response rates as well, including sponsorship by a university or other respected institution;

Table 10.2 Mail Survey Timeline

---

1. Pre-notification card: Typically received 1 week before the questionnaire.
2. Cover letter and Questionnaire: Sent out following the pre-notification card
3. Thank you card or letter: Sent out 1 week to 10 days after the cover letter and questionnaire.
4. New letter and Questionnaire: Typically sent 2–3 weeks after the arrival of the initial questionnaire.
5. Additional questionnaires (optional): Some researchers will send additional cover letters and questionnaires to give potential respondents more opportunities.

---

mailing questionnaires in envelopes with stamps rather than metered or bulk rate markings; enclosing a stamped, self-addressed return envelope with the survey; and using relatively modest monetary incentives such as a $2 or $5 bill sent with the initial cover letter and questionnaire.

Other ways exist for researchers to increase response rates, but some attempts to produce increased participation may actually reduce participation. Using personalized envelopes or questionnaires—for example, when respondent anonymity is important or the topic of a survey is sensitive—can be counterproductive. This shows it is critical for researchers to understand as much as possible about the topic and sample members and to pretest all aspects of a survey in order to increase their ability to obtain valid, reliable results from sample members.

The representativeness of mail survey results is increased through probability sampling methods, as discussed in Chapter 6. One benefit of mail surveys is that practitioners can purchase the names and addresses of randomly selected members of a population from vendors who sell samples, often at a reasonable price. These same companies typically can provide highly specialized samples at a somewhat higher price. Such samples often are invaluable because they allow research team members to complete a survey using a probability-based sample, helping to increase the reliability and external validity of survey results. Some organizations and associations use their own mailing lists as the basis for a probability sample. The mailing list serves as the *sampling frame* (a list of population members from which researchers draw a sample), and researchers can randomly draw names and addresses from the list to form the sample. In this way, it is a relatively simple process for researchers to generate a probability-based sample to use when conducting a mail survey.

Practitioners should take care in the interpretation of research results, however, when mailing lists serve as the basis for a sample. Even though the sample is probability based, practitioners can legitimately generalize the results only to members of the mailing list. Ideally, a mailing list contains all of the members of a population. In this case, the results of the survey are likely to accurately reflect the true opinions and attitudes of all population members (given a certain range of error at a specific level of confidence; see Chapter 6 for these calculations).

In other instances, however, a mailing list does not provide a complete list of all members of a population. This might be the case, for example, if researchers are trying to survey members of a professional association using the association's mailing list. Any sample generated using such a mailing list would produce results that are directly generalizable only to members of the association and not to all members of the profession. This matter may seem small and technical, but study results are as trustworthy as the sample on which they are based. Researchers must use mailing lists with care and consider the ramifications of sampling decisions before plunging into data collection. Practitioners cannot increase the generalizability of a survey's results once a study is complete.

Mail Survey Critique

For many applications, mail surveys are relatively inexpensive. This benefit alone contributes greatly to their use. Although there are situations in which other survey methods cost less, in most instances, mail surveys provide the ability to cover a large geographical area at a relatively low cost per respondent. Regardless of the survey method, there generally are similar costs associated with developing and producing a questionnaire, securing a sample, and analyzing and interpreting the results. Two methodological benefits can reduce the cost of mail surveys relative to other research methods. The first is postage which is relatively inexpensive. The second cost-saving benefit results from lower administrative costs. Project managers do not need interviewers to collect data; therefore, these surveys generally require fewer people to complete the data collection process. Although it is important to have knowledgeable staff members assemble materials, track responses, mail follow-ups, and edit and code returned questionnaires as necessary, mail surveys generally require relatively few administrative resources.

In addition, mail surveys allow for probability sampling through specialized mailing lists. Although researchers must be concerned about the limited generalizability of survey results when they use a list as a sampling frame, mailing lists can make excellent sampling frames in appropriate research settings. Researchers may use a selected list, for example, when they need to sample a highly specialized, professional population. Researchers also can use mail surveys to collect information from sample members such as this because they are busy and are unlikely to participate in a telephone or personal interview.

Researchers may find mail surveys useful when they desire a high degree of respondent anonymity. Respondents may be more likely to provide candid answers to questions concerning sensitive subjects because they are not speaking directly to an interviewer (Wimmer & Dominick, 2014). In addition, researchers are not concerned about the effect of interviewer bias on study results when they use mail surveys. Respondents typically are sensitive to both verbal and nonverbal cues during the interview process, and sometimes they interpret these cues as supportive or unsupportive of their opinions, attitudes, and behaviors. Respondents may change their answers as a result. Survey results concerning racial prejudice, for example, would be ruined if participants changed their answer because they sensed interviewer disapproval for their prejudicial opinions and attitudes. Instead of an accurate measure of racial prejudice, study results would be skewed by participants who provide socially desirable responses because of perceived interviewer influence. Researchers who are studying sensitive subjects, or who have concerns regarding the potential for interviewer bias, can use mail surveys to help eliminate such problems.

Perhaps the greatest concern practitioners have when they use mail surveys is their low rate of response which has become a problem common to most survey research. It is not uncommon for mail surveys to have response rates ranging widely from 5% to 40% (Wimmer & Dominick, 2014). Although mail surveys can achieve higher response rates (Dillman, et al., 2009), a low return rate casts doubt on the validity and reliability of a survey's findings by introducing nonresponse bias into survey results among other problems. For example, project managers are less likely to receive returned surveys from respondents who are low in educational attainment, who do not like to read or write, and who are not interested in the survey subject (Blair, Czaja & Blair, 2014; Wimmer & Dominick, 2014). The differences between respondents and non-respondents potentially bias a survey's results.

In addition, mail-survey projects tend to take longer to complete than other survey-project methods. Typical mail surveys may require 8 weeks or longer to complete, given the need for pre-notification and multiple questionnaire mailings, along with the slower rate of questionnaire return via regular mail. While this length of time may not be unreasonable for some applications such as academic research, it often is too long given the time constraints of many applied research projects.

Another significant problem with mail surveys concerns the need for questionnaires to be self-explanatory and relatively short to encourage survey participation. Because no one is available to explain questions or provide additional information, researchers must make survey instructions, question wording, and question skip patterns—necessary when certain questions apply to some but not all participants—extremely simple and clear. Even when questions and instructions are clear, some respondents skip questions or even entire sections of a questionnaire.

Additionally, researchers can never be sure who has actually completed a questionnaire. Even though research project managers usually direct surveys to specific individuals, these sample members may ask or allow other individuals who are not a part of the sample to fill out their questionnaires. Any of these concerns, working individually or together, may reduce the desirability of mail as a survey method and potentially introduce inaccuracies and/or bias into study results.

Online Surveys Including Opt-In and Panel Surveys

The World Wide Web and Internet have dramatically altered survey research. The number of surveys administered electronically, as well as online survey tools and service providers, has grown rapidly. A variety of options exist for contacting potential respondents when conducting electronic surveys and the best choice largely depends on sample members. In some cases, it is best to contact participants directly via e-mail with an embedded link, perhaps after they have received some form of pre-notification to help establish trust in the researchers. In other instances, it may be best to contact sample members via regular mail with survey-related information and ask them to go to a website to complete a questionnaire (technically, this would be a mixed-mode survey). For other projects, both forms of contact may be necessary. As a result, it is important to understand the preferences of potential sample members to the extent that is possible.

In addition, our increasingly wired and interconnected world has resulted in increased time demands on individuals, along with increased fraud attempts. As a result, many people are rightfully distrustful of unsolicited e-mails and more guarded about providing private information to others. These issues have greatly increased the challenge of completing electronic surveys. Ultimately, it is important for researchers to find ways to overcome these challenges to ensure the successful completion of electronic survey research projects (Dillman, et al., 2009).

Online Survey Considerations

Although there are different procedures researchers can use to conduct Web-based surveys these are self-administered questionnaires and require care in their development and planning. As with regular-mail surveys, research-team members must carefully write the cover letter and questionnaire to optimize the participation rate of sample members. Poorly conceived, planned and constructed questionnaires are likely to suffer from participation rates so low they are useless for practical purposes. Unfortunately, as with mail surveys, a well-written cover letter and questionnaire are not enough to ensure the success of a Web-based survey.

Fortunately, the Web offers flexible and sophisticated design options to research managers enabling them to design surveys with a number of features to encourage sample-member participation. Web-based surveys allow participants to answer questions involving complicated skip patterns, for example, without their knowledge that questions are even part of a skip pattern. In addition, with proper tools and/or technical support, researchers can design surveys with a variety of features including graphics and pop-up instructions, which they can use to encourage respondents to complete a questionnaire resulting in high-quality data.

The number of online research tools and service providers, such as Qualtrics or SurveyMonkey, has increased dramatically over the past several years, as Figures 10.2 and 10.3 demonstrate. Using these tools, researchers can compose and send Web-based surveys with relative ease because they are user friendly and generally require few technical skills. In addition, researchers can produce highly customized surveys with proper skills or support. Even without such support, online survey tools typically provide project managers with the ability to produce and distribute a relatively high-quality questionnaire using standard measurement scales simply, easily, and at a low cost per respondent.

The ability to produce questionnaires easily does not guarantee the success of a survey project. Instead, many of the procedures that contribute to the success of regular mail surveys also contribute to the success of surveys conducted via the Web but there are important differences between the methods. Dillman and colleagues (2009), widely recognized for their expertise in survey research, note a number of keys to the successful implementation of Web-based surveys.

Initially, project managers may contact sample members using some form of pre-notification sent via e-mail, regular mail, or both. When possible, researchers should use some forms of message personalization because research indicates personalization—simply using the name of the sample member in an e-mail, for example—helps to increase survey responses. In addition, an incentive sent as a token of appreciation also helps increase survey participation. While this is difficult to do via e-mail, a prepaid incentive such as a $5 electronic gift certificate potentially will help increase participation and some experts recommend a prepaid cash incentive sent via regular mail when possible (Dillman, et al., 2009).

In addition, the use of multiple contacts containing varied messages is likely to contribute to increased participation. While sending the same message repeatedly to sample members is unlikely to produce anything besides annoyance, varied messages—especially if they are pretested and perhaps sent via different modes—have a greater likelihood of appealing in some way to respondents. Equally as important, avoiding the use of words such as "free," "cash," or "prize" also may help increase the chances that at least some messages will survive spam filters.

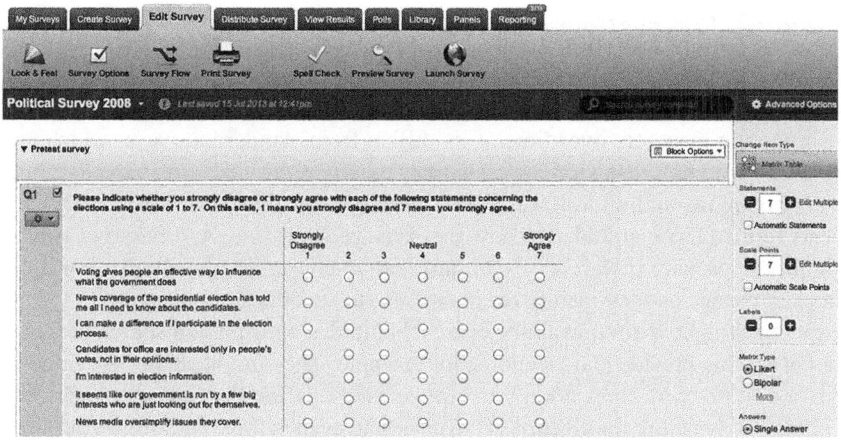

FIG 10.2. Online survey platforms such as Qualtrics allow users to create surveys with relative ease and typically include tutorials and technical support.

The Edward R. Murrow
College of Communication

Please indicate whether you strongly disagree or strongly agree with each of the following statements concerning the elections using a scale of 1 to 7. On this scale, 1 means you strongly disagree and 7 means you strongly agree.

	Strongly Disagree 1	2	3	Neutral 4	5	6	Strongly Agree 7
Voting gives people an effective way to influence what the government does	○	○	○	○	○	○	○
News coverage of the presidential election has told me all I need to know about the candidates.	○	○	○	○	○	○	○
I can make a difference if I participate in the election process.	○	○	○	○	○	○	○
Candidates for office are interested only in people's votes, not in their opinions.	○	○	○	○	○	○	○
I'm interested in election information.	○	○	○	○	○	○	○
It seems like our government is run by a few big interests who are just looking out for themselves.	○	○	○	○	○	○	○
News media oversimplify issues they cover.	○	○	○	○	○	○	○

0% [   ] 100%

>>

FIG. 10.3. This is the finished Qualtrics survey.

Finally, Dillman and his coauthors (2009) recommend some standard practices to communicate professionalism to sample members and to help build trust among participants. These include following the standard rules of spelling and grammar—typically prevalent in most forms of writing but often relaxed in electronic communication—and avoiding acronyms such as LOL or FYI.

Opt-in Internet Surveys/Panel Studies

Panel studies are a type of longitudinal survey that permit researchers to collect data from the same participants on a repeated basis. Because of this, panel studies allow researchers to examine changes in sample members over time. This differs from standard surveys, which are cross-sectional in nature. As cross-sectional research, a survey provides an immediate picture of participants' opinions and attitudes as they currently exist but little information about how participants formed those attitudes or how they change over time. A strength of panel studies is their ability to provide researchers with information concerning how participants' attitudes and behaviors change as they mature or in response to specific situations.

Researchers might want to examine citizens' attitudes, information source use, and voting behavior concerning presidential elections, for example. They might survey the same group of people in late summer of an election year, immediately before the first televised presidential debate, immediately before the elections take place and even in the weeks following an election. Such a longitudinal study can reveal change among participants as they engage in media use and political decision making over time rather than examining their attitudes and behaviors at a single point in time.

Today, some research organizations conduct sophisticated, large-scale consumer panel studies which are made possible through online participation. These studies can be based on sizeable samples and provide organizations with a variety of useful information that has been nearly impossible for organizations to collect in the past. There are different types of panels that exist currently so generalizing to all panel studies is difficult. While some panel studies use probability-based samples, the vast majority of online panels rely on nonprobability-based sampling. Commonly, these are opt-in panel studies—often conducted in market research applications—in which individuals voluntarily choose to participate in surveys as a way to earn money or other rewards. While many in government, academic and even market research have resisted online panel studies because of concerns over the accuracy of the results they provide, there has been a tremendous growth in the use of this method and its growth likely will continue.

In an attempt to provide study results more closely reflecting results from probability-based samples and reflective of population parameters, panel studies typically rely on quotas to match the demographic characteristics of study participants to the characteristics of population members. Organizers of a panel study might work to ensure their study participants reflect members of a population in terms of age, race or ethnicity, gender, education levels, income levels, political ideology, and more. In this way, panel-study results may be more likely to enjoy a high degree of generalizability. Unfortunately, some research results indicates panel-based studies have quite a bit more error than studies using probability-based samples (e.g., Yeager, et al,, 2011) while other studies have produced results with more reasonable amounts of error (e.g., Ansolabehere & Schaffner, 2011).

Practitioners considering conducting a panel study or purchasing information based on panel research should be careful, however. Although the information panels provide may be extremely useful, the samples organizations use for most panel research are not representative because they are based on a nonrandom-selection process, are too small to be representative, or both. Because of this, the results of panel research may suffer from low external validity, or generalizability. This problem may be compounded by high rates of attrition, or mortality over time. That is, panel members may drop out of studies because they become busy or simply lose interest. When panel studies suffer from large-scale attrition, practitioners need to consider and use the results they produce carefully because they may lack representation.

Having said this, online panel surveys appear to be gaining increased acceptance among researchers and some panels are quite sophisticated producing results that are consistent with probability-based surveys. For these reasons and because they are a form of Internet-based survey, we have included panel studies in our discussion of formal, Web-based survey research. Having said this, readers should be careful in their interpretation and application of panel-based research. Despite the clear benefits and tremendous potential of this research method, there is a fair amount of uncertainty regarding panel surveys and practitioners should consider the results of panel studies with a clear understanding of their limitations.

Online Survey Critique

The advantages of online electronic surveys are numerous (Table 10.3). In particular, electronic surveys often cost less to produce and distribute than regular-mail surveys and many population subgroups such as professionals and government employees have near 100% Internet access. Web-based research tools and service providers generally make it inexpensive and easy for

Table 10.3 Characteristics of Online Surveys

Selected Benefits	Selected Limitations
• Generally inexpensive • Many population subgroups have near 100% Internet access including professionals, college students, and government employees • Reaches widely dispersed sample members easily • Nearly immediate delivery and potentially quick data collection • No interviewer bias	• Internet access still is limited; it is impossible to conduct a probability-based survey of the U.S. general population, for example • Potential participants need reasonably equipped computer and basic computer competence • It is difficult for researchers to encourage survey participation • Volunteer samples are likely to produce results low in generalizability • May suffer from very low response rates

those interested in research to put together and distribute a survey. Web-based surveys also can have some degree of flexibility. Because of the benefits of widespread and near-immediate delivery, researchers can use these surveys when sample members are widely dispersed geographically. In addition, the substantially shortened time it takes researchers to deliver and receive questionnaires generally reduces the time it takes to complete a project. Interviewer bias is not a concern to project managers when they use online surveys, and the availability of sampling lists and password-protected websites allows researchers to conduct probability sampling with key population subgroups.

In spite of these advantages, however, researchers' use of online surveys is tempered by some important limitations. Perhaps most important, research indicates that only 62% of U.S. adults have broadband Internet access at home (Zickuhr & Smith, 2013). As a result, it is impossible for project managers to conduct a representative, general-population study of U.S. adults online because a sizeable portion of the population cannot participate. This does not mean researchers should avoid using electronic surveys, but it does mean they should use them selectively. Internet use among some population subgroups such as college students, for example, is quite high and online surveys of these group members have a greater likelihood of being representative. In other instances, however, such as when researchers post surveys on bulletin boards and simply invite participation, the resulting sample is self-selected and not representative of any population.

Problems with low response rates also are a potential concern to researchers who conduct Web-based surveys. Wimmer and Dominick (2014) report a surprisingly large 5%–80% range of response for Web-based surveys. Without careful planning and execution based on a clear understanding of sample members, response rates for Web-based surveys typically will be in the low single digits. Increasing participation requires additional time and resources, which increases the cost it takes researchers to complete online surveys. As already discussed, a low participation rate potentially introduces bias into survey results and raises concerns about the external validity and reliability of a survey's findings.

Finally, online projects typically require respondents to have a reasonably equipped computer and they must possess a basic level of computer competence to participate in a

Web-based survey. As a result, while Web-based surveys have tremendous potential and a number of important benefits, researchers must use online surveys carefully and interpret their results with care.

Telephone Surveys

Telephone surveys involve contacting potential respondents and conducting personal interviews by telephone. This method of data collection represents a middle ground between mail surveys and personal interviews in that telephone surveys offer many of the advantages of personal interviews at a cost that often is competitive with that of mail surveys (Wimmer & Dominick, 2014). Although they do not offer the high degree of flexibility present in personal interviews, telephone surveys offer researchers more control and, until the early 2000s, often higher response rates than surveys conducted via regular mail or the Internet. Research team members also can complete telephone survey data collection in less than half the time it takes to complete many mail surveys. Historically, telephone surveys provided substantially the same information as a face-to-face interview at a much lower price (Groves, 1989) making them a common choice for academic and market researchers in the 1980s and 1990s.

Unfortunately, about the same time researchers were increasing their use of the telephone for research purposes telemarketers were increasing their telephone-sales efforts. The result was a significant increase in the number of unsolicited calls households received and an increase in people's wariness toward callers (Dillman, et al., 2009). In addition, telephone survey response rates began to fall precipitously as technology gave potential respondents a way to avoid unsolicited calls, first through unlisted numbers and answering machines and then through call blocking and caller identification. Finally, many citizens began to eliminate their land-line telephone service completely and online surveys started to emerge as a viable survey-research option. As a result, telephone survey use began to fall significantly in the early 2000s. Nevertheless, it remains a potentially useful tool for a variety of applications and is important for practitioners to understand and use effectively, as a result.

Telephone Survey Considerations

Telephone surveys (Table 10.4) require interviewers to introduce the survey to sample members or perhaps reintroduce the survey if research managers have mailed pre-notification cards or letters. Interviewers must then obtain cooperation, present instructions, ask survey questions, provide answer categories, and motivate participants to answer questions, all in a relatively brief time span. Throughout this process, interviewers are to operate as a channel through which to collect information from respondents without influencing their answers. It is a complex process that requires carefully trained interviewers. Telephone surveys require well-written questionnaires and instructions because they rely solely on verbal communication. Because of this, survey design and construction are based on utility rather than on aesthetics, as Figures 10.4. and 10.5. demonstrate. The interviewers' job is more difficult and the quality of the data collected is reduced if instructions, questions, and response categories are unclear.

Respondents are likely to have problems answering questions if the survey does not proceed in an obvious manner with the aid of transitional statements, if question placement is irregular or lacking apparent topical organization, or if the survey lacks easily understood instructions (Frey, 1989). A survey typically starts with introductory questions designed to

Table 10.4 Characteristics of Telephone Surveys

Selected Benefits	Selected Limitations
Relatively inexpensive (reasonable cost per completed interview) Data collection can be completed quickly Reaches widely dispersed sample members relatively easily Lists or random digit dialing make it possible to generate probability-based sample Rapport established with respondent can help gain compliance	Interviewer bias may occur Not every household has a land-line telephone and cell-only users are less likely to participate (potential source of bias) Households with land lines are likely to be equipped with answering machines and/or caller identification Short, relatively simple questionnaire required Limited interview flexibility Respondents may not answer thoughtfully

maximize respondents' interest and moves to issue-oriented questions concerning respondents' opinions, attitudes, and behaviors. The survey typically concludes with routine demographic questions that are important but also have the potential to reduce participation because respondents may find them offensive (e.g., questions concerning age or income).

In telephone surveys, project managers use open-ended questions sparingly because they interrupt questionnaire flow and require additional coding during data analysis. Given the importance of a well-designed survey instrument, questionnaire pretesting and comprehensive interviewer training are a pivotal part of the success of telephone surveys.

Although each survey is different and typically requires specialized interviewer training, there are common threads to the successful training of telephone interviewers. First, project managers want interviewers to pay particular attention to the survey introduction because this is the first point of caller contact. Second, interviewers need to learn to read questions exactly as they are written or appear on a computer screen; practice answering respondents' questions; practice selecting survey participants after they have made initial phone contact, if necessary; and learn how to encourage respondents to continue their survey participation and to use appropriate response categories as necessary. They must accomplish all of this while providing neutral feedback and probes so that they will not influence participants' responses.

Finally, interviewers must complete a call record. This is a record of the result of each call attempt, and it provides project managers with information they need to determine sample members who receive additional call attempts and to determine the response rate for a survey. The number and complexity of these and other issues necessitate thorough interviewer training before ever calling sample members (we provide tips for training interviewers in Chapter 12). Also, this training enables interviewers to provide participants with a pleasant interview experience and helps encourage higher rates of response.

When conducting mixed-mode research, pre-contact in the form of letters or cards effectively increases response rates in a manner similar to mail survey research. Pre-notification letters or cards also can help legitimize a study by providing information about why researchers are contacting sample members, the kind of information interviewers will request, and the

QUEST. ID#: _____   CALLER: _____

DATE: _____   PH#: _____

MEDIA AND POLITICAL DECISION MAKING SURVEY, FALL 2008

On a scale of 1–7, please indicate whether you strongly disagree or strongly agree with each of the following statements concerning the elections. On this scale, 1 means strongly disagree and 7 means strongly agree, so the lower the number the more you disagree with a statement, and the higher the number the more you agree with a statement. [REPEAT CATEGORIES AS NECESSARY.]

		ST DISAGREE				ST AGREE			
1e.	Voting gives people an effective way to influence what the government does.	1	2	3	4	5	6	7	RF/DK
2ms.	News coverage of the presidential election has told me all I need to know about the candidates.	1	2	3	4	5	6	7	RF/DK
3e.	I can make a difference if I participate in the election process.	1	2	3	4	5	6	7	RF/DK
4c.	Candidates for office are interested only in people's votes, not in their opinions.	1	2	3	4	5	6	7	RF/DK
5i.	I'm interested in election information.	1	2	3	4	5	6	7	RF/DK
6c.	It seems like our government is run by a few big interests who are just looking out for themselves.	1	2	3	4	5	6	7	RF/DK
7ms.	News media oversimplify issues they cover.	1	2	3	4	5	6	7	RF/DK

FIG. 10.4. Researchers construct telephone surveys to serve a utilitarian purpose and are less concerned about aesthetics because participants never see the survey. In this type of survey, researchers' primary concern is clear, unbiased communication via telephone. Questions include topic codes.

benefits of participation to sample members. Providing general information concerning the timing of survey phone calls helps to reduce the surprise associated with receiving an unanticipated phone call from an unknown source. Depending on the sample, many interviewers place initial calls on weeknight evenings (excluding Friday) from 6:00 p.m. to 8:30 p.m. Interviewers make callback attempts when they are unable to reach sample members during an initial call attempt. Although the number of callbacks differs according to survey characteristics, Wimmer and Dominick (2014) reported three callbacks produce contact about 75% of the time.

The Edward R. Murrow
College of Communication

Please indicate whether you strongly disagree or strongly agree with each of the following statements concerning the elections using a scale of 1 to 7. On this scale, 1 means you strongly disagree and 7 means you strongly agree.

	Strongly Disagree 1	2	3	Neutral 4	5	6	Strongly Agree 7
Voting gives people an effective way to influence what the government does	○	◉	○	○	○	○	○
News coverage of the presidential election has told me all I need to know about the candidates.	○	○	○	◉	○	○	○
I can make a difference if I participate in the election process.	○	○	◉	○	○	○	○
Candidates for office are interested only in people's votes, not in their opinions.	○	○	○	○	○	○	○
I'm interested in election information.	○	○	○	○	○	◉	○
It seems like our government is run by a few big interests who are just looking out for themselves.	○	○	◉	○	○	○	○
News media oversimplify issues they cover.	○	○	○	◉	○	○	○

0% [   ] 100%

[>>]

FIG. 10.5. This is the same survey created using Qualtrics for distribution via the Internet. It is more aesthetically pleasing, contains simple, direct instructions and participants can complete it at their own pace.

As with all research methods, the external validity, or generalizability, of telephone survey results depends on researchers' use of probability-based sampling methods, which are explained in Chapter 6. One benefit of telephone survey research is that, similar to mail surveys, research managers can purchase names and phone numbers of randomly selected members of a population from commercial vendors at a reasonable price, allowing them to use a probability-based sample relatively easily. These same companies typically can provide specialized samples at a higher price.

When researchers choose not to purchase a sample, they often can use a random-digit dialing (RDD) technique to overcome problems with unlisted telephone numbers and produce a random sample. The importance of randomization is explained in Chapter 6. Theoretically, RDD provides an equal probability of reaching a household with a telephone-access line regardless of whether its telephone number is listed or unlisted, and it replicates what would occur if a complete sampling frame existed (Lavrakas, 1993). There are several RDD techniques and most of them rely on standard area codes and telephone number prefixes, along with a randomization technique, to produce a telephone number suffix (the last four digits of a phone number). Although such techniques produce unusable telephone numbers such as numbers for businesses or government offices, they also produce a sample that provides coverage of unlisted telephone numbers.

Once interviewers make initial telephone contact, some studies require random selection of a respondent from within each household and interviewers must use a systematic process for selecting the member of the household to interview. If staff members do not use selection procedures, the resulting sample may include disproportionately high numbers of women and older adults, who are most likely to be home when interviewers call (Lavrakas, 1993).

Scholars and research practitioners have developed various selection procedures to avoid possible bias resulting from interviewing the person who answers the telephone. Unfortunately, they can be unwieldy to use. When interviewers use selection procedures, they typically increase survey costs because of the extra time required to identify and select respondents and the need to make additional callbacks when selected respondents are unavailable. In addition, interviewers may experience additional refusals because interviewees are confused or frustrated by the procedures they must follow before an interview begins.

One method that has gained widespread acceptance for randomizing respondent selection is to ask for the eligible person in the household whose birthday was most recent or who will have the next birthday (Salmon & Nichols, 1983). Although some researchers have expressed concerns these methods do not always produce a completely randomized sample, scholars and research professionals generally have embraced the birthday-selection method because it is generally effective, easy to use, and not time consuming or intrusive (Lavrakas, 1993).

Finally, computer-assisted telephone interviewing (CATI) now is common among universities and commercial-research firms. When research projects rely on CATI systems, interviewers use computers to facilitate nearly every aspect of the interview process. The computer dials the telephone number and the interviewer reads the introduction, respondent-selection procedures, and questionnaire off the screen. Interviewers use the computer to record and code responses and to help with statistical analysis. A CATI system is particularly useful if a questionnaire has complicated skip patterns or if researchers desire randomization of questions within a survey. The development of computer technology in connection with data collection is growing rapidly, and when a research organization properly implements a CATI system, it has the ability to improve the quality of telephone survey research.

Telephone Survey Critique

The benefits of telephone surveys contributed to a rapid increase in their use in the 1980s and 1990s but changes in technology have changed this. In terms of advantages, telephone surveys are relatively cost effective. They generally compete well with mail surveys in terms of cost and usually are less expensive than personal interviews. In addition, the short time in which researchers can complete a telephone survey is highly advantageous to practitioners. Given the importance of cost and time factors in many research-project decisions, these factors make telephone surveys a potentially advantageous choice of research professionals and public relations practitioners. In addition, research staff can collect data from a widely dispersed sample and it is relatively easy to purchase or generate a probability-based sample using random digit dialing. Telephone surveys also have enjoyed strong participation in the past. Generally, participation in telephone surveys has been much higher than participation in typical mail surveys, although this now has changed.

Unfortunately, technology such as answering machines, caller identification, and cell phones are making it more and more difficult for researchers to complete interviews via the phone. Ultimately, telephone surveys raise concerns about bias resulting from nonresponse (because of those who refuse to participate) and bias resulting from non-coverage (because of the growing number of individuals who no longer use landline telephones). While survey researchers can conduct surveys via cell phone, participation tends to be lower for sample members using cell phones than for those using landline phones (AAPOR Cell Phone Task Force, 2010).

What does all of this mean for the future of telephone survey research? No one knows for certain. While researchers' use of telephone interviews has declined, telephone surveys still appear viable as a research method (e.g., Ansolabehere & Schaffner, 2011). By conducting interviews via both landline phones and cell phones, researchers typically can reduce coverage errors. In addition, research concerning differences among participants and nonparticipants in surveys indicate that, while error increases as nonresponse increases, increasing rates of nonparticipation generally do not appear ruinous to the quality of survey research data (Groves, 2006; Keeter, Kennedy, Dimock, Best & Craighill, 2006). As a result, indications are that much nonparticipation in telephone surveys currently is not detrimental to survey research.

Even so, it still is important for project managers to do all they can to encourage as much participation as possible. Telephone surveys are likely to enjoy stronger participation when research staff members write and pretest survey introductions and questionnaires carefully, send pre-notification cards or letters, and use callbacks as needed. Survey sponsorship by a university or respected institution also helps to increase participation. Some organizations conducting telephone surveys even offer respondents small monetary incentives for participation.

Well-trained and experienced interviewers are indispensable in securing participation and help increase the quality of data studies produced. Interviewers contribute significantly to the accuracy and reliability of study results by answering participants' questions, encouraging participation in a professional manner, and moving data collection forward in an orderly fashion. In addition, interviewers may be able to establish rapport with respondents to help them obtain more complete and accurate information. At the same time, the use of interviewers potentially introduces bias into survey results. Interviewers should have no influence on respondents' answers, but instead serve only as a means of data collection. Interviewers require thorough training to learn how to provide neutral feedback and answer respondents' questions in a non-biasing manner.

Finally, telephone interviews suffer from some important limitations. Perhaps most obviously, researchers' use of visuals and similar interview aids is severely hampered. In addition, project managers' instructions, questions, and response categories must be easy for sample members to understand because interviewers are reading them over the telephone. Participants must be able to remember the question and the response categories, and they typically have no time to examine personal records or other information before responding to a question.

Open-ended questions are complicated for researchers to use in a telephone survey because they require research-team members to engage in additional coding and are sometimes difficult to interpret. In addition, researchers have no control over the survey environment—incoming calls, the doorbell, children, or other distractions commonly interrupt an interview. These interruptions and distractions sometimes require interviewers to schedule a callback that may result in an incomplete interview.

Project managers also must keep interviews relatively short. Most respondents are unwilling to complete a long survey over the telephone. Today, many market researchers try to keep their telephone interviews under 10 minutes. It can be difficult or impossible to collect a reasonable amount of high-quality data in such a short interview. Despite these difficulties, telephone surveys still are used by scholars, pollsters, and market researchers.

Personal Interview Surveys Including Mall Intercepts

When investigators conduct personal interviews, they may invite respondents to a research firm or collect information in a respondent's home or office. Research staff members administer questionnaires in a face-to-face interview, record respondent's answers, and possibly collect other information. There generally are two types of personal interviews: unstructured and structured.

In an *unstructured,* in-depth interview, interviewers ask broad questions and give respondents freedom to respond as they wish. The results of these interviews are challenging to analyze because of the unstructured nature of the interview. Because these interviews fail to measure participants' responses using standard scales and the interviews often involve individualized follow-up questions, the results they produce may lack a high degree of reliability and generalizability. As a result, personal surveys using in-depth interviews generally produce informal research results (discussed in Chapter 7).

In a *structured* interview, interviewers ask questions in a predetermined order and have little freedom to deviate from the questionnaire, also called a *survey schedule*. The result is an interview process that often produces high-quality data, has a reasonable response rate, and lends itself well to various topics and question types. For these reasons, many scholars and market research professionals have historically favored personal interviewing as a survey research method.

Several factors, however, have reduced the use of personal interviewing for survey research. These factors include a high cost per completed interview, the length of time researchers need to complete a research project, and the need for a high degree of administration and coordination. Nevertheless, personal interviewing is a flexible and effective survey method that serves some research-project settings effectively.

Personal Interview Considerations

In many research situations, several important benefits result from having an interviewer collect data in a one-on-one meeting with a survey participant (Table 10.5). A face-to-face meeting allows interview staff to interact and build rapport with potential participants, helping to increase survey response rates. Although this no longer is true, personal interview surveys historically have had the highest response rates of any of the primary research methods (Blair, et al., 2014). A high level of personal interaction also increases the likelihood that interviewers will obtain complete and accurate information by creating a comfortable interview atmosphere. This factor is important when interviews are long or questionnaires contain complex questions or skip patterns. In this instance, the interviewer has a great deal of influence over the administration of the questionnaire and other aspects of the data-collection process.

Personal interviews also are highly flexible, much more so than other survey methods. Research staff can answer respondents' questions; seek additional information to clarify ambiguous responses; show charts, pictures, or graphs; and even estimate respondent information such as general appearance. Finally, personal interviews do not depend on the literacy or education level of respondents, and they are not limited to persons with telephones, computers, or Internet access. These factors can significantly improve the reliability and external validity of survey results.

Personal interviews, however, are highly susceptible to bias. Interviewer-related bias, or error, occurs in face-to-face interviews when participants vary their answers because of the

Table 10.5 Characteristics of Personal Interviews

Selected Benefits	Selected Limitations
Interviewers establish rapport with participants	Often expensive; typically highest cost per respondent
Often results in high-quality data	Requires high degree of administration and interviewer training
Bias from sampling frame often is low	Data collection may take a relatively long time
High degree of interview/questionnaire flexibility	Strong potential for interviewer bias
	Some sample members difficult to reach

person conducting the interview (Fowler & Mangione, 1990). Participants who sense that interviewers agree or disagree as they respond to certain questions, for example, may knowingly or unknowingly alter their answers to survey questions. Respondents also may hesitate to report sensitive information and may be more likely to provide socially desirable responses in personal interviews. In research concerning racial attitudes, for example, participants are more likely to give socially desirable responses when the interviewer and interviewee are of different races (Campbell, 1981).

The need for extensive interviewer training and standardized interview techniques is important in personal-interview surveys given the importance of the interviewer in the data-collection process. A standardized research protocol helps all interviewers conduct their work in a consistent manner and reduces interview-related error (Fowler & Mangione, 1990). In addition, well-trained staff members help encourage survey participation among sample members; draw thoughtful, relevant responses to survey questions; and produce data that are high in accuracy, reliability, and external validity. Poorly trained staff members, in contrast, are more likely to collect poor-quality data and even bias survey results through their actions and statements. Problems may occur when poorly trained interviewers fail to probe inadequate answers, record respondents' answers incorrectly, ad lib questions rather than reading them as written, and behave in a way that could bias respondents' answers.

Personal Interview Variations

Group-Administered Surveys

Group-administered surveys combine some of the features of personal interviews and some of the features of mail or Web-based surveys. Researchers give the survey to members of a group who complete the survey individually, usually with minimal input from a survey administrator. Research staff typically give group-administered surveys to existing groups of people who are part of a selected sample, such as students, employees, or members of the armed forces. Sometimes, project managers recruit participants at shopping malls and take them to a vacant store location or in-mall research facility where they give them a survey. In this case, staff members typically thank respondents for their participation with a small gift. In each case, research staff members administer the survey in a group setting.

The research setting raises some concerns about group-administered surveys. Group members may feel coerced to participate, and if they fear their anonymity will be compromised, may not answer questions honestly. If a survey is sponsored by organizational management, for example, participants may be less likely to answer questions honestly fearing for their jobs. In addition, many preexisting groups do not lend themselves to probability-based sampling procedures. Although it is possible to use probability sampling for group-administered surveys— in particular, cluster sampling—it may be difficult for project managers to execute such sampling. When investigators do not use probability sampling, survey results generally suffer from limited reliability and external validity. Group-administered surveys have useful applications, but like all research methods, researchers must use them carefully to produce data that are accurate and reliable.

Computer-Assisted Interviewing

With the advent of mobile technology, some research organizations conduct personal interviews with the help of laptop computers or other mobile devices. In this form of interview, researchers might load questionnaires directly onto a computer, for example. Computer assisted personal interviewing (commonly called CAPI) occurs when research-team members conduct the interview. Computer assisted self-interviewing (commonly called CASI) occurs when respondents enter their own answers to questions—that is, complete a self-administered interview—using a computer or mobile device.

The main advantage of this type of interview is that computers aid in the standardization of survey administration and data collection. In some situations, they also may help reduce bias resulting from participant–interviewer interactions. In addition, researchers can use CAPI or CASI when survey questions are complicated, and photographs, computer graphics, or other visual aids will help participants understand questions and successfully complete an interview.

A primary drawback of computer-assisted interviewing is its expense. Even though the price of laptops and mobile devices has fallen considerably, the startup and maintenance costs associated with this form of personal interviewing are potentially quite high, especially when researchers need a sizeable number of devices to complete a large number of interviews.

In addition, CASI requires participants to have at least a minimal level of computer literacy so they can complete a questionnaire accurately, which raises concerns about the ability of researchers to locate a representative sample for some projects. Even though most people now use computers on a regular basis, CASI can present researchers with difficult challenges in some research settings.

As a final note, some researchers (e.g., Wimmer & Dominick, 2014) have raised concerns that computer-assisted interviewing is needlessly slow. Although this is not always the case, every research project typically has a time–cost tradeoff. In this instance, using more collection devices reduces the time it takes for researchers to collect data, but also costs more money. CAPI and CASI have clear benefits in some interview situations and some researchers are enthusiastic about their use, but the limitations of these interview methods have hindered their development as a primary interview method in many survey settings.

Mall-Intercept Surveys

Mall-intercept surveys, or simply mall intercepts, are a common method of collecting data in a personal interview format. Well-dressed interviewers, typically wearing matching-colored blazers and carrying clipboards, are a common sight in most malls today. Researchers also use different locations for intercept studies, including downtown areas, college campuses, and other areas that attract large numbers of people. When a field service provider conducts a mall intercept, project managers position interviewers at strategic locations throughout a mall and they verbally administer a survey to shoppers. Interviewers may ask shoppers to fill out a survey in a manner similar to group-administered surveys. They also typically provide a small inducement for participation.

Mall intercepts offer several benefits that have made them relatively popular, particularly among market researchers. Perhaps most important, researchers can complete a study relatively quickly if necessary, and mall intercepts are inexpensive relative to other research methods. Combined, these two benefits make mall intercepts an attractive research method given the time and budgetary constraints that hinder many research projects. In addition, the method is relatively uncomplicated and provides some flexibility in data collection.

Mall intercepts have some key limitations researchers should consider before undertaking a project, however. Perhaps most important, although it is possible for researchers to generate a probability-based sample in an intercept study, it is difficult as a practical matter. Even if researchers used a probability-based sampling method, the results would generalize to shoppers at a single mall. For these reasons, researchers normally use nonprobability sampling methods that, although convenient, limit the external validity and reliability of a study's findings. In addition, many shoppers actively avoid mall interviews, raising further concerns about the validity and reliability of study results. Interviews typically suffer from poor interview conditions because of noise, foot traffic, and other distractions, and researchers must keep questionnaires short and to the point. Although intercept studies offer benefits in certain circumstances and are popular among research practitioners, researchers must use them carefully because their results suffer from limited reliability and generalizability.

Personal Interview Critique

Researchers use personal interviews for several reasons, many of which concern data quality. Historically, face-to-face interviews produced high response rates, enhanced through the ability of interviewers to interact with sample members. When interviewers establish a strong rapport with survey participants, this gives them an easy opportunity to probe respondents' answers and seek clarification as necessary. Typically, personal interviews take place in comfortable interview environments. This encourages response and tends to make respondents less sensitive to questionnaire length. In addition, sampling bias can be low for personal interview surveys when researchers use Census Bureau data as a basis for the sampling frame. As a result of these characteristics, researchers can use personal interview surveys to produce high-quality data.

Personal interview surveys also offer interviewers a high degree of flexibility in obtaining research information. One-on-one interviews lend themselves to questions requiring in-depth answers and the interviewer can use visual aids or other interview devices as necessary. Interviewers also can explain questionnaire items that are confusing to respondents, particularly if the respondent misunderstands the intent of a question or is confused by a response category. Researchers can even estimate some information, although they should do this sparingly because of the potential to introduce error into survey results. The flexibility of one-on-one interviews also allows interviewers to use complex questionnaires with difficult skip patterns. The flexibility and quality of data produced through personal interview surveys have historically made this research method highly desirable to researchers.

Unfortunately, personal interview surveys suffer from significant drawbacks that have limited researchers' use of this survey method. Probably the greatest drawback to personal interview surveys is cost. Personal interviews generally are the most expensive survey research method (Blair, et al., 2014; Wimmer & Dominick, 2014). Depending on the specific project, these costs may result from the need for extensive interviewer training, field supervisors, travel expenses and other costs. In addition, personal interviews generally take longer than telephone interviewing because of logistical complexities. The administration of a personal interview survey is costly and complex when sample members are geographically dispersed. These are significant limitations given the importance of time and cost factors in many research decisions.

Another significant disadvantage in the use of personal interviews is the possibility of interviewer bias. The physical appearance, age, dress, race, sex, and verbal and nonverbal communication skills of the interviewer may influence respondents to provide answers that do not accurately reflect their feelings. In addition, participants may be hesitant to report highly personal behavior. The resulting bias hinders the reliability and generalizability of research results. A high degree of careful interviewer training and field supervision is required to avoid interviewer bias, which also contributes to survey cost and length. Finally, some samples are difficult to access for personal interviews. Busy work schedules make it difficult to schedule interviews with many adults, for example. In other cases, sample members live in areas with high crime rates. Each of these sample members is important as potential respondents and researchers must interview them if possible, but reaching them presents a special challenge when conducting personal interview surveys.

Mixed-Mode Surveys

Historically, researchers have conducted the vast majority of survey research via a single mode. Typically, researchers would look at their budgets, time constraints and information needs, as well as the characteristics of their sample. When designing the survey, they would select the method they believed was most likely to provide the information they needed at a reasonable level of quality within time and budgetary limits of a project.

As survey participation began to decline, many survey researchers began to consider using more than one survey mode, primarily in an attempt to increase response rates. In many instances, the use of multiple modes reflected the needs of survey-project managers who were desperate to reach sample members who would not answer a telephone, threw away mail surveys and generally were too busy to take the time to complete a survey. In addition, Internet penetration increased quickly among important population subgroups in the U.S. and researchers began to develop and study best practices for Web-based interviews. When combined with the low cost and quick distribution and collection potential of Internet surveys, researchers' use of mixed-mode surveys began to grow quickly. As a result, many researchers now design surveys with more than one mode.

Why did it take so long for researchers to embrace mixed-mode research? While the answers potentially are numerous, two reasons are critical. First, it wasn't necessary in most situations. Historically, single-mode survey participation has been relatively strong so there has been no need for researchers to consider expanding to multiple modes for interviews. Second, research indicates different modes of research can produce different answers to questions (Dillman, 2000) increasing the likelihood of measurement error.

There are a variety of ways to combine survey modes and any one of them might be useful for a specific research project (Dillman, et al., 2009). Perhaps the most common form of multiple-mode study involves making initial contact with sample members via one mode, such as through regular mail, and then collecting data via a different mode, such as through a Web-based survey. This type of mixed-mode research has the potential to increase response rates helping to reduce *nonresponse error* and also *coverage error*. Recall that nonresponse error occurs when members of a sample fail to complete a questionnaire. By not completing a questionnaire, non-respondents potentially are introducing error or bias into survey results. Coverage error occurs when not every member of a population has an equal (nonzero) chance of being included in a sample. A survey's results cannot represent everyone in a population if some people are systematically excluded from a sample. Increasing contact and participation using a mixed-mode study is likely to help reduce these errors.

In a second type of common mixed-mode survey, researchers use different survey modes to collect information from respondents as part of the same research project. This might be the case, for example, when college students receive a Web-based survey to complete and members of older population subgroups receive the same survey via regular mail. As an alternative, researchers might use one typically less-expensive mode to collect information from most participants in a survey and a second, often more-expensive mode to try to collect information from remaining sample members who are more difficult to contact. By limiting the need to use more-expensive survey modes to reach all sample members, researchers may be helping to reduce their overall costs. In addition, by combining methods, researchers will likely improve response rates and reduce error from coverage and nonresponse.

Final Thoughts

Survey research is an indispensable part of organizations' attempts to monitor their internal and external environments, solve complex problems, and plan and evaluate communication campaigns. Despite what some have suggested, there is no best method of survey research, and the potential advantages and disadvantages of each method do not apply equally, or even at all, to every research situation. The best method for a project depends on various situation-specific factors, and because of this, project managers must consider the use of a survey research method in relation to the needs and constraints of each situation.

It is important for practitioners to fully understand each survey research method because of this. Practitioners serve their own interest by understanding not only the key issues associated with the use of one survey method over another, but also issues associated with using mixed-mode surveys. In addition, practitioners should be well-versed in other aspects of survey implementation, such as the use of probability versus nonprobability sampling. This knowledge allows practitioners to make informed research decisions and engage in sophisticated problem solving and campaign-management activities.

11

Making Research Decisions
Questionnaire Design

Chapter Contents

- Understanding Reliability and Validity
- Levels of Measurement and Why They Matter
- Types of Questions and the Information Each Type Provides
- Ensuring Clarity and Avoiding Bias
- Questionnaire Layout and Design
- Handling "Don't Know" Responses
- Design Features that Affect Response Rate
- Final Thoughts

Writing a questionnaire seems simple. As the famous survey researcher G. W. Allport once said, "If we want to know how people feel: what they experience and what they remember, what their emotions and motives are like, and the reasons for acting as they do—why not ask them?" (Selltiz, Jahoda, Deutsch, & Cook, 1959, p. 236).

Unfortunately, just asking them is not as easy as it sounds. To avoid obtaining misleading results, questions must be clear, must elicit honest and reliable answers, and must keep the respondent interested in providing answers. The construction of questions must differ according to whether the questions are being read or heard, and the researchers can ask only as many questions as respondents have the time and energy to answer. It is easy to write bad questions and difficult to write good ones. Guidelines for questionnaire design typically focus on the importance of clarity, simplicity, and objectivity. Other important considerations include making questions interesting and letting the questionnaire progress logically so that respondents feel motivated to answer carefully.

Given the myriad of details that can make or break a questionnaire, the best questionnaires often turn out to be those you would have written once it is too late and you have the answers to the one you already used. To avoid post-survey regrets, questionnaires need to be pretested with attention to every detail and with members of the intended sample of respondents. Important issues to consider when writing questionnaires include the following:

- Validity and reliability concerns as they relate to the sample, the topic, and the client
- Levels of measurement and why they matter
- Ways to ensure clarity and avoid bias
- Types of questions and how the information each type provides differs
- Questionnaire layout and design to ensure logical flow and visual clarity.

Understanding Reliability and Validity

What is a "fast" city? If you are the communication manager for the local chamber of commerce, would you want your city rated as "fast" or as "slow"? National and regional rankings of cities, universities, corporations, and other organizations are published all the time. Depending on your interpretation, "fast" could mean exciting or it could mean stressful. Meanwhile, "slow" could mean boring or it could mean mellow and comfortable. One feature on fast cities included the rates of coronary heart disease in the city population. A ranking of 1 on this list probably would not make city leaders happy. But how can your organization effectively refute ratings based on objective data?

The answer is that measures need to be *valid* and *reliable*. A valid measure is one that seems to represent a particular idea in a convincing way. If people generally can agree that the things used to measure something such as a fast city are appropriate, the measures are considered valid. A reliable measure has consistency. If virtually anyone can replicate the study using the same measures and come out with similar answers, the measures are considered reliable. The fast city measures could be attacked as invalid by arguing that rates of coronary heart disease have no logical connection to other things the researchers measured, such as bank-teller speed.

For measures to be valid, the *concept* or idea they represent must be clear and the *operationalizations,* the actual measures themselves, must seem appropriate. To a great extent, determining validity is an exercise in persuasion. Reliability is easier to verify objectively.

Threats to validity and reliability sometimes are subtle, making it important to think carefully about the context in which surveys will be answered and interpreted. The measure itself must seem appropriate, and the scale used to measure it must seem appropriate. For example, operationalizing a concept such as a "livable" city might seem fairly straightforward. *The Economist* (2013)*, Business Week* (Konrad, 2013), and *U.S. News and World Report* (2013a) all publish regular features on this issue, focusing on characteristics such as crime rates, leisure options, housing costs, air quality and employment rates. Most people would agree that a more livable city would feature a lower crime rate, lower housing costs, and higher employment rates. But wait: Rising housing costs make a city more attractive, not less attractive, to those investing in real estate. So a high score on housing costs could mean less livable to some people and more livable to others. Meanwhile, some might argue that the most appropriate measure of livability would be people's perceptions of safety and satisfaction, rather than more objective measures of crime rates, numbers of parks, and so on.

Moreover, the measures chosen to operationalize livability might be criticized as insufficient to measure the concept appropriately. Perhaps factors such as average commute times, numbers of cultural events, and the quality of public schools (as indicated by standardized tests or availability of special services?) also need to be included to provide a valid measure. The three-quarters of the population who do not have school-age children, however, may not consider public school quality a primary determinant of a city's livability. In addition, some people might consider other factors such as nearby access to parkland as critical to quality of life, whereas others might consider a booming nightlife a higher priority. *U.S. News & World Report* (2013b) based "best cities for public transportation" on public transit ridership, safety and government spending, but some might equate high rates of ridership with overcrowding, and some might frown on high rates of government spending. And what about weather? Is a warm temperature an advantage or a disadvantage? It depends on whether you prefer to snow ski or water ski. Thus, to measure a fairly simple idea such as a livable city, the measures chosen must be the following:

- Sufficient in number to represent enough about the concept
- Appropriate as indicators of the concept
- Unambiguous, so that a high score on a measure clearly represents a high level of the concept.

Reliability, too, is an important characteristic for measures, with two primary components. First, the indicator of a concept must be replicable, that is, reusable with a similar result. The second component of reliability is how consistently the various operationalizations of a concept measure it. The operationalizations are the ways the researcher measures an idea, such as by counting the number of adults employed in the community during a single year. Consistency of the measures is important because observers tend to find a group of measures more convincing than any single measure. For example, if a city that scores highly on employment rates and cultural events also scores highly on individuals' reports of perceived safety and happiness with the town, these measures as a group representing "livability" can be called reliable. Some people may think employment rates are more important than personal reports of happiness, others may consider personal reports more important, but they all may accept the others' measures if convinced that the measures "hang together" consistently. This type of reliability can be measured statistically. Cities rightly emphasize the measures on which they look the best, as Pittsburgh, Pennsylvania has done (Sidebar 11.1).

Sidebar 11.1

Pittsburgh, Pennsylvania's Overall Quality of Life

(Imaginepittsburgh.com, 2013)

- Recently named "America's Most Livable City" for the second time (*Places Rated Almanac*); the only place to earn this honor twice
- The No. 1 "Most Livable City in the Nation" (*The Economist*)
- Among "Top 10 Cities for Job Growth in 2009" (*Forbes*)
- A "Top Travel Destination for 2008" (*Frommers*)

- The No 8. "Fun City" among the top 50 U.S. metro areas (*Bizjournals*)
- A "Top 10 Best City for Couples" (*Forbes*)
- The No. 1 "Best City for Relocating Families" in the nation (*Worldwide ERC*) and the No. 1 "Best Place to Raise Children" in Pennsylvania (*BusinessWeek*)
- Voted No.8 "Best U.S. Cities for Working Mothers" (ForbesWoman)
- While our friendly region was the inspiration for Mr. Rogers' Neighborhood, it was recently recognized for having the nation's No. 2 "Most Courteous Drivers" (*AOL Autos*)
- A "Top 10 Cities for Commuters" (*Forbes*)
- Ranked among the "Economically Strongest Metropolitan Areas" (*Pittsburgh Business Times: Brookings Institution*)
- Among the "Top 20 Cities that Eat Smart, Be Fit and Eat Well" (*Cooking Light Magazine*)

Rankings such as "most livable cities" can have major repercussions for organizations that score well or poorly or just better or worse than expected. According to Monks and Ehrenberg (1999), educational institutions that receive a less favorable rating from the *U.S. News and World Report* annual rankings of colleges and universities end up with a lower-quality pool of applicants and have to use bigger financial incentives to attract desirable students. As shown in Table 11.1, rankings of universities can vary dramatically depending on the methods used to develop the ranking scores. As Gater (2002) has asserted, it is nearly impossible to identify, quantify, and measure characteristics that fairly compare colleges and universities because they have wide-ranging sizes, scopes, missions, and disciplinary emphases. Nevertheless, many parents of potential students, students themselves, faculty considering potential employers, and donors considering potential beneficiaries look for rankings to help them in their decision making.

As Table 11.1 shows, rankings change depending on the types of institutions included in the analysis, how the organizations collect data about "quality" or "value," and when they collect the data. Some raters, for example, analyze institutional-level data such as admission and graduation rates. Some include surveys of university administrators. Some include surveys of alumni or current students. In addition, some surveys rely on volunteer samples rather than representative samples. Table 11.1 shows that even the same organizations rank universities differently depending on whether they focus on a particular issue (e.g., academic excellence or cost) or include a range of issues important to most applicants (e.g., academic excellence *and* cost) in the ranking criteria. Meanwhile, other organizations may focus on criteria important only to some, such as political activism.

In addition, rankings can change depending on whether they focus exclusively on schools that meet criteria for "national" universities or mix public and private colleges along with public and private universities. Communication managers at educational institutions must understand validity and reliability issues to deal effectively with these rankings, which frequently receive a great deal of news coverage and attention from important constituents. Universities that wish to publicize rankings that make them look good while de-emphasizing those that portray them less positively have to defend the validity and reliability of one survey credibly while attacking the validity and reliability of another.

Levels of Measurement and Why They Matter

Survey questions fall into four general levels, shown in Table 11.2, that dictate how researchers can and should analyze the questions. It is important to know your level of measurement because the level dictates the types of statistical tests you can perform on the data. Usually, clients hope to determine how certain beliefs or behaviors relate to other beliefs and behaviors. If researchers collect measures at a low level of measurement, this seriously limits the analyst's ability to investigate relationships of interest.

To choose the appropriate level, questionnaire designers need to consider how they will use the information gathered. Sometimes, for example, a client may wish to know whether people first heard about an organization from the newspaper or from a friend. Other times, however, the organization may need to know how often newspapers and friends are sources of information or how credible the information received from these sources seems. Each of these needs requires a different level of measurement.

The first level of measurement is called the *nominal* level, referring to names or categories of things. This level of measurement can show how many people fit into particular categories. The possible answers for a nominal variable should be mutually exclusive and exhaustive. In other words, they should not overlap and should include all possible responses. For example, a question assessing sex of the respondent would include "male" and "female" (social scientists consider "gender" a socially constructed identity rather than a category dictated by chromosomes). A question assessing information sources could include "media" and "interpersonal sources." Including "media" and "newspapers" would be redundant instead of mutually exclusive because the newspaper is a form of media. Eliminating "interpersonal sources" or including "friends" but not "coworkers" or "family" would not be exhaustive. Nominal variables can be useful, but little statistical analysis can be performed using this type of variable. In other words, they have little explanatory power, because people either fit a category or do not fit. They cannot fit a little bit or a lot.

The second level of measurement is called the *ordinal* level, indicating that some meaningful order exists among the attributes. These questions should have answers that are mutually exclusive, exhaustive, and ordered in some way. A popular type of ordinal question is the ranking question, as in "Please rate the following five publications according to how much you like them, with the best one rated 1 and the worst one rated 5." It would be possible to know which publications do best and worst, but it would not be possible to know whether Publication 2 is liked a lot better than Publication 3 or is liked just a little bit better.

The ranking question often creates problems and researchers generally should avoid it. It not only provides information of limited use but also frequently confuses or frustrates respondents. Because respondents often find ranking difficult to do, it tends to discourage them from completing a questionnaire. Sometimes respondents may consider two or more items to be ranked in a tie, and other times they may not understand the basis on which they are supposed to determine differences. When asked to rank the corporate citizenship of a group of companies, for example, respondents may not feel they have enough information on some companies to distinguish them from others. Respondents often rate several things as the same number. This renders their response to the entire question useless to the analyst, because if two or more items are tied, they no longer are ranked. In other words, the answers no longer are mutually exclusive, which makes the question of less use than even a nominal variable would be.

Table 11.1 Year 2012 Rankings of Universities Based on Varying Criteria from Different Organizations

	Sierra Club	Washington Monthly	Forbes	Princeton Review	Kiplinger	U.S. News & World Report
	"Greenest Colleges"	"Best Liberal Arts Colleges Based on Contribution to the Public Good"	"Best Return on Investment"	"Most LGBT Friendly"	"Best In-State Public College Values"	"Best National Universities"
1.	University of California, Davis	Bryn Mawr College	Harvey Mudd College	New York University	University of North Carolina – Chapel Hill	Harvard University
2.	Georgia Institute of Technology	Swathmore College	California Institute of Technology	Stanford University	University of Virginia	Princeton University (tied for 1st)
3.	Stanford University	Berea College	Massachusetts Institute of Technology	Emerson College	University of Florida	Yale University
4.	University of Washington, Seattle	Carleton College	Stanford University	Wellesley College	College of William and Mary	Columbia University
5.	University of Connecticut	Harvey Mudd College	Princeton University	Bennington College	University of Maryland – College Park	University of Chicago
6.	University of New Hampshire	New College of Florida	Harvard University	University of Wisconsin-Madison	University of California – Los Angeles	Massachusetts Institute of Technology

7. Duke University	Williams College	Dartmouth College	Macalester College	New College of Florida	Stanford University
8. Yale University	Macalester College	Duke University	New College of Florida	University of California – Berkeley	Duke University
9. University of California, Irvine	Wellesley College	University of Pennsylvania	Prescott College	SUNY – Geneseo	University of Pennsylvania (tied for 8th)
10. Appalachian State University	Amherst College	University of Notre Dame	Sarah Lawrence College	University of California – San Diego	California Institute of Technology
Scoring Method					
Self-report survey scoring rubric in several areas	Self-report and publicly available national data in social mobility, research, and service	Self-report survey data on cost of attendance and earnings	Student response to single survey item as part of a larger survey	Admission and graduation rates; cost of attendance; average debt at graduation	Acceptance, retention, and graduation rates; small class sizes; ACT/SAT scores
Reference					
(Sierra Club, 2013)	(Washington Monthly, 2013)	(Forbes, 2013; Payscale.com, 2012)	(DegreeSearch.org, 2012)	(Kiplinger, 2013)	(U.S. News and World Report, 2013)

Table 11.2 Levels of Measurement for Credibility

Nominal Level	Which of the following companies do you find credible?
Ordinal Level	Rank the following companies from most credible to least credible, with the most credible company receiving a 5 and the least credible company receiving a 1.

Interval Level	How credible are the following companies?				
	Not at all credible			Very credible	
	1	2	3	4	5

Ratio Level	How many times in the last year have you wondered whether the following companies were telling you the truth?				
	0	1	2	3	4	5 or more

Organizations that want to rank a group of things may find it better to let rankings emerge from the data rather than trying to convince respondents to do the ranking themselves. They can do this by creating a question or a group of questions that can be compared with one another, such as, "Please rate each of the following information sources according to how much you like them, with a 4 indicating 'a lot,' a 3 indicating 'some,' a 2 indicating 'not much,' and a 1 indicating 'not at all.'" The mean score for each information source then can be used to create a ranking.

The third level of measurement is the *interval* level. This is the most flexible type of measure to use because it holds a lot of meaning, giving it a great deal of explanatory power and lending itself to sensitive statistical tests. As with the previous levels of measurement, the interval measure's responses must be mutually exclusive, exhaustive, and ordered. The order, however, now includes equal intervals between each possible response. For example, a survey could ask people to indicate how much they like a publication on a 10-point scale, on which 10 represents liking it the most and 1 represents liking it the least. Researchers can assume that the respondent will think of the distances separating 2 and 3 as the same as the distances separating 3 and 4, and 9 and 10.

Most applied research—and some scholarly research—assumes that perceptual scales such as strongly agree–strongly disagree or very important–not important at all can be considered interval-level scales. Purists disagree, saying they are ordinal because respondents might not place an equal distance between items on a scale such as *not at all . . . a little . . . some . . . a lot* in their own minds. Fortunately, statisticians have found this usually does not present a major problem. Nevertheless, researchers must construct such measures carefully and pretest them to ensure they adhere to the equal-distance assumption as much as possible.

The fourth level of measurement is the *ratio* scale, which is simply an interval scale that has a true zero. This means the numbers assigned to responses are real numbers, not symbols representing an idea such as "very much." Ratio scales include things such as the number of days respondents report reading news on a particular website during the past week (0–7 days), the number of minutes spent reading the business section, or the level of confidence they have that they will vote in the next presidential election (0–100% likelihood of voting). This type of scale is considered the most powerful because it embodies the most meaning.

Types of Questions and the Information Each Type Provides

Various strategies exist for eliciting responses at each level of analysis. Keep in mind that respondents will find complex questions more difficult and time consuming to answer. As a result, the survey designer has to make trade-offs between obtaining the most meaningful information and obtaining any information at all. For example, a lengthy and complex mail survey may end up in the trash can more often than in the return mail. Even if the questions are terrific, the few responses that come back may not compensate for the loss of information resulting from the number of nonresponses.

Likewise, people answering a telephone survey will find complicated questions frustrating because they tend to comprehend and remember less when hearing a question than when reading a question. This is the reason telephone surveys often use generic response categories such as the Likert scale type of response, in which the answer range is: strongly agree, agree, neutral, disagree, strongly disagree. People on the telephone often have distractions in the background and other things they would rather be doing, making them less involved in the survey. This makes it easier for them to forget what a question was, what the response options were, or how they answered a previous question on the survey.

For ease of response and analysis, questions on surveys usually are closed ended, meaning respondents choose their preferred answer from a list of possibilities. Open-ended questions, which ask a query but provide space for individual answers instead of a response list, invite more information but are often skipped by respondents and are time consuming to analyze afterward. As a result, surveys typically limit the number of open-ended questions to 2 or 3 out of 50. The primary types of closed-ended questions are the checklist, ranking scale, quantity/intensity scale, Likert-type scale, frequency scale, and semantic differential scale.

Checklists

The checklist is a nominal variable, providing categories from which respondents can choose. They can be asked to choose only one response, or all that apply.

Checklist example:

Please indicate whether you are male or female:

☐ Male   ☐ Female

Please indicate which of the following news apps you have read this week (check all that apply):

☐ Newspaper   ☐ TV or cable news   ☐ News aggregating   ☐ Other
   apps   apps   apps

Ranking Scales

Ranking scales are ordinal variables, in which respondents are asked to put a set of items in the order they think is most appropriate. Ranking scales are problematic because they require respondents to perform a complex and often confusing task. They must decide which choice should come first, which should come last, which comes next, and so on until the whole series of comparisons is completed.

> *Ranking example:*
>
> Please rank the following issues according to how important they are to your decision to support a congressional candidate this year. Put a 1 by the issue most important to you and a 5 by the issue least important to you:
>
> ☐ Taxes
> ☐ Economy
> ☐ Environment
> ☐ Education
> ☐ Crime

Questionnaire designers can help respondents answer a ranking question by breaking it into a series of questions, so that the respondents do not have to do this in their heads. Although this method makes it easier for respondents to answer ranking questions, it uses a lot of valuable questionnaire space.

> Among the following issues, which is the *most* important to your decision about a congressional candidate this year?
>
> ☐ Taxes
> ☐ Economy
> ☐ Environment
> ☐ Education
> ☐ Crime
>
> Among the following issues, which is the *next most* important to your decision about a congressional candidate this year?
>
> ☐ Taxes
> ☐ Economy
> ☐ Environment
> ☐ Education
> ☐ Crime
>
> Among the following issues, which is the *least* important to your decision about a congressional candidate this year?
>
> ☐ Taxes
> ☐ Economy
> ☐ Environment
> ☐ Education
> ☐ Crime

Quantity/Intensity Scales

The quantity/intensity scale typically is an ordinal- or interval-level variable in which respondents choose a location on the scale that best fits their opinion on a list of options that forms a continuum.

Quantity/intensity example:

How much education have you completed?

- ☐ Less than high school degree
- ☐ High school diploma or GED
- ☐ Some college (no degree; may be currently enrolled)
- ☐ Vocational certificate or associate's degree
- ☐ College graduate (bachelor's degree)
- ☐ Some graduate work (no degree)
- ☐ Master's or other graduate professional degree
- ☐ Doctoral degree

Likert-Type Scale

The most frequently used scale is known as the Likert scale.

Likert scale example:

Please indicate whether you strongly agree, agree, disagree, or strongly disagree with the following statement:

The Bestever Corporation is responsive to public concerns

- ☐ Strongly agree
- ☐ Agree
- ☐ Disagree
- ☐ Strongly disagree

Other variations on the Likert scale appear frequently on questionnaires. Some popular response ranges include the following:

- Very satisfied/Somewhat satisfied/Somewhat dissatisfied/Very unsatisfied
- Strongly oppose/Oppose/Support/Strongly support
- Very familiar/Somewhat familiar/Somewhat unfamiliar/Very unfamiliar
- A lot/Somewhat/Not much/Not at all
- A lot/Some/A little/None
- Always/Frequently/Seldom/Never
- Often/Sometimes/Rarely/Never
- Excellent/Good/Fair/Poor

Quantity/Intensity example:

Please indicate if the following reasons have been *very important* (VI), *somewhat important* (SI), *not very important* (NVI), *or not at all important* (NAI) to your decision whether to give to the Big-Effort Association in the past.

The tax benefits resulting from giving	VI	SI	NVI	NAI
Because you like being involved with the BEA	VI	SI	NVI	NAI

Another variation of the Likert scale is known as the *feeling thermometer*, which can be modified to measure levels of confidence, degrees of involvement, and other characteristics. The feeling thermometer as presented by Andrews and Withey (1976) used 10- or 15-point increments ranging from 0 to 100 to indicate respondents' warmth toward a person, organization, or idea.

Feeling thermometer example:

100	Very warm or favorable feeling
85	Good warm or favorable feeling
70	Fairly warm or favorable feeling
60	A bit more warm or favorable than cold feeling
50	No feeling at all
40	A bit more cold or unfavorable feeling
30	Fairly cold or unfavorable feeling
15	Quite cold or unfavorable feeling
0	Very cold or unfavorable feeling

Yet another variation of the Likert scale uses pictorial scales, which can be useful for special populations such as children, individuals lacking literacy, or populations with whom language is a difficulty. Often, the scales range from a big smiley face (very happy or positive) to a big frowny face (very unhappy or negative), or from a big box (a lot) to a little box (very little):

Frequency Scales

The frequency scale is an interval or ratio scale. Instead of assessing how much a respondent embraces an idea or opinion, the frequency question ascertains how often the respondent does or thinks something.

Frequency example:

How many days during the past week have you watched a local television news program?

- ☐ 7 days
- ☐ 6 days
- ☐ 5 days
- ☐ 4 days
- ☐ 3 days
- ☐ 2 days
- ☐ 1 day
- ☐ 0 days

About how many times have you visited a shopping mall during the past month?

☐ 16 times or more
☐ 11–15 times
☐ 6–10 times
☐ 1–5 times
☐ 0 times

Sometimes frequency scales are constructed in ways that make it unclear whether equal distances exist between each response category, which makes the meaning of the measure less clear and the assumption of interval-level statistical power questionable.

Frequency example:

In the past month, how many times have you done the following things?

	Never	1–2 times total	3–4 times a week	1–3 times a week	1 time a week	More than once a week
Visited an REI location	____	____	____	____	____	____
Visited the REI website	____	____	____	____	____	____
Purchased an item for myself from REI	____	____	____	____	____	____
Purchased a gift from REI	____	____	____	____	____	____

Semantic Differential Scales

The semantic differential scale is an interval-level variable, on which respondents locate themselves on a scale that has labeled end points. The number of response categories between the end points is up to the questionnaire's designer, but it is useful to have at least four response options. More options make it possible for respondents to indicate nuances of opinion; beyond a certain point, which depends on the context, a proliferation of categories becomes meaningless or even confusing. An even number of response categories forces respondents to choose a position on the issue or refuse to answer the question, whereas an odd number of response categories enables respondents to choose the neutral (midpoint) response.

Semantic differential example:

Please rate your most recent experience with the Allgetwell Hospital staff:

Incompetent	_ _ _ _ _ _ _ _ _ _ _ _ _ _ _ _ _ _ _ _	Competent
Impolite	_ _ _ _ _ _ _ _ _ _ _ _ _ _ _ _ _ _ _ _	Polite
Helpful	_ _ _ _ _ _ _ _ _ _ _ _ _ _ _ _ _ _ _ _	Unhelpful

Semantic differential questions can provide a lot of information in a concise format. Written questionnaires especially can include a list of semantic differential items to assess the performance of an organization and its communication activities. Because this type of question includes information as part of the answer categories themselves, some consider these items more valid than Likert scale items. For example, a Likert scale question asking if the staff seemed competent could bias respondents who do not want to disagree with the statement, whereas a semantic differential question that gives equal emphasis to "competent" and "incompetent" as end points may elicit more honest answers. Psychologists have demonstrated that agree/disagree question batteries can suffer from acquiescence (Warwick & Lininger, 1975, p. 146), which occurs when people hesitate to express disagreement.

Measuring Knowledge

Often, an organization wants to determine what people know about a topic. One option is to give a true/false or multiple-choice test. The advantage of the multiple-choice test is that, if carefully written, it can uncover misperceptions as well as determine the number of people who know the correct answers. The wrong answers, however, must be plausible. A second option is to ask open-ended questions in which people must fill in the blanks. This requires a lot of work from the respondent but potentially provides the most valid answers. A third option is to ask people how much they feel they know, rather than testing them on what they actually know. This technique seems less intimidating to respondents. Finally, follow-up questions can ask people how sure they are of a particular answer.

Ensuring Clarity and Avoiding Bias

Wording can affect the way people respond to survey questions. As a result, it is important to pretest for clarity, simplicity, and objectivity. Using standardized questions that have been pretested and used successfully can help prevent problems. Of course, because every communication issue has unique characteristics, standardized batteries of questions suffer from lacking specific context. Often, a combination of standard and unique items serves the purpose well. When designing questions, keep the following principles in mind:

1   *Use words that are simple, familiar to all respondents, and relevant to the context.* Technical jargon and colloquialisms usually should be avoided. At times, however, the use of slang may enhance the relevance of a questionnaire to a resistant target public. For example, asking college students how often they "prefunk" could elicit more honest responses than asking them how often they "use substances such as alcohol before going out to a social function," which is both wordy and could have a more negative connotation to the students than their own terminology. When using specialized terms, it is important to pretest them to ensure the respondents understand them and interpret them as intended. Try to choose words that will not seem patronizing, class specific, or region specific. Choosing to ask about "pasta" instead of "noodles" when assessing audience responses to messages about an Italian restaurant could alienate some respondents who think "pasta" seems pretentious.

2   *Aim for precision to make sure the meaning of answers will be clear.* Avoid vague terms. For example, the word often may mean once a week to some people and twice a day to others. *Recently* could mean "this past week" or "this past year." Terms such as here and there do not set clear geographic parameters.

Do not leave room for interpretation. People responding to a question about how often in the past year they have donated to a charitable organization may consider each monthly contribution to a church a separate donation. The sponsor of the survey, however, may have intended for respondents to indicate to how many different organizations they have made donations during the past year. Avoid hypothetical questions because people often are not very good at, or may have trouble being honest about, predicting their own behavior. Direct questions about cause or solutions also may be difficult for respondents to answer validly (Fowler, 1995). It is better to let the reasons for things emerge from the data analysis by looking at the associations between attitudes and behaviors instead of asking respondents to make those associations for the researcher.

Finally, because the use of negatives in a question can create confusion, use positive or neutral statements while providing respondents with the opportunity to disagree. For example, instead of asking, "Do you think the Neverong Corporation should not change its partner benefits policy?" a survey can ask, "Do you think the Neverong Corporation's partner benefits policy should change or stay the same?"

3 *Check for double-barreled questions.* Each question must cover only one issue. Asking if respondents rate staff as "polite and efficient," for example, makes it impossible for respondents to choose "polite but inefficient" or "impolite but efficient" as their answer. Sometimes a double-barreled question is subtle, and the problem occurs because a phrase requires respondents to embrace an assumption they may not hold. For example, asking "How likely are you to use this service on your next visit to Funpark?" assumes there will be a next visit.

4 *Check for leading or loaded questions.* A leading question prompts the respondent in one direction instead of treating each possible response equally. Asking the question, "How much did you enjoy your visit?" leads respondents in the direction of a positive answer, whereas the question, "How would you rate your visit?" allows enjoyment and disappointment to be equivalent answer categories, making it easier for respondents to choose the negative answer.

A loaded question biases the answer through the use of emotionally charged words, stereotypes, or other words that give a subtle charge to a phrase. Loading can occur in the question or in the answer. For example, the question given earlier asking respondents to indicate which issues are most important to them in an upcoming election mentions only some of the possible alternatives about which voters may care. Health care, abortion, social security, welfare, agricultural issues, and race/gender equality are among the many issues not even mentioned. In addition, loading can occur by using words that have positive or negative connotations, such as "unwed moms" versus "single mothers." Loading also can occur in frequency scales. Asking people whether they had 0, 1, 2, 3, 4, 5, 6, 7 or more alcoholic drinks during the past week, for example, gets more people to acknowledge having 3 or 4 drinks than asking people whether they had 0, 1, 2, 3 or more alcoholic drinks during the past week (Fowler, 1995). People often feel marginalized by picking what seems like an extreme response.

5 *Check for social-desirability effects.* Some people find it difficult to express an opinion or report a behavior they think is inconsistent with what most other people think or

do. Some also find it difficult to give a response they think the surveyor disagrees with or disapproves of. It is well documented, for example, that a higher percentage of people claim to have voted in an election than actually turn out at the polls. Try to write questions so that people find it easy to give a negative or potentially unpopular response.

One technique for reducing social-desirability bias is to include an introduction to a sensitive question that makes any response seem normal and acceptable. For example, Fowler (1995) noted that asking people if they own a library card can seem threatening because a "no" response could be perceived as a lack of interest in reading, which might seem socially unacceptable. As a result, Fowler suggested the following introduction: "Many people get books from libraries. Others buy their books, subscribe to magazines, or get their reading material in some other way. Do you have a library card now, or not?" (p. 36).

6   *Provide enough context to enable people to respond realistically or remember accurately.* On the whole, questions should be as brief as possible so that they can be digested with the least effort. Nevertheless, the goal of questionnaire design is to construct questions such that answers will provide the most meaningful information possible. As a result, adding some context can be useful. It helps, for example, to ask people to recall behaviors over a limited time or from a recent time, such as during the past week.

In general, questionnaire designers must avoid yes/no items. Besides providing information of limited usefulness for statistical analysis (dichotomous questions are nominal variables), this type of question leaves no room for a respondent to answer "maybe" or "well, it depends." Answers to dichotomous questions, as a result, can be misleading. Similarly, questions usually need to avoid "always" and "never" as categories. "Almost always" and "almost never" give people the opportunity to be more context specific.

Questionnaire Layout and Design

Most discussions of survey design focus on how to construct the questions themselves, but other aspects of design, such as how items appear on a page or the order in which questions appear, also can make a difference to respondents.

Ease of Reading

It helps to give respondents "chunks" of questions at a time. A series of questions without a break can become boring and confusing. People may get lost in a written questionnaire that has 10 items in a row, for example, checking off their responses to Question 6 on the line for Question 5. Assessing respondents' interest in different types of university-related news, for example, is difficult to follow in a continuous format.

The following are topics that might be covered in a publication from Central State University. For each one, please tell me whether you are *very interested* (VI), *somewhat interested* (SI), *not very interested* (NVI), or *not at all interested* (NAI) in receiving information about each topic*:

1.	The university's branch campuses	VI	SI	NVI	NAI	RF/DK
2.	Student accomplishments	VI	SI	NVI	NAI	RF/DK
3.	The financial needs of the university	VI	SI	NVI	NAI	RF/DK
4.	The work of the administration	VI	SI	NVI	NAI	RF/DK
5.	How donations are being used	VI	SI	NVI	NAI	RF/DK
6.	News about teaching	VI	SI	NVI	NAI	RF/DK
7.	Athletic accomplishments	VI	SI	NVI	NAI	RF/DK
8.	News about university research	VI	SI	NVI	NAI	RF/DK
9.	University nostalgia and history	VI	SI	NVI	NAI	RF/DK
10.	News about alumni	VI	SI	NVI	NAI	RF/DK
11.	News about campus life	VI	SI	NVI	NAI	RF/DK

*RF/DK = refused or don't know.

Questions are easier to answer in chunks. Generally, chunks of three or four items at a time work well.

The following topics that might be covered in a publication from Central State University. For each one, please tell me whether you are *very interested, somewhat interested, not very interested*, or *not at all interested* in receiving information about each topic*:

12.	The university's branch campuses	VI	SI	NVI	NAI	RF/DK
13.	Student accomplishments	VI	SI	NVI	NAI	RF/DK
14.	The financial needs of the university	VI	SI	NVI	NAI	RF/DK
15.	The work of the administration	VI	SI	NVI	NAI	RF/DK
16.	How donations are being used	VI	SI	NVI	NAI	RF/DK
17.	News about teaching	VI	SI	NVI	NAI	RF/DK
18.	Athletic accomplishments	VI	SI	NVI	NAI	RF/DK
19.	News about university research	VI	SI	NVI	NAI	RF/DK
20.	University nostalgia and history	VI	SI	NVI	NAI	RF/DK
21.	News about alumni	VI	SI	NVI	NAI	RF/DK
22.	News about campus life	VI	SI	NVI	NAI	RF/DK

* RF/DK = refused or don't know.

Respondents on a telephone survey also can become fatigued by a long list of items and will benefit from a break during which the surveyor gives a new introduction, even if the questions in the next section do not focus on anything new.

Example from a phone survey:

OK, now I need to know if you [READ SLOWLY] *strongly agree* (SA), *agree* (A), *disagree* (D), or *strongly disagree* (SD) with each of the following statements about politics and the media.* [REPEAT CATEGORIES AS NECESSARY.]

	(5)	(4)	(3)	(2)	(1)	(9)
19. The media rarely have anything new to say.	SA	A	n	D	SD	RF/DK
20. I'm interested in campaigns and election information.	SA	A	n	D	SD	RF/DK
21. The news media only pay attention to bad news about political issues and candidates.	SA	A	n	D	SD	RF/DK
22. Candidates for office are interested only in people's votes, not in their opinions.	SA	A	n	D	SD	RF/DK
23. My vote makes a difference.	SA	A	n	D	SD	RF/DK

This won't take much longer and we really appreciate your help. These next few questions also are about politicians and the media. Do you *strongly agree* (SA), *agree* (A), *disagree* (D), or *strongly disagree* (SD) that:

	(5)	(4)	(3)	(2)	(1)	(9)
24. Politicians are out of touch with life in the real world.	SA	A	n	D	SD	RF/DK
25. I pay attention to campaign and election information.	SA	A	n	D	SD	RF/DK
26. There's often more to the story than you hear in the news.	SA	A	n	D	SD	RF/DK
27. Political campaigns are too mean spirited.	SA	A	n	D	SD	RF/DK
28. I actively seek out information concerning the government and politics.	SA	A	n	D	SD	RF/DK
29. I have a say in what the government does.	SA	A	n	D	SD	RF/DK

*n = neutral; RF/DK = refused or don't know.

It also is important to remember how easily people answering telephone surveys can get lost. Because they do not see the questions, they can forget what a series of questions is about or what the response options are. In addition, changing response options frequently will slow them down and may make it difficult for them to keep track of what they are supposed to be doing. Forcing them to slow down can help improve the validity of answers by making sure they think carefully about their answers, but it also can hurt validity by causing utter confusion. Pretesting, over the phone, is essential.

Clarity of Graphics

Work by Christian and Dillman (2004) has shown that respondents to self-administered surveys pick up important cues from the visual design of survey questions and answers. For example, Christian and Dillman demonstrated that respondents become confused if a scale is broken up into two columns instead of being presented in a single row or in a single column.

Clear:

Overall, how would you rate the quality of education that you are getting at SU?

- ☐ Excellent
- ☐ Very Good
- ☐ Good
- ☐ Fair
- ☐ Poor

More confusing:

Overall, how would you rate the quality of education that you are getting at SU?

| ☐ Excellent | ☐ Good | ☐ Poor |
| ☐ Very Good | ☐ Fair | |

Directionality and Response Set

Another issue that can affect validity is known as *directionality* and refers to the order in which response categories are presented. It helps both respondents and analysts to associate negative opinions with lower numbers and positive opinions with larger numbers. Some questionnaires, for example, ask respondents to choose a numbered response instead of checking a box. This can make a questionnaire easier to read—it makes the middle of a scale more obvious—and it also makes data entry easier because the computer usually has to receive numbers.

Example of numbered responses on a written survey:

How important are the following for helping you choose your preferred candidates or issues?

	Not at all important						Very important
Newspapers	1	2	3	4	5	6	7
Radio	1	2	3	4	5	6	7
Television	1	2	3	4	5	6	7
Blogs	1	2	3	4	5	6	7
Friends	1	2	3	4	5	6	7
Family	1	2	3	4	5	6	7

Questionnaire designers also need to pretest for response set, which is a form of response bias. If response categories always have the negative response first (on the left if on a written questionnaire) and the positive response last (on the right), people may begin to answer questions too quickly, without thinking them through. Response set can make a group of questions seem related simply because they appear near each other on the questionnaire. In other words, people may have marked similar answers on the questions out of convenience or habit, instead of because they thought deeply about each question and agreed that a similar answer applied to each.

Using "Skip Patterns" Effectively

Sometimes a question will not apply to all respondents. In this case, researchers use a screening question, or a series of screening questions. This series of questions is known as a *skip pattern*. On a written questionnaire, it is important to make it clear when and which questions should be skipped. Often instructions such as "GO TO Q. 6" appear next to the appropriate response to the screening question. Sometimes, questionnaires include graphic elements such as boxes or arrows to guide respondents. Such devices can make a questionnaire look cluttered and confusing, however, so skip patterns need to be pretested carefully. Christian and Dillman (2004) found that directional arrows help prevent confusion, as does placing instructions to skip a question *before* the response options instead of after them. Their example looked something like this:

Clear:

A. Have one-on-one meetings with professors contributed significantly to your SU education?

If you haven't had many one-on-one meetings, just skip to Question 9.

☐   Yes
☐   No

Confusing:

A. Have one-on-one meetings with professors contributed significantly to your SU education?

☐   Yes
☐   No

If you haven't had many one-on-one meetings, just skip to Question 9.

Handling "Don't Know" Responses

One subtle but major issue in the use of surveys is how to handle people who do not have an opinion on a particular question. One of the problems with survey research is that most people do try to offer an opinion for the researchers, even if they must manufacture an opinion on the spot. For example, the average American respondent queried about the economic situation in Mozambique probably knows little about Mozambique's economy, unless it has been in the news. Few people knew much about Chechnya until two brothers originally from Chechnya decided to plant bombs at the finish of the Boston Marathon in 2013. Nevertheless, if asked for an opinion many people offer one, even though some may decline to answer the question. Such opinions, based on little or no information, mean little because they are unstable. They are pseudo data, not real data.

Researchers must be ready to handle respondents' potential lack of opinion. The most common way is to include a "don't know" response among the answer categories. The drawback of making it easily available is that respondents may be tempted to use it. Making it subtly available is easy to do on a telephone survey because the interviewer can be instructed not to read that option. On a written survey, the respondents will see the option if it is available. Respondents will use the "don't know" option for one of two reasons: either they truly do not know, or they do not feel like answering the question. To prod people who are not motivated to think about an issue to report an opinion, even if it is top of the mind, surveyors may eliminate the "don't know" option, forcing respondents to leave the question entirely blank if they do not want to answer it.

It is important to consider two issues here. The first is that "don't know" can be a meaningful response, of great usefulness to the communication manager. For example, if a large proportion of participants respond "don't know" to a question about corporate reputation, the organization can conclude that it does not have a bad reputation even if it does not have a good reputation. In other words, the company may learn that instead of running a persuasion campaign, it needs to launch an awareness campaign. This frequently is the case, but organizations must be skilled at collecting and interpreting "don't know" responses to make the appropriate diagnosis.

Another important issue about "don't know" responses is that "don't know" cannot be interpreted the same way as "neutral." Likert scales, for example, often feature a neutral category, which can tempt people to avoid taking a position on an issue. Nevertheless, "neutral" does not necessarily mean the respondent lacks information on which to base an opinion. A neutral opinion is an opinion. Responding "neutral" to a question about providing child care in the workplace, for instance, may mean "I don't care; this doesn't affect me," or "I am satisfied either way," rather than "I have no information on which to base an opinion." Both options can be made available to respondents to avoid misinterpreting the findings. Another way to handle the possibility of "don't know" responses is to provide information in the introduction to a question that gives the respondent background on which to base an opinion. This has important advantages and disadvantages. For example, three members of the state legislature in Washington state included the following questions on a survey of their constituents:

> About 9 in 10 Washington voters in a recent nonpartisan survey said education was their number one issue this year. About 2 in 3 people surveyed said education was underfunded and worse than it was 4 years ago. How would you address this?
>
> - Divert funding from other areas of state government and put it into higher education?
>
>   YES   NO
>
> - Increase enrollment and on-campus opportunities at our state's colleges and universities?
>
>   YES   NO

Increase enrollment opportunities at branch campuses?

YES   NO

Increase the number of courses available to students at off-campus sites via television, e-mail, and the Internet?

YES   NO

Build more classrooms, laboratories, and other facilities for off-campus instruction?

YES   NO

The value of this strategy is that it gives a client the opportunity to see how respondents will react to an issue of emerging importance, about which they may not yet know much. This can help the client respond to the issue effectively.

The risk associated with this strategy is that it can bias the question in the direction of the information selected for inclusion. Some organizations do this intentionally on bogus questionnaires sent out as fund-raising appeals or to attract media attention through "created" opinion. This is a blatantly unethical practice that is denounced by the American Association of Public Opinion Researchers (2003), and it violates the principles of the PRSA code of professional ethics (Sidebar 11.2).

Sidebar 11.2

Push Polls*
(Not to be confused with legitimate polling)

What is a push poll?

- A push poll is an insidious form of negative campaigning disguised as a political poll that is designed to change opinions, not measure them.

How do push polls differ from legitimate political polls?

- Legitimate polls measure existing opinion among representative samples of the public and voters.
- Push polls contact large numbers of voters in order to change their opinions.
- Legitimate polls accurately describe candidate characteristics in order to understand voter reactions.
- Push polls frequently distort candidate characteristics in order to influence voters.
- Push polls go beyond the ethical boundaries of political polling and bombard voters with problematic statements about candidates in an effort to manufacture negative voter attitudes.

For example, push polls mostly ask questions like:

"Would you be more or less likely to vote for (NAME OF RIVAL CANDIDATE) if you knew he had avoided the draft / falsified his resume / been arrested / gone through bankruptcy / patronized prostitutes / failed to pay child support / failed to pay income taxes?"

How do you spot a push poll?

- The organizations conducting these "polls" are not usually recognized as professional pollsters.
- Push polls typically call thousands of people. The people called are not a representative sample of voters. Instead, they're people who are targeted because they're thought to be undecided voters or supporters of a rival candidate.
- The truth of the questions is stretched or fabricated.
- Usually people's answers are not tabulated; the intent is to create a negative effect on potential voters.

What is the position of the American Association for Public Opinion Research on push polls?

- AAPOR Councils have repeatedly warned members and the public about the iniquity of push polls.
- The 1996 and 2000 Councils issued formal condemnations of push polls.
- AAPOR has reacted to complaints about suspected push polls and made investigations.
- AAPOR urges its members and the media to uncover push-polling and help us alert the public.

How can you help in combating push polls?

- Attempt to get the name and location of the organization doing the "interviewing."
- Ask about the sponsors, the number of people called, the questions asked, and how the information from the poll is being used.
- Contact AAPOR at AAPOR-info@goAMP.com.

*Reprinted with permission from AAPOR. For more information on the American Association for Public Opinion Research, go to www.AAPOR.org.

Some organizations do this in hopes of educating the public; the problem is that only a small sample of the public is answering the survey. Surveys are opportunities to gather unbiased information to guide a campaign, not an opportunity to educate the public. Still others use them to see if providing certain information on a survey can change people's responses. This type of survey is known as a "push poll" and often is used by political campaigns. Not only is the information provided on such "surveys" biased in favor of the sponsoring candidate but also the survey often ends with a fundraising appeal. Turning surveys into vehicles for persuasion and fundraising defeats the purpose of collecting objective data and compromises the reputation of surveyors trying to do authentic research. It is no wonder, with such unethical practices going on, that a declining number of people agree to answer market research (or any other) surveys.

Design Features that Affect Response Rate

Every survey requires an introduction to inform respondents of the study's purpose. The introduction also represents an opportunity to motivate respondents to cooperate. Mail surveys and telephone surveys have different introductions, especially suited to the context. Nevertheless, the primary information to include in an introduction remains the same and includes the following:

- What the study is about
- Who the sponsor is
- How the results will be used
- Why respondents should be a part of the study (how they were chosen and why they should care about this)
- The extent to which their responses will be confidential or anonymous.

Anonymous means that no one, including the researchers, will know respondents' identities. *Confidential* means that the researchers will have identifying information for some purpose, such as matching respondents from the same household or calling back to gather more information later, but their identities will be kept secret from everyone else. Some organizations have "human subjects committees" or "institutional review boards" that must approve of study materials and may require additional elements as well.

The Mail Survey Introduction

Despite the popularity of the Internet, mail surveys still can be useful tools. Mail surveys must have a cover letter introducing the study. It should be brief (never longer than one page), on a letterhead (to identify the sponsoring institution and lend credibility to the study), include a contact person for questions or concerns, indicate how long the survey will take to fill out (be honest), and make it clear how to return the questionnaire (providing a self-addressed, stamped, return envelope is essential). Researchers must thank respondents for cooperating and tell them their participation is important. It also helps to give respondents a deadline for returning the questionnaire, of no more than a week, so they do not forget about it. Finally, the letter may include information about an incentive provided for cooperating with the study.

The Telephone Survey Introduction

Introductions by telephone need to be even shorter than those by letter. If possible, keep the introduction to two sentences. In those two sentences, identify the sponsor and the purpose of the study, the way respondents have been selected, the length of time required for answering the survey, and the importance of the respondent's part in the study. It also helps to have the callers identify themselves by name so respondents do not think the caller has anything to hide.

At the end of the introduction, proceed directly to the first question on the survey. Do not ask permission to begin explicitly because this invites participants to tell you that you have called at an inconvenient time. Instead, solicit their permission to begin through the explanation of the survey and the assurance that their answers are important. This introduction makes it obvious you plan to ask questions and you hope they will answer them. Because respondents probably will be skeptical of your motives and more interested in whatever they were doing before you called, you want to get right to the first question on the survey to gain their confidence and capture their interest. You want to make the first question nonthreatening, general, and interesting so that the respondents will think the questionnaire is easy and worth their time (Sidebar 11.3).

Nuances can make a difference. For example, identifying the organization at the outset gives the project more credibility and can make it clear you are not a sales person. In addition, calling the project a *study* instead of a *survey* makes it sound less threatening and makes it clear that this will be not be one of those sales calls masquerading as a survey. Also, saying you have called them long distance (if you really are) or that your study is being sponsored by a university or respected institution can make their selection and the study itself seem more special (Dillman, 2000).

Pre-notification Cards or Letters

The use of pre-notification cards to tell respondents that a survey will be happening soon helps boost response rates. If they understand the purpose of the study ahead of time, they will be less likely to throw away an envelope that looks like a direct mail solicitation or to hang up on a call from an individual who sounds like a telephone solicitor. Letters or postcards both suffice, but postcards offer the advantage of being readable at a glance and less costly to mail. Envelopes may go unopened into the trash.

SIDEBAR 11.3

A Standard Telephone Introduction With a Screening Question

Hello, my name is _____ . I'm calling long distance from _____. We're conducting a study of _____ and I have a few questions for a registered voter 18 years of age or older.

Are you registered to vote?

[IF YES: BEGIN SURVEY. DO *NOT* STOP TO ASK PERMISSION TO BEGIN.]

[IF NO:

Is someone else in your household registered to vote?

May I speak with that person please?

BEGIN AGAIN WITH NEW RESPONDENT.]

IF NO: Thanks for your time. Good-bye.

Follow-up Mailings

Mail surveys typically achieve a wide-ranging 5% to 40% response rate with a single mailing (Wimmer & Dominick, 2014). Research has found, however, that reminders can boost response rates to 75% or better. It may take a number of reminders with additional questionnaires to achieve a 75% return, with each reminder netting fewer responses. As a result, the research manager needs to decide the extent to which the cost of reminders is worth the additional responses. Generally, each reminder garners half the number of responses that the previous mailing achieved. As a result, a single reminder can increase a 30% response rate to a 45% response rate or a 40% response rate to a 60% response rate.

Incentives

It is difficult to give telephone respondents a concrete reward for their participation, although credit card companies have tried promising a bonus credited to the respondent's account in return for answering a survey. Mail and Internet surveys, however, frequently include incentives. Usually the incentive is provided ahead of time to motivate the person to respond, instead of afterward as a reward. Monetary incentives ranging from $2 to $5 are especially popular, with amounts over $10 rare. Other incentives can include a gift certificate or product samples. Organizations sometimes promise donations to a charity in hopes of appealing to respondents' sense of altruism. Questionnaires returned in person or using the Internet can include a raffle ticket to enter respondents into a drawing for a valued prize such as an electronic gadget. These drawings are kept separate from the questionnaire container to preserve the anonymity of the respondent.

Sensitive Questions

Sensitive questions should never appear at the beginning of a survey. Instead, the most sensitive questions come at the end so that respondents who may quit the study because of a particularly offensive question will already have answered most of the questionnaire. This is why demographic questions almost always appear at the end of a survey. Many people especially dislike identifying their income levels, ethnic background, and age.

Encouragement

Because respondents to telephone surveys cannot see the questionnaire, they will be worrying about how long the interruption will take. If the questionnaire seems to go on too long, they will lose interest. As a result, it helps to thank them every so often for continuing, as well as assuring them that the survey will end soon. For example, one phone survey about the media and politics includes the phrase, around Question 23, "This won't take much longer and we really appreciate your help. These next few questions . . . " Then, anticipating increasing impatience from the respondent, the survey includes more encouragement at Question 30, "I have just a few more questions about your use of the media . . . " before beginning the introduction for the next set of questions. Before the demographic questions at the end of the survey, a last bit of encouragement ensures respondents that these are the final set of queries.

Response Set

When constructing a questionnaire, it is important to scatter questions that measure a concept instead of clustering them together. The reason for this is that people's answers can suffer from *response set*, which means they answer a set of questions similarly because they are answering too quickly or not thoughtfully enough rather than because they think similarly about each question in the set. Response set can make measures look statistically reliable but can render them meaningless or invalid. When commissioning a survey from a research firm, managers should make sure the outfit's findings provide both reliable and meaningful information.

Length

No perfect length exists for a questionnaire, although a good bit of research focuses on the topic. For example, people seem more likely to participate in a mall-intercept survey limited to a 5″ × 8″ card. It is difficult to keep people on the phone longer than 5 to 8 minutes, which means a telephone survey of more than 40 to 50 questions will suffer from attrition as people begin to hang up. Questions appearing at the end of the survey will end up with a smaller sample of responses than questions appearing at the beginning of the survey.

In mail surveys, a longer mail survey will receive less cooperation than a shorter survey, but the number of pages is not always the deciding factor. For example, respondents may prefer the ease of reading and feeling of accomplishment that comes from having fewer questions and more white space, even if that necessitates using more pages. Some survey designers find a two-column format makes questionnaires more reader friendly. Disagreement exists about the use of single-sided versus double-sided printing. Double-sided printing cuts the number of pages but can confuse respondents, who may end up accidentally skipping pages. As with everything else, it helps to pretest surveys using different formats to see which works the best.

Interviewer Directions

Untrained or confused interviewers can ruin a survey. Interviewers must sound enthusiastic, polite, and confident. They also need to present questions clearly, which means they need to enunciate carefully and speak slowly. To prevent interviewer bias from affecting the validity of the responses, they need to present the surveys in a consistent way. As a result, interviewer directions must be clear. Chapter 12 discusses interviewer training in some detail.

Generally, instructions to the interviewer appear in all capital letters or in brackets to set off the information from the parts that are read aloud. Words that require special emphasis can be italicized or put in boldface. Information read by an interviewer needs to sound conversational in tone rather than formal.

> *Sample interviewer instruction:*
> As I read the following list of information sources, please tell me whether the source is [READ SLOWLY] very important, important, unimportant, or very unimportant to you: [REPEAT CATEGORIES AS NECESSARY.]

Cultural/Language Sensitivity

Knowing the target public well can aid design and secure a better response. For example, question wording may need to change depending on the age of the participants. Translators may be needed if a phone survey aims to interview people who do not speak English. Mail surveys, too, can benefit from making translations available.

Final Thoughts

Clearly, a myriad of design issues contribute to the effectiveness of a questionnaire. Research managers need to write questions in a way that will provide the most meaningful and unbiased information. The order of questions must seem logical and interesting to the respondent, and the directions to respondents and interviewers must prevent confusion. Researchers need to use pretesting to check for the existence of subtle bias in word choice.

No perfect survey exists, but various strategies can boost response rates and increase the validity of responses. The details can make the simple task of asking questions seem overwhelmingly complicated, but the use of preexisting instruments or batteries of questions can provide useful models to follow. For the manager working within a tight budget, the principles laid out make it possible to run a reliable, valid, and useful survey. In addition, various books and online survey tools can guide managers through the process. Meanwhile, for managers able to hire experts to do the job, the principles presented here can make it easier to monitor a survey research firm to ensure top-quality results.

12

Collecting, Analyzing, and Reporting Quantitative Data

Chapter Contents

- Designing Surveys for Easy Data Entry
- Training Interviewers
- Call Tracking
- Timing of Telephone Surveys
- Response Rates
- Reporting Univariate Relationships
- Reporting Relationships among Variables
- Final Thoughts

We all know the saying: "Garbage in; garbage out." For communication managers, this means "collect data effectively to report data effectively." The best survey will seem easy to answer, straightforward to analyze, obvious to report, and intuitive to the reader. Although most of the work goes into the writing of questions themselves, research managers also need to think ahead to analysis and reporting strategies. Designing surveys and training interviewers with data entry in mind can improve the speed and reliability of results. Prioritizing how and what results will most convincingly guide and justify proposed communication strategies can aid analysis and ensure that managers collect data in a way that makes it possible to create necessary tables and figures. Once the results become available, the manager can think about how to share good, bad, or surprising news with the client.

Designing Surveys for Easy Data Entry

Computer-assisted data collection techniques often make it simple to create easily analyzed questionnaires. Many survey research centers, for example, use CATI (computer-assisted telephone interviewing) systems, in which telephone or personal interviewers enter data directly into the computer as they talk with respondents. Managers also increasingly use do-it-yourself online systems such as Qualtrics (Qualtrics.com), Zoomerang (zoomerang.com) and Survey Monkey (surveymonkey.com), which provide question templates for survey designers that range in sophistication (and cost) and can be customized. Statistical packages that go far beyond Excel® provide powerful analysis tools. The cost for these packages ranges from several hundred dollars to tens of thousands of dollars.

CATI or computer-assisted data collection (CADC) eliminates the need for cumbersome data entry procedures. Interviewers using a CATI system typically wear a headset and ask questions prompted by the computer. As they type in the answers from each participant, the computer automatically updates the database to incorporate the new information. This type of system also is growing more popular for personal interviews, particularly for sensitive issues. Computer-aided data entry can reduce data entry errors by 77%. In addition, it can reduce confusion on complicated questionnaires that include conditional, or branching, questions. *Conditional questions* separate participants into groups depending on their response. For example, consumers who answer "yes" to a question about having previously purchased a company's product can go on to answer questions about the product's quality and the company's responsiveness. Consumers who answer "no" answer a different set of questions that may focus on the potential interest in the company's or the competitors' products.

If survey questionnaires must be entered manually, several design issues can make data entry more efficient. A familiarity with these issues also can help researchers using automated systems, because just as spellcheck will not prevent certain types of writing mistakes, automated systems will not prevent certain types of data-collection errors. For example, you will waste everyone's time if you ask respondents "how satisfied are you" with a client's new consumer interface when you have neglected to ask if they ever have used it in the first place. As a result, the following principles can make it easier to analyze and interpret the results even if researchers have access to automated data collection systems.

Directionality

As mentioned in Chapter 11, attention to directionality can make results more intuitive to report. *Directionality* refers to the match between the numbers that represent answers to questions in the computer and the idea they symbolize. For example, on a Likert scale, a 5 should represent "strongly agree" and a 1 should represent "strongly disagree" to ensure that a high score means more agreement instead of less agreement. Always use a high number to indicate a positive response, even if the question is negatively worded. For example, a higher number should represent "very often" on a scale measuring "how often have you had difficulty receiving your order on time?"

Coding and Code Books

Questionnaire designers usually include the numbers representing the data on the questionnaires themselves, but when that is not possible they rely on a separate code book. The *code book* is a copy of the questionnaire with annotations that direct data entry personnel and analysts. The annotations include short variable names—abbreviations for the questions—along with information about where in a computerized data set the answers appear and what numbers represent each answer. We address each of these issues separately.

The advantage to including numbers within the questionnaire is that data analysts (and entry personnel in situations requiring manual data entry) see a constant reminder of the codes they must use, making memory lapses less likely. This can help considerably on complicated questionnaires. Numbers also can help respondents follow along when answers include a lot of response options. In the example below, note how much easier it is to find the center of the scale when it includes numbers instead of blanks:

Which of the following best describes our customer service representatives?

Incompetent	1	2	3	4	5	6	7	8	9	Competent
Impolite	1	2	3	4	5	6	7	8	9	Polite
Unhelpful	1	2	3	4	5	6	7	8	9	Helpful

Which of the following best describes our customer service representatives?

Incompetent	–	–	–	–	–	–	–	–	–	Competent
Impolite	–	–	–	–	–	–	–	–	–	Polite
Unhelpful	–	–	–	–	–	–	–	–	–	Helpful

Questionnaire designers avoid permitting the questionnaire to become so cluttered with numbers that it becomes difficult to read or appears impersonal. As a result, some codes appear only in the code book. It also helps both interviewers and data entry personnel to have sets of answers clustered in small groups, such as in the following example:

OK, thinking again about some election issues, please think now about the public schools where you live, and tell me about the job your schools are doing educating students in each of the following areas. Use a scale from 1 to 5, with 1 meaning *very poor* (VP) and 5 meaning *very good* (VG):

	VP				VG	
26. The first area is basic subjects such as reading, writing, and math	1	2	3	4	5	DK/RF
27. Training students for a specific job?	1	2	3	4	5	DK/RF
28. Preparing students for college?	1	2	3	4	5	DK/RF
29. Teaching moral values?	1	2	3	4	5	DK/RF

On an Internet-based survey, this means having a set of questions appear on a Web screen that does not require scrolling. This presents special challenges when designing questionnaires that can be read on small mobile devices. Note that the example includes abbreviations for the interviewers (such as DK/RF for "don't know or refused to answer") that respondents will not need to hear or see. When using an Internet survey database you may need to program the survey to include "don't know" as a separate option from "refused" or "neutral."

Edge Coding

Usually, variable names and locator information for the data set in the computer appear only in the code book, or in the margins for an interviewer-assisted phone or in-person survey. The behind-the-scenes use of codes to provide important contextual information is known as *edge coding.* These codes include the following:

1   *Tracking information.* Often, survey supervisors want to keep a record of which interviewer completed each questionnaire, on which day the survey took place if data collection occurs over several days or weeks, where the survey took place if data collection occurs in several locations, which type of survey someone answered in a mixed-mode project (such as mail or Internet-based survey), and any other information of background importance. Each set of answers is given an identification number, which makes it easier to check for and correct mistakes in data entry.

2   *Question information.* On hard copy codebooks, most information regarding placement of question answers go in the left margin next to the questions, as shown below:

We're already halfway through our survey, and we really appreciate your help. Now, if you have declined to give money to SU at any time in the past, please tell me if each of the following issues have been *very important, somewhat important, not very important*, or *not at all important* reasons for your decision.

(N/A, Have never refused to give)   __ (8) __

			4	3	2	1	8	9
(32) GETTO	27. You just didn't get around to it		VI	SI	NVI	NAI	N/A	RF/DK
(33) AFFORD	28. You felt you couldn't afford it		VI	SI	NVI	NAI	N/A	RF/DK
(34) DISSAT	29. You are dissatisfied with the quality of education at SU		VI	SI	NVI	NAI	N/A	RF/DK
(35) NODIFF	30. You feel your gift would not make a difference to students at SU		VI	SI	NVI	NAI	N/A	RF/DK

Note that the abbreviations for each question appear in all capital letters and are greatly abbreviated. The information in parentheses refers to the location of the question responses in the data set. Most often this number points to the column in a spreadsheet.

3   *Answer codes.* The numbers at the top of each column refer to the codes used by the computer to indicate the answers to the questions regarding barriers to giving. Automated survey programs differ in whether and how they shows these codes to the survey respondent and often can be programmed to the researcher's specific needs. In the sample shown above, a 2 indicates "not very important," a 4 indicates "very important," and so on.

It is important to be able to find a particular respondent's questionnaire quickly in case of data-entry mistakes. For example, a respondent may type an "O" instead of a "0" into a field intended to accept numbers. The identification number associated with each respondent makes it possible to isolate the questionnaire researchers need to fix. Keep in mind that nearly every data set will require some corrections or recoding for intuitive reporting of results; thus the process of fixing mistakes in the data set has a name: *data cleaning*.

Data Entry Conventions

You can assign any number to any answer, but people become accustomed to seeing things a certain way. For example, it is common to assign a 1 to a "yes" answer and a 0 to a "no" answer. In a series of items for which respondents "check all that apply," each checked response would get a 1, and each blank response would get a 0.

Most questions do not need more than seven or eight response categories. As a result, another conventional number code is 8, to indicate "don't know." Researchers often use either a 9 or a blank for refusals.

Remember that the codebook must account for each answer. When questions have multiple answers possible ("check all that apply"), each possible answer must be coded as a separate item, as shown below:

50. What is your race or ethnicity? (MARK ALL THAT APPLY)

_____ American Indian or Alaska Native
_____ Asian
_____ Black or African American
_____ Hispanic/Latino/Spanish origin
_____ White
_____ Other
_____ REFUSED ALL [Code all other choices as 9]

[Coded as No = 0 / Yes = 1 / Refused = 9]

Open-Ended Questions

Most computer programs do not lend themselves to *qualitative analysis*, meaning the analysis of words or pictures instead of numbers. As a result, analysis of open-ended data usually requires a special program or procedure. Open-ended questions usually are skipped during data entry of closed-ended questions. A separate word processing file can be used to keep track of identification numbers and open-ended comments for each question. A file or notebook also must be kept for interviewers and data entry personnel to log problems or anomalies that will require decisions from the research manager, such as what to do with a respondent who wrote in "lots of times" for a question asking how often he or she used a particular product in the past month, instead of writing in a number from 0–31.

Training Interviewers

Interviewers must act polite even when respondents do not. They also must read slowly and clearly, avoid lengthy conversations, and read each question in a consistent way. As a result, interviewer training is an essential part of reliable data collection. Interviewer instructions vary slightly depending on the organization, the project, and the facilities, but some general guidelines apply to most situations. In their classic survey research text, Warwick and Lininger (1975) suggested several keys to standardized personal interviewing, which apply equally well to telephone interviews.

1   *Use the questionnaire carefully, but informally.* The questionnaire is a tool for data collection. Interviewers must be familiar with the purposes of the study and the questionnaire, including question order, question wording, skip patterns, and the like. Interviewers who are well prepared can take a relaxed, informal approach to their work. This helps maximize interviewers' ability to collect high-quality data and avoid carelessness in the interview process.

2   *Know the specific purpose of each question.* Interviewers need to understand what constitutes an adequate response to each question to satisfy the purposes of the research project and to improve their use of the questionnaire. This information must be discussed as a part of interviewer training and reviewed before data collection begins.

3   *Ask the questions exactly as they are written.* Even small changes in question wording can alter the meaning of a question and a participant's response. Researchers must assume each participant has answered the exact same question. The consistent, unbiased wording of each question provides a strong foundation for the accuracy and reliability of study results. Neutral comments such as, "There are no right or wrong answers; we just want to know your opinion," should be used sparingly and only when interviewer feedback is required.

4   *Follow the order indicated in the questionnaire.* The order of questions in a survey instrument has been purposefully determined and carefully pretested. Arbitrary changes made in question order reduce the comparability of interviews and potentially introduce bias into questions that are sensitive to question order.

5   *Ask every question.* Interviewers need to ask every question, even when participants have answered a previous question or made comments that seem to answer a later question. Respondents' answers to questions often change as a result of small changes in question wording. In addition, the intent of questions that seem similar often are different. Researchers develop and pretest question wording carefully and with a specific purpose in mind. Unless respondents terminate an interview early, each question must be asked of each respondent.

6   *Do not suggest answers.* Interviewers must never assume to know a respondents' answer to a question, even after a respondent has answered seemingly similar questions in a consistent manner. All answers must be provided by the respondent.

7   *Provide transitions when needed.* A well-written questionnaire needs to contain transitional phrases that help the respondent understand changes in topics, question types, or question response categories. Interviewers use these transitional phrases to help guide a respondent through a questionnaire.

8   *Do not leave any question blank.* Interviewers need to make every effort to have participants answer every question, except those intentionally left blank because of skip patterns. Although researchers may choose to use a questionnaire even if questions are left blank, omitted questions reduce the reliability and external validity of survey results. It is best if each respondent answers every applicable question.

Call Tracking

Telephone surveys typically use call sheets or tracking files that have lists of numbers and places to record the outcome of each call attempt. Sometimes call sheets include special information such as giving history for donors or an individual's code number if an organization is calling a different individual—such as a spouse or a parent—to obtain more complete information from a household. The basic information appearing on most call sheets or in tracking files is similar to the following, which is based on a telephone survey:

CM	=	Completed interview
RF	=	Refused
NA	=	No answer (sometimes AM appears separately to indicate answering machine)
BUS	=	Business/beeper/fax/modem
BZ	=	Busy signal
TM	=	Terminated
DIS	=	Disconnected/out of service
LB	=	Language barrier
NE	=	No eligible respondents at this number
CB	=	Call back appointment (interviewers fill in the details)
OTH	=	Other (interviewers fill in the details)

Timing of Telephone Surveys

The optimum times of day and days of the week for doing telephone surveys vary depending on geographic region, time of the year and target audience. Although calling on Sunday evenings usually works well, a manager will not want to plan a survey for Super Bowl Sunday, for example. Generally, however, weeknights between 6:00 p.m. and 8:30 p.m. are considered reasonable hours for calling the general public.

Response Rates

Research reports must include information regarding how many people approached for the survey actually completed it. People evaluate the validity of conclusions based partly on the response rate obtained. Because so many survey and response-rate calculation methods exist, the American Association for Public Opinion Research (AAPOR) monitors a myriad of specialized issues and methods relevant to reporting outcome rates for surveys based on Internet-based surveys, mail surveys, random-digit dialing (RDD), in-person interviews, and other methods (AAPOR, n.d.; also see Sidebar 12.1). It also has made a convenient Excel-based response rate calculator available at http://aapor.org/Response_Rates_An_Overview1/3720.htm. Most practitioners generally will find the following several pieces of information sufficient to report outcomes in a way that complies with AAPOR's ethical guidelines:

1   *The total sample size.* This is the total number of people (or phone numbers or addresses) used in the study. For example, for an RDD survey, a manager might draw a sample of 2,500 random phone numbers to achieve a final *n* of 800. Table 12.1

provides an example of how you might compute the valid sample size for an Internet-based survey.

SAMPLE SIZE COMPUTATION WORKSHEET
(Example for Online Surveys)

		VALID CONTACTS?
Number of E-mails or other contacts (initial sample size):	_____	No
Number of bounce-backs (Undeliverable addresses):	_____	No
Number of unconfirmed receipt (if available) after at least ____ attempts)	_____	No
Number of ineligible responses (if available):	_____	No
Number of no responses with insufficient attempts:	_____	Yes
Number of refusals/nonresponse:	_____	Yes
Number of partial completes (< ___ qs):	_____	Yes
Number of "completed interviews":	_____	Yes
TOTAL (should equal # of attempts):	_____	
TOTAL VALID SAMPLE:	_____	

Chapter 6 addresses how to draw the right size of total sample to achieve the desired valid sample.

2   *The valid sample size.* This is the number of sample elements (e.g., individuals, households, companies) in the total sample that remain after removing invalid phone numbers or addresses. These include nonworking phone numbers, respondents who do not fit the profile necessary to be included in the sample (e. g., not registered to vote), and respondents who do not speak English when surveyors do not speak other languages. In addition, research managers typically remove phone numbers and addresses from a sample if interviewers have made three to five attempts to reach someone at that location. The eliminated numbers are considered unreachable. Some market research firms only make one or two attempts, called *call-backs* in phone-survey lingo, but this practice is questionable scientifically. If an insufficient number of attempts have been made before the completion of the study, the location is considered a noncontact location and must remain in the valid sample. It is in the research manager's interest to minimize the number of noncontacts because they lower the response rate and can raise questions about the study's quality:

Valid Sample Size = Total Sample Size – Ineligibles – Unreachables

3   *The completion rate.* This is the number of people who complete a survey out of the *total* sample size. If the researcher can anticipate the completion rate, sometimes called the *minimum response rate* (AAPOR, 2011), this will determine how big a sample must be drawn to achieve the desired number of completed surveys. For example, if the completion rate is 31% and a sample of 384 is needed, the manager determines, by dividing 384 by 0.31, that 1249 numbers will be required to end up with 384 completed surveys:

$$\text{Total Sample Size} = \frac{\text{Target } n \text{ of Completed Surveys}}{\text{Completion Rate in Decimal Form}}$$

$$\text{TSS} = \frac{384}{.31} = 1249$$

4   *The response rate.* In its simplest form, the response rate refers to the percentage of people contacted who complete a questionnaire. Survey researchers have had to address a variety of issues resulting from technology, changing social mores and the like that have combined to greatly reduce citizens' participation in surveys. As a result, the formulas many researchers are using have grown more complicated and even controversial. Some response rate formulas are more conservative—or careful—than others. The America Association for Public Opinion Research (AAPOR) has developed a report containing standard definitions and explanations of the formulas AAPOR recommends (go to aapor.org and search the site for standard definitions to learn more).

Even though AAPOR is a leader in the field, survey researchers do not have to use AAPOR's formulas and definitions and often use other formulas to calculate and report a response rate. The formula many researchers have used in the past to calculate a response rate, for example, AAPOR calls a *cooperation rate* (or *participation rate*). This rate is the least conservative way to calculate survey participation because it results in the highest possible rate of response. Because it makes surveys look stronger and most managers want to know a survey's response rate, researchers strive to keep the response rate as high as possible. Unfortunately, phone surveys these days often have response rates as low as 5%, although some achieve rates as high as 80% (Wimmer & Dominick, 2014). Mail surveys typically garner a 5% to 40% response rate although their response rates can be much higher (Dillman et al., 2009), and Internet-based surveys garner response rates ranging from 5% up to 80% (Wimmer & Dominick, 2014):

$$\text{Response Rate} = \frac{\text{Completed Questionnaires}}{\text{Valid Sample Size}}$$

5   *The refusal rate.* This is the number of people who declined to answer the survey out of the valid sample size. Research managers strive to keep this number low:

$$\text{Refusal Rate} = \frac{\text{Refusals}}{\text{Valid Sample Size}}$$

6   *The noncontact rate.* This is the number of people who could not be reached out of the total sample and, therefore, never had the opportunity to complete the survey or refuse to do so:

$$\text{Noncontact Rate} = \frac{\text{Noncontacts}}{\text{Total Sample Size}}$$

Sidebar 12.1

American Association for Public Opinion Research

III. Standards for Minimal Disclosure

Good professional practice imposes the obligation upon all public opinion researchers to include, in any report of research results, or to make available when that report is released, certain essential information about how the research was conducted. At a minimum, the following items should be disclosed:

1   Who sponsored the survey, and who conducted it.
2   The exact wording of questions asked, including the text of any preceding instruction or explanation to the interviewer or respondents that might reasonably be expected to affect the response.
3   A definition of the population under study, and a description of the sampling frame used to identify this population.
4   A description of the sample selection procedure, giving a clear indication of the method by which the respondents were selected by the researcher, or whether the respondents were entirely self-selected.
5   Sample sizes and, where appropriate, eligibility criteria, screening procedures, and response rates computed according to AAPOR Standard Definitions. At a minimum, a summary of disposition of sample cases should be provided so that response rates could be computed.
6   A discussion of the precision of the findings, including estimates of sampling error and a description of any weighting or estimating procedures used.
7   Which results are based on parts of the sample, rather than on the total sample, and the size of such parts.
8   Method, location, and dates of data collection.

From time to time, AAPOR Council may issue guidelines and recommendations on best practices with regard to the release, design and conduct of surveys.

Reporting Univariate Relationships

The minimum information usually required for a research report includes frequencies, percentages, means, and, for some clients, standard deviations. The frequencies tell the client how many people answered each question using each response. Frequency tables usually include percentages as well, so the reader can make informed comparisons across questions.

As shown in Table 12.2, a frequency table includes both the number of people who answered the question and the number who did not (called *missing*). The valid percentage is based on the number of people who answered the question (338), whereas the unadjusted percentage refers to the total sample size (400). In this example, the numbers used on the survey appear along with the descriptions of the responses, but most research reports include only the descriptions.

Table 12.1 Sample Frequency Table: Purpose of Most Recent Visit to Convention Center

Valid		Frequency	%	Valid %
1	Attend a sporting event	121	30.3	35.8
2	Attend a musical or theater performance	54	13.5	16.0
3	Attend a fair or exhibit	51	12.8	15.1
4	Attend a rally or workshop	30	7.5	8.9
5	Attend a graduation ceremony	17	4.3	5.0
6	Attend a private social function	13	3.3	3.8
7	Get information	10	2.5	3.0
8	Other	42	10.5	12.4
Valid Total		338	84.5	100.0
Missing		62	15.5	
Total		400	100.0	

Researchers also can present frequencies visually, using tables, bar charts, histograms, or pie charts. Figure 12.1 displays a bar chart, which often can give clients a better grasp of the range and strength of responses than they might get from just a recitation of mean and standard deviation.

Pie charts, meanwhile, can communicate the contrasts and similarities between the usefulness of information sources, as shown in Figure 12.2. This particular example illustrates that registered voters tended to consider both daily news reports and interpersonal contacts as important sources of election information, but they were less likely to discount interpersonal sources than mediated ones.

Reporting Relationships among Variables

Often, a client wants to compare results for several groups, such as by education levels, sex, ethnicity, or membership. The crosstab table usually provides the most intuitive presentation format. Crosstab tables usually present frequencies and column or row percentages. The layout of the table will encourage readers to interpret the data in a particular way. Note that in the first

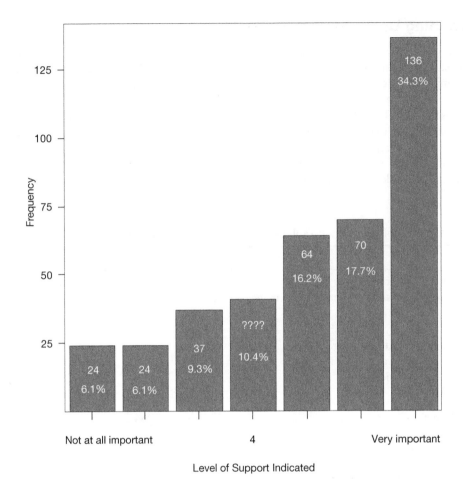

Note: Responses range from 1 (not at all important) to 7 (very important), with 4 representing the midpoint of the scale.

FIG. 12.1. Support for tobacco use prevention among registered voters.

example, shown in Table 12.3, the table is arranged so the row percentages display how many participants of each political orientation support tobacco use prevention efforts. In the second example, the row percentages display how many of the low, medium, and high supporters come from each political orientation. The first table shows more dispersed support among conservatives but strong support among moderates and liberals. This information can help communication managers understand which target groups need persuasion and which need reinforcement. The second table, shown in Table 12.4, shows that high supporters tend to cross the political spectrum fairly equally but that low support is disproportionately conservative. This information suggests that tobacco prevention represents an issue on which people from varied political orientations tend to agree. This could make tobacco use prevention a useful issue to emphasize when trying to unify the electorate.

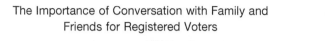

The Importance of Conversation with Family and
Friends for Registered Voters

The Importance of Daily News

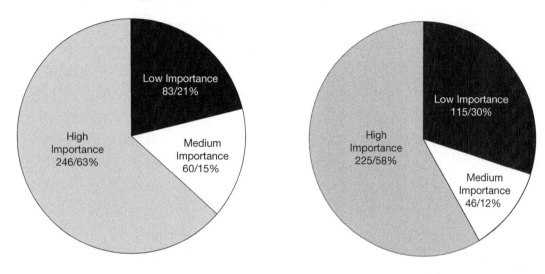

FIG. 12.2. Pie charts displaying registered voters' use of interpersonal and mass media information.

Table 12.2 Political Orientation and Level of Support for Tobacco Prevention Among
Registered Voters: Row Percentage Example

Tobacco Use Prevention

Political Orientation	Low Support	Medium Support	High Support	Total
Conservative				
Count	44	15	78	137
Row Percentage	32.1%	10.9%	56.9%	100.0%
Moderate				
Count	27	10	102	139
Row Percentage	19.4%	7.2%	73.4%	100.0%
Liberal				
Count	12	16	79	107
Row Percentage	11.2%	15.0%	73.8%	100.0%
Total				
Count	83	41	259	383
Row Percentage	21.7%	10.7%	67.6%	100.0%

Table 12.3 Political Orientation and the Level of Support for Tobacco Prevention: Column
Percentage Example

Tobacco Use Prevention

Political Orientation	Low Support	Medium Support	High Support	Total
Conservative				
Count	44	15	78	137
Column Percentage	53.0%	36.6%	30.1%	35.8%
Moderate				
Count	27	10	102	139
Column Percentage	32.5%	24.4%	39.4%	36.3%
Liberal				
Count	12	16	79	107
Column Percentage	14.5%	39.0%	30.5%	27.9%
Total				
Count	83	41	259	383
Column Percentage	100%	100%	100%	100%

Data from a random telephone survey of registered Washington State voters ($N = 397$) conducted during
October 24–28, 2004 (Pinkleton & Austin, 2005).

The research manager needs to determine which presentation provides the most helpful
information to the program planner. Although it is possible to include both types of information
in the same table, by displaying both row and column percentages and even total percentages,
too much information can create confusion. Evaluate the communication programming needs
carefully before creating the tables.

Crosstab tables only lend themselves to breakdowns across a limited number of categories,
such as low/medium/high or male/female. For a variable such as age, which in a standard public
opinion survey can range from 18 to 94 or more, managers need to condense it into decades
or market-oriented categories (such as 18–34) to make the crosstab table interpretable. Strive
to make tables readable at a glance.

Statistics such as the *Chi-square* can be used to highlight especially notable differences
across groups. Many clients, however, do not want to see the statistics themselves and may
find too much statistical information intimidating. Keep the presentation interpretable while
ensuring statistical rigor behind the scenes. Meanwhile, always be prepared for the client who
appreciates statistical depth.

Another way to present relationships is through a correlation coefficient. Correlations are
useful for examining the strength and direction of relationships between two interval-level (e.g.,
"very interested" to "not at all interested") or ratio-level (e. g., "0 times to 7 times") variables.
Correlations are less intuitive for a client without a statistical background, however. It can be
useful, therefore, to run correlations as background while presenting condensed versions of the
scales in a crosstab table. Condensing the data may mask subtle relationships; check the tables
to make sure they do not seem to tell a different story from the original statistics.

A correlation coefficient ranges between –1 and +1. A –1 indicates that the two variables
are exact opposites. For example, if younger children always like an event featuring Dora the
Explorer more than older people do, people always dislike Dora the Explorer more as they get

older. A + 1 indicates the two variables are perfect matches, for example, if the price people will pay for a product increases exactly in proportion to how valuable they think the product is.

Of course, such perfect relationships do not exist. The statistician, therefore, looks to see whether the coefficient is "significantly" different from 0, which would indicate that two variables change with no relevance to each other. The closer the coefficient is to +1 or –1, the stronger the relationship is between the two variables. In the information-seeking example, examining the relationship between age and interest level, the correlation between the two original variables is about –.17, indicating a small and negative association between age and interest: Older people, in other words, have slightly less interest than younger people have, but the difference is not dramatic.

Research managers may encounter times when they need to consider complex relationships using sophisticated multivariate statistics. For the most part, this sort of analysis still needs to be translated into results interpretable by a statistical novice or math phobe. Keep in mind that even the most sophisticated analysis is useful only if it is understandable, and the most prescient research is helpful only if it gets used. Keep the presentation as simple and compelling as possible.

Final Thoughts

In the blur of program-planning deadlines, the communication manager can be tempted to plunge into a research project without thinking through the details of data entry or later presentation. The more communication managers think ahead, however, the more useful the final report is likely to be. The research plan can serve as an invaluable tool for determining what a research report should look like. Managers often map out the final report before doing the research, demonstrating—without the numbers, of course—what the answers to the questions raised in a situation analysis should look like. Planning to this level of detail can help ensure that the questions asked on a survey are designed to make it possible to create the tables desired. In addition, planning ahead for data entry and analysis helps focus the research manager's work and can save both time and money. Just as effective communication program plans focus on the final outcomes—the goals and objectives—from the start, the most effective research projects envision the final report well before the first survey responses are collected.

PART III

Using Theory for Practical Guidance

13

What Theory Is and Why It Is Useful

Chapter Contents

- What Is a Theory?
- Finding a Good Theory
- A Theoretical Framework for "Symmetrical" Public Relations
- A Theoretical Framework for "Asymmetrical" Campaigns
- Final Thoughts

Despite the admonition of a famous social scientist named Kurt Lewin that "nothing is as practical as a good theory" (Marrow, 1969), practitioners and students of public relations often seem skeptical. After all, the term *theory* sounds academic, not applied, and theories usually emanate from academics in ivory-tower institutions, seemingly insulated from real-world complications. But Lewin was right: A good understanding of a few "good theories" enhances the strategic manager's success. Theories—essentially generalizations about how people think and behave—help determine appropriate goals and objectives for a communication program. Scientifically tested theories also help communication programmers develop effective strategies to achieve those goals and objectives.

Because applying theory makes communication planning more scientific and less haphazard, it helps ensure effectiveness. The value of being scientific does not diminish the need for creativity. Instead, science makes it possible to (a) *predict* what will happen, such as anticipating the results from a mailing versus a social-media campaign; (b) *understand* why something has happened, such as why attendance was poor at a special event; and (c) *control* what will happen (to the extent possible). To achieve success, the manager wants as much control as feasible and applied theory provides the most control possible in a field notorious for its uncertainty.

What Is a Theory?

Theories explain why people behave in certain ways and how people are likely to respond to something. This gives the strategic manager the ability to make predictions based on an understanding of communication processes and effects. This is especially important to communication managers because much public relations communication takes place through gatekeepers such as reporters, opinion leaders and online bloggers instead of through paid advertising, increasing the opportunities for plans to go awry. In addition, many communication results seem difficult to quantify. These difficulties force managers to choose: Either accept the inability to control process and outcome or find a way to exert more control. Doing so requires developing the best understanding of likely explanations and predictions of communication processes and effects.

In truth, we all operate on the basis of theories every day. Many predictions come from personal experience. Savvy practitioners know that pitching a story to a reporter on deadline breeds failure. Localizing a story makes it more attractive. Media relations experience teaches practitioners what sorts of things to say (and not say) when pitching a story to an editor and what types of outlets will find a story about a pastry chef or a celebrity interesting.

All of these predictions illustrate theories. For example, the need to avoid the reporter's deadline pressure illustrates the larger point, or theory, that "timing affects receptivity." The need to localize a story exemplifies the theory that "relevance affects acceptance." Finally, the appropriateness of specialized outlets, such as culinary websites, to the pastry chef story demonstrates the theory that "proximity increases relevance." To the extent that the manager can control the variables of timing, relevance, and proximity, the better the manager can control the result of media relations activities. To the extent that the manager learns from others' experiences instead of from personal trial and error, the manager will endure fewer opportunities to learn from mistakes.

Finding a Good Theory

Theories cannot offer guarantees; instead, they improve the probability of success. Because of the way the scientific method works, theories are never proven beyond any doubt. They gain support, and they can be disproved. A scientific test of a theory sets up a situation in which the theory has to either succeed or fail. To gain support (never "proof"), a theory must demonstrate success at least 95% of the time in a given statistical test. The more times a theory gets tested and the more methods and contexts used to test it, the more confidence a practitioner can place in the theory's predictions. As a result of testing, theories often evolve; for example, testing may show that a theory applies better in some contexts than in others. This makes it important to keep up to date on what is new in communication, organization, and persuasion theory to know the nuances that give theories the most professional relevance. This becomes particularly important when a theory creates controversy or fails too many tests.

One of the most popular theories used by practitioners, also the most criticized, is called the *linear model* of communication or the *bullet theory* of communication (Figure 13.1). Although the model originally was developed to illustrate the constraints that messages encounter when sent electronically through wires, too many people have embraced the illustrative model as an explanatory device, a theory of how communication works. Much research has shown that the bullet theory is too simplistic. Nevertheless, publicity-based communication programs

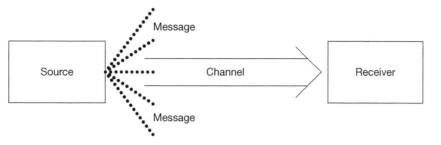

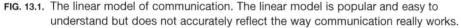

FIG. 13.1. The linear model of communication. The linear model is popular and easy to understand but does not accurately reflect the way communication really works.

essentially operate on that outdated theory, assuming that just getting the message out will have desirable effects. We still hear many practitioners brag about how many media impressions they have achieved. Achieving "impressions," however, does not tell you whether what you have sent out has gotten any attention from your target audience and whether their reaction is positive, negative or indifferent. A study of 1,000 consumers and 250 marketers by Adobe Systems, Inc., for example, found that consumers overwhelmingly found online advertising annoying and avoided paying attention to it (Adobe Systems, Inc., 2012).

Gaining exposure through media platforms can serve a valuable purpose. But a reliance on publicity greatly limits the practitioner's ability to achieve and measure success for important persuasive goals such as behavior change or important relational goals such as trust and commitment. Just because a message receives a lot of exposure does not mean anyone will pay attention to it, understand it, believe it, or act differently because of it. As a result, clip counts and Twitter statistics can be meaningless to a program focused on attitude change, behavior change, or even knowledge change. Because activities that do not contribute demonstrably to goal achievement waste time and resources, programs must include publicity only to the extent that reasons exist to predict and explain how publicity will help achieve stated goals. These reasons are theories.

Theories often use fancy social science terms that have special meaning to scholars looking for nuances, but good theories usually can be boiled down into sensible language that is fairly simple to apply. Some theories especially relevant to public relations focus on how relationships work, and others focus on persuasion. Theories focused on relationships correspond to what Grunig and Hunt (1984) called the *symmetrical model* of public relations, and theories focused on persuasion correspond to Grunig's (1989) *asymmetrical model* of public relations. According to Grunig, strategic managers often operate on the basis of both models, instead of on one exclusively. Two remaining models of public relations management—the publicity model and the public information model—operate on the basis of the outdated bullet theory, focusing solely on distributing messages. These two models cannot be considered strategic management.

A Theoretical Framework for "Symmetrical" Public Relations

Several useful theories explain how the symmetrical model of public relations works, as well as what makes it work so well. These theories explain why public relations is relevant and useful for an organization. They also guide problem identification and goal setting because they help the manager understand when and why issues should be considered problems or achievements. Four theories are especially important for the public relations manager, whose ultimate focus rests on long-term relationship building.

Systems Theory—Adaptation and Adjustment

According to systems theory, organizations are most effective when they acknowledge that they interact with, affect, and are affected by their environment. They need to bring in resources that enhance their success and deflect threats that can compromise their survival. Organizations in *open systems* (which means, in real life) exchange information, energy, and material with their environments. Organizations operating in *closed systems* exist in a vacuum without interacting with or exchanging things with any other organization or person. In an open system, the organization sometimes implements changes (e.g., flextime hours) to adjust to changes in the environment (e.g., increasingly difficult commute traffic). The organization also tries to obtain accommodations from the environment (e.g., having the county pay for access road maintenance) that help it operate effectively. According to the open systems model (Broom & Dozier, 1990; Broom & Sha, 2013; Grunig & Hunt, 1984), organizations that close themselves off from this exchange process become inert or disintegrate. In other words, they become irrelevant or ineffective.

Activities necessary to succeed, according to systems theory, include surveillance, interpretation, and advising management (Table 13.1).

Table 13.1 Necessary Activities According to Systems Theory

Surveillance	Interpretation	Advising Management
Gather information about environment	Prioritize issues	Suggest concrete actions
Gather information about opportunities and challenges	Prioritize publics	Suggest measurable objectives
	Anticipate changes Develop recommendations	

Surveillance—also called *scanning*—means gathering information about the environment and possible challenges or opportunities (data collection). Interpretation means having the ability to make sense of the information gathered to be able to prioritize issues and publics, anticipate how the situation may change in ways that may help or hurt the organization, and develop recommendations for action (theorize). Advising management means making credible suggestions for concrete actions that will achieve measurable objectives consistent with organizational goals. To sum up systems theory, organizations do not exist in a vacuum. They need to perform ongoing research to understand changing environmental constraints and possibilities.

Co-Orientation Theory

This theory helps to delineate what makes communication productive. According to co-orientation theory (McLeod & Chaffee, 1972; Newcomb, 1953), people and organizations relate to one another successfully to the extent they think similarly about ideas. The co-orientation model shows the ways two parties may relate to the same idea (Figure 13.2). Each party will have impressions both about the idea and about what the other party thinks about the idea. On one hand, the two parties can agree and know that they agree, but they also can think they disagree. On the other hand, they may disagree but think they agree. Even more confusing, they may think they are discussing the same idea, such as improving customer service responsiveness, when in fact they are thinking about different ideas, such as a need for new procedures versus a need for additional training. According to co-orientation theory, the most effective communication takes place when both parties agree and when they know they agree, which means they have achieved consensus.

Grunig & Huang (2000) wrote that the application of co-orientation theory promotes long-term success, but its usefulness may not seem obvious when examining only short-term outcomes. Clients and CEOs may not understand how measures such as agreement, accuracy, and understanding relate to the achievement of organizational goals such as increased sales,

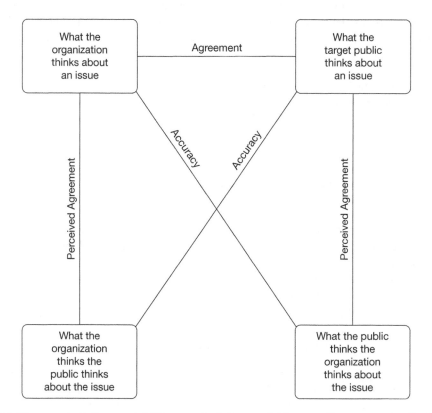

FIG. 13.2. The co-orientation model. The co-orientation model focuses the manager's attention on relationships, consistent with the overall mission of public relations.

increased membership renewals, or passage of an important bill in Congress. As a result, managers trying to demonstrate long-term communication effectiveness need to focus on outcomes such as trust and control mutuality, relational commitment, and relational satisfaction (Table 13.2). *Trust* is defined as the belief that the other party will not exploit one's goodwill. *Control mutuality* refers to the degree to which the parties believe that they have enough control over the relationship and the other party's goals and activities. *Relational commitment* means the desire to maintain the relationship, including level of interest in maintaining membership, level of acceptance of the organization's goals, willingness to exert effort on behalf of the organization, and extent to which the party believes the benefits of maintaining the relationship outweigh the costs of discontinuing it. Finally, *relational satisfaction* is defined as the degree to which a relationship seems fulfilling. Stafford and Canary (1991) suggested that relational satisfaction may be the most important measure of an effective relationship, but measures such as trust and commitment seem especially well suited to the demonstration of communication's contributions to organizational goals. Discover Card applied co-orientation theory to try to preserve its relationship with customers even as it pursued their overdue accounts. The company changed the way it contacted some customers about their late payments. According to Scott Robinette, president of Hallmark Loyalty, "Discover didn't want to alienate those customers" (Associated Press, 2004). As a result, Discover started sending customers a greeting card encouraging them to "give us a call so we can work through this together" instead of sending a threatening business letter. Whole websites now exist to advise companies on how to write friendly reminder letters to first-time delinquent clients without sacrificing a potentially beneficial long-term relationship.

Table 13.2 Measurable Outcomes of a Mutually
Beneficial Relationship

- Trust
- Control mutuality
- Relational commitment
- Relational satisfaction

According to co-orientation theory, organizations must try to maximize levels of agreement, understanding, and accuracy among the organization's communicators and stakeholders. These indicators of successful communication contribute to long-term success measured by outcomes such as trust and commitment. Co-orientation theory demonstrates the importance of taking a long-term view of the organization's relationship with its stakeholders despite the temptation to focus on short-term goals such as the success of the next product promotion.

Situational Theory of Strategic Constituencies

This approach responds to the truism that "You cannot please all of the people all of the time." An organization must prioritize its efforts, and that includes the publics on which it focuses. Higher priority goes to publics whose opposition or support can either help or hinder the organization's ability to achieve its goals and mission. Publics can be internal to the organization (e.g., union employees), external to the organization (e.g., environmental groups), or both (e.g., employees who are members of environmental groups). According to Grunig and Repper (1992), strategic constituencies can be segmented into categories of active, potentially active (latent), and passive publics.

An *active public* is made up of individuals who perceive that what an organization does matters to them (called *level of involvement*), that the consequences of what an organization does affects them (called *problem recognition*), and that they have the ability to do something to affect the organization's actions or the consequences of those actions (called *constraint recognition*). Actions can be positive, such as purchasing stock or maintaining memberships, or negative, such as engaging in boycotts and lawsuits.

A latent public is one whose members have the potential to become active. These are people who should care about an issue because it could affect them but who may not be interested, may not know about the issue, or may not have the ability to take action.

Active publics can be divided into three types:

1   *The long haul.* Those interested in all aspects of the issue.
2   *Special interests.* Those interested only in certain aspects of the topic.
3   *Hot button.* Those who get interested only if an emotional debate ensues.

A fourth category—apathetic publics—do not care about any aspect of the issue and have no relevance to the organization.

Excellence Theory

According to excellence theory, building mutually beneficial relationships with strategic constituencies saves money by preventing problems such as lawsuits, boycotts, and strikes and by increasing employees' satisfaction, which enhances productivity and quality. According to Dozier, Grunig, and Grunig (1995), excellence theory integrates systems theory and the situational theory of strategic constituencies explained in the previous section. It proposes that managed communication helps achieve organizational goals because it helps reconcile organizational goals with the expectations of its relevant publics (Grunig, Grunig, & Ehling, 1992). Excellence theory proposes that public relations is most effective when the senior communication manager helps shape organizational goals and helps determine which external publics are most important strategically. Communication management will be most successful when it operates strategically by identifying (segmenting) active publics and developing symmetrical communication programs that have measureable success. (Grunig & Huang, 2000; Grunig & Repper, 1992).

Summarizing the Symmetrical Perspective

The combination of theories integrated into excellence theory takes a holistic view of communication and organizational success. According to this viewpoint, organizations must operate with an understanding of and respect for others who coexist in their social system. Because the system constantly evolves, the environment can change in ways that can affect the organization in beneficial or detrimental ways. Publics operating in the environment also evolve, which means their *relevance* to the organization—the degree to which their support makes a difference to organizational success—also will change. Organizations' success depends

Table 13.3 Comparison of the Us–Us and Us–Them Operating Styles

	Us–Us	*Us–Them*
View of strategic publics	Publics are stakeholders or partners	Publics are adversaries
Character of communication	Integrate publics' values into organizational goals	Communication lacks shared understanding
Focus of goals	Win–win situations (consensus)	Self-preservation (consensus unlikely)
Communication style	Focus on responsiveness (accommodation and advocacy)	Indifference or counteraction (advocacy only)

on their ability to integrate the needs and desires of relevant publics into organizational goals and activities to gain and maintain their trust and commitment.

In summary form, this view is an "us and us" (us–us) philosophy. It also can be summarized as the practice of social responsibility. According to this philosophy, the mission of public relations is to develop and maintain "win–win" situations for the organization and the publics on whose goodwill its success depends. This stands in contrast to an "us and them" (us–them) philosophy, which often devolves into an "us versus them" situation (Table 13.3). The reason for this is that the us–them philosophy fails to integrate strategic publics' values into organizational goals. Instead, it views organizational values and goals as distinct from publics' values and goals.

According to systems theory, the us–them approach is likely to fail because it discounts the organization's interdependence with its environment. According to co-orientation theory, the us–them approach is likely to fail because communication will lack shared understanding and will be less likely to achieve consensus. According to situational theory, the us–them approach does not recognize that active and latent publics can take action damaging to the organization's ability to succeed and will do so if they feel the need and find the opportunity. According to excellence theory, the us–them approach fails to appreciate that responsiveness is less expensive and more effective than indifference.

In keeping with the us–us philosophy, symmetrical public relations benefits the organization because strategic communication programs are essential to existence in an interdependent social system. The communication manager's ability to understand strategic publics, communicate successfully with them, and advise management about the implications of evolving relationships can have long-term, measurable effects on the bottom line.

Pure Advocacy   Symmetry   Pure Accommodation

Constraints:
Decision-making independence
Power of relevant publics
Climate of media coverage
Regulatory or legal constraints

FIG. 13.3. Cameron's continuum of symmetrical contingencies.

What Makes the Symmetrical Ideal "Practical"

Grunig (1989) noted that few organizations put the symmetrical philosophy into practice, although the idea is not new. These organizations may not believe sufficient evidence supports the symmetrical imperative, or they may view the approach as impractical or difficult to apply. Cameron (1998) suggested that practitioners' ability to practice symmetrical public relations depends on various contingencies, such as independence in decision making, the power of relevant publics, the climate of media coverage, and regulatory or legal constraints (Figure 13.3). According to Cameron, companies operate on a continuum that ranges from pure advocacy to pure accommodation. Pure advocacy refers to developing and delivering messages in support of a position without seeking feedback for compromise. Depending on the situation, companies' location on the continuum will vary. Although perfect symmetry may not exist between an organization and its publics, striving for symmetry demonstrates the willingness to meet another viewpoint part way and to at least seriously consider alternative perspectives on an issue. To attempt this is to practice social responsibility.

Plenty of evidence supports the view that communication management as the practice of social responsibility reaps measurable success. Although managers with a social conscience may embrace socially responsible management for its intuitive appeal, even the most hardcore pragmatist can seize on its bottom-line benefits, summarized by Feldstein (1992) and demonstrated more recently by many others. The CEO of Verizon in 2010, for example, said, "Our belief is that corporate philanthropy expands the business. If you do the right thing over time, you expand the capabilities of your customer base, business, and society" (Committee Encouraging Corporate Philanthropy, 2010, p. 20). An increasing number of companies now produce annual "social reports" disclosing their corporate social responsibility activities. Companies engaging in the practice, sometimes referred to as *public reports, sustainable development reports,* or *corporate citizenship reports,* find it valuable. Starbucks, for example, releases an annual social responsibility report.

According to many professionals, corporate social responsibility has become an essential part of doing business, with a big shift in this direction since 2008. The Edelman Trust Barometer (Edelman, 2012), for example, showed that among over 5,000 adults aged 25–64 surveyed across 23 countries, the most important drivers of corporate reputation included trust, honesty and transparency along with quality. Their follow-up study (Edelman, 2013) of 31,000 adults across 26 countries found that engagement with constituents and integrity mattered most heavily for building and maintaining trust. An article in the *Wall Street Journal* claiming the "CSR" (Corporate Social Responsibility) approach made no sense created a firestorm of comments, many citing research, and attracted an official response from the Committee Encouraging Corporate Philanthropy, which claimed to represent 150 CEOs (Coady, 2010; Karnani, 2010).

The benefits of the social responsibility approach, according to Feldstein (1992) and as borne out by more recent research such as the Trust Barometer and the Committee Encouraging Corporate Philanthropy (CECP), include the following:

1   *Consumer loyalty.* Increasingly, studies have demonstrated that consumer loyalty has value to an organization that translates into measurable profits. It has long been understood that consumers are 90% more likely to buy products or services from a socially responsible company ("In Focused," 1996) and that even small reductions in

consumer defection rates have remarkable effects on profits ("Building Customer," 1996). For example, reducing client defections by 5% increased profitability to an auto service chain by more than 20%, to insurances brokerages by more than 40%, to software by about 30%, and to credit cards by more than 80%. On the other hand, one survey found that 91% of Americans who dislike a company's citizenship practices would consider taking their purchasing elsewhere ("Numbers Don't," 2004). "Sustainable Value Creation" refers to an emphasis on prosocial corporate behavior that delivers mutually beneficial results of bottom-line benefit, competitive advantage, and community benefits (CECP, 2010).

2   *Employee morale.* Businesses have discovered that employee morale is not a nicety but an important factor affecting recruitment, retention, quality, and profitability. For example, fear of job loss can hurt morale, which can contribute to accidents, mistakes, and decreased productivity. Helping morale, on the other hand, can increase productivity and loyalty. For example, Johnson and Johnson's Balancing Work and Family Program ("A Look," 1997) demonstrated that 71% of employees who used the company's flexible time and leave policies cited the policy as a "very important" reason for staying with the company (also see Figure 13.4). Two years into the program, employees maintained that their jobs were interfering less with their family lives even while the number of hours worked on average had increased. The program has helped keep Johnson and Johnson on *Working Mother's* top-100 list of family-friendly companies ever since, along with IBM (Working Mother, 2012). Meanwhile, companies such as Xerox and IBM also have found that potential employees like the idea of working for a company that promotes volunteerism among employees. Some companies such as Allstate even provide managers with training—in Allstate's case, 3 days' worth—on how to foster a supportive work environment. Good employee relations can help recruitment as well as retention, with a variety of magazines now ranking companies on issues such as family friendliness and work environment. When they have a choice, the vast majority of potential employees will refuse to work at a company that they consider socially irresponsible ("Numbers Don't," 2004). As a result, when Marissa Mayer, the new CEO of Yahoo in 2012, announced an end to telecommuting among employees (Swisher, 2013), she was risking an exodus among those with work records strong enough to secure a job elsewhere with more flexible policies. A frequent criticism of her decision asserted that telecommuting has been shown to increase productivity when managed properly and that ending it would not address Yahoo's core problem of performance (O'Leary, 2013). A recent study showed that 98% of U.S. employers have some sort of worker flexibility program (Rhodes, 2011). Figure 13.4 illustrates specific benefits of worker flexibility programs.

3   *Shareholder value.* Retaining efficient and creative employees increases profits because quality and productivity increases, and organizations spend less money on recruitment and on problems related to quality control or employee grievances. Retaining loyal customers reduces the need for attracting new customers and can sharply increase profits. One study of 600 Morgan Stanley Capital International companies between 1999 and 2003 found that companies scoring well on environmental and social performance measures outperformed others financially by 23% ("Numbers Don't," 2004). More recently, when IBM celebrated its 100th anniversary by coordinating an international "Celebration of Service" year, linking employee volunteerism with local

FIG. 13.4. Flexpays Infographic.

(Courtesy of Working Mother Research Institute)

organizations, 89% of their employees participated in 5,000 projects across 120 countries, contributing an estimated 1,070 years of volunteerism valued at $100 million and benefitting an estimated 10 million people. It also produced a jump of 8 points in brand value in the annual Interbrand Most Valuable Global Brand study, on which they already were ranked number 2 (PRSA, 2012d).

4   *Community goodwill.* Another apparent nicety that is essential, community goodwill or support, can make or break a company in times of crisis. For example, when Los Angeles erupted in rioting following the Rodney King beating by police officers in 1991, McDonald's found its restaurants standing unscathed in neighborhoods that had been essentially razed and looted. McDonald's attributed its survival to the company's long-standing involvement in activities intended to benefit the communities in which they operated and the employees who worked for the company in those communities. The Basilica of St. Mary in Minneapolis acted quickly to preserve community goodwill

when a clash between church leaders and gay rights activists in 2011 threatened to derail the annual Basilica Block Party music festival, which annually raises funds to provide housing, employment, food and clothing to more than 2,500 local people each month. They succeeded in bringing the protestors back on board with the festival and raised a near-record $400,000 (PRSA, 2012f).

5   *Community well-being.* Because employees, customers, and potential employees all live in the community, the health of the community affects the well-being of the company. Many indirect effects, such as good schools, safe streets, thriving arts, and health promotion all benefit the company by improving the environment in which the organization exists. As Feldstein (1992) wrote, 90% of the $144 billion given to charity in 1990 came from individuals, and only 5% came from businesses. He reported estimates that 87% of Americans give to charities and 78% volunteer their time. It meant that many companies were divesting themselves of a major opportunity to help their communities and thereby help themselves. Both large- and small-scale projects make a difference. For example, the PR firm 206 Inc. in Seattle enables each employee to contribute 40 hours of their work time each year to the philanthropic initiative of their choosing. That and other policies landed 206 Inc. on *Seattle Metropolitan's* list of best places to work (Williams, 2012). Other companies such as Columbia Sportswear have well-developed employee volunteerism programs and matching-fund programs to encourage employees to donate to charitable causes. The consumer goods company, Tom's of Maine, for example, runs a 5%-for-volunteering program, which allows employees to spend 5% of their work time helping nonprofit organizations. Starbucks encourages customers to join in their embrace of issues by providing their own grants and promoting purchases that benefit selected causes. Working Assets performs an annual survey of its customers to select the causes it will promote during the following year.

Keys to Making the Symmetrical Ideal Sensible

Managers need not worry that acting socially responsible can lead to giving away the store, which would be asymmetrical and counterproductive. As Richmond (1990) wrote, stakeholders will understand that the organization must ensure its own success. Indeed, as McDonald's learned so dramatically, stakeholders who see their values incorporated into the organization's values and goals have a vested interest in helping ensure the organization's survival. The manager can operate on several principles drawn from Richmond's sensible approach to corporate responsibility, what he called "putting the public in public relations":

1   *Be honest.* There is no shame in being straightforward about the fact that your organization needs to profit from its relationship with its publics.
2   *Be creative.* There is no need to give away huge amounts of resources to promote mutually beneficial relationships. A hotel, for example, can offer special services such as a tour of an award-winning kitchen and a meal as a door prize for a nonprofit group holding a special event at the hotel. Or the hotel can provide the room free, provided the organization agrees to include a no-host bar.
3   *Do your research.* The manager must know the public to find common ground on which to build understanding that leads to mutually beneficial goals. Richmond (1990),

for example, knew that a major southwest association was determining where to hold its next Seattle-based conference. Richmond learned that one of the two major charities supported by the organization also was supported by his client, the Seattle Sheraton. The charity was happy to encourage the organization to support the business of another benefactor, and the organization was pleased to give its business to an organization that shared its philanthropic priorities.

4   *Find the right fit.* Philanthropic efforts must be strategic, but this means they need to reflect genuine concerns of the sponsoring organization and must not seem insincere or mercenary. Programs should reflect the organization's business interests and offer opportunities for its expertise to make a difference. Efforts also need to be relevant to the values and interests of active and latent publics. Philanthropic programs must reflect an organization's core beliefs, actively involve individuals at all levels of employment within the company, and correspond to the organization's behavior. Focusing efforts in a small number of areas can magnify the organization's impact.

5   *Always monitor and evaluate the relationship.* Never assume plans will carry through as expected or that the health of a relationship is assured indefinitely. This often requires simple actions instead of sophisticated research techniques. Richmond (1990), for example, advised the Sheraton to buy some tables at events hosted in the hotel both to show support for the organization and to ensure quality control during the event.

6   *Remember that little things can count big.* Small donations can come back to an organization many times over. Richmond's Seattle Sheraton, for example, had a company move its function from another hotel to its hotel because the Sheraton unknowingly had donated a room to a key decision-maker's son's elementary school for a raffle in a town located in the suburbs. Likewise, small insults can cost big business. It is a good idea to remember that, in a social system always in flux, every relationship has the potential to affect other relationships.

A Theoretical Framework for "Asymmetrical" Campaigns

Another set of theories can help guide the manager developing a campaign. These theories, from communication, psychology, sociology, and marketing, take a more short-term, so-called "asymmetrical" view and emphasize persuasion. Although theories focused on campaign issues emphasize the asymmetrical approach, managers need to use them with long-term relational goals in mind. For example, although campaigns focus on changing a public's attitude or behavior, such as approving zoning changes beneficial to an organization, managers must recognize the organization's need to respond to the public as well, such as by helping develop a solution to neighborhood traffic concerns. Theories of public relations strongly suggest an organization's long-term success depends on its ability to develop and maintain good relationships with key stakeholders. Even organizations taking the long view, however, need to engage in persuasion.

Persuasion (O'Keefe, 2002) is a "successful, intentional effort at influencing another's mental state through communication in a circumstance in which the persuadee has some measure of freedom" (p. 17). This aspect of freedom distinguishes persuasion from coercion, which is an attempt to force compliance by taking away the target's freedom to disagree. The definition of *persuasion* includes other important elements to consider:

Success. Persuasion does not occur unless the effort to influence another succeeds.

Intent. Persuasion occurs on purpose. Change can occur accidentally, but that is not persuasion.

Mental state. Persuasion often focuses on changing a behavior, such as increasing sales or the number of votes in favor of a particular issue, but changing behavior is not enough if attitudes do not correspond to the behavior. If attitudes and behavior conflict, coercion may have taken place instead of persuasion. On the other hand, sometimes attitude change, such as increased trust, is enough to satisfy organizational goals, without an associated specific behavior.

Through communication. Persuasion uses communication instead of force to achieve goals.

Persuasion and Ethics

After a long discussion of the importance of symmetrical practices and social responsibility, students of public relations often worry that engaging in persuasion somehow is unethical. Indeed, the asymmetrical approach to communication management often gives public relations a bad reputation because of its us-them embrace of persuasion as unidirectional change. The media and other publics notice the lack of reciprocity on the part of the organization and resent what can seem like efforts to take advantage of others.

Nevertheless, just as every individual operates according to personal theories, everyone engages in efforts to persuade. Even babies quickly learn that they must communicate their needs and desires to others in an attempt to have those needs and desires fulfilled. As grown-ups and communication professionals, we often need to persuade others to help us achieve our goals. But just as we learn to give as well as receive in our personal relationships, organizations at times must permit themselves to be persuaded by others, to be responsive to strategic publics' needs and desires. In other words, persuasion on behalf of an organization must occur in the context of the symmetrical approach to public relations. The PRSA Code of Professional Standards for the Practice of Public Relations provides a useful yardstick for evaluating whether persuasive efforts remain within ethical bounds (Sidebar 13.1; see also Appendix A; Public Relations Society of America, 2013).

The values in the PRSA code of standards highlights this issue, noting that a member needs to act in accord with "the public interest." Several provisions address the importance of the message recipient's freedom to disagree by acknowledging that the withholding of important information violates a message recipient's freedom to evaluate the veracity of a message. As a result, the communication practitioner is expected to "deal fairly . . . giving due respect to the ideal of free inquiry and to the opinions of others." The member must act with honesty and integrity, communicate truthfully and accurately, refrain from knowingly spreading false or misleading information, refrain from representing conflicting interests, and be prepared to identify publicly the client or employer on whose behalf public communication is made. In addition, the practitioner may not corrupt "the integrity of channels of communications or the processes of government" or accept fees or other remuneration from anyone except clients or employers who must fully disclose facts.

In simple language, the PRSA code of standards means that persuasion must occur without resorting to lying or misrepresentation. Indeed, research shows that persuasion is more effective and has longer lasting effects when persuaders acknowledge and refute the other side of an issue. It is not necessary to use dishonesty to persuade someone; after all, if the organization holds a particular view, its reasons for the view are real. The key to persuasion is to communicate successfully the reasons why members of a target public should share the organization's view on an issue or should want to participate in a behavior the organization thinks is a good idea.

Sidebar 13.1

PSRA Member Statement of Professional Values

This statement presents the core values of PSRA members and, more broadly, of the public relations profession. These values provide the foundation for the Member Code of Ethics and set the industry standard for the professional practice of public relations. These values are the fundamental beliefs that guide our behaviors and decision-making process. We believe our professional values are vital to the integrity of the profession as a whole.

Advocacy

We serve the public interest by acting as responsible advocates for those we represent. We provide a voice in the marketplace of ideas, facts, and viewpoints to aid informed public debate.

Honesty

We adhere to the highest standards of accuracy and truth in advancing the interests of those we represent and in communicating with the public.

Expertise

We acquire and responsibly use specialized knowledge and experience. We advance the profession through continued professional development, research, and education. We build mutual understanding, credibility, and relationships among a wide array of institutions and audiences.

Independence

We provide objective counsel to those we represent. We are accountable for our actions.

Loyalty

We are faithful to those we represent, while honoring our obligation to serve the public interest.

Fairness

We deal fairly with clients, employers, competitors, peers, vendors, the media, and the general public. We respect all opinions and support the right of free expression.

In support of this perspective, a theory has developed based on research that has shown that the most effective campaigns treat persuasion as a relational situation in which everyone can benefit, instead of as a contest in which the organization desires victory and the public must concede. Managers must not view a campaign as an attempt to push a public to accept something the organization wants distributed, such as a product or an attitude. Instead, the manager should view a campaign as an opportunity to demonstrate to a public that the organization has something from which it will want to benefit. Public relations calls this a receiver orientation; marketers call it a consumer orientation. A theory called *social marketing* illustrates the value of this perspective.

Social Marketing Theory

According to social marketing theory, purveyors of ideas need to think more like purveyors of products, who view a purchase as an equal exchange. The consumer deciding whether to buy a product must weigh the cost of the product against the benefits of having the product. If the benefits outweigh the costs, the consumer will buy the product. Similarly, the public deciding whether to embrace an idea must weigh the costs associated with embracing the idea against the benefits. For example, the cost of turning out to vote could include lost time, a missed opportunity to do something else, the need to go outside in bad weather, the need to move a car from a hard-won parking space, and so on. The benefits—the possibility of helping a favored candidate or proposal win at the polls—must outweigh those costs. This cost–benefit analysis is known as a *profit orientation*, and social marketing theory acknowledges that the consumers of ideas evaluate the degree to which they will profit from the ideas.

Social marketing theory views the consumer as the center of the universe. As with product marketing, success hinges on a successful exchange relationship with the consumer. The marketing of ideas, however, presents a tougher challenge than does the marketing of products. Although the gain of a small market share in product marketing can translate into large profits for a company, stakes often are much higher in social marketing, the need for 51% of the vote, for example. Solomon (1989) listed several other differences:

1   Social marketing often targets the toughest audiences instead of the most easily profitable. A rule of thumb for persuasion is that on a continuum of support, persuasive efforts are most likely to reinforce positive opinions, crystallize neutral opinions to become more positive, and neutralize negative opinions (see Figure 13.5). To move negative opinions to the positive side represents a huge, probably unrealistic, leap for a single campaign. Persuasion likely must take place in increments. As a result, social marketing often must acknowledge that change will take time.

2   Social marketing consumers often do not pay in dollars for services and products. The costs to them are perceptual, such as in time, reputation, ego, or guilt.

3   Political dimensions often exist in social marketing campaigns.

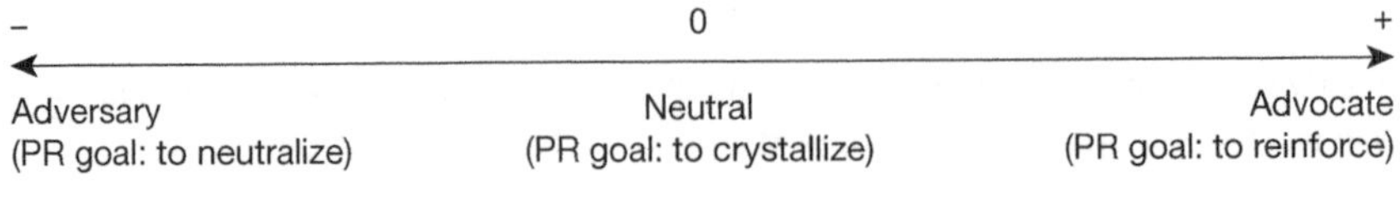

−	0	+
Adversary (PR goal: to neutralize)	Neutral (PR goal: to crystallize)	Advocate (PR goal: to reinforce)

FIG. 13.5. The continuum of public support.

4   The products or services marketed often are not seen as valuable by the target public. It can be tough to sell the idea of a new school to the 80% of the public who do not have school-age children but who will have to pay for it in taxes.

5   Social marketers often have small budgets and need to acquire both clients and funding sponsors.

6   Too much success can prove disastrous if the marketer cannot handle the demand. Colleges implementing new automated registration systems have had entire systems fail because of the sudden overload. An 800 number can be overwhelmed so that no one can get through. An organization can run out of brochures, or pizzas, if too many people show up.

To apply social marketing theory successfully, the communication manager can refer to the model of the *six Ps* to answer the questions that give the campaign focus. The six Ps encompass the traditional four Ps of marketing—Product, Place, Price, And Promotion—but also include the Public (instead of the consumer) and Positioning. The combination of elements is known as the *marketing mix* (Figure 13.6). Managers determine each element through research, given that each choice to guide a campaign must respond to public perceptions.

FIG. 13.6. The marketing mix. Elements of the social marketing model as applied to communication programs. The marketing mix includes the six Ps of public, product, price, promotion, positioning, and place.

1   Who is the *public*? Everything else in the campaign hinges on the target public's needs, interests, and perceptions.
2   What is the *product*? The product is the focus of the transaction between an organization and a public. In social marketing, the product is the goal, whether this involves the embrace of an item or an idea or the adoption of a behavior.
3   What is the *price*? The price represents the cost of embracing the idea or behavior from the public's point of view. This can include time, sacrifices, cultural misgiving, and psychological discomfort.
4   What is the *promotion*? The promotion represents the benefits of the idea or behavior from the public's point of view. What benefits outweigh or decrease the costs it associates with the behavior? Promotion does not mean a simple advertising slogan but represents a summary of the cohesive message strategies that are used in a campaign.
5   What is the *positioning?* Positioning refers to what makes a product special or unique. What makes one event especially worthy of the public's attention? What will make yet another anti–drunk-driving campaign be noticed among the crush of other messages about driving, drinking, and safety? Positioning answers the "why should anyone care?" question and distinguishes the idea, service, or product from competitors in ways the public appreciates.
6   What is the *place*? The place refers to the distribution channels by which the public gains access to information about the product, service, or idea. Where can the public best receive a message about the product?

Figure 13.7 illustrates a social marketing mix based on the Truth campaign against tobacco use developed in Florida. The goal was to reduce tobacco use among Florida teenagers. Through a review of existing research and tobacco-use statistics in the late 1990s, the campaign designers had learned that teenagers already know that tobacco use presents serious health risks but that adolescent smoking rates nevertheless had increased by about one third in the previous decade. Much of tobacco's allure seemed to stem from the perception of smoking as a rebellious activity against adult authority. The strategists decided they needed a *product* that would "drive a wedge" between teens and the tobacco industry: Activism against tobacco use. What would acceptance of the "product" cost this target public, and what promotion could convince them to buy into it?

For the target *public*—teens 12 to 17 at risk for using tobacco—the health dangers of tobacco use clearly did not present a relevant cost. Despite their knowledge of tobacco's physical effects, smoking rates had increased. To them, the social success gained from daring to embrace the danger and defy adults outweighed the health risks. From this perspective, the cost of *not* smoking could be high, because it represented caving in to adult directives (Hicks, 2001). The *price* of acting against adult authority usually is punishment from adults, but this activity invited praise from peers. The best way to *position* the campaign, strategists realized, was to enable young people to motivate each other to take on adults through *placement* of messages via grassroots advocacy, merchandising, and a mass media campaign. The *promotion*, therefore, was glorifica- tion of actions against the tobacco industry. The campaign designers held a youth summit with 500 teens and continued to include teens as partners throughout the campaign.

According to Porter Novelli (Ruiz, 2000), the campaign achieved 92% awareness among Florida teens within 9 months. An evaluation by Farrelly and colleagues (Farrelly, et al., 2002)

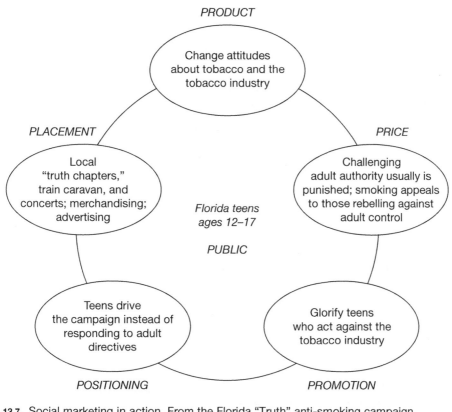

FIG. 13.7. Social marketing in action. From the Florida "Truth" anti-smoking campaign, implemented by the Office of Tobacco Control, Tallahassee, Florida.

indicated that the campaign increased the belief among teens that cigarette companies want young people to smoke and lie about tobacco's health risks. The interpretation of campaign results has sparked some controversy because of the difficulties of isolating the effects of a massive, multipronged strategy, but the campaign eventually was implemented nationwide and appeared to contribute to a 22% decline in youth smoking from 1999 to 2002.

Choosing a Level of Effect

Campaign designers must determine what type of effect they intend to achieve. As Chapter 14 illustrates in more detail, it is much harder to change someone's attitudes or opinions than to change their level of awareness, shown as the base of the level of effects pyramid in Figure 13.8. Changing someone's value system, shown as the pinnacle of the pyramid, offers a nearly impossible challenge. The communication manager must know a huge amount about the target public and the social environment to choose a realistic level of effect on which to base measurable objectives for a communication program.

Attitudes are learned, enduring, and affective evaluations of a person, thing, or idea (Perloff, 2013). Attitudes show that someone feels positively or negatively about something or someone.

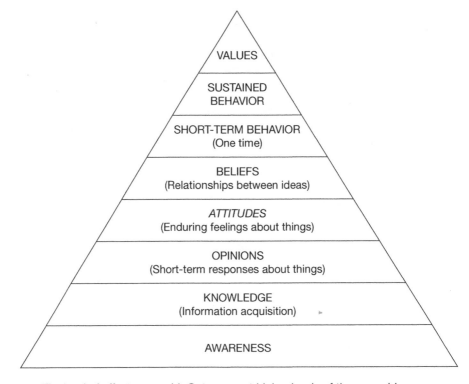

FIG. 13.8. The level of effects pyramid. Outcomes at higher levels of the pyramid are progressively more difficult to change.

Beliefs, on the other hand, are pieces of information about things or people, whether or not these pieces of information are accurate. Beliefs can trigger emotional reactions—attitudes—but generally are considered to be more logically based. Attitudes not only often grow out of beliefs but also can contradict beliefs because people are not purely logical. On the pyramid in Figure 13.8, beliefs appear above attitudes because beliefs are more clearly based on information (or misinformation), and some theories of attitude and behavior change suggest that it is more difficult to change people's minds if they are more systematic (information-oriented) in their responses to messages (Chen & Chaiken, 1999). Yet, product advertising typically depends on short-term change based on affective responses. This body of research suggests that more affectively based attitudes change more easily than logically grounded beliefs. Nevertheless, managers must realize that attitudes supported by strongly held beliefs can be just as challenging to alter as the beliefs.

Some scholars and practitioners consider opinions to be equivalent to attitudes, but others find it useful to make distinctions between them. *Opinions* generally are considered to be somewhat like beliefs because they incorporate cognitive judgments (information). According to Perloff (2013), opinions also differ from attitudes because opinions are simpler and more specific. In addition, opinions can be more short-lived. For example, people asked a question on a survey may produce an opinion on the spot in order to answer the question. They may not

Table 13.4 Terminal and Instrumental Values

Terminal Values	Instrumental Values
Comfortable life	Ambitious
Equality	Broad minded
Exciting life	Capable
Family security	Caring
Freedom	Cheerful
Happiness	Clean
Health	Courageous
Inner harmony	Fair
Mature love	Forgiving
National security	Good citizen
Pleasure	Helpful
Salvation	Honest
Self-respect	Imaginative
Sense of accomplishment	Independent
Social recognition	Intellectual
True friendship	Logical
Wisdom	Loving
World peace	Obedient
	Polite
	Respectful
	Responsible
	Self-controlled
	Trustworthy

hold that opinion deeply or for long. As a result, some survey specialists ask respondents how strongly they feel about an issue along with how positively or negatively they feel.

Organizations often make the mistake of trying to change people's values, which is usually unnecessary and unrealistic. Values are like life goals. According to Rokeach, who developed a famous values scale still in use today (Rokeach, 1973), people adopt *terminal values*, which embody their ultimate life goals, and *instrumental values,* which represent desired strategies for achieving those goals. As shown in Table 13.4, terminal values include freedom, world peace, security, pleasure, health, excitement, and comfort. Instrumental values include politeness, ambition, obedience, helpfulness, self-control, and fairness. A person's *value system* dictates which values are more or less important in relation to one another.

Because values develop early and tend to remain stable, targeting values for change is a divisive strategy, whereas appealing to people's values tends to be a more constructive approach. Attacking the target public's values is especially common among single-issue advocacy groups, such as those focused on animal rights, gun control and control, abortion, homosexuality, and environmental issues. As Plous wrote (1990), however, value-based campaigns often offend the people they aim to persuade. Some political analysts, for example, suggested that Republicans severely damaged their appeal to mainstream voters in their 1992 national convention when they attacked nontraditional families and embraced a traditional family values platform. The Democrats, on the other hand, used their convention to promote the alternative message—that family values means every family has value. The Democrats had economic issues in their favor, commonly considered a major political asset, which meant that Republicans could ill afford a strategy that alienated a large portion of the population.

Both parties, as well as third parties such as Libertarians, continue to "appeal to their base" with messaging and policy proposals intended to represent the core values of their most ardent constituents. Such campaigns, however, tend to alienate others and contribute to polarization and gridlock. In response, a group spanning the political spectrum, called No Labels, launched in 2010 and attracted high-profile Republican and Democratic leaders in 2013 who agreed to facilitate regular meetings of diversely oriented politicians. The group promotes proposals such as "no budget, no pay" for members of Congress, aimed at removing structural barriers to collaboration (No Labels, 2013).

Organizations need to exercise caution both in trying to change values and in interpreting data about values. Accusations that people who disagree with an organization's preferred view hold substandard values make those people defensive and less willing to entertain other viewpoints. Demonstrating a shared value, on the other hand, can enable adversaries to find common ground on which to build understanding and, ultimately, consensus. It is not easy and it takes time to build trust, but it can be done. In 2012, the Humane Society and the United Egg Producers lobbying group, longtime adversaries, co-sponsored legislation that would require larger cages for egg-laying hens. They began their journey toward the discovery of common ground when Gene Gregory, of the United Egg Producers, sent a note through an intermediary to Wayne Pacelle, the president of the Humane Society of the United States, asking, "Can the two of us just talk?" They discovered that despite their different backgrounds and nearly opposite dietary orientations, they could find reasons to respect one another. They also realized, as Pacelle said, "We could fight the United Egg Producers for another 10 or 15 years, and spend millions of dollars on both sides. But the other option is, we could sit down together and figure out a pathway that's good for industry and better for animals" (Charles, 2012, ¶ 16).

For communication managers seeking to bridge differences to build partnerships, the Public Conversations Project (2013) can provide helpful resources. The project's mission is to foster a more inclusive, empathic, and collaborative society by promoting constructive conversations and relationships among those who have differing values, world views, and positions about divisive public issues. It provides training, speakers, and consulting services with support from more than two dozen private foundations.

Final Thoughts

Efforts to build on common ground embody Plous's (1990) point that "activists will be more effective if they are able to understand and empathize with people whose views differ from their own" (p. 2). Even a pure advocacy campaign can benefit from a symmetrical theoretical perspective on communication. This theoretical framework guides goal setting and planning. Then, within this theoretical perspective, the manager can turn to more specific theories that explain the communication process and communicators themselves. An understanding of these theories can guide strategy development, give a program proposal credibility, and increase the probability of program success. They are the focus of Chapter 14.

14

Theories for Creating Effective Message Strategies

In the 1950s and early 1960s, communication experts noticed that mass communication campaigns were having little effect, and many believed the situation to be hopeless. One scholar caused an uproar with an article calling mass media campaigns essentially impotent, and another published an influential book asserting that information campaigns tended to reinforce existing opinions but rarely changed anybody's minds. These followed on the heels of two other scholars who blamed the receivers of messages for failing to be persuaded by them. This pessimistic view still prevailed a decade later, when a man named Mendelsohn responded with a more realistic diagnosis and a more optimistic prognosis. His ideas have had an enormous impact on the communication field.

Mendelsohn's Three Assumptions for Success

Mendelsohn (1973) believed campaigns often failed because campaign designers over-promised, assumed the public would automatically receive and enthusiastically accept their messages, and blanketed the public with messages not properly targeted and likely to be ignored or misinterpreted. As McGuire (1989) wrote later, successful communication campaigns depend on a good understanding of two types of theories: those that explain how someone will process and respond to a message and those that explain why someone will or will not respond to a message in desirable ways.

After more than three decades, Mendelsohn's diagnosis still applies. Surveys and interviews with communication professionals have shown consistently that one of the major reasons clients and superiors lose faith in public relations agencies and professionals is because the agencies overpromised (Bourland, 1993; Harris & Impulse Research, 2004; Ketchum, 2012). In 2003, the failure to keep promises was the biggest reason cited by clients for declining confidence in public relations agencies (Harris & Impulse Research, 2004). An inability to demonstrate measurable results was still rated one of the top three issues facing communication leadership worldwide in 2012 (Berger, 2012), and ineffective communication of realistic expectations often is at the root of this problem. The Ketchum Leadership Communication Monitor, in a survey of over 3700 individuals in 12 countries, found a 28% gap between what people expected of their leaders and what they perceived that their leaders actually delivered (Ketchum, 2012). Overpromising often occurs when program planners do not have a good understanding of their publics and of the situation in which program messages will be received. People from varied backgrounds and with varied interests are likely to interpret messages differently. Moreover, a good understanding of the problem, the publics, and the constraints affecting the likelihood of change (remember social marketing's "price") helps the program planner set goals and objectives that can be achieved using the strategies available in the time allotted. Mendelsohn (1973) offered a trio of campaign assumptions:

1   Target your messages.
2   Assume your target public is uninterested in your messages.
3   Set reasonable, midrange goals and objectives.

On the one hand, Mendelsohn's admonition that message receivers will not be interested in a campaign and that campaigns setting ambitious goals are doomed to failure can cultivate pessimism. On the other hand, Mendelsohn's point is that campaign designers who make his three assumptions can make adjustments in strategy that will facilitate success both in the short term and in the long run. The implication of Mendelsohn's tripartite is that research is necessary to define and to understand the target publics and that an understanding of theory is necessary in order to develop strategies that acknowledge the publics' likely lack of interest and that point to strategies that will compensate for it. Mendelsohn illustrated his point with an example from his own experience, which, depending on your perspective, could be viewed either as a major success or a dismal failure.

Mendelsohn's campaign tried to increase traffic safety by addressing the fact that at least 80% of drivers considered themselves to be good or excellent drivers, yet unsafe driving practices killed people every day. Long holiday weekends were especially gruesome. Meanwhile, most drivers ignored the 300,000 persuasive traffic safety messages disseminated each year in the print media.

Mendelsohn's team, in cooperation with the National Safety Council and CBS, developed "The CBS National Driver's Test," which aired immediately before the 1965 Memorial Day weekend. A publicity campaign distributed 50 million official test answer forms via newspapers, magazines, and petroleum products dealers before the show aired. The show, viewed by approximately 30 million Americans, was among the highest rated public affairs broadcasts of all time to that point and resulted in mail responses from nearly a million and a half viewers. Preliminary research showed that almost 40% of the licensed drivers who had participated in the broadcast had failed the test. Finally, 35,000 drivers enrolled in driver-improvement programs across the country following the broadcast. The producer of the program called the response "enormous, beyond all expectations." Yet no evidence was provided that accident rates decreased because of the broadcast, and the number of people enrolled in driver improvement programs reflected only about .07% of those who had been exposed to the test forms. How was this an enormous success?

Mendelsohn realized that bad drivers would be difficult to reach because of their lack of awareness or active denial of their skill deficiencies, and he realized that to set a campaign goal of eliminating or greatly reducing traffic deaths as the result of a single campaign would be impossible. As a result, Mendelsohn's team chose more realistic goals in recognition of the fact that a single campaign could not be expected to completely solve any problem. The goals of the campaign included the following:

1   To overcome public indifference to traffic hazards that may be caused by bad driving (increasing awareness).
2   To make bad drivers cognizant of their deficiencies (comprehension).
3   To direct viewers who become aware of their driving deficiencies into a social mechanism already set up in the community to correct such deficiencies (skill development).

How People Respond to Messages (McGuire's Hierarchy of Effects or "Domino" Model of Persuasion)

Evaluating Mendelsohn's success illustrates both the pitfalls of dependence on the traditional linear model of the communication process and the advantages of adopting a more receiver-oriented view, commonly known as the *domino* model or *hierarchy of effects* theory of persuasion (Figure 14.1). The domino model acknowledges that campaign messages have to achieve several intermediate steps that intervene between message dissemination and desired behavior changes. According to McGuire, the originator of the domino model, effective campaigns need to acknowledge the following steps, which have been modified here to reflect recent research findings and the symmetrical public relations perspective. Each step is a repository for dozens, if not hundreds, of studies that have shown the importance of the step in people's decision making, along with the factors that enhance or compromise the success of campaign messages at each step.

1   *Exposure.* This, unfortunately, is where most communication programs begin and end, with getting the message out. Obviously, no one can be persuaded by a message they have had no opportunity to receive. Simply placing a message in the environment, however, is not enough to ensure its receipt or acceptance. Recall that some 300,000 safe driving messages had been ignored consistently by the target public before Mendelsohn's campaign.

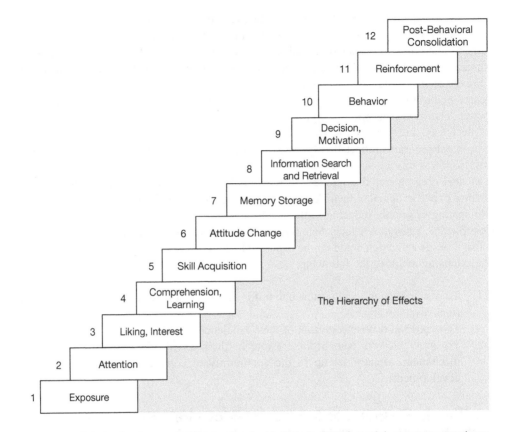

FIG. 14.1. McGuire's domino model. According to McGuire's (1989) model, message receivers go through a number of response steps that mediate persuasion decision making. Managers setting program goals at the top of the hierarchy may be unrealistic.

2 *Attention.* Even a paid advertisement broadcast during the Super Bowl will fail if the target publics have chosen that moment to head to the refrigerator for a snack, paying scant attention to the spot ostensibly broadcast to millions. A message must attract at least a modicum of attention to succeed, and campaign designers must not forget the obvious: complex messages require more attention than simple messages. Production values such as color can make a difference: Color can attract attention, communicate emotion and enhance memory ("Breaking Through," 1999; Felton, 1998). Production values, however, do not guarantee success even if they do attract attention. Color must be used carefully, for example, because the meaning of color may vary with the context and cultural environment. Although orange may signify humor, Halloween, and autumn, it also can mean quarantine (United States) or death (Arab countries). Red can mean danger or sin (United States), passionate love (Austria and Germany), joy and happiness (China and Japan), and death (Africa). Quite a range! As a result, the International Red Cross, sensitive to this issue, uses green in Africa instead of red (Felton, 1998). According to the Y&R Brand Futures Group ("Survey Finds," 1998),

blue has become a popular color to signify the future because people across cultures associate it with the sky and water, signifying limitlessness and peace.

Message designers need to know that some aspects of attention are controlled by the viewer, and some are involuntary responses to visual and audio cues. A sudden noise, for example, will draw attention as a result of what scientists call an orienting response, a survival mechanism developed to ensure quick responses to danger. A fun activity, on the other hand, will draw attention because the viewer enjoys seeing it. Many communication strategists find it tempting to force viewers to pay attention by invoking their involuntary responses, such as through quick cuts and edits (e.g., the style often used in music videos). The problem with this tactic is that people have a limited pool of resources to use at any one time for message processing tasks. If viewers must devote most or all of their cognitive energy to attention, they will have little left over for putting information into memory. In other words, they may pay lots of attention to your message but remember little or nothing about it.

3 *Involvement (liking or interest).* Although research has shown people will orient themselves to sudden changes in sounds or visual effects, other research has shown that they stop paying attention if a message seems irrelevant, uninteresting, or distasteful. Messages that seem relevant sustain people's interest, making people more likely to learn from the message. Social marketing theory acknowledges the importance of this step in its placement of the audience, or public, in the center of the planning profile. Everything about the campaign goal—its benefits, costs, and unique qualities— must be considered from the target public's point of view. They care much more about how a proposal will affect them than how it will affect your company. The City of Tacoma, Washington, for example, wanted to extend the life of its landfill and promote recycling. A survey of customers found that people would recycle more if they did not have to sort and separate items. As a result, the city responded by offering a new comingled recycling program that enabled customers to throw all recyclables into the same bin. Recycling increased 300% to 400%, far exceeding the research-based objective of 200% to 300% and earning the city a Silver Anvil Award from PRSA.

An unusual characteristic to an otherwise familiar story often can attract people's interest. The relatively unknown issue of pulmonary hypertension achieved its goal of improving awareness by obtaining the cooperation of the U.S. Secretary of State and, as a result, a great deal of publicity. A fund-raising concert became an especially significant event when it took place at the Kennedy Center in Washington, D.C. and featured Condoleezza Rice, an accomplished pianist as well as the Secretary of State at that time, as one of the performers. According to Representative Tom Lantos of California, who had mentioned to the Secretary that his granddaughter suffered from the disease, Rice told him, "We have to do something about this and enhance public consciousness. Let's have a concert and I'll accompany her at the piano" (Schweld, 2005). According to Orkideh Malkoc, the organization's associate director for advocacy and awareness, more than 450 people attended the event and the organization received coverage in more than 250 publications, including some outside of the United States (personal communication, June 20, 2005).

4 *Comprehension (learning what).* Sustained attention increases but does not guarantee the likelihood of comprehension. Messages can be misinterpreted. For example, a cereal

company promotion suggested more than a dozen whimsical ideas for getting a cookie prize, named Wendell and shaped like a person, to come out of the cereal box. Having a cookie for breakfast appealed to children, as did the silly ideas, such as telling him he had to come out because he was under arrest. Unfortunately, one of the ideas—call the fire department to rescue a guy from your cereal box—backfired when some children actually called 911, which confused, alarmed, and irritated the rescue teams. The boxes had to be pulled from the shelves in at least one region of the country.

5 *Skill acquisition (learning how).* Well-intentioned people may be unable to follow through on an idea if they lack the means to do so. Potential voters without transportation to the polls will not vote; intended nonsmokers will not quit smoking without social support; interested restaurant patrons will not come if they cannot afford it; parents interested in a civic betterment program will not attend a meeting if they do not have child care. An effective campaign anticipates the target public's needs to provide the help they require. The National Fire Protection Association (NFPA), for example, found, through a Burke Marketing survey, that many people had a passive attitude about fire, many believed they had much more time to escape than they really do, and only 16% had developed and practiced a home fire escape plan (PRSA, 1999a). As a result, NFPA developed a Fire Safety Week promotion focused on teaching students about fire escape planning and practice, with incentives to encourage them to participate in a documented practice drill with their families. Although the Silver Anvil Award-winning campaign generated an enormous amount of publicity, the most dramatic result was that at least 25 lives were saved as a direct result of the families' participation in the promotion.

6 *Persuasion (attitude change).* Although McGuire listed this step following skills acquisition, attitude change often precedes skill development. People who lack the skills to follow through on an idea may tune out the details, figuring it is not relevant for them. Attitude change is another of the necessary but often insufficient steps in the persuasion process. Sometimes, however, attitude change is all that is necessary, particularly if the goal of a campaign is to increase a public's satisfaction with an organization in order to avoid negative consequences such as lawsuits, strikes, or boycotts. Usually, however, a campaign has an outcome behavior in mind. In that case, remember that people often have attitudes inconsistent with their behaviors. Many smokers believe smoking is a bad thing but still smoke. Many nonvoters say voting is important and that they intend to vote, but they still fail to show up on Election Day.

7 *Memory storage.* This step is important because people receive multiple messages from multiple sources all day, every day. For them to act on your message, they need to remember it when the appropriate time comes to buy a ticket, make a telephone call, fill out a form, or attend an event. They need to be able to store the important information about your message in their memory, which may not be easy if other messages received simultaneously demand their attention. Key elements of messages, therefore, need to be communicated in ways that make them stand out for easy memorization.

8 *Information retrieval.* Simply storing information does not ensure that it will be retrieved at the appropriate time. People might remember your special event on the correct day but forget the location. Reminders or memory devices such as slogans, jingles, and refrigerator magnets can help. Mobile phone apps have become especially

popular tools for providing reminders and for keeping critical information handy at a moment's notice.

9 *Motivation (decision).* This is an important step that many campaign designers forget in their own enthusiasm for their campaign goals. Remember Mendelsohn's (1973) admonition that people may not be interested in the campaign? They need reasons to follow through. The benefits need to outweigh the costs. In addition, the benefits must seem realistic and should be easily obtained. The more effort required on the part of the message recipients the less likely it is that they will make that effort. If the message recipients believe a proposed behavior is easy, will have major personal benefits, or is critically important, they are more likely to act. The challenge for the program is to discover what will motivate the target successfully, an issue addressed later in this chapter. DDB of Seattle, when asked to help reduce Puget Sound curbside disposal of grass clippings by 5%, realized motivation would be an important focus. Focus groups and phone surveys indicated that the target group, male homeowners aged 25 to 65, had an interest in grasscycling but needed the proper tools to make it easy and practical. As a result, they arranged to recycle consumers' old polluting gas mowers for free at a special event and sell Torro and Ryobi mulch mowers at below the normal retail price, with an additional rebate. With a goal of selling 3,000 mowers, they sold 5,000. They hoped to remove 1,500 gas mowers from the market and ended up recycling approximately 2,600. And as for their original goal of reducing curbside disposal of grass clippings by 5%? They more than tripled the target amount, reducing grass clippings by 17%, winning a Silver Anvil Award (PRSA, 1999b).

10 *Behavior.* Success often is measured in terms of behaviors such as sales or attendance figures. Marketing experts, however, know that getting someone's business once does not guarantee long-term success. One study ("Building Customer," 1996) found that keeping customers loyal can boost profits up to 80%. As a result, the program planner needs to do everything possible to ensure that behavior attempts meet with success. The Massachusetts Office of Energy and Environmental Affairs, for example, wound up with thousands of frustrated citizens when it promoted a cash-for-appliances rebate program only to find its phone and Web-based systems overwhelmed with bargain seekers who maxed out the $6 million available in rebate reservations in less than two hours. The site had been designed to accommodate only 5,000 users at a time. Anticipating demand and preparing to handle unsuccessful attempts in a positive way can help cement relationships for the long term.

11 *Reinforcement of behavior, attitude, or both.* Most people are familiar with the phrase *buyer's remorse*, which is what people feel if they have second thoughts about a decision they made. Sometimes buyer's remorse results from a bad experience with an organization, such as an unresponsive telephone operator, which is quite unrelated to the product or idea that was the focus of a campaign. Program planners need to anticipate possible reasons for buyer's remorse in a campaign and make follow-up communication part of the campaign to ensure targeted publics continue to feel good about the organization's products or ideas.

12 *Post-behavior consolidation.* This is the final step in a message receiver's decision-making process. At this point, the receiver considers the campaign messages, the attitudes and behaviors involved, and the successes or failures encountered in implementing the targeted attitudes or behaviors, to incorporate this new information

into a preexisting world view. By attending a special event promoting both a company and a cause, such as feeding the homeless, a message recipient may develop a long-term connection with both the company and the cause. In this spirit, medical schools such as at Georgetown University hold memorial services to honor the families of individuals who donate their bodies to the university. The event helped family members feel more comfortable about the choice their loved one had made (Sun, 2012). Affecting the targeted public's worldview is the most challenging result for a communication campaign, but for programs focused on building long-term, mutually beneficial relationships, this result also is the most coveted.

Just How Difficult Is It?

McGuire (1989) suggested a success rate of 50% at each stage in a typical mass media campaign would be improbably optimistic. Given that level of attrition, a campaign exposed to 1 million people would gain the attention of 500,000, would hold the interest of 250,000, would be understood as intended by 125,000, would address the necessary skills and needs of 62,500, would be persuasive to 31,250, would be remembered at the time of the communication by 15,625, would be recalled later by 7,813, would be sufficiently motivating to 3,907, would achieve behavior change among 1,954, would achieve repeat behavior among 977, and would gain long-term "consolidation" among 489. No wonder campaign designers in the 1950s and 1960s thought campaigns were doomed to failure. The good news, however, is that this pessimistic view assumes each step has an equal chance of success, each step is equally important to the campaign, and the steps must proceed in the order delineated by McGuire's matrix. Fortunately, these assumptions do not always apply.

If we think back to Mendelsohn's (1973) campaign, in which 50 million people were exposed to promotions regarding the CBS National Driver's Test, 30 million viewed the program to become aware of the hazards of unsafe driving, nearly 40% of licensed drivers failed the test, and approximately 35,000 drivers enrolled in driver improvement programs, should we consider Mendelsohn's campaign a success or a failure? The campaign only achieved close to 0.1% success throughout the hierarchy of effects.

Given Mendelsohn's points about assuming that the target is uninterested, the need for targeting the audience, and the need to set reasonable goals, we must consider the situation before assigning credit or blame.

> *Uninterested target.* Bad drivers are not likely to be interested in being told their driving is deficient; indeed, they are likely to be defensive. Everyone thinks everyone else is the bad driver. In fact, Mendelsohn found that 80% of drivers thought they were good drivers, yet almost half of licensed drivers failed the National Driver's Test. That means that one of every two bad drivers either did not know or would not acknowledge their deficiencies. This means that Mendelsohn was correct, even understated, on the first point.
>
> *Targeting the audience.* The CBS National Driver's Test did not broadcast exclusively to bad drivers. It needed to find them among all other viewers of the program, some of whom were not licensed drivers, were not old enough to drive, or were safe drivers. As a result, the campaign could not reasonably expect, nor did it desire, all 50 million people exposed to the campaign to enroll in driver improvement programs. Indeed, if that many people signed up for class, there would not have been enough teachers to serve them all.

Reasonable goals. If 40% of the drivers who watched the program took the test and failed it in the privacy of their own homes, many of them probably changed their attitudes about their own driving and perhaps took some extra precautions the next time they drove, regardless of whether they enrolled in a formal driver improvement program. The 35,000 drivers who did sign up for formal programs represented a 300% increase, in a 3-month period, over the previous annual enrollment in the programs.

Any public relations agency promising 50 million exposures and 50 million behaviors would be dismissed as naive and absurd. Any public relations agency promising a 300% increase in targeted behaviors, particularly for a challenging behavior to change, probably also would be dismissed as arrogant and unrealistic. In this context, Mendelsohn's campaign looks terrific. So from Mendelsohn we can learn that the definition of success depends on the viewer's perspective. Defining success in terms of desired receiver-oriented outcomes is more appropriate than defining success in terms of source-oriented outputs such as reach or impressions

Problems With a Source-Oriented Perspective

The common strategy of promising clients huge exposure can tempt clients to expect more impressive behavioral outcomes than would be realistic. With such dangers in mind, McGuire (1989) explained various fallacies that can doom a campaign, along with principles for counteracting challenges along the way.

Common Problems in Application of the Domino Model

McGuire (1989) noted three fallacies that dog campaign designers with an insufficient grasp of persuasion theory.

1 *The attenuated-effects fallacy.* Clients and agencies alike want to assume that exposure will produce success in terms of reputation, sales, or other desirable outcomes. The likelihood of continued success along each successive decision-making step, however, is probably less than 50% in a mass market campaign, making the final outcome likely to be less than 0.1% of the original number exposed to the campaign. For example, when Chase Card Services introduced its new Sapphire credit card in the San Francisco market, it needed to achieve solid applications, not just media impressions (Public Relations Society of America, 2012c). The company did accomplish nearly 70 million media impressions, but it also demonstrated a 72% level of awareness among affluent target-market members and netted a 12% increase in new credit card applications. The 12% increase in behavior was nowhere near the 70 million impressions, of course, but the campaign won a Silver Anvil Award for its effectiveness. As the Ketchum representatives wrote, this level of response represented a "huge feat," particularly given the dour economic climate at the time of the campaign.

2 *The distant-measure fallacy.* Sometimes program planners report results for attitude change as if it represents behavior change, or they may report changes in awareness as a representation of attitude change. If a program hopes to achieve behavior change, it must measure behavior, not attitudes, as an outcome. Using so-called clip counts as an indicator of awareness by collecting the amount of publicity accumulated misrepresents campaign effects.

The experience of the pop bands Backstreet Boys and 'N Sync, who released albums the same year, provides a dramatic example of this. The bands had quite different levels of success depending on how observers measured it. The Backstreet Boys garnered a *Publicity Watch* score of 1,372 during the 2 months including and following the release of their album, *Black & Blue*. This number represents a special method for media tracking exposure in print, broadcast, and consumer and trade publications from Delahaye Medialink. 'N Sync, meanwhile, managed only a score of 951 for the months including and following the release for its album, *No Strings Attached*. On the measure of exposure, therefore, the Backstreet Boys demolished 'N Sync. 'N Sync, however, sold 2.4 million copies of its recording in its first week, compared with 1.6 million copies for the Backstreet Boys' recording. Although both recordings sold well, 'N Sync clearly did better on the behavior measure at the cash register (Stateman & Weiner, 2001). To say, based on publicity, that the Backstreet Boys had the more successful release would misrepresent what actually happened.

3   *The neglected-mediator fallacy.* Well-meaning program planners can make unwitting mistakes if they assume elements that enhance success at one step in the process will continue to enhance success at every step. For example, using Nancy Reagan as a spokesperson for the "Just Say No" antidrug programs of the 1980s helped the campaigns achieve tremendous exposure nationwide. But Nancy Reagan's credibility among the targeted audience of at-risk adolescents was not high. Likewise, having police officers deliver messages to school children in the "DARE to Say No to Drugs" campaigns might capture the children's attention, but it would do little to provide them with the skills needed to face being ostracized by their peers. A spokesperson more relevant to their own needs and interests is important to such a campaign.

McGuire also offered several recommendations designed to help maximize success at each step. Even if a campaign cannot achieve 300% increases in behavior, as Mendelsohn's campaign did, it probably can do better than 0.1% of those initially exposed to a program message if the designer successfully implements the following principles:

1   *The compensatory principle.* The good news is that sometimes things can balance out such that something working against your campaign at one step may work in favor of it at another step. If a simple, graphics-heavy message on television captures people's attention but communicates little information about a complex issue, a companion message, perhaps in a medium such as print or Web-based technologies more amenable to careful consideration, can provide the necessary details. Not everyone will pursue the details, but if the initial message piques the public's interest, more people probably will pay deeper attention to the companion message than would have done so otherwise. If a political figure helps a campaign achieve exposure but is irrelevant to the ultimate target public, a campaign can include more appropriate message sources for different targeted publics.

2   *The golden-mean principle.* Usually, a moderate amount of something, rather than extreme levels, has the maximum effect (Figure 14.2). The program designer's challenge is to determine more precisely what level is optimal for each target public and situation. This principle seems like common sense but can be difficult to apply

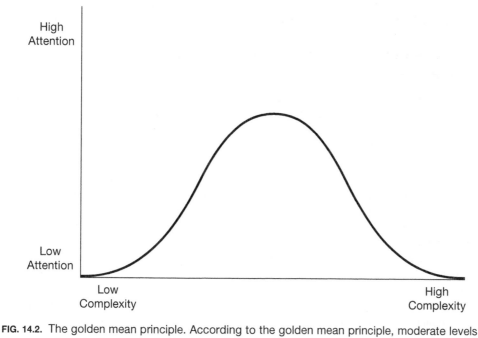

FIG. 14.2. The golden mean principle. According to the golden mean principle, moderate levels of production- or content-related strategies tend to have more effectiveness than extreme levels.

because it can be challenging to determine what levels of humor or fear, for example, seem extreme to the target public. Similarly, the campaign designer needs to know what level of complexity makes a message incomprehensible, versus what level of simplicity makes the message boring. The golden mean principle, therefore, illustrates why pretesting is vital to message development.

The program designer's challenge is to determine more precisely what level is optimal for each target public and situation.

3   *The situation-weighting principle.* According to McGuire (1989), achieving the hierarchy of effects is not as difficult as it may seem at first glance because some steps will probably be easier to achieve than others. For example, publicity campaigns continue to hold such popularity because they often reach enough people who already have the interest and motivation to follow through on a message about a new product or service opportunity. Most people will not be interested, but if enough interested people read a well-placed piece on a new restaurant, they will need little additional impetus to get them to the restaurant, as long as the location is easy to remember. They already may possess the skills (transportation and money), the attitude (liking to eat out at that type of restaurant), and the motivation (perhaps an anniversary or birthday dinner is coming up). Likewise, people who want to do something they never thought possible may jump at the opportunity if a campaign addresses their needs (the skill development step).

The result, according to the domino model and Mendelsohn's (1973) assumptions, is that a well-researched, carefully targeted campaign will make more dominos fall without going awry.

Limitations of the Domino Model—Acknowledging that People are Not Always Logical

Because the domino model provides such a useful campaign planning tool, it is the most popular theory of persuasion among communication program planners. In fact, Ketchum Public Relations fashioned a public relations *effectiveness yardstick*. The yardstick approximates the hierarchy of effects for easy application, by combining the steps of the domino model into three levels of effect (Figure 14.3).

The first level, called the *basic level*, measures *outputs*, or exposure in McGuire's (1989) terminology, such as total placements and number of impressions. The second level, called the *intermediate level*, measures *outgrowths*, such as whether target audiences have received messages directed at them, whether they have paid attention to them, whether they have understood them, and whether they have retained them. This corresponds to the steps of attention, comprehension, interest, and memory storage in McGuire's model. The third level, called the *advanced level*, measures communication *outcomes*, such as opinion, attitude, or behavior change.

The domino theory, however, has one important limitation: It incorporates an assumption that the recipients of campaign messages will process them in a logical way, carefully considering

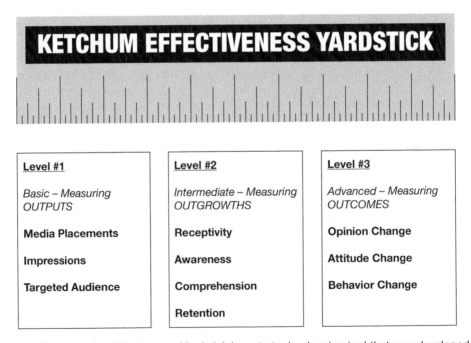

FIG. 14.3. The Ketchum Effectiveness Yardstick is a strategic planning tool that was developed by the Ketchum Research and Measurement Department.

the veracity of campaign messages to evaluate whether they wish to perform the proposed behavior. The truth is people are not always logical, and we do some things not because they seem right but because they feel good. As a result, it is important to consider another theoretical perspective on persuasion that explicitly acknowledges our logical lapses.

The most popular alternative to the hierarchy of effects theory is called the *elaboration likelihood model* (ELM). Developed by Petty and Cacioppo (1986) using tightly controlled experiments with limited samples of college students, this theory has its detractors and needs to be applied with respect for its limitations (Chen & Chaiken, 1999). Its basic principles, however, echoed by other theorists pursuing so-called heuristic and systematic routes to decision making, provide a useful framework for communication program application, regardless of how the scholars sort out the details. According to the ELM, people process messages differently depending on their level of involvement with the issue. In this way, the ELM dovetails with Grunig and Repper's (1992) situational theory of publics. People uninterested or uninvolved in a topic will not process messages deeply, but those more interested will be more likely to elaborate, to think more carefully about, the message.

The result is that the campaign designer can think broadly of two routes to persuasion. The first route is called the *central approach* and emphasizes logic and careful consideration. This is known more broadly as *systematic processing*. The second route is called the *peripheral approach* and forgoes logical arguments in favor of more emotionally or heuristic-based strategies. These strategies include elements such as likable, attractive, powerful, and credible sources. According to the ELM, decisions achieved using the central approach are more likely to last, whereas decisions achieved using the peripheral approach are more likely to fade or decay. The peripheral approach, however, can achieve changes more quickly because less thoughtful consideration is necessary from the message recipients.

The central approach requires a larger investment of energy from the message recipient, making it more likely to succeed if recipients are highly involved or interested in the topic. If it succeeds, it has longer-lasting effects because people feel more invested in a decision that took more effort to make and that is based on facts instead of on surface cues. The peripheral approach is more appropriate for low-involvement issues or among target publics who do not care much about the issue. Again, it requires research to determine the extent to which target publics feel involved and ready to participate in thoughtful decision making.

McGuire (1989) called the ELM an alternative route to persuasion because it acknowledges that the central approach follows all the steps in the domino model, whereas the peripheral approach bypasses several steps, concentrating on elements such as attention, liking, and motivation to the exclusion of elements such as attitude change and skill development. Both the central approach and the peripheral approach require that the program planner understand what will attract and hold message recipients' attention, along with what will motivate them to follow through the hierarchy of effects necessary to achieve behavior change.

Why People Respond to Messages—Finding the Right Motivating Strategy

To help campaign designers sort through the possible strategies for motivating target publics, McGuire created a matrix that summarizes hundreds of scientific studies on attitudes and persuasion into 16 categories. A modified version of McGuire's matrix is presented in Figure 14.4 to help the communication professional. Managers may notice that the top half of the chart,

Nature of Motivation / State		Need for Stability		Need for Growth	
		Active	Reactive	Active	Reactive
Cognitive	Internal	1. Consistency (cognitive dissonance)	2. Categorization	5. Autonomy	6. Problem solver
	External	3. Noetic	4. Inductional	7. Stimulation	8. Teleological
Affective	Internal	9. Tension-reduction (fear appeals)	10. Ego-defensive	13. Assertion	14. Identification
	External	11. Expressive	12. Repetition	15. Empathy	16. Contagion (bandwagon)

FIG. 14.4. McGuire's dynamic theories chart. The chart illustrates different types of motivations that affect the ways people respond to persuasive messages.

Adapted with permission from Public Communication Campaigns (2nd ed., Table 2.2, p. 54), R. E. Rice & C. K. Atkin (Eds.). Copyright ©1989 by Sage Publications, Inc.

labeled *cognitive theories*, roughly corresponds to the central approach of the ELM theory, or so-called systematic processing strategies, whereas the bottom half of the chart, labeled *affective theories*, roughly corresponds to the peripheral approach, or so-called heuristic processing strategies. Although heuristics such as credibility can be quite logically based, they often rely on the tug of emotion. As a result, the bottom half of the matrix also tends to emphasize emotionally based appeals. The top half relies more on logic and evidence, whereas the bottom half makes more use of raw fear, anger, love, and desire.

The top and bottom halves of the chart are divided again, to acknowledge that sometimes people are motivated by the need for stability because utter chaos would make life too unpredictable and uncomfortable, and sometimes people are motivated by the desire to grow, such as by the desire to become smarter, or more successful, or more independent, or more happy.

The most effective campaign probably will combine various strategies from the matrix to address the needs and interests possessed by different target publics or to address the challenges presented at different steps in the persuasion process. For example, a campaign might use an affective strategy (i.e., a heuristic drawn from the bottom half of the matrix) to pique the public's interest in an issue and follow that with a more logically-based message (from the top half of the matrix) to deepen the public's understanding of the issue. Remember that virtually no effective campaign will forgo emotional appeals as part of its strategic mix. A dry recitation of information attracts little attention, interest, or motivation except from the most dedicated target publics. As a result, even logically-based strategies tend to incorporate affective elements. This is why it is better to think of the top half of the matrix as systematic approaches (not emotion-free approaches) and the bottom half as heuristic (primarily but not exclusively emotion based). Again, research and pretesting are required to determine which among the following strategies is most appropriate for a given communication program or campaign.

Logical Strategies

The first half of McGuire's (1989) dynamic theories matrix focuses on primarily logic-based appeals. On the whole, logical appeals serve as useful strategies for publics who have an interest in a topic and some motivation to ponder it. For issues about which they care less or feel defensive, rational arguments may not work. Even logic-based arguments include some affective elements to make target publics think better of themselves or to encourage them to avoid thinking less of themselves. As a result, they include a range of positive and negative strategies, as follows:

1   *Consistency*. People desire to have consistency in their lives. If the campaign demonstrates they have two conflicting beliefs, they will feel cognitive dissonance, meaning discomfort from the contradictions in their belief system, which they will want to resolve (Figure 14.5). The consistency-based message is one of the most popular campaign strategies because it offers a straightforward way to communicate that the public is mistaken for disagreeing with the client's point of view. The Family Violence Protection Fund, for example, challenged its target public that "if the noise coming from next door were loud music, you'd do something about it," implying that if the noise is coming from something much more serious such as spousal abuse, there is no excuse for domestic violence and no excuse for failing to report it. The idea that the reader would intervene for something trivial but bothersome yet not for something serious aims to create dissonance by making the reader feel selfish.

2   *Categorization*. The categorization approach responds to people's desire to organize their world into sensible categories such as good and bad, real and unreal. If the campaign designer can change the way people view a situation, it may change the way they evaluate issues relevant to the situation. For example, a moderate Republican challenging a Democrat for office may apply the label *liberal*, or *tax and spend* to the Democrat to evoke a reliable response from targeted segments of the electorate, but the same Republican can fall victim to a more conservative Republican challenger who may relabel the moderate Republican as *too liberal* or as *tax and spend* to associate him or her more with the Democrats than with the Republicans. Such strategies, however, can stretch the truth or ethical boundaries and must be used with care. Former presidential candidate Rick Santorum went so far as to relabel the firearms issue problem for Pennsylvania gun-favoring voters as being the existence of his opponent, Harris Wofford, during an early run for one of Pennsylvania's U.S. senate seats.

     Santorum's direct mail piece suggested Wofford should be targeted to rid Pennsylvania of the gun control problem. The piece, with Wofford's name imprinted in the center of a target, not only looked as if it was meant for real target shooting but also was offered for sale as such. The idea of using gun targets to represent political opponents became especially controversial after a gunman killed and injured a number of people at a constituent services event held by former Arizona congresswoman, Gabrielle Giffords.

     A more positive and innovative use of this strategy was used to promote art school, by the College for Creative Studies. The posters created by Team Detroit, with slogans such as "1 in 5 teenagers will experiment with art," cost little but quickly became a sensation on the internet as a hilarious parody of anti-drug messages (Figure 14.6).

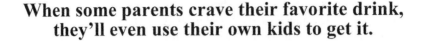

When some parents crave their favorite drink, they'll even use their own kids to get it.

When you tell your kids to get you a beer, are you unconsciously giving them permission to handle alcohol?

To kids, your most casual gestures involving alcohol can take on great importance. So examine any messages your behavior concerning this drug might be sending. And talk to them early about the responsibilities that go along with alcohol use.

Call 1-800-662-911, or send for our free guide, "Talking To Your Kids About Alcohol."

And make sure what you're teaching your kids about alcohol is what you want them to learn.

Washington State Substance Abuse Coalition
Talking To Your Kids About Alcohol Brochure
12729 N.E. 20th, Suite 18, Bellevue, WA 98005

FIG. 14.5. Example of a consistency appeal. This ad motivates behavioral change by pointing out the inconsistencies that exist between parents' inherent desire to parent well and their behavior when they do things like asking their children to get a beer for them.

Courtesy of the Division of Alcohol and Substance Abuse, Department of Social and Health Services, Washington State.

FIG. 14.6. Example of a categorization appeal, with a humorous twist.

Courtesy of the College for Creative Studies.

> After we created this series of low-tech posters, something amazing happened. They went **viral**. People started sharing them though blogs, Facebook and Twitter. People chuckled, then passed them along to their friends. Who knew you could blow up the Internet with a campaign full of print material?
>
> (College for Creative Studies, 2013, ¶ 3)

3 *Noetic or attribution.* Sometimes the campaigner prefers to take a more positive approach to people's desire for consistency. The noetic approach relies on highlighting an association that gives the target public and the organization some common ground on which to share their perspectives, to encourage the target public to view the organization or its proposed behaviors in a more favorable light. One use for attribution theory is to point out a simple association between two things the public may not have connected previously, such as CARE, a social assistance organization, and Starbucks coffee. Credo phone service has used the strategy to appeal to consumers who favor nonprofit causes such as Greenpeace, Human Rights Watch, and Planned Parenthood. Each year they accept nominations and survey their customers to choose the beneficiaries for the following year.

Of course, communication managers must use such strategies carefully. Appealing to consumers who favor Greenpeace and Planned Parenthood can alienate others who despise those organizations. Another use is to attribute the cause of a problem to a desired issue instead of an undesired issue. For example, some businesses might prefer to attribute the reason for a problem, such as diminished salmon runs, to dammed-up rivers instead of to a complex variety of environmental factors. In this way an organization can deflect blame from its own environmental practices to one cause.

In another creative application of this strategy, the Learning to Give project encourages schools to teach children to make philanthropy a priority by associating it with the regular curriculum. In one case, a Jewish day school in Palo Alto, California, has tried to instill a philanthropic mind-set in its students by creating an association between charitable giving and celebrations upon which the children commonly *receive* gifts. The students research potential recipient organizations, contribute money into a common fund instead of giving each other gifts, make presentations to each other about the prospective charities, and then make decisions about how to allocate the money (Alexander, 2004).

Figure 14.7 shows an example of the Learning to Give's noetic campaign approach, encouraging youth as young as 8 years old to get involved and envision a better world, and to devise strategies to make their ideas happen.

FIG. 14.7. Example of noetic approach.

Used with permission courtesy of Peace First, Inc., and Benchmark Studio Group.

4   *Inductional.* This approach can be called the *coupon* approach because it endeavors to arrange a situation to induce the desired behavior without changing an attitude first. Instead, the campaign follows the behavior change with an appeal to change corresponding attitudes. For example, people might attend a rock concert benefiting the homeless out of a desire to hear the music and see the stars. Once at the concert, they might receive a pitch to support the targeted charity.

One technique that became popular in the late 1990s and early 2000s incorporated customized address labels into direct-mail solicitations. For this tactic to succeed from a public relations standpoint, designers must remember to include the organization's easily identifiable name, slogan, or symbol on the labels. Even if the prospective donor does not contribute, they can help to spread the organization's message simply by using the labels. They also receive a personal reminder of the (albeit tiny) investment the organization has made in them every time they use the labels. Labels may increase awareness and involvement and therefore the potential for a delayed return on investment.

A more unusual approach to an inductional appeal was used by the group Exit Deutschland, which helps people extricate themselves from Neo-Nazi groups. The organization provided free t-shirts to fans at an extremist rock festival in Germany (Figure 14.8). At first glance the t-shirts seemed appropriately right wing, but when the fans washed their new shirts, they discovered a different message had been revealed. "If your T-shirt can do it, so can you. We'll help to free you from right-wing extremism," it read, followed by contact information for the advocacy group. A representative of the groups acknowledged that committed neo-Nazis would be unlikely to switch sides based on the t-shirts, "But our name will be stored in their minds. And when they consider leaving the scene at some point, they will remember us," he said. The group intended that the message would reach those who wanted to be reached while they were at home alone. The group reports that they have helped approximately 400 right-wing extremists to escape since their formation in 2000 (Spiegel Online International, 2011).

5   *Autonomy.* This strategy appeals to people's desire for independence. Particularly in the United States, individualist-minded publics do not want to be told what to do. Appealing to their desire to be self-sovereign sometimes can help an organization develop a convincing message. Organizations that believe their own sovereignty is under attack often resort to this strategy, hoping that targeted publics will share their outrage. For example, Voters for Choice told readers of the *New York Times* that "you have the right to remain silent," displaying a tombstone with the name of Dr. David Gunn, who had been killed for practicing abortion, "but your silence can and will be used against you by anti-choice terrorists." Sometimes the strategy can work with an ironic twist, in an attempt to convince people that giving up some freedom, such as by following the rules in a wilderness park, actually will gain them more freedom by ensuring they can enjoy the peace and quiet themselves.

6   *Problem solver.* Another favorite campaign strategy, the problem-solver approach, simply shows a problem and demonstrates the favored way to solve the problem. Not enough people can afford to go to college; give to the United Negro College Fund. Not enough children have safe homes; be a foster parent. Use of this strategy assumes the target public will care enough about the problem to respond, which is a big assumption to make. Recall Mendelsohn's (1973) advice to assume the opposite—that the audience is uninterested. Campaigns that neglect to confirm this assumption through research risk failure. Google and Wikipedia tried to make people care about potential Internet censorship by changing their landing pages and by interrupting the Wikipedia site functions briefly in 2012 (Figure 14.9). By *creating* a problem temporarily, they hoped their stakeholders would be motivated to help prevent it from becoming permanent, and Congress took notice of the attention it received.

FIG. 14.8. Two hundred fifty of these "Trojan t-shirts" were given out by Exit Deutschland at the Neo-Nazi-organized "Rock for Germany" festival. At first, the shirt reads, "Hardcore Rebels – National and Free," but after it is washed, it changes to "What your shirt is able to do, you can do as well – We help you to drop out from right-wing radicalism."

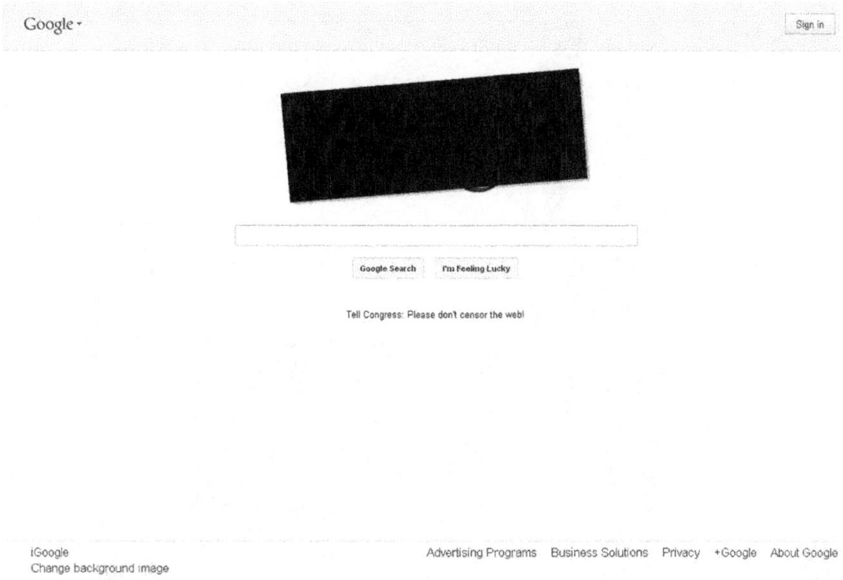

FIG. 14.9. An example of the problem solver approach, as used by Google, concerning Internet censorship.

Google and the Google logo are registered trademarks of Google Inc., used with permission.

When the assumption holds, the results can be impressive. It worked for Beaufort County, South Carolina, which had to persuade voters to approve a 1% sales tax increase to pay for improving a dangerous 13-mile stretch of road and bridges when the measure had failed by a 2-to-1 margin twice before. The carefully coordinated, Silver Anvil Award-winning campaign overwhelmed the vocal opposition in a 58% to 42% victory when White retirees, young workers, employers, and older African-Americans became familiar with the problem, that "The Wait Is Killing Us," and mobilized in support of the measure.

7 *Stimulation.* Sometimes the right thing to do seems boring and some excitement can make it seem more appealing. Stimulation strategies appeal to people's curiosity or their desire to help create or preserve something with an exciting payoff, such as a wilderness area that can offer outdoor adventures. A group of police officers in Washington state, for example, although visiting middle schools with a serious antidrug message, transformed themselves into rap stars to deliver their message with rhythm instead of force. As they chanted about things students should not do or "you're busted!" the students gyrated and yelled the punch line back to the officers. The message got through.

8 *Teleological.* Just as noetic theories offer the opposite strategy from consistency approaches, teleological approaches offer the positive alternative to problem-solver approaches. Teleological means heaven-like, and the approach relies on showing what the world would look like if a problem already had been solved (Figure 14.10). This

FIG. 14.10. This example of the teleological approach by a campaign for Adopt US Kids encourages teen adoption by envisioning a loving, positive family future.

© The AdCouncil and Department of Health and Human Services.

is a useful strategy for incumbent candidates for political office who wish to show their service has made a positive difference for their constituents. In other cases, the target public is shown the ideal result of implementing a desired behavior, along with a script advising how to make the ideal result become reality. For example, a fund-raising promotion for the National Wall of Tolerance not only provided a sketch of the proposed monument but also provided a mock-up of the wall with the solicited donor's name already inscribed on it. Figure 14.10 illustrates another example of the teleological approach, promoting the adoption of U.S. teenagers using future-oriented positive imagery.

Affective/Heuristic Strategies

The second half of McGuire's (1989) dynamic theories matrix focuses on heuristic-based, often more emotionally charged, appeals. On the whole, emotional appeals serve as useful nudges for undecided or uninterested target publics. For issues that require complex consideration, however, or for which a target public has a deeply held view that counters the sponsoring organization's view, emotional appeals can accomplish little or, even worse, can backfire. They, too, include a range of positive and negative approaches:

1 *Tension-reduction (fear appeals).* This strategy attempts to produce tension or fear in the message recipient, which makes the target public uncomfortable and in need of a solution that will reduce the tension. It is the emotional parallel to the consistency-cognitive dissonance approach, which aims to create or highlight a contradiction in the target public's beliefs and behaviors they will want to resolve. The tension-reduction strategy is particularly popular among health campaigners, who try to scare the public into more healthy habits.

   The problem with fear appeals, however, is that they can backfire badly if not applied with precision. One weakness in fear appeals is a failure to resolve the tension in the message. Threatening a target public with a dire outcome (usually death) linked to a behavior, such as drug use or eating habits, without showing how the problem can be fixed can make the target public resent the message and the messenger. Another problem is the use of extreme or unrealistic levels of fear, such as the Partnership for a Drug-Free America's admonition that equated the use of marijuana with Russian roulette. Because the production of fear appeals is filled with so many pitfalls and the effects of fear appeals are so difficult to predict, they are best avoided when possible. Although appropriate in some situations, such appeals must be well researched. Clients who cannot be dissuaded from using a fear appeal simply must build a large pretesting budget into the project.

   When using a fear appeal it is essential to provide a solution to the problem presented. For example The Federal Emergency Response Administration (FEMA, n.d.) commissioned a campaign to encourage small business owners to prepare for emergencies. The multimedia campaign included a billboard targeting commuters with the stark message, black and white and red type with no further illustration: "At least one in four businesses never reopen after a disaster. MAKE A PLAN." The campaign included an easy-to-remember Web address for more information: ready.gov. The site included information for other target audiences as well, such as older Americans, pet owners, and children, and could be viewed in over a dozen languages.

FIG. 14.11. The Flat Stanley/Flat Stella campaign offers a child-friendly tension-reduction appeal.

Used with permission. Visit the Flat Stanley Project at www.flatstanleyproject.com.

The promotions for children did *not* use fear appeals but instead promoted fun and games, showing images such as happy children wearing hardhats and possessing radios (see Figure 14.11). Children could test their wits by playing a "pack it up" match game, word searches, and a "hidden treasures" game to identify things that could help with them in an emergency. Flat Stanley and Flat Stella could come with them as they practiced emergency drills.

2   *Ego defensive.* The ego-defensive approach sets up a situation in which the target public will associate smartness and success with the desired attitude or behavior, whereas failure is associated with the refusal to adopt the message. This approach can be used in both a positive and a negative application. For example, the Greater Good campaign launched by a coalition of business leaders and education advocates in Washington state challenged residents with messages such as: "Is Third from the Bottom Good Enough for You?" blaming Washington's rank of 48th in per capita enrollments in higher education on the state's trend of disinvestments in education over the previous years (Figure 14.12). Meanwhile, the Illinois Department of Public Health and Golin/Harris International focused on making safe-sex decisions "cool" in awkward situations. Research designed to ensure the appeal would not backfire included mall intercepts of 200 teens, a 33-member teen advisory panel, feedback from high-risk adolescents via state-funded organizations, and message testing using quantitative and qualitative methods.

Similarly, the Washington State Department of Health in its "Tobacco Smokes You" campaign showed a young woman trying to impress her peers and gain acceptance by smoking. Instead of looking cool, however, the ad showed her face morphing into a severely tobacco-damaged visage, which grossed out her peers and led them to reject her. Among 10 to 13-year-olds, 73% considered the ad convincing, 71% said it grabbed their attention, and 88% said it gave them good reasons not to smoke (Washington State Department of Health, 2004). The ad had a slightly lower impact on 14 to 17-year-olds.

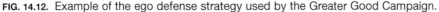

FIG. 14.12. Example of the ego defense strategy used by the Greater Good Campaign.

Courtesy of the *Seattle Times*.

3 *Expressive.* Just as noetic strategies take the opposite tack of consistency strategies
   and teleological approaches reflect the mirror image of problem-solver approaches,
   the expressive approach takes a positive twist on the tension-reduction approach. The
   expressive appeal acknowledges that a target public may find the organization's
   undesired behavior desirable. For example, many drug users perceive real benefits to
   the use of drugs, such as escape from reality or peer acceptance. From a social
   marketing point of view, these benefits simply must be acknowledged, along with
   the real perceived costs of physical and mental discomfort associated with "saying no"
   to drugs. These costs can include the loss of social status and even physical danger.
   In perhaps the most well-known campaign incorporating the expressive approach,
   communities across the country hold all-night graduation celebrations for high school
   students that require students to stay locked in the party for the entire night to make
   themselves eligible for extremely desirable prizes. The goal: Keep the celebrants from
   endangering themselves and others with alcohol and other drugs. The reason it works:
   The party and its incentives fulfill the students' need for a major celebration and their
   desire to keep it going all night long.

Expressive strategies probably have the greatest potential for making difficult behavior-change campaigns effective, but they are rarely used because they do not reflect the campaign sponsor's perspective. Various theories, however, ranging from co-orientation theory to excellence theory to social marketing theory, discussed in Chapter 13, all lend strong support to the value of the expressive approach. Unfortunately, clients often run campaigns using strategies more persuasive to themselves than to their target publics.

4   *Repetition*. If you simply say the same thing over and over enough times, sometimes it gets through. According to McGuire (1989), three to five repeats can help a message get through, especially if the message is presented in a pleasant way. Many campaign designers interpret the three-to-five rule as a magic bullet guaranteeing a message will be successfully propelled into waiting target publics. Repetition, however, constitutes a useful supplemental strategy for an otherwise well-designed campaign and cannot be considered a sufficient strategy in itself.

5   *Assertion*. The emotional parallel to autonomy appeals, the assertion strategy focuses on people's desire to gain power and status. A popular appeal for low-involvement issues or products, the assertion appeal promises increased control over others or a situation in return for adopting the proposed attitude or behavior. During the Iraq war, the U.S. Army tried to recruit young people by creating a video game called "America's Army" (America's Army, 2013), designed to be realistic and fun and which had attracted more than 5 million users by mid-2005. The video game far exceeded the Army's expectations. The purpose was to pique players' interest, after which they could be encouraged to request more information from their local recruiter. The strategy seemed to work until the casualty count in the Iraq war began to diminish young people's desire to serve their country by fighting terrorism. The game, however, remained hugely popular and may have helped to prevent a further reduction in recruits.

One campaign that successfully combined categorization with assertion portrayed appealing images of youth achieving athletic greatness while contrasting the odds of becoming an Olympic athlete (1 in 28,500) with the odds of a child developing autism (1 in 150). The Autism Speaks campaign that year achieved a 43% increase in public awareness (Figure 14.13).

6   *Identification*. People aspire to feel better about themselves and frequently aspire to be like someone else. Often, they look to other role models who embody positive characteristics (Figure 14.13). Campaigns commonly use this to create positive associations between a proposed idea or product and a desirable personality. Negative associations also can be made, but as with most negative appeals, they require careful pretesting to ensure relevance and credibility with the target public.

7   *Empathy*. Empathy strategies appeal to people's desire to be loved. Although most applications of the empathic strategy focus on how target publics can achieve personal acceptance from others, this approach can appeal to people's altruism and desire to feel good for helping others they care about. A simple but eloquent American Red Cross appeal, for example, noted that "when you give blood, you give another birthday,

Odds of a child becoming an Olympic athlete: 1 in 28,500

Odds of a child being diagnosed with autism: 1 in 150

Some signs to look for:

| No big smiles or other joyful expressions by 6 months. | No babbling by 12 months. | No words by 16 months. |

To learn more of the signs of autism, visit autismspeaks.org

AUTISM SPEAKS
It's time to listen.

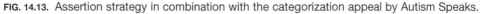

FIG. 14.13. Assertion strategy in combination with the categorization appeal by Autism Speaks.

Courtesy of the Ad Council

another anniversary, another day at the beach, another night under the stars, another talk with a friend, another laugh, another hug, another chance." In a campaign evoking similar emotions, Spokane, Washington-area animal welfare agencies and local businesses paid for a four-page insert in the local newspaper of classified ads featuring photographs of pets needing homes. Adoptions at the four local shelters shot up to record levels. One shelter director said, "We placed every single animal we had" (Harris, 2002).

8   *Bandwagon*. Making an idea seem contagious can make the idea seem even better. If 2,000 community leaders and neighborhood residents have signed a petition favoring the construction of a new city park, shouldn't you favor it, too? The bandwagon strategy does not do much to change strongly held opinions, but it can sway the undecided and serve as a useful reminder and motivator for those in agreement with a campaign message. According to the domino model of persuasion, increased awareness can (even if it does not always) lead to increased knowledge, skill development, persuasion, and behavior change.

In a remarkable example of the bandwagon effect, the Lance Armstrong Foundation created a craze when it initially launched yellow, plastic LIVESTRONG wristbands to honor the famous bicyclist and raise money for cancer research. The goal of the campaign, cosponsored by Nike, was to raise $5 million by selling the wristbands for $1 each. A year later they had sold 47.5 million wristbands (raising $47.5 million) and had inspired a myriad of spinoff campaigns featuring bracelets to promote everything from breast cancer to political statements. Quite the bandwagon effect.

The bandwagon strategy also can be used to demonstrate that a behavior must be "normal," because so many people like you do it, think it, or look like it. The Oregon Dairy Council, for example, developed a poster-based educational campaign with the slogan, "What's normal supposed to look like, anyway?" showing teenage boys and girls spanning the range of healthy sizes and shapes according to the body mass index. The purpose was to counter stereotyped media images that distort what everyone looks like or should look like. Strategists need to apply a norms campaign with caution, however, because—as with identification—the target public must believe in the personal relevance of the norm presented.

Other Theories that Explain Special Situations

Diffusion of Innovations

Another popular variation on the domino model provides useful guidance for campaign designers hoping to promote the adoption of an innovation. Innovations can be products such as a new computing tool or ideas such as recycling or changing eating habits. According to diffusion of innovations theory (Rogers, 1983), people considering whether to adopt an innovation progress through five steps that parallel the hierarchy of effects in the domino model. The innovation-decision process follows the way an individual or decision-making unit passes from a lack of awareness to use of the new product or idea. The likelihood of someone making progress through the steps depends on prior conditions such as previous experiences, perceived needs, the norms of the society in which the target public lives, and the individual's level of innovativeness. The steps include knowledge, persuasion, decision, implementation, and confirmation. Innovations are evaluated on the basis of their relative advantages, which Rogers called compatibility, complexity, trialability, and observability. Simply put, an innovation is more likely to be adopted if it seems to have clear benefits that are not difficult to harvest, particularly if giving it a try is not particularly risky.

Diffusion of innovations theory teaches that most innovations occur according to a fairly predictable S-curve cycle. First, a few brave souls give the new idea a try, and then the innovation picks up speed and becomes more broadly accepted. More specifically, people begin to imitate opinion leaders who have tried the innovation, and gradually a bandwagon effect gets started. Finally, most people likely to adopt the innovation do so, and the rate of change slows down again. Campaigns advocating relatively innovative ideas or products benefit from tailoring their messages according to where the innovation is on the S-curve.

Campaigns advocating adoption of an innovation must consider that people who are more innovative will have different needs and interests from people who are less innovative. According to diffusion of innovations theory, campaigners can think of five broad target publics: innovators, who are the first 2.5% to adopt a new product or idea; early adopters, who are the next 13.5%; the early majority, who represent 34% of the total potential market; the late majority, who represent another 34%, and laggards, who are the final 16%. People who fit in each of these categories have characteristics in common with each other. According to diffusion of innovations theory, people associate mainly with people who share key characteristics with themselves (called *homogeneous*), but they learn new things from people who are slightly different (called *heterogeneous*). People who are completely different will probably not be able to relate well with the target public and will have less persuasive potential.

Inoculation

Inoculation theory looks like the mirror image of diffusion of innovations theory. The idea behind inoculation (Pfau, 1995) is to address potential trouble before it starts so that potential problems never gain enough momentum to create a crisis. Just as a flu shot can prevent a full-blown attack of the flu bug, a small dose of bad news early can prevent an issue from turning into a full-blown crisis. For example, political candidates expecting bad news to hit the media can present the news themselves, from their own perspective. Taking away the element of surprise or confrontation makes the news less sensational and, therefore, less damaging.

Final Thoughts

Theories explaining how and why message recipients make decisions in various circumstances demonstrate that purely informational messages and messages that appeal mainly to the client instead of the message recipient can doom a communication program. Remember that if the target public already shared the organization's point of view perfectly, a communication program probably would not be necessary. Because the goal of a public relations program is to increase the degree to which a target public and an organization share common perspectives and priorities, the organization controlling the message needs to make overtures inviting collaboration with the target public, instead of expecting the target public to invite the organization's perspective into their lives. Making a change is not the target public's priority. Understanding how and why message receivers think the way they do can greatly enhance the communication professional's ability to build constructive relationships with them by pinpointing the strategies target publics find relevant, credible, and compelling.

15

Practical Applications of Theory for Strategic Planning

Chapter Contents

- About Sources
- About Messages
- About Channels
- Which Channels Are Best?
- Media Advocacy (Guerilla Media)
- Making Media Advocacy Work
- Making the Most of Unplanned Opportunities
- Social Media Campaigns
- Final Thoughts

The generalizations acquired from hundreds of studies about how communication programs work lead to some interesting conclusions about the parts of a communication program the manager can control. This chapter summarizes some of what research has demonstrated about sources, messages, and channels of communication. In general, the research has shown that, despite the complexities of communication program design, managers can follow a set of general rules to guide their tactical planning. In fact, most successful practitioners appear to take advantage of the lessons derived from formal social science research. The astute practitioner also realizes, however, that no rule applies to every situation, making a reliance on generalizations dangerous. As a result, managers should not consider the generalizations offered in this chapter an alternative to performing original program research and understanding theories such as those reviewed in Chapters 13 and 14. Instead, the principles that guide the use of the following tactics can aid strategic planning preparatory to pretesting. We address the familiar elements of the linear model—source, channel, message and receiver—but with a twist because everything ultimately depends on the receiver.

About Sources

Research has shown that one of the most important attributes of a source is its *credibility*. Some say it takes a long time to build credibility but only a short time to lose it, making credibility an organization's most precious asset. Although various perspectives exist, experts generally agree credibility includes two main characteristics: *trustworthiness* and *expertise*. Some add a third characteristic called *bias*. Because credibility of the source exists in the mind of the receiver, credibility can be tricky to determine.

Despite the importance of credibility, some research has suggested that it matters more for short-term attempts at persuasion than for long-term campaigns. The reason for this is that, after a while, people can forget where they heard a bit of information although they still recall the information. For long-term campaigns, research suggests people rely more on aspects of the message than its source, considering factors such as how well the evidence presented in a message supports the viewpoint advocated.

A second characteristic of a source is perceived *similarity*. Both credibility and perceived similarity exist in the mind of the receiver. Similarity matters because people trust (i.e., think more credible) people who seem to be like themselves in a relevant way. Message recipients may judge similarity on the basis of membership or attitudes. This is why presidents will go to work in a factory for a day, or presidential candidates will wear a flannel shirt or a T-shirt instead of a suit. They hope that doing such things will increase their appeal to the average person.

This technique also can help persuade people to do things such as take their medicine, wear their helmets when boarding, or obey rules. In an airport, for example, an announcer advises that he has been a baggage handler for years "and I've never lost a bag." He continues on to admonish travelers that they will be more likely to hang on to theirs if they keep them close by and under constant supervision. The message, intended to reinforce airport policy, seems more personal than an anonymous disembodied voice threatening to confiscate unsupervised bags. Another announcer identifies himself as a smoker and tells travelers, in a cheerful voice, where he goes to smoke. In the first case, the announcer identified himself as an expert who can be trusted on matters of baggage; in the second case, the announcer established similarity by identifying himself as a member of the group he is addressing. Another announcer could establish similarity on the basis of attitudes by noting how much he hates long lines, just like other travelers, before encouraging them to have their tickets and identification out and ready before lining up at a security gate.

A third characteristic of the source that can make a difference is *attractiveness,* which can refer to physical or personality traits. Research indicates that visually appealing sources hold more sway over a target public than less-attractive sources. Some scholars think that this is because people want to imagine themselves as attractive, too; thus they establish similarity with an attractive source through wishful thinking. Because they do not want to seem unattractive, they do not want to do or think the same things that an unattractive source does or thinks. As with credibility and perceived similarity, attractiveness exists in the eye of the beholder, making audience-centered research essential for successful communication programs. Cultural differences, for example, can affect what seems attractive, and it is more important for a campaign to use sources that seem attractive to the target public than to use sources that seem attractive to the campaign sponsors (within limits). For example, a source with green hair, a myriad of pierced body parts, and tattoos will appeal to rebellious teenagers more than a dark-suited executive in a tie.

About Messages

Much research provides managers with guidance regarding the development of messages. Just as the Elaborated Likelihood Model and other dual-process theories assume two possible routes to persuasion within a person's mind, the findings from message research focus on two aspects of meaning: logical aspects and emotional aspects. The basic theme behind these findings is that messages need to be accurate, relevant, and clear. Effective messages include the right mix (determined through research, of course) of evidence and emotion.

The Importance of Evidence

Evidence is important only to the extent that a target public will feel motivated to evaluate the authenticity of the evidence presented, but accuracy is a minimum requirement for any message. Messages with unintended inaccuracies communicate incompetence; messages with intentional inaccuracies are unethical, and can be illegal as well. Beyond accuracy, the most important generalization about evidence is that messages have more influence when they acknowledge and refute viewpoints that contradict the preferred position advocated by a sponsoring organization. Consistent with inoculation theory (see Chapter 14), scholars have found that two-sided messages are about 20% more persuasive than one-sided messages, provided the other side is refuted after having been acknowledged. If the message includes no refutational statement, the two-sided message is about 20% less effective than a one-sided message (Allen, 1991).

The Importance of Emotion

Emotion enhances the appeal of a message because it increases the relevance of the message. Through emotions, people can feel something as a result of a message even if they do not take the trouble to think about the information presented. Fear is probably the emotion most often elicited by health campaign designers, but as noted in Chapter 14, it also is the emotion most likely to backfire. Although fear appeals are popular for campaigns aimed at adolescents, such as to keep them off of drugs or out of a driver's seat when alcohol impaired, research has shown that fear appeals are more effective with older people than with children or adolescents (Boster & Mongeau, 1984). In addition, research has shown that people only respond favorably to fear appeals when they feel that they have the power to deal effectively with the danger presented (Witte, 1992). As a result, campaigns that do things such as warning adolescents about the dire consequences of becoming infected with HIV without providing realistic ways for avoiding it probably will fail.

Another popular negative emotion among campaign designers is anger. Political ads, in particular, use anger, much like a variation on a fear appeal, to encourage voters to mobilize against a villainous enemy. Anger can be a powerful motivator because people instinctively desire to protect themselves against danger. As with fear appeals, however, attack strategies can backfire. Political candidates know, for example, that attacks citizens perceive as unfair will hurt the sponsoring candidate. Another danger arises from the possibility of cultivating cynicism and distrust in message recipients, which will reflect badly on the sponsoring organization and can dampen the target public's motivations and interests (Pinkleton, Um, & Austin, 2001).

Positive emotions are easier to use effectively than negative emotions, provided people do not already have negative feelings about an issue or product. Positive emotions are particularly helpful when people are unfamiliar with a campaign topic, undecided, or confused. Feel-good messages are less apt to change strongly held negative attitudes. Two kinds of positive emotional appeals can be used by campaign managers. The first, the *emotional-benefit appeal*, demonstrates a positive outcome to compliance with a campaign message. Positive emotional-benefit appeals can be effective if they grab people's attention, but they are not compelling unless they incorporate tactics such as attractive spokespeople and production features. These tactics, called *heuristics*, are the second kind of positive-emotional appeal. They abandon logical reasoning and simply associate positive images or feelings with an attitude, behavior, or product (Monahan, 1995). Heuristic appeals sell a mood or a feeling instead of more rational benefits. Research has shown that positive-heuristic appeals are effective attention getters, but they do not encourage deep involvement or thought on the part of the receiver. People tend to remember the good feeling the message produced rather than any information provided. As a result, positive heuristics have only short-lived effects on attitudes and are unlikely to produce long-term behavioral change. Overall, a combination of positive benefits and positive heuristics garners the most success.

About Channels

It may seem obvious that different communication vehicles lend themselves most effectively to different purposes. Traditional mass communication vehicles have advantages and disadvantages that make them serve different purposes from interpersonal channels and social media. In addition, managers find that communication channels are not interchangeable; sources such as family members have advantages and disadvantages over other sources such as teachers or religious leaders. Interactive technologies such as social media have become very popular and serve as a hybrid of interpersonal and mass communication, but that does not guarantee their effectiveness.

The Mass Media

The traditional definition of a mass medium is one that reaches many people at once but does not make immediate feedback possible. Increasingly, of course, many forms of mass media not only reach many people at once but also allow varying degrees of feedback. Feedback is important because it makes it possible for message recipients to clarify information and for organizations to understand how people are reacting to a message. Organizations must be able to adapt to feedback as well as encourage accommodations from others. Recall that the co-orientation model illustrates that people need to agree and know they agree. To aid this process, radio offers talk shows; the Internet offers blogs and e-mail; television offers polling tie-ins and instant purchasing; newspapers include reader editorials, letters to the editor and online comments. Some generalizations based on the differences among traditional media types, however, still apply. For example, print media can carry more complex information than television or radio can, because people can take the time to read the material slowly or repeatedly to make sure they understand it. On the other hand, television can catch the attention of the less interested more effectively than newspapers or magazines can because of the combination of visual and auditory production features that make it entertaining. Radio, meanwhile, is accessible to people in their cars, in their homes, at work, in stores, and even in the wilderness. This makes it possible to reach target audiences quickly, making it a particularly effective medium in crisis situations when news needs frequent updating and mobile networks can get overwhelmed. The drawback of radio, however, is that messages must be less complex than messages in print media or on television because people depend solely on their hearing to get the message. They cannot see pictures or printed reminders to reinforce or expand on the message, and it goes by quickly.

Additional generalizations can be made about mass media overall. First, they can reach a large audience rapidly, much more quickly than personally going door to door. As a result, they can spread information and knowledge effectively to those who pay attention. In terms of the hierarchy of effects or domino model, these characteristics make mass media appropriate for gaining exposure and awareness. The mass media also can combine a message with entertainment effectively, which helps message designers get people's attention. It is important to note that while trendy technologies such as Twitter can spread news and rumors quickly, their reach is more limited than it may appear. According to the Pew Research Center (Mitchell & Hitlin, 2013), only 13% of adults use or read Twitter, and only 3% say they tend to tweet news or news headlines. Twitter users—at least in 2013—tend to be younger and more liberal than the general public. Keep in mind that usage patterns change quickly as new communication tools debut and grow stale.

Another benefit of mass media and more recent innovations in digital communication such as YouTube can be the remoteness of the source and situation portrayed from the receiver. Some things, such as scary or embarrassing topics (e.g., drug use) are better broached from a distance. Mass media can safely introduce such topics, which can be helpful to organizations ranging from hospitals to zoos. One experiment showed that people afraid of snakes could overcome their fear by being introduced to snakes through media portrayals, gradually progressing to the real thing in the same room. Meanwhile, hospitals have found that videos explaining surgical techniques to patients before they experience the procedures can reduce anxiety.

Something experienced vicariously often becomes less alarming in real life. One reason is because the vicarious experience has removed the element of uncertainty from the situation. Research has shown that many of our fears come from uncertainty and from feeling a lack of control. Information, meanwhile, removes uncertainty and can provide more control. The results can be impressive. One classic study found that children who watched videos that took them through the process of having a tonsillectomy or other elective surgery—including visits to the operating and recovery rooms and some discussion of likely discomforts—actually got better more quickly, had fewer complications, and were more pleasant patients (Melamed & Siegel, 1975).

The mass media, online or offline, suffer from weaknesses, however. Anytime a message reaches a lot of people at once, it risks misinterpretation by some and provides less opportunity for two-way communication. The less feedback in a channel, the more potential there is for unintended effects to occur. In addition, people find it much easier to ignore or refuse a disembodied voice or a stranger who cannot hear their responses than to ignore someone standing in the same room or talking with them on the telephone. The ability to motivate people, therefore, is less strong with mass media than with interpersonal sources.

Interpersonal Sources

Real people can do many things mass media cannot. They can communicate by way of body language and touch, instead of only through sound and pictures. They also can receive questions and even can be interrupted when something seems confusing. As a result, interpersonal sources can help make sure messages are received without misinterpretation. They also can offer to make changes. For example, company presidents speaking with consumers who are threatening a boycott can eke out a compromise that satisfies both parties, whereas a mass-mediated message could make the consumers angrier.

Personal attention demonstrates that the target public's views have value. In addition, interpersonal sources can provide encouragement in difficult situations and can serve as models of a desired attitude or behavior. These abilities can be crucial for difficult behavior-change campaigns that require skill development and reinforcement. Thus, although interpersonal communication lacks reach, it often makes an excellent support strategy to a mass-mediated campaign, especially when targeting narrow audience segments. In terms of the hierarchy of effects or domino model, interpersonal sources can help with comprehension, skill development, attitude change, motivation, and reinforcement. This makes interpersonal sources especially important for communication programs addressing strongly held attitudes or challenging behaviors.

Online technologies have made it easier for communication programs to approximate having interpersonal sources. For example, online support groups can enable people with rare medical conditions to provide information and encouragement to one another. In 2012, the annual Rare Disease Day sponsored by an international organization called EURODIS brought together people in 63 countries to support the medical and social needs of people suffering from the approximately 7,000 diseases that might affect only 1 of every 5,000 people (IIP Digital, 2013).

Digital Media

Because the Internet makes it possible for people to seek out the sources that make them most comfortable and also frequently provides opportunities for interactivity, it can provide a helpful bridge between the mass media and interpersonal channels. For example, online print sources such as Web-based aggregators and the home pages of traditional news outlets emphasize read-at-a-glance, visually stimulating stories on their landing pages. More depth often is available within the site for those motivated to click through, along with opportunities for comment and hosted discussions in real time.

Managers using online technologies need to consider how long-standing principles and theories such as the information on credibility and accessibility pertain or differ when applied to digital technologies. Usage and credibility patterns for online technologies can shift quickly and dramatically, making pretesting for relevance of great importance. Twitter, for example, debuted in 2006 and initially operated in relative obscurity among technology specialists (Dugan, 2011). By 2009 Twitter had annual growth of 1,382% and then just as quickly appeared to have stalled (Hernandez, 2011). By 2012, however, it had become important enough for the Pope to open his own Twitter account. Nevertheless, certain analysts were cautiously reporting that Twitter is scorned by teens (Carlson, 2012) while others were reporting that teens actually tweet more than the general public (Cook, 2009).

Which Channels Are Best?

The information from Chapters 13–15 should make it clear that communication is a complex process that lends itself to few generalizations applicable to all situations. The search for the best solutions to a communication problem can tempt managers to draw broader conclusions from selected successes than are warranted, leading to risky, one-size-fits-all solutions. According to Chaffee (1982), communication experts sometimes assume that because interpersonal sources are more persuasive than mass media sources, or at least more difficult to rebuff, this means they also are more credible. And credibility is an extremely important attribute for a source. Chaffee, however, pointed out that studies have found interpersonal networks notoriously unreliable—this includes a Twitter feed—and some studies have found people making up their minds based solely on information from the media, ignoring or rejecting interpersonal sources.

As Chaffee pointed out, it is silly to pit mass communication against interpersonal communication to determine which is more effective, and in the digital age it often is difficult even to tell the difference between the two. The reality, according to Chaffee, is that *opinion leaders*—the sources from which people seek information or find influential—depend on the context. For information about the quality of local daycares, local parents may be the expert sources. For information about peace negotiations in another country, professional reporters or trusted advocates are more likely to be the experts. Nevertheless, Chaffee noted that a few generalizations can be made about communication that still can help the program designer today.

1   *People seek information from the most accessible source.* Research has shown that if people are highly involved in a topic, meaning deeply interested, they will go to the trouble to find information from the most credible sources available. When people care little about a topic, however, they rarely go out of their way. Some people develop habits of checking multiple sources of information, but others do not have the opportunity, ability, or desire to do so. This means communication programs should endeavor to make information easily accessible to target publics, instead of expecting them to seek out information.

2   *People give opinions more often than they seek opinions.* People like to make their opinions known. They do not like having other people's opinions foisted upon them. As a result, the most effective persuasion is *self-persuasion*, in which people reach their own conclusions, guided by information made available to them. To the extent communication programs can set the agenda for what people think about and provide the basis on which they evaluate issues, called *framing*, the more likely target publics will be to draw conclusions compatible with those of the sponsoring organization.

3   *People seek information more often than they seek opinions.* People search for information, not opinions. In fact, they often search for information to back up their existing opinions. If they succeed, they may try to convince others to agree with them. When a communication program can make information available while establishing a common ground of shared values or opinions with a target public, the public will be more likely to accept the information as credible and make use of it in ways consistent with the sponsoring organization's viewpoint.

4   *Interpersonal social contacts tend to be similar (homophilic).* This has various implications for the communication manager. People tend to associate with people who are like themselves because they share a frame of reference. Establishing similarity with a target public tends to enhance credibility. Credibility and closeness can motivate change, and people who are close can provide reinforcement when change takes place. This makes interpersonal sources critical for motivating and consolidating behavior changes.

5   *Expertise, followed by trustworthiness, is the most persuasive attributes of a source.* Both expertise and trustworthiness are aspects of credibility. Although similarity can help facilitate open communication and can enhance credibility, credibility itself is still more important. The key is to determine on what criteria message recipients will be evaluating a source's expertise and trustworthiness. Remember that interpersonal sources are not necessarily more expert or trustworthy than mass communication sources, meaning that they will not necessarily be more persuasive.

6   *The biggest effect of the media is more communication.* The previous generalizations necessarily lead to this conclusion. People receive information from accessible sources, and media can make a message highly accessible. People like to receive information instead of opinions, which means media are better at spreading credible information than at changing opinions. People tend to associate with people similar to themselves and often use information received from the media to try to convince others to share their opinions. Finally, people can motivate others similar to themselves to act and can provide reinforcement of those actions. The biggest strength of the media, therefore, is their ability to spread information and spark interpersonal communication that can change opinions and lead to action. Although this means media campaigns are unlikely to prove sufficient for a social marketing-style advocacy program, they are definitely good for something. This has inspired the development of media advocacy, which has led further to the development of "social media campaigns."

Media Advocacy (Guerilla Media)

Changing people's minds is no easy task, and just getting their attention can be a challenge. As a result, social marketing campaigns intended to change attitudes or behaviors usually require funds that enable a long-term, gradual adjustment process. Sometimes organizations simply do not have the time or the money to underwrite such a campaign. Instead of giving up, however, they can address the issue from a different theoretical viewpoint, called *media advocacy.*

The media advocacy approach acknowledges the hierarchy of effects model, but it does so from a different angle than social marketing approaches, often striving for shock value and the social pressure that results from it, more than for motivating careful consideration of issues and attitude change. Social marketing campaigns make three crucial assumptions that distinguish them from media advocacy campaigns:

1   Campaigns ultimately aim to change individual attitudes and behaviors.
2   Individuals ultimately have control over and are responsible for their own attitudes and behaviors.
3   Campaigns must convince and motivate individuals in order to change attitudes and behaviors.

Media advocacy campaigns, on the other hand, make different assumptions:

1   People's attitudes and behaviors depend on environmental opportunities and constraints.
2   Organizations and governmental institutions control critical environmental factors.
3   Organizations and governmental institutions respond to the public's agenda.
4   The agenda for public opinion can be affected by the media.

5 Public opinion needs to force organizations and institutions to alter environmental factors such as public policy in order to change attitudes and behaviors.

Both sets of assumptions have validity because human behavior is complex. The communication manager, however, must decide which theoretical strategy is most appropriate for a given situation. Both social marketing and media advocacy have advantages and disadvantages, and both have strengths and limitations. For example, because social marketing targets individuals, people who do change attitudes or behaviors will feel invested in the changes they have made. In addition, because social marketing tries to establish common ground with the initially differing target public through source and message strategies, social marketing is less likely than media advocacy to backfire (provided sufficient preprogram research and pretesting has been performed). Social marketing campaigns, however, are likely to require more time and funding than media advocacy campaigns because they strive for incremental changes that rarely happen quickly and can require a large investment of funds. People also resist change, particularly if they are made to feel defensive about their own attitudes or behaviors.

Media advocacy campaigns, meanwhile, focus on getting people's attention and motivating them to communicate further in some way, instead of on persuading people to change their own attitudes or behaviors. They encourage people to blame a company, public official, or institution for a problem instead of accepting personal responsibility, which can eliminate a good deal of potential resistance among the target public. Media advocacy campaigns often use shock or anger to grab people's attention and motivate them to turn on a perceived enemy under the assumption that public pressure may force the opponent to make a desired change.

Although media advocacy campaigns focus on media coverage, thriving on negative emotions and, therefore, on controversy, this also presents some drawbacks. As with any strategy based on negative emotions, the media advocacy strategy can backfire, with the public blaming the sponsoring organization. In addition, heated public debates rarely continue for long, and the media or target publics soon become bored and turn to another topic for discussion. The shorter time frame and strategy of creating newsworthy controversy can make media advocacy campaigns less expensive to run than social marketing campaigns, but they also mean the campaigns are shorter and changes can lack staying power. In other words, the attack strategy of media advocacy, sometimes called *guerilla media* because of the attack tactics used, makes it lower cost but higher risk.

Media advocacy, therefore, is the strategic use of mass media to advance a social or public policy initiative, applying the strategy of reframing public debate. Social marketing, in contrast, is the strategic use of mass and interpersonal channels to achieve change among individuals, applying strategies directed at individual responsibility and motivations.

For example, contrast the two campaigns illustrated in Figures 15.1 and 15.2, both of which targeted second-hand smoking as a cause of lung diseases. The social marketing version targeted parents, encouraging them to take responsibility for exposing their children to tobacco smoke in the home (Figure 15.1). The media advocacy approach appealed to people's potential outrage over an unregulated work environment framed as abusive (Figure 15.2). A spokesperson for BreatheND explained, "We believe that our secondhand smoke ads were instrumental in getting the North Dakota voters to pass a statewide smoke-free law" (personal communication, August 2013).

FIG. 15.1. An anti-secondhand smoke campaign using a social marketing approach in the U.K., targeting parents to keep their children away from secondhand smoke.

Used with permission from the Roy Castle Lung Cancer Foundation.

FIG. 15.2. An anti-secondhand smoke campaign using a media advocacy approach, emphasizing the unfair and unhealthy choice that many employees around secondhand smoke are forced to make.

Making Media Advocacy Work

Media advocacy recognizes that media are a primary forum for challenging policies. As a result, a successful media advocacy campaign depends on the sponsoring organization's ability to make news. An organization may buy advertising space, for example, but the goal often is for the ad to make news rather than for the ad itself to persuade many people. Organizations buying such ads usually have much less to spend than the companies or institutions they attack. For example, Kalle Lasn, president of a group that ran a parody of an Absolut Vodka ad that resulted in prominent coverage in the *New York Times*, has said, "Even though we're little, we take a big, large corporation, and we use these images to slam them on the mat like a judo move." To do this effectively requires several skills.

1   *Research.* It is essential when using swift and risky guerilla tactics to have confidence in their effectiveness. The media advocate needs to know what story angles will interest the media, what messages will motivate the public, and what messages may backfire. Practitioners need data to demonstrate convincingly the extent of a problem, including whether some people are affected more than others (people respond when something seems unfair). Research can suggest useful solutions such as policy initiatives, regulations, or the elimination of regulations. Research also can guide efforts to build coalitions, which can make a small organization seem more powerful.

2   *Creative epidemiology.* Creative epidemiology is the use of creative strategies to make dry information such as statistics more interesting. Often, policy issues are complex, and statistics demonstrating the extent of a problem or the value of a solution can be boring. Big numbers can be convincing but hard to digest. As a result, media advocates need to make abstract data seem more relevant and interesting through vivid examples and sound bites. For example, antismoking advocates can draw yawns with the statement that some 350,000 people die each year from smoking-related causes. On the other hand, they can create a vivid image in people's minds if they say instead that "1,000 people quit smoking every day—by dying. That is equivalent to two fully loaded jumbo jets crashing every day, with no survivors," or 920 crashes per year (Faxton St. Luke's Healthcare, n. d.; American Cancer Society, 1988).

   Techniques for creating such vivid imagery abound. Media advocates can turn the abstract into the concrete by *localizing* information (e.g., indicating how many in a community have died from smoking, or AIDS, or drunk-driving accidents); using *relativity techniques* by re-characterizing numbers into a more meaningful form (e.g., saying the alcohol industry spends approximately $225,000 every hour of every day to advertise, instead of saying they spend more than $2 billion per year); and *showing effects of public policy* by highlighting individuals who have been affected. For example, the Smart Grid Consumer Collaborative created an infographic ("Smart Grid," n.d.) to illustrate that annual energy savings from the desired smart grid would produce enough savings to enable 70 million trips around the world by an electric car, or 199 million years of refrigerator use. Those images make a far greater impression than simply stating that the smart grid would increase U.S. energy efficiency by 9%.

3   *Issue framing.* Usually, media advocacy campaigns challenge the public's complacency on an issue. To jar people into listening to a perspective they have not heard before requires finding an angle that will attract attention. For this reason, media advocates

often focus on industry practices instead of on individual behavior, or attempt to delegitimize the opponent by exposing their supposedly exploitative and unethical practices.

This requires using familiar symbols to create an advantage. Industries and organizations targeted by media advocates often have carved out a comfortable niche in society through the skilled use of symbols to associate themselves with values shared by the public. For example, tobacco companies often appeal to the public's desire for freedom by claiming censorship or an assault on the First Amendment. Increasingly, media advocates have found it more productive to co-opt their opponent's symbols than to use their often-meager resources to try to carve out their own. For example, the symbol of "Joe Chemo" was developed as a satirical imitation of the Joe Camel tobacco symbol (Adbusters, 2011).

4   *Gaining access to media outlets.* According to Wallack, Dorfman, Jernigan, and Themba (1993), reporters need a compelling story to tell that has something newsworthy. Newsworthiness *pegs* or *news hooks* can include associating the issue with an anniversary, a season, or a milestone; localizing the story in some way; demonstrating irony, injustice, or a breakthrough of some sort; attaching a celebrity to the story; or creating controversy.

Media advocacy usually requires guerilla-style tactics. It requires more creativity to gain attention, make news, and mobilize public opinion without going negative. The trend toward negativity makes media advocacy a powerful but dangerous tool. The media advocate must bear in mind that once news has been created it can take on momentum in directions damaging to the sponsoring organization. The media advocate must be able to anticipate counterarguments from targeted organizations and be ready to handle a crisis situation should guerilla tactics go awry (Figure 15.3).

Making the Most of Unplanned Opportunities

Even traditional practitioners should be ready to jump on media advocacy opportunities that present themselves unexpectedly. For example, an anti-obesity campaign in Georgia had to shift its strategy when its social marketing campaign attracted backlash from "fat-acceptance groups" claiming obesity does not cause health issues and that the campaign shamed fat children and made them easy prey for bullying. The social-marketing campaign had included a community relations plan that featured relationship building with other organizations, building community trust, engaging community leaders to speak out with ready facts on the issue, and social media to allow for discussion. When activists tried to hijack the social media conversations, the Strong4Life campaign organizers launched a crisis communications plan focused on speedy response, substantive messaging and strong spokespersons. They also launched a new, regularly monitored Facebook page that featured "rules of engagement" promising "protection" from those "not interested in discussing the medical crisis facing Georgia's kids." They also provided facts and tactics to donors and partners who suffered attacks from the activists. The controversy attracted national media coverage, which raised awareness of the issue and attracted the support of a few high-profile journalists and talk-show hosts. Campaign evaluations showed that 80% of parents in Atlanta who had seen the campaign had a positive reaction to it, with 88% agreeing that being overweight puts individuals at risk for

1. Identify and prioritize key decision maker(s).

2. How to build pressure on key decision makers to act.

3. Identify the right influencers and how to reach them.

4. Design pressure tactics to fit your organizational strengths.

5. Identify priorities among possible tactics.

6. Develop a plan for timing tactics for greatest effect.

7. Plan for additional tactics if necessary, to build momentum over the long-term.

FIG. 15.3. Planning questions for media advocacy campaign design.

Adapted from http://www.frogloop.com/care2blog/2012/6/14/the-secret-ingredient-to-winning-advocacy-campaigns. html#ixzz2P9ZNepEX

illness. They also demonstrated that 80% of the social media comments to the campaign were positive (PRSA, 2012h).

The way Jackson Spalding and Children's Healthcare of Atlanta successfully pushed back against the media advocacy campaign launched against its social marketing campaign shows how strategic planning and informed flexibility can enable communication managers to deal with the unexpected. Strategists considering the media advocacy approach nevertheless must weigh its risks against the potential payoffs. According to Wallack et al. (1993), an advocacy campaign will probably make enemies because by drawing attention to a controversy "it points a finger, names names, and starts a fight" (p. 40). This means the communication managers must consider the likelihood of victory against the costliness of failure and must remember that, above all, an organization needs to maintain its credibility in any communication program. If a guerilla-style campaign costs an organization its credibility, even a short-term victory will not merit the cost. Advocacy campaigns still must operate in ways consistent with an organization's long-term mission.

Communication managers must be prepared to defend their organizations against advocacy campaigns waged by other groups. Media advocates target institutions that have power in a community. If an organization becomes a target of an advocacy campaign, it must fight back with its own guerilla tactics or somehow demonstrate the campaign has no merit. For example, American Forests found itself under attack for a promotion that used Dr. Seuss's environmentalist Lorax character, which cautions against cutting down Truffula trees. According to the Heritage Forests Campaign in Portland, which aims to preserve roadless wilderness areas, American Forests advocated clear-cutting, which made its campaign disingenuous. Focusing on the contradiction between the Lorax character and the company's policies provided an easy way for the anti-clear-cutting group to gain media attention. Deborah Gangloff of American Forests responded in Seuss-like language: "Shame on you. Shame. Shame. You think publicity by deceit is a feat!" and then provided evidence that the group's congressional testimony on the subject had been misinterpreted, that it is not an advocate of clear-cutting, and that the organization often disagrees with timber companies (Hughes, 1999). In doing so, American Forests managed to turn the attack into positive publicity. The ability to launch a credible defense in such crisis situations depends on an organization's relationship with media personnel and past performance—a history of honesty, openness, and accessibility makes reporters more amenable to an organization's side of a story. Good humor seems to help, too.

With this in mind, remember that even though media advocacy can make enemies, successful media advocacy nevertheless requires the cultivation of relationships. Key publics include gatekeepers such as reporters and bloggers, as well as potential collaborators or program co-sponsors. Wallack et al. (1993) wrote that the best media advocacy campaigns build a sense of community and of community-based power. Media advocacy campaigns aim to enact change at the community level instead of at the individual level. This, in turn, can help individuals in the community. By shaping the public agenda, shaping the way the agenda is debated, and advancing a policy-oriented solution, media advocacy can help improve the environment in which an organization and its key publics operate.

Social Media Campaigns

As the anti-obesity campaign in Georgia demonstrates, media advocacy and social marketing campaigns increasingly focus on social media. As Amnesty International has pointed out in its training materials, the social media campaign organizer should consider best practices for:

1   educating the public
2   engaging and mobilizing current supporters
3   recruiting and mobilizing new supporters.

(Stoddard, n.d.).

This includes listening to and learning from campaign participants, because an interactive campaign cannot limit itself to pushing predetermined message points. All the while, organizers strive to promote brand awareness and drive traffic to their campaign sites and partners.

Many public relations specialists now offer an array of social media campaign tactics that provide opportunities to deepen stakeholders' engagement with an organization. Campaign designers need to stay abreast of quickly changing trends, along with planning to counter the potential for losing control of their messages. While content platforms keep changing, training and promotional tools widely available from advocacy groups and marketing/public relations firms can help identify current best practices (e.g. Valeo Online Marketing, 2013). Increasingly, opportunities for micro-targeting can help practitioners navigate difficult situations. For example, one campaign launched in 2013 made use of the ability to alter an image as seen from different angles (Figure 15.4). The Aid to Children and Adolescents at Risk (ANAR) Foundation, based in Spain, produced an ad that a person taller than four feet (presumably an adult) would see as a sad child with the message, "sometimes, child abuse is only visible to the child suffering it," while a shorter person (a child) would see the image quite differently. The secret message seen by children showed bruises on the child's face with the accompanying message, "if somebody hurts you, phone us and we'll help you," along with the foundation's phone number. The message was ostensibly designed to reach children who needed to escape an abusive situation, even with the potentially responsible adult standing right next to them. The message, which originally had been displayed only in a few locations in five cities, went viral, attracting 2,250,000 views

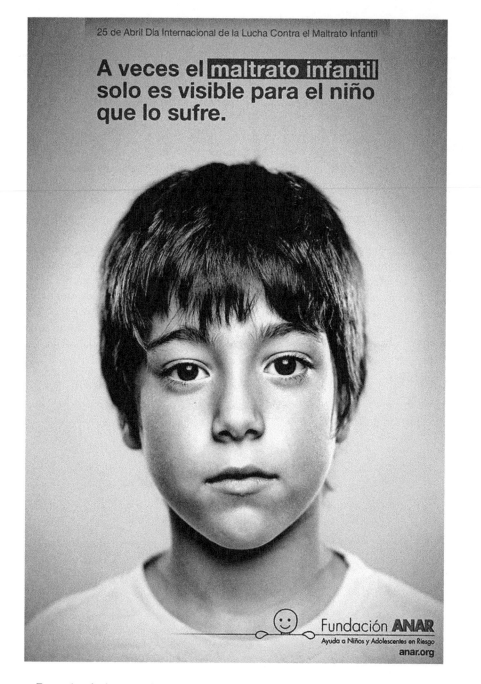

FIG. 15.4. Example of what an adult would see in Fundación ANAR's child abuse campaign.

in nine days (Fundación ANAR, 2013). The Foundation acknowledged that it had not received more calls for help from children than usual and had not considered it likely that they would. Instead, they had hoped the unusual technique would raise awareness and increase discussion of an increasing problem in Spain (Rodriguez, 2013). "We are delighted and overwhelmed," said Antonio Montero, from the agency that created the displays. "'We had a minimal budget, but we had to do something with high impact." (¶ 3, 5). It worked.

Final Thoughts

Communication research can contribute much to the professional's understanding of how people look for and make use of information. Decades of study have led to helpful generalizations about sources, messages, and communication channels that can help practitioners develop effective program strategies. The principles can help managers identify when a situation calls for an accommodation- or social marketing-oriented strategy and when a situation calls for an advocacy-oriented or even guerilla-style strategy. Many of the generalizations presented in this chapter come intuitively to the seasoned communication professional, but one lesson may seem less obvious. The effectiveness of each tactic—characteristics of source, channel, and message— ultimately depends on how it will be perceived by intended and unintended audiences. This lesson, therefore, comprises the overarching rule of how communication works: It depends. No message, strategy, channel, or source has the same effect in every situation or for every person. This is why an understanding of theories about message receivers is essential, as explained in Chapter 14, and preliminary research and pretesting represent such vital parts of effective program planning.

PART IV

The Successful Pitch and Follow-Through

16

Presenting Campaigns, Program Proposals, and Research Reports

---

Chapter Contents

- Communication Plans, Public Relations Proposals, and Research Reports
- The Successful Writer's Mind-Set
- About Grammar and Usage
- Oral Presentations
- Final Thoughts

Communication practitioners can expand their role in organizational decision making based on their important contributions to the organization's success, but they need to present their ideas effectively to do so. The communication manager's ideas achieve success only when they appear credible and successful to those who must approve project plans, budgets, and personnel decisions. Clients who cannot understand your research or who remain unconvinced that your ideas will work will not hire you for the job. Managers, therefore, need to treat the campaign plan or public relations program proposal as a kind of communication campaign. For those presenting research reports rather than complete plans, keep in mind that the client wants to understand the implications and limitations of the research you have done. Both situations require clear, confident, and forthright communication.

Communication Plans, Public Relations Proposals, and Research Reports

Every agency and organization has its own customs and expectations for oral and written presentations. Some expect a lot of detail in written form, and some prefer brief proposals in an outline format. This chapter presents a generic, detailed format for a complete communication plan, shown in Table 16.1, so practitioners have guidelines for the most formal campaign or program proposals. The format can be modified to fit a specific organization's needs. The parts include appropriate introductory material, an executive summary, a situation analysis and explanation of research needs, a list of research goals, a list of research objectives, a statement of research hypotheses, an explanation of research strategies, a description of the research results, a revised situation analysis that provides an explanation of the implications of the research findings, a proposed communication plan, a conclusion, and any relevant references and appendixes. The *research report* is similar to the communication plan or program proposal but excludes the proposed communication plan. Instead of including a detailed plan, the research report includes the revised situation analysis or implications section and then segues straight to the conclusion.

Introductory Material

Communication plans often will include a brief cover letter, sometimes called a *transmittal letter*. The cover letter for an internal document, such as a report submitted to a CEO by a department, can take the form of a memo. The cover letter states that the proposal requested is being submitted. As shown in Figure 16.1, the letter expresses appreciation to clients for the opportunity to work with them. It also makes it possible to highlight unique, surprising, or especially notable findings or recommendations that should interest the client. Finally, the cover letter invites the client to contact the agency with questions or concerns and provides contact names, phone numbers, fax numbers, and e-mail addresses as appropriate. It is constructed using the writing conventions of formal business style.

The plan includes customary introductory material, such as a title page that includes the client's name, the agency or department's name, the date, and a title identifying the purpose of the report. Giving the client's name more prominence than the agency on the title page conveys a more receiver-oriented impression, consistent with social marketing's focus on the target audience. Emphasizing the agency or department producing the report can seem arrogant. Clients gain a first impression of the strategic planning team based on these details.

The introductory material also includes a detailed table of contents, along with separate lists of tables and figures so clients can find material of special interest quickly. The team lists items included in appendixes individually so readers know what they will find there and in what order. Appendixes, however, often do not have page numbers. Instead, each piece receives a different heading, or slip-sheet divider, identifying it as Appendix A, Appendix B, or Appendix C along with a title that identifies the content more specifically, such as "community survey questionnaire." Some stylistic guidelines call for the table of contents and illustrative material to appear before the executive summary, whereas others call for them to appear after the executive summary.

Executive Summary

The executive summary addresses the needs of busy clients and executives who want to learn critical information at a glance. Many readers never have the motivation or opportunity to read a report all the way through. Indeed, committees evaluating a series of proposals may look first for reasons to weed out proposals as inappropriate, unresponsive, or impractical before reading

Table 16.1 Elements of the Campaign Plan, Program Proposal, or Research Report

---

Title page
(include client's name, agency or department name, date, and report title)

Cover letter

Table of contents
List of tables and figures

I.   Executive Summary
- Purpose of report or proposal
- Overview of method and results
- Overview of conclusions (recommendations) (about a sentence or two for each)
length: 1 to 2 pages

II.   Research needs
- Problem statement
- Situation analysis
    - the issue (problem statement)
    - what was known about the client and the issue
    - history
    - reporting lines for budget and policies
    - internal and external opportunities and challenges
    - assumptions (things we thought we knew but had not verified)
    - information needs (questions)
length: ranges considerably, often 4 to 8 pages

III. Research goals (What were you trying to find out?)
- Formal statements of research goals
- Further explanation of each goal, as needed
length: usually 1 page or less

IV.   Research objectives (How you found out, and by when)
- Formal statements of objectives
length: usually 1 page or less

V.   Research hypotheses (hunches or evidence-based expectations)
- Anticipated answers to questions
- Reasoning for answer anticipated
length: usually 1 to 2 pages

VI.   Research strategies
- Explanation of methodology, sampling approach
    - reasons for choices based on time, budget expertise, and need for precision
    - advantages and limitations of each choice against alternatives
- Operationalization of concepts (how ideas were measured)
    - wording of questions
    - relevance of questions to hypotheses
- Procedures for data analysis
length: usually 2 to 4 pages

Table 16.1 continued

VII. Results
- Discussed as answers to research questions or hypotheses
- Includes tests of assumptions
- Includes surprises
- Includes explanatory tables and figures as necessary
- Can integrate findings from different methods or discuss sequentially

length: usually several pages, plus illustrative material

VIII. Implications of the results (revised situation analysis)
- Overview of strategic recommendations with supporting evidence
- Identification of (only for campaign or program proposals; not included in research reports)
  - target publics
  - media/communication vehicles
  - messages/themes
  - evaluation strategies

length varies: parts may be in outline form with annotations for supporting evidence

IX. Proposed communication plan (only for campaign or program proposals; not included in research reports)
- Goals
- Objectives
- Strategies
- Tactics
- Calendar (time line)
- Budget

length varies; may be in outline form

X. Conclusion
- Summary of
  - original situation analysis and problem statement
  - revised situation analysis
  - recommended strategy
  - anticipated results
  - implications for a longer-term view

XI. References (as needed)

XII. Appendixes
- Research instruments
- Raw results
- Sample campaign materials (only for campaign or program proposals; not included in research reports)
- Other relevant background materials

```
[ON LETTERHEAD]




DATE

RECIPIENT'S NAME
RECIPIENT'S TITLE
RECIPIENT'S ADDRESS

Dear Ms. Client:

I am pleased to present you with a campaign proposal to [STATE OVERALL CAMPAIGN
GOAL]. It has been a privilege to work with you.

The proposal includes an overview of the situation, an explanation of the data collected
to direct strategic planning, and a detailed campaign implementation and evaluation plan.
[INCLUDE 1–3 PROPOSAL AND/OR RESEARCH HIGHLIGHTS HERE]. The campaign
has been designed to [STATE KEY OBJECTIVES FOR ACCOUNTABILITY].

Thank you for engaging our services. Please let us know if you have any questions.

Sincerely,

NAME OF LEAD CONSULTANT
TITLE OF LEAD CONSULTANT
```

FIG. 16.1. Sample cover letter template.

any further. As a result, managers must make a strong case for a credible proposal in just a few words.

The executive summary therefore usually acts as a special form of abstract. The executive summary serves as the business parallel to scientific papers that often have abstracts of 75 to 125 words to synopsize complicated procedures and findings. Companies have different customs for executive summaries; some organizations use the executive summary more as an overview chapter than as a true abstract, especially for long and complex reports. Such executive summaries can go on for 10 to 25 pages. Once an executive summary goes beyond 2 pages, however, it is considered a summary chapter and not an abstract. Obviously, nobody can read it at a glance. In this case, an additional 1- or 2-page abstract may be helpful.

EXECUTIVE SUMMARY

Researchers conducted a series of six focus groups (N=37) in four locations over a two-month period to explore parents' perceptions of attitudes toward commercial, government-sponsored and nonprofit Internet websites focused on healthy eating and food preparation. The purpose of the focus groups was to identify and evaluate features of of Internet websites that resonate with and effectively inform parents about food preparation and nutrition. Participants discussed their personal and family's uses of the Internet, including for gathering nutrition and recipe information. They also explored and discussed a set of 11 pre-selected websites. Each group explored 4–5 websites.

Results of the focus groups indicated that participants commonly use the Internet to learn about topics of interest to them including food and health. These include health and food/recipe-focused websites. The most common theme regarding participants' reported Internet use was as a resource for interests related to family and health.

Website credibility was important to participants but understanding the specifics of what makes a website credible to participants was more challenging. When pressed, participants indicated they have learned to trust certain websites from experience, because they use them frequently. In other instances, participants indicated they may visit a number of websites looking for specific, accurate information. They attempt to corroborate their findings to achieve a sense of information accuracy. Sponsorship by a university tended to improve perceptions of credibility.

Participants made distinctions between the usefulness and the usability of websites. Useful websites contained at least some information participants found interesting and instructive. A useable website, however, had visual appeal, ease of navigation, family friendly formats, and target-relevant content. Content ideas participants disliked included lessons and certificates, blogs and prominent mission statements. In general, participants avoided registering on websites and did not want to subscribe to any service. They also wished to avoid regular e-mails and reminders from website providers and expressed concerns about websites that triggered problems with computers' security software. They validated the importance of regular content updates.

Overall, participant responses emphasized the importance of providing a visually appealing, navigable, personally relevant site that takes into consideration the dietary needs and financial challenges of the target audience. Because these recommendations may be difficult to implement with limited funding and time for site development and maintenance, a simpler site that provides key information effectively may be more useful than a multilayered site that is more difficult to create and maintain.

FIG. 16.2. Sample executive summary.

Used with permission, Austin & Pinkleton 2012

As shown in Figure 16.2, the executive summary should present the purpose of the report or proposal, the procedures used to evaluate and address the needs presented by the situation, the findings of the research performed, the conclusions drawn from the research, and an overview of specific recommendations for action. A concise executive summary outlines every crucial section of the report or proposal, giving one or two sentences to each section. Some especially helpful summaries include page numbers directing readers to the sections of the proposal that contain the details.

The situation analysis demonstrates agency members' understanding of the issue and situation under consideration. In some cases, this section presents research findings, but in other cases, this section provides an overview of how a situation appeared before commissioned research was performed. If an agency has performed research, this provides an opportunity to highlight the purpose of the research so clients can understand why it was necessary.

The section opens with a statement of the problem, just like the lead to a news story. It then summarizes everything known about the client and the issue. This includes the client's mission, history, personnel and decision-making structure, locations, facilities, and a summary of other priorities and projects. It also includes a history of the issue itself, such as whether it is an international problem of concern to many organizations or a problem only for the client. The description of the issue describes the extent to which the issue is emerging, declining, stable, or cyclical. As explained in Chapter 2, the situation analysis provides a detailed explanation of the opportunities and challenges that exist within the organization and its environment. It also identifies what additional information is required to design a successful campaign. Agencies and organizations often have their own preferred format for presenting this information, such as using the SWOC/SWOT (strengths, weaknesses, opportunities, challenges, or threats) analysis. Whether presented in narrative, outline, or tabular form, background on the situation represents an essential element for campaign planning. This section usually ranges from about 4 to 8 pages.

Research Goals

The campaign proposal then turns to the presentation of research goals. A proposal to perform research preparatory to the development of a campaign must explain the purpose of the research. If preparing the reader for the results of completed research, it usually will appear in past tense. Although this section presents research goals in a formal style, the purpose of the goal statements is to explain what the agency or department was (or will be) trying to find out. Some explanation of the goals can be provided, but this section usually requires only 1 page or less, most often in an outline form.

Research Objectives

Present research objectives in formal, objective style in an outline. These objectives state what research was (or will be) performed in response to the research goals. The goals and objectives can be presented in one interwoven section instead of two separate sections if doing so makes the purpose of the research more clear. This section usually requires only 1 page.

Research Hypotheses

Although communication managers do not need to act like academic scientists, they still can present informed hunches to clients. These hunches guide both data collection and data analysis. In response to the questions that need answers (the research goals), this section provides insight into what answers the manager may expect to find, along with the reasons for these expectations. If a manager expects to present surprising or disconcerting results to the client, this section can help prepare the client by presenting possible results scenarios. This section usually requires 1 or 2 pages.

Research Strategies

All research requires a thorough explanation of the methods used to collect data. For quantitative research, refer to the Standards for Minimal Disclosure of Opinion Polls (American Association for Public Opinion Research, 2010) (see Sidebar 12.1); further details are available in Appendix C. Because every research project suffers from limitations of some sort, the client needs to understand what guided your decision making as you performed the research. For example, if you present a mail survey, the client may want to know why a telephone or Internet survey would not have been a better choice. If you surveyed residents of one town when the client operates in seven towns, the client will wonder why only one town was used.

This section discusses the specifics of methodology, along with the reasons for making choices of method, sample, question design, and procedure. Include steps taken to ensure quality control throughout data collection. Describe the wording of all questions used in surveys, focus groups, and formal interviews, although long data-collection instruments can be described briefly using examples, and complete details can be provided in the appendixes. This section also includes a discussion of the limitations of the research performed, as well as a defense of its usefulness given its limitations.

For example, an e-mail-based survey of individuals who declined to donate to an organization during previous fund-raising campaigns could ask what might prevent a respondent from donating to an organization like the client's, instead of asking what prevented the respondent from giving in the past. The disadvantage is that the question is less direct, but the advantage is that respondents may give a more honest, less defensive answer if they do not feel singled out for having refused to donate previously. This section includes information about response rates, refusal rates, and data analysis procedures, explained in Chapter 12. This usually requires about 2 to 4 pages, depending on the scope of the project.

Results (With Minimal Interpretation)

This section presents a straightforward recitation of the research findings, putting each finding into the context of the research goals and hypotheses. It helps to restate each research goal and hypothesis before providing the results. This allows a client to read the results section independent of the rest of the document. Providing context also ensures that the results will make sense to the reader; managers should never simply list results. Consider that the client will read this section to find out what questions have answers, what assumptions have support, and what surprises have emerged. Research for a client with an apparent credibility problem, for example, may reveal that the client suffers from a lack of awareness rather than a lack of trust.

It helps to provide tables and figures to highlight particularly important findings. Too many tables and figures, however, overwhelm the reader and reduce their impact. A judicious selection of tables and figures integrated into the text instead of relegated to the appendixes helps clients who do not have the time, motivation, or inclination to flip back and forth between the two sections. The length of this section depends on the scope of the research and the complexity of the findings.

When reporting several research projects, such as a survey and a series of focus groups, the manager must decide whether the information will have the greatest effect presented as discrete sections (e.g., Survey, Focus Group 1, Focus Group 2, Focus Group 3) or in a consolidated discussion format organized in terms of research questions and hypotheses. Often, the consolidated format works well. For example, a survey finding on low credibility can be supplemented by focus group responses, which should take the form of themes illustrated by specific quotes, describing impressions of the client's recent communication activities.

Revised Situation Analysis

This section discusses the implications of the research results. After the research is complete, the communication manager will have a more definite view of the reasons for a problem experienced by the client, along with directions to guide strategy development. This section summarizes the results, indicating how they change or confirm the original view of the situation. The section goes on to provide an overview of recommendations for a public relations program or communication campaign. Each recommendation must seem appropriate and realistic. To convince the client, each recommendation is accompanied by: reasons that describe why it is appropriate; why it will be effective; and why it is worth the cost, in time and money, of implementation. Supporting evidence can take the form of findings from the research, public relations principles, and communication theory. Clients expect concrete reasons for action rather than esoteric discussions of theory, however, so keep it simple.

Coming after the summary of the situation and recommendations, this section presents a clear breakdown of the elements for the communication program. These include a discussion of appropriate target publics, communication channels, recommended messages and themes, and methods to evaluate program success. This section can be presented in outline form, provided each recommendation is explained and defended in a companion section. The length varies depending on the scope of the campaign.

Proposed Communication Plan

This section, frequently presented in outline format, presents the complete communication program plan. This includes goals, objectives, strategies, tactics, a calendar for implementation and completion, and a proposed budget. Some managers prefer to present all of the goals, followed by the objectives, followed by strategies and tactics. Others integrate all of the components needed to achieve each goal with that particular goal, like a series of strategic planning ladders (see Chapter 3) presenting strategies and tactics specific to each objective along with the objective itself.

Conclusion

A brief conclusion provides a summary of the problem, the discoveries, and the solutions. The conclusion can put the project into a larger context, showing how achieving the goals of this program will contribute to the organization's overall mission. A long-term view will demonstrate that the communication manager has a deep understanding of the client's needs and challenges, which can help build credibility both for the project proposed and for the long term. The conclusion should remain brief, rarely stretching beyond 1 or 2 pages.

References and Appendixes

Some communication plans include references, but managers must determine the extent to which clients will appreciate background material as opposed to finding it distracting or, even worse, self-important. Appendixes, however, usually are essential. The appendixes include copies of all research instruments used, a summary of the raw results, and other illustrative sample campaign materials such as brochures.

The Successful Writer's Mind-Set

One of the most important skills a manager can possess is the cultivation of a confident demeanor, both on paper and in person. Managers often sell themselves short by appearing hesitant, portraying self-doubt. You want to portray confidence combined with a respectful attitude. Meanwhile, you must avoid seeming arrogant.

In writing, hesitance reveals itself through use of the first person to advance ideas. Using phrases such as "I believe" and "we recommend" signals to the reader that managers do not have evidence on which to base opinions. As a result, written reports and proposals need to avoid using "I" and "we," which appear to advance tentative opinions instead of authoritative facts. A better strategy has the writer using the third person to state ideas directly and plainly, remembering to back up every idea with evidence, such as public relations principles and theory, and data from research, a source, or experts. Assertions have much more credibility when the manager can demonstrate their veracity with facts and sources, instead of "believing" or "feeling" them to be true.

Reports and proposals also must avoid passive voice, which gives the appearance of hesitance or, worse, evasiveness. Passive voice makes it seem as if an action is being done to another thing by something, instead of something doing an action to another thing. In other words, it reflects reactive writing instead of proactive writing because it emphasizes the receiver of the action instead of the initiator. Active voice and active verbs give power to communication efforts. As shown in Figure 16.3, active voice appears authoritative.

Throughout the document, the manager must display confidence, expertise, and empathy with the client. To communicate effectively, writing must be clear, interesting, and correct. As shown in Figure 16.4, reprinted from *The Effective Writer's Mind Set* (Austin, 1989) the writer must ask the following questions:

1   *What do I want to get across?* Know your main communication objective. The opening argument or lead forms the foundation for a communication piece. A strong lead helps the rest of a piece fall into place and shows readers why they should continue to read.

WEAK

Participants can be more likely to return to food- and nutrition-based websites when they are seen as attractive, are viewed as nicely formatted, are considered as clear and easy to navigate, and when content is filled with pertinent family-friendly content consisting of easy recipes with basic nutritional and cost information, the option of a personalized space tailored to household grocery needs, and a how-to section with short, embedded videos. Visitors are more likely to register or subscribe to a site when it is affiliated with a school or nonprofit organization and when it is providing material incentives and assurances of information privacy.

STRONG

Participants' return to food- and nutrition-based sites would depend on a successful merging of an attractive site format, clear and easy site navigability, and pertinent family-friendly content consisting of easy recipes with basic nutritional and cost information, the option of a personalized space tailored to household grocery needs, and a how-to section with short, embedded videos. Site affiliation with a school or nonprofit organization would increase the likelihood of site registration and/or subscription, as would material incentives and assurances of information privacy.

FIG. 16.3. Using active voice to communicate authoritatively.

A good lead uses direct sentence construction and addresses who, what, where, when, how, and why. A main argument for a report or speech shows a commitment to the subject through a clear, strong position statement. A strong opening argument statement will inspire and focus your writing and will inspire the reader as well.

2 *Can I visualize my audience?* Writing must target an audience. Try to imagine the audience and its expectations. Show an awareness of its interests and level of expertise. Show respect for audience members: assume they are intelligent. But do not assume they know what you are talking about: spell everything out using simple language. Tell them only what they care to know. If you want them to know something, make sure you show them why they should want to know it (i.e., demonstrate its relevance to them).

3 *Is my main point obvious?* Get to the point quickly. You do not have room or time to get wordy. Busy readers will not bother to wade through extra verbiage. Use the active voice (not the passive voice that relies on words such as "is," "was," and "to be"), look out for lots of little words such as "then," "in," "to," "so," "as," and so on because they often signal clutter, and worry more about providing supporting statements for your arguments than about adding embellishments and description.

4 *Am I vague?* Get specific. Without sufficient support, even the best ideas remain generalizations. At worst, the reader will think the communicator is trying to hide

QUESTIONS FOR THE WRITER

1. **What do I want to get across?**
   A strong opening statement will inspire and focus your writing and will inspire the reader as well.

2. **Can I visualize my audience?**
   Writing must target an audience. Make sure you show them why they should pay attention.

3. **Is my main point obvious?**
   Busy readers will not bother to wade through extra verbiage. Use active voice.

4. **Am I vague?**
   Get specific. Do not just tell; instead, show, by using evidence and examples.

5. **Am I logical?**
   Readers must see easily how every new bit of information relates to what came before it.

6. **Do I provide enough (too much) explanation?**
   Use supporting evidence: the perfect example, the exemplary quotation, the clinching statistic.

7. **Am I interesting?**
   Vary sentence structure. But avoid a lot of complexity.

8. **Does my writing read naturally?**
   Write as you would speak, but avoid conversational expressions.

9. **Is my writing free of errors?**
   No matter how good your ideas, no one will take them seriously if your writing includes basic errors.

10. **What impression do I leave at the end?**
    In report, feature, proposal, and speech writing, your conclusion makes as strong an impact as your introduction.

11. **Am I my worst critic?**
    Do not fear multiple rewrites. Good writing appears deceptively easy, just like good gymnastics. Do not get discouraged!

Fig. 16.4. The effective writer's mindset.

something. Try to develop main ideas to their fullest extent; explore the areas of a subject in relevant detail. Do not just tell; instead, show, by using evidence and examples. Remember that you need to convince the reader with your argument, so avoid merely describing your position.

5 *Am I logical?* Make strong transitions. Written ideas need to progress in a continuous, logical manner. Readers must see easily how every new bit of information relates to what came before it. Do not assume any relationships are obvious; you have to make these connections obvious for the reader as you write. Present new news before old news.

6 *Do I provide enough (too much) explanation?* Use supporting evidence effectively. Use only what you need: the perfect example, the exemplary quotation, the clinching statistic. When using quotes, remember to introduce the quote and explain its significance or implications (i.e., what it shows or proves). Do not just drop it in. Readers need to know why you want them to read a quote.

7 *Am I interesting?* Vary sentence structure. Variety comes naturally in our thoughts and spoken words, thus variety in your writing will read more naturally and will seem more interesting. How do you do it? Vary short and long sentences. Try mixing the order of subordinate clauses or subject and verb. Read your writing aloud to hear how it sounds. But avoid a lot of complexity, particularly in news items that generally have few embellishments.

8 *Does my writing read naturally?* Write as you would speak, but avoid conversational expressions. Good writing read aloud sounds like good conversation. In conversation, however, we use shortcuts and embellishments that appear sloppy in print. Avoid meaningless qualifiers such as "really," "very," "pretty," "so," "sort of," and "kind of." Also avoid colloquialisms and clichés. If you have original thoughts, they deserve original words to describe them. Make sure you follow the appropriate style guidelines for your piece: Associated Press style for news releases, newsletters, and newspapers; Chicago style for magazine articles; American Psychological Association style for scientific documents, and so on.

9 *Is my writing free of errors?* Eliminate mechanical and grammatical errors. Always proofread. No matter how good your ideas, no one will take them seriously if your writing includes basic errors. If in doubt of spelling or grammar, look it up or ask a colleague. Always proofread at least once just for grammar and spelling errors.

10 *What impression do I leave at the end?* Write a strong conclusion. In report, feature, proposal, and speech writing, your conclusion makes as strong an impact as your introduction. Here you sum up your evidence and show how it all inevitably validates your main argument. This also provides you with the opportunity to take the reader to the next step. You can expand on the topic, suggest where all this may lead, or show how it all contributes to an overarching mission.

11 *Am I my worst critic?* Revise and rewrite. Become your toughest critic. Do not fear multiple rewrites. Good writing appears deceptively easy, just like good gymnastics. It takes a lot of practice and wrong moves to get it right. Do not be discouraged!

About Grammar and Usage

Virtually all organizational units specializing in communication will expect professional-level grammar and stylistic skill from their employees. Effective communicators can rise through the ranks quickly, while those without stagnate if they can get hired in the first place. Many excellent grammar and style guidebooks, online articles and websites exist to guide the novice and to refine skills of the experienced.

Sidebar 16.1 provides an example of a compilation of frequently misused words. Do not consider this list exhaustive. Other lists frequently appear in professional journals and newspapers, demonstrating the continuing frustration of communication managers tired of encountering such mistakes (e.g. Gray-Grant, 2012, for Ragan's PR Daily).

Sidebar 16.1
Commonly Misused Words

Sometimes the wrong words appear like land mines to weaken your writing. Misuse of words such as these reduces your credibility with those who know how to use them correctly.

Less/Fewer

Less refers to an amount (which is single).

Example: There is less coffee in the pot.

Fewer refers to numbers (which are plural).

Example: There are fewer coffee beans.

Thus, fewer coffee beans make less coffee. But you can't have less beans.

Presently/Currently

The present is now, but presently is soon. Current and currently both refer to the present!

Example: I'll be there presently because I'm working on something else currently (or at present).

Affect/Effect

Affect is a verb meaning to alter (except in psychology jargon when it means emotion), but effect is a noun. You cannot "effect" something (except in rare cases such as "effecting a change." Here it means a certain change was accomplished. The reason: you can't alter—or "affect"—change, because that's redundant.)

Example: If you affect something you produce an effect.

However

However, when used to mean nonetheless, does *not* belong as the first word in a sentence. It should be set off with commas like a subordinate clause. Its misuse is common, but it signals weak writing.

It also, however, may be used immediately following a semicolon. This provides as much punch as if it were beginning a sentence; however, it does not break up the flow of your writing as much.

Hopefully

Like however, hopefully often is used to begin a sentence. Hopefully, however, is an adverb that must have a verb to modify. Using it at the beginning of a sentence to mean "We hope" is incorrect.

Example: You can do something hopefully, but you won't, "hopefully," do this.

Who/That/Which

Who refers to people. That refers to things. Which can refer to either.

Example: We recommend reading about the people who wrote the book that shows which strategy to use.

Comprise/Compose

Comprise means "embrace" or "include," and compose means "together make the whole of." Comprise is an active verb, and compose is used as a passive verb.

Example: The puzzle comprised pieces composed of cardboard.

Ensure/Insure

Ensure means "to make sure," whereas insure means to "possess insurance."

Example: You can ensure your loved one's security by insuring your life.

Its/It's

Its means something belongs to "it," whereas it's means "it is."

Example: It's amazing how many times people confuse its usage.

Between/Among

Between refers to two things only. Among refers to three or more things.

Example: Between the two of us, I see trouble among the 30 members of this cooperative.

Their/Her/His/Its

Remember that their is plural; his, hers and its all are singular.

When referring to a reader, he and she are never "they"; only when referring to the readers can we say "they."

Medium/Media; Datum/Data

"Media" are plural. "Medium" is singular. Data are plural. Datum is singular.

When we report data, we say "they" show results.

When we call members of the media, we are talking about more than one media outlet.

Oral Presentations

Presentations themselves require research. Presentations differ depending on the size of the room and the number of people attending a presentation, for example. It helps to know as much about the audience as possible to understand their interests, their needs, and their expectations of formality. It also helps to know their competition and your own competition to put recommendations into a context that will maximize the presenters' credibility. Familiarity with room lighting and seating arrangements helps presenters construct a presentation with the appropriate degree of formality or intimacy. Always have strategies ready to adapt because timing, room locations, and other characteristics of the presentation situation may change on a moment's notice. If you plan to use PowerPoint, online video links or other presentation technology, have backup plans in case equipment breaks, the Internet signal malfunctions, or the power goes out. In one case, presenters to a regional public relations breakfast meeting brought two computers, each with the presentation on the hard drive, as well as a backup file in case someone else's equipment had to be used. When the interfaces to the room's projection technology failed to work with any of the equipment, including a third computer supplied by the event planners, no technicians were on duty to help out. Fortunately, the presenters had brought old-fashioned transparencies that worked with the outdated equipment available in the room and also had handouts.

Oral presentations often take the form of a 10- to 15-minute pitch, after which clients ask questions. The sale of a project ultimately depends on the quality of its presentation, including the ability of the presenters to deal with unexpected situations and challenging questions. Effective presentations require substance more than bells and whistles, but some sizzle helps demonstrate professionalism and creativity. A successful pitch depends on effective organization, clarity, and completeness; clear concrete illustration of key points; and a professional demeanor.

1 *Organization of ideas.* As with a written document, clients appreciate it if managers present ideas in a logical order. Clients who become confused will blame the communicator rather than themselves. They will look for another agency that makes more sense. In other words, if the presentation loses the client, the agency loses the job.

2 *Clarity and completeness of presentation.* Ideas need to seem concrete, efficient, and effective. They must build on each other to create a cohesive plan, without redundancy.

A brief presentation can never present every detail of a proposal; careful choices must be made. The client needs to know he or she has heard the key ideas, recommendations, and evidence. The manager's challenge is to demonstrate a deep understanding of the client that enables the agency or department to anticipate the client's priorities, concerns, and reservations about the project. The client should not have any nagging questions or doubts following the presentation. It helps to practice answering tough questions to anticipate dealing with reservations a client may have.

3   *Illustration of key points.* Presenters need visual aids to illustrate key points and to add interest to a presentation. Illustrations also can help relieve the presenter's nerves by providing clients with a focus other than the presenter. Illustrations such as outlines of key points can pull a presentation back on track if a presenter forgets the script or becomes distracted by questions or disturbances. Visual aids must serve an explanatory purpose, instead of seeming pointless. Pointless illustrations risk leading clients to believe agencies will recommend pointless program tactics as well. Because illustrations represent the presenters in a prominent way, they must be neat and free of errors. Charts and tables require large type and few words to be readable and easy to interpret. Give the audience at least 3 to 5 seconds to digest even the simplest visual aid. Clients often expect computer-aided presentations, but they aid a presentation only if they make sense. Keep in mind that equipment frequently malfunctions, making it necessary to have a "low-tech" backup plan for any "high tech" presentation.

4   *Presentation style.* Presenters need to look and act professional, which requires rehearsal. Most clients expect presenters to dress in business attire, but some agencies have success with a more *avant garde* approach that distinguishes them from the norm. This is a risky strategy, however, and can communicate sloppiness or arrogance if it backfires. To demonstrate confidence and empathy, presenters need to make eye contact with audience members. The presentation of bad news requires a gentle demeanor, and in some situations eye contact can seem overly aggressive: avoid making clients feel defensive. To soften bad news, open with a bit of good news and then present bad news without assigning blame and in a way that gives the client realistic hope that problems can be resolved. Figure 16.5 provides an example of this approach.

NOT RECOMMENDED

The website has a lot of problems that need attention. Specifically, users criticized the website for the following reasons.

RECOMMENDED ALTERNATIVE

Survey results indicate that site users consider it an important, helpful and easy-to-use tool for their work. Survey results also indicate users would appreciate the following changes.

FIG. 16.5. Two ways to frame bad news.

Presenters need to show enthusiasm for and confidence in their material. If something goes wrong during the presentation, the client probably will not worry about it if the presenters show good humor and continued confidence in their material.

Final Thoughts

The communication plan serves as the manager's sales pitch. The manager demonstrating expertise at promoting an organization's mission must illustrate this expertise in the promotion of the communication department or agency itself. Each public relations pitch constitutes a communication campaign in miniature. The manager wants to appear confident, credible, enthusiastic, and creative, but never hesitant, insincere, uninterested, or arrogant. Public relations and communication principles apply just as much to plan writing and presentation as to programming itself.

Appendix A

Code of Professional Standards for the Practice of Public Relations

Preamble

Public Relations Society of America Member Code of Ethics 2000:

- Professional Values
- Principles of Conduct
- Commitment and Compliance

This Code applies to PRSA members. The Code is designed to be a useful guide for PRSA members as they carry out their ethical responsibilities. This document is designed to anticipate and accommodate, by precedent, ethical challenges that may arise. The scenarios outlined in the Code provision are actual examples of misconduct. More will be added as experience with the Code occurs.

The Public Relations Society of America (PRSA) is committed to ethical practices. The level of public trust PRSA members seek, as we serve the public good, means we have taken on a special obligation to operate ethically.

The value of member reputation depends upon the ethical conduct of everyone affiliated with the Public Relations Society of America. Each of us sets an example for each other as well as other professionals—by our pursuit of excellence with powerful standards of performance, professionalism, and ethical conduct.

Emphasis on enforcement of the Code has been eliminated. But, the PRSA Board of Directors retains the right to bar from membership or expel from the Society any individual who has been or is sanctioned by a government agency or convicted in a court of law of an action that is not in compliance with the Code.

Ethical practice is the most important obligation of a PRSA member. We view the Member Code of Ethics as a model for other professions, organizations, and professionals.

PRSA Member Statement of Professional Values

This statement presents the core values of PRSA members and, more broadly, of the public relations profession. These values provide the foundation for the Member Code of Ethics and set the industry standard for the professional practice of public relations. These values are the fundamental beliefs that guide our behaviors and decision-making process. We believe our professional values are vital to the integrity of the profession as a whole.

ADVOCACY

We serve the public interest by acting as responsible advocates for those we represent. We provide a voice in the marketplace of ideas, facts, and viewpoints to aid informed public debate.

HONESTY

We adhere to the highest standards of accuracy and truth in advancing the interests of those we represent and in communicating with the public.

EXPERTISE

We acquire and responsibly use specialized knowledge and experience. We advance the profession through continued professional development, research, and education. We build mutual understanding, credibility, and relationships among a wide array of institutions and audiences.

INDEPENDENCE

We provide objective counsel to those we represent. We are accountable for our actions.

LOYALTY

We are faithful to those we represent, while honoring our obligation to serve the public interest.

FAIRNESS

We deal fairly with clients, employers, competitors, peers, vendors, the media, and the general public. We respect all opinions and support the right of free expression.

PRSA Code Provisions

FREE FLOW OF INFORMATION

Core Principle: Protecting and advancing the free flow of accurate and truthful information is essential to serving the public interest and contributing to informed decision making in a democratic society.

Intent:

To maintain the integrity of relationships with the media, government officials, and the public.

To aid informed decision-making.

Guidelines:

A member shall:

Preserve the integrity of the process of communication.

Be honest and accurate in all communications.

Act promptly to correct erroneous communications for which the practitioner is responsible.

Preserve the free flow of unprejudiced information when giving or receiving gifts by ensuring that gifts are nominal, legal, and infrequent.

Examples of Improper Conduct Under this Provision:

A member representing a ski manufacturer gives a pair of expensive racing skis to a sports magazine columnist, to influence the columnist to write favorable articles about the product.

A member entertains a government official beyond legal limits and/or in violation of government reporting requirements.

COMPETITION

Core Principle: Promoting healthy and fair competition among professionals preserves an ethical climate while fostering a robust business environment.

Intent:

To promote respect and fair competition among public relations professionals.

To serve the public interest by providing the widest choice of practitioner options.

Guidelines:

A member shall:

Follow ethical hiring practices designed to respect free and open competition without deliberately undermining a competitor.

Preserve intellectual property rights in the marketplace.

Examples of Improper Conduct Under This Provision:

A member employed by a "client organization" shares helpful information with a counseling firm that is competing with others for the organization's business.

A member spreads malicious and unfounded rumors about a competitor in order to alienate the competitor's clients and employees in a ploy to recruit people and business.

DISCLOSURE OF INFORMATION

Core Principle: Open communication fosters informed decision making in a democratic society.

Intent:

To build trust with the public by revealing all information needed for responsible decision making.

Guidelines:

A member shall:

> Be honest and accurate in all communications.
> Act promptly to correct erroneous communications for which the member is responsible.
> Investigate the truthfulness and accuracy of information released on behalf of those represented.
> Reveal the sponsors for causes and interests represented.
> Disclose financial interest (such as stock ownership) in a client's organization.
> Avoid deceptive practices.

Examples of Improper Conduct Under this Provision:

Front groups: A member implements "grass roots" campaigns or letter-writing campaigns to legislators on behalf of undisclosed interest groups.

Lying by omission: A practitioner for a corporation knowingly fails to release financial information, giving a misleading impression of the corporation's performance.

A member discovers inaccurate information disseminated via a website or media kit and does not correct the information.

A member deceives the public by employing people to pose as volunteers to speak at public hearings and participate in "grass roots" campaigns.

SAFEGUARDING CONFIDENCES

Core Principle: Client trust requires appropriate protection of confidential and private information.

Intent:

To protect the privacy rights of clients, organizations, and individuals by safeguarding confidential information.

Guidelines:

A member shall:

> Safeguard the confidences and privacy rights of present, former, and prospective clients and employees.
> Protect privileged, confidential, or insider information gained from a client or organization.
> Immediately advise an appropriate authority if a member discovers that confidential information is being divulged by an employee of a client company or organization.

Examples of Improper Conduct Under This Provision:

A member changes jobs, takes confidential information, and uses that information in the new position to the detriment of the former employer.

A member intentionally leaks proprietary information to the detriment of some other party.

CONFLICTS OF INTEREST

Core Principle: Avoiding real, potential or perceived conflicts of interest builds the trust of clients, employers, and the publics.

Intent:

To earn trust and mutual respect with clients or employers.

To build trust with the public by avoiding or ending situations that put one's personal or professional interests in conflict with society's interests.

Guidelines:

A member shall:

> Act in the best interests of the client or employer, even subordinating the member's personal interests.
>
> Avoid actions and circumstances that may appear to compromise good business judgment or create a conflict between personal and professional interests.
>
> Disclose promptly any existing or potential conflict of interest to affected clients or organizations.
>
> Encourage clients and customers to determine if a conflict exists after notifying all affected parties.

Examples of Improper Conduct Under This Provision:

The member fails to disclose that he or she has a strong financial interest in a client's chief competitor.

The member represents a "competitor company" or a "conflicting interest" without informing a prospective client.

ENHANCING THE PROFESSION

Core Principle: Public relations professionals work constantly to strengthen the public's trust in the profession.

Intent:

To build respect and credibility with the public for the profession of public relations.

To improve, adapt and expand professional practices.

Guidelines:

A member shall:

> Acknowledge that there is an obligation to protect and enhance the profession.
>
> Keep informed and educated about practices in the profession to ensure ethical conduct.
>
> Actively pursue personal professional development.
>
> Decline representation of clients or organizations that urge or require actions contrary to this Code.
>
> Accurately define what public relations activities can accomplish.

Counsel subordinates in proper ethical decision making.

Require that subordinates adhere to the ethical requirements of the Code.

Report practices not in compliance with the Code, whether committed by PRSA members or not, to the appropriate authority.

Examples of Improper Conduct Under This Provision:

A PRSA member declares publicly that a product the client sells is safe, without disclosing evidence to the contrary.

A member initially assigns some questionable client work to a non-member practitioner to avoid the ethical obligation of PRSA membership.

PRSA Member Code of Ethics Pledge

I pledge:

To conduct myself professionally, with truth, accuracy, fairness, and responsibility to the public; To improve my individual competence and advance the knowledge and proficiency of the profession through continuing research and education; And to adhere to the articles of the Member Code of Ethics 2000 for the practice of public relations as adopted by the governing Assembly of the Public Relations Society of America.

I understand and accept that there is a consequence for misconduct, up to and including membership revocation.

And, I understand that those who have been or are sanctioned by a government agency or convicted in a court of law of an action that is not in compliance with the Code may be barred from membership or expelled from the Society.

_____

Signature

_____

Date

Code of Professional Ethics and Practice

The Code of Professional Ethics and Practices (Revised May, 2010)

We—the members of the American Association for Public Opinion Research and its affiliated chapters—subscribe to the principles expressed in the following Code. Our goals are to support sound and ethical practice in the conduct of survey and public opinion research and in the use of such research for policy- and decision-making in the public and private sectors, as well as to improve public understanding of survey and public opinion research methods and the proper use of those research results.

We pledge ourselves to maintain high standards of scientific competence, integrity, and transparency in conducting, analyzing, and reporting our work; establishing and maintaining relations with survey respondents and our clients; and communicating with those who eventually use the research for decision-making purposes and the general public. We further pledge ourselves to reject all tasks or assignments that would require activities inconsistent with the principles of this Code.

The Code describes the obligations that we believe all research professionals have, regardless of their membership in this Association or any other, to uphold the credibility of survey and public opinion research.

It shall not be the purpose of this Code to pass judgment on the merits of specific research methods. From time to time, the AAPOR Executive Council may issue guidelines and recommendations on best practices with regard to the design, conduct, and reporting of surveys and other forms of public opinion research.

I. Principles of Professional Responsibility in Our Dealings with People

A. Respondents and Prospective Respondents

1. We shall avoid practices or methods that may harm, endanger, humiliate, or seriously mislead survey respondents or prospective respondents.

2. We shall respect respondents' desires, when expressed, not to answer specific survey questions or provide other information to the researcher. We shall be responsive to their questions about how their contact information was secured.

3. Participation in surveys and other forms of public opinion research is voluntary, except for the decennial census and a few other government surveys as specified by law. We shall provide all persons selected for inclusion with a description of the research study sufficient to permit them to make an informed and free decision about their participation. We shall make no false or misleading claims as to a study's sponsorship or purpose, and we shall provide truthful answers to direct questions about the research. If disclosure could substantially bias responses or endanger interviewers, it is sufficient to indicate that some information cannot be revealed or will not be revealed until the study is concluded.

4. We shall not misrepresent our research or conduct other activities (such as sales, fundraising, or political campaigning) under the guise of conducting survey and public opinion research.

5. Unless the respondent explicitly waives confidentiality for specified uses, we shall hold as privileged and confidential all information that could be used, alone or in combination with other reasonably available information, to identify a respondent with his or her responses. We also shall not disclose or use the names of respondents or any other personally-identifying information for non-research purposes unless the respondents grant us permission to do so.

6. We understand that the use of our research results in a legal proceeding does not relieve us of our ethical obligation to keep confidential all respondent-identifying information (unless waived explicitly by the respondent) or lessen the importance of respondent confidentiality.

B. Clients or Sponsors

1. When undertaking work for a private client, we shall hold confidential all proprietary information obtained about the client and about the conduct and findings of the research undertaken for the client, except when the dissemination of the information is expressly authorized by the client, or when disclosure becomes necessary under the terms of Section I-C or III-E of this Code. In the latter case, disclosures shall be limited to information directly bearing on the conduct and findings of the research.

2. We shall be mindful of the limitations of our techniques and capabilities and shall accept only those research assignments that we can reasonably expect to accomplish within these limitations.

C. The Public

1. We shall inform those for whom we conduct publicly released research studies that AAPOR Standards for Disclosure require the release of certain essential information about how the research was conducted, and we shall make all reasonable efforts to encourage clients to subscribe to our standards for such disclosure in their releases.

2. We shall correct any errors in our own work that come to our attention which could influence interpretation of the results, disseminating such corrections to all original recipients of our content.

3. We shall attempt, as practicable, to correct factual misrepresentations or distortions of our data or analysis, including those made by our research partners, co-investigators, sponsors, or clients. We recognize that differences of opinion in analysis are not necessarily factual misrepresentations or distortions. We shall issue corrective statements to all parties who were presented with the factual misrepresentations or distortions, and if such factual misrepresentations or distortions were made publicly, we shall correct them in as commensurate a public forum as is practicably possible.

D. The Profession

1. We recognize our responsibility to the science of survey and public opinion research to disseminate as freely as practicable the ideas and findings that emerge from our research.

2. We can point with pride to our membership in the Association and our adherence to this Code as evidence of our commitment to high standards of ethics in our relations with respondents, our clients or sponsors, the public, and the profession. However, we shall not cite our membership in the Association nor adherence to this Code as evidence of professional competence, because the Association does not so certify any persons or organizations.

II. Principles of Professional Practice in the Conduct of Our Work

A. We shall exercise due care in developing research designs and instruments, and in collecting, processing, and analyzing data, taking all reasonable steps to assure the reliability and validity of results.

1. We shall recommend and employ only those tools and methods of analysis that, in our professional judgment, are well suited to the research problem at hand.

2. We shall not knowingly select research tools and methods of analysis that yield misleading conclusions.

3. We shall not knowingly make interpretations of research results that are inconsistent with the data available, nor shall we tacitly permit such interpretations. We shall ensure that any findings we report, either privately or for public release, are a balanced and accurate portrayal of research results.

4. We shall not knowingly imply that interpretations should be accorded greater confidence than the data actually warrant. When we use samples to make statements about populations, we shall only make claims of precision that are warranted by the sampling frames and methods employed. For example, the reporting of a margin of sampling error based on an opt-in or self-selected volunteer sample is misleading.

5. We shall not knowingly engage in fabrication or falsification.

6. We shall accurately describe survey and public opinion research from other sources that we cite in our work, in terms of its methodology, content, and comparability.

B. We shall describe our methods and findings accurately and in appropriate detail in all research reports, adhering to the standards for disclosure specified in Section III.

III. Standards for Disclosure

Good professional practice imposes the obligation upon all survey and public opinion researchers to disclose certain essential information about how the research was conducted. When conducting publicly released research studies, full and complete disclosure to the public is best made at the time results are released, although some information may not be immediately available. When undertaking work for a private client, the same essential information should be made available to the client when the client is provided with the results.

A. We shall include the following items in any report of research results or make them available immediately upon release of that report.

1. Who sponsored the research study, who conducted it, and who funded it, including, to the extent known, all original funding sources.

2. The exact wording and presentation of questions and responses whose results are reported.

3. A definition of the population under study, its geographic location, and a description of the sampling frame used to identify this population. If the sampling frame was provided by a third party, the supplier shall be named. If no frame or list was utilized, this shall be indicated.

4. A description of the sample design, giving a clear indication of the method by which the respondents were selected (or self-selected) and recruited, along with any quotas or additional sample selection criteria applied within the survey instrument or post-fielding. The description of the sampling frame and sample design should include sufficient detail to determine whether the respondents were selected using probability or non-probability methods.

5. Sample sizes and a discussion of the precision of the findings, including estimates of sampling error for probability samples and a description of the variables used in any weighting or estimating procedures. The discussion of the precision of the findings should state whether or not the reported margins of sampling error or statistical analyses have been adjusted for the design effect due to clustering and weighting, if any.

6. Which results are based on parts of the sample, rather than on the total sample, and the size of such parts.

7. Method and dates of data collection.

B. We shall make the following items available within 30 days of any request for such materials.

1. Preceding interviewer or respondent instructions and any preceding questions or instructions that might reasonably be expected to influence responses to the reported results.

2. Any relevant stimuli, such as visual or sensory exhibits or show cards.

3. A description of the sampling frame's coverage of the target population.

4. The methods used to recruit the panel, if the sample was drawn from a pre-recruited panel or pool of respondents.

5. Details about the sample design, including eligibility for participation, screening procedures, the nature of any oversamples, and compensation/incentives offered (if any).

6. Summaries of the disposition of study-specific sample records so that response rates for probability samples and participation rates for non-probability samples can be computed.

7. Sources of weighting parameters and method by which weights are applied.

8. Procedures undertaken to verify data. Where applicable, methods of interviewer training, supervision, and monitoring shall also be disclosed.

C. If response rates are reported, response rates should be computed according to AAPOR Standard Definitions.

D. If the results reported are based on multiple samples or multiple modes, the preceding items shall be disclosed for each.

E. If any of our work becomes the subject of a formal investigation of an alleged violation of this Code, undertaken with the approval of the AAPOR Executive Council, we shall provide additional information on the research study in such detail that a fellow researcher would be able to conduct a professional evaluation of the study.

May, 2010

Appendix C

Guidelines and Standards for Measuring and Evaluating PR Effectiveness

THE INSTITUTE FOR PUBLIC RELATIONS COMMISSION ON PR MEASUREMENT AND EVALUATION University of Florida * PO Box 118400 * Gainesville, FL 32611–8400 (352) 392–0280 * (352) 846–1122 (fax) www.instituteforpr.com

GUIDELINES FOR MEASURING THE EFFECTIVENESS OF PR PROGRAMS AND ACTIVITIES

This booklet was first published in 1997 under the title, "Guidelines and Standards for Measuring and Evaluating PR Effectiveness." It was originally written by Dr. Walter K. Lindenmann, based on guidance, input and suggestions from a task force of PR practitioners, counselors, academicians and research suppliers that included the following individuals: Forrest W. Anderson . . . Albert J. Barr . . . Dr. Mary Ann Ferguson . . . Dr. James E. Grunig . . . Thomas Martin . . . Geri Mazur . . . Willard Nielsen . . . Charlotte Otto . . . Katharine D. Paine . . . David Silver . . . Kathleen Ward . . . Mark Weiner . . . and Dr. Donald K. Wright.

The booklet was updated and revised in 2002 and given a new title, "Guidelines for Measuring the Effectiveness of PR Programs and Activities," to more accurately reflect its contents. The revised version is primarily the work of Dr. Walter K. Lindenmann, with input and suggestions from Fraser Likely.

CONTENTS

FOREWORD

For years we have been told that we can never expect to get proper credit for what we do in public relations until we can find an effective way to measure our effectiveness.

Most other professions have recognized measuring tools—engineering devices, chemical reactions, case law, charts and figures. But public relations efforts have always been gauged in a variety of ways—each using a different kind of measuring stick.

In an attempt to begin to find a uniform "ruler" we can all use for measurement, a Public Relations Evaluation Summit was called in October, 1996 in New York City. This gathering of top leaders interested in public relations research was sponsored by the Institute for Public Relations, *INSIDE PR*, and the Ketchum Public Relations Research and Measurement Department.

As a result of that Summit, a booklet was published and distributed in 1997 under the title, *Guidelines and Standards for Measuring and Evaluating PR Effectiveness* as a first attempt to establish guidelines for how we might begin to agree on uniform ways to measure public relations by using the same measuring sticks. In the light of new developments relating to PR measurement overall, this booklet was revised in 2002 and given a new title, *Guidelines for Measuring the Effectiveness of PR Programs and Activities,* to more accurately reflect its contents. We view the revised version of this book as a companion to *Guidelines for Measuring Relationships in Public Relations,* and *Guidelines for Setting Measurable Objectives,* both of which were published in 1999.

We believe you can use the ideas and suggestions in this booklet as a working document of ways we can continue a dialogue on measuring the effectiveness of public relations.

Jack Felton
President & CEO

OVERVIEW

What is public relations measurement and evaluation?

Basically, it is any and all research designed to determine the relative effectiveness or value of what is done in public relations. In the short-term, PR measurement and evaluation involves assessing the success or failure of specific PR programs, strategies, activities or tactics by measuring the *outputs, outtakes and/or outcomes* of those programs against a predetermined set of objectives. In the long-term, PR measurement and evaluation involves assessing the success or failure of much broader PR efforts that have as their aim seeking to improve and enhance the *relationships* that organizations maintain with key constituents.

More specifically, *PR measurement* is a way of giving a result a precise dimension, generally by comparison to some standard or baseline and usually is done in a quantifiable or numerical manner. That is, when we measure *outputs, outtakes* and *outcomes*, we usually come up with a precise measure—a number; for example, 1,000 brochures distributed . . . 60,000 hits on a website . . . 50% message recall . . . an 80% increase in awareness levels, etc.

PR evaluation determines the *value* or importance of a PR program or effort, usually through appraisal or comparison with a predetermined set of organization goals and objectives. *PR evaluation* is somewhat more subjective in nature, or softer, than *PR measurement*, involving a greater amount of interpretation and judgment calls.

Interest in public relations measurement and evaluation has surged in recent years, as the public relations field has grown in size and sophistication, and as those who practice in the field have found themselves more often than ever being asked to be accountable for what they do.

Those who supervise or manage an organization's total communications activities are increasingly asking themselves, their staff members, their agencies and consulting firms, and their research suppliers questions such as these:

- Will those public relations and/or advertising efforts that we initiate actually have an effect—that is, "move the needle" in the right direction—and, if so, how can we support and document that from a research perspective?
- Will the communications activities we implement actually change what people know, what they think and feel, and how they actually act?
- What impact—if any—will various public relations, marketing communications, and advertising activities have in changing consumer and opinion-leader awareness, understanding, retention, attitude and behavior levels?

As questions such as these have increased in number in recent years, many public relations practitioners—as they seek to justify what they, themselves, do—have sensed a need to establish guidelines or criteria that the industry can follow, when it comes specifically to public relations measurement and evaluation.

This guidebook, which has been revised and edited under the auspices of the Institute for Public Relations Commission on PR Measurement and Evaluation, seeks to set minimum standards when it comes to measuring and evaluating the effectiveness of specific short-term PR programs, strategies, activities and tactics against pre-determined *outputs, outtakes* and *outcomes.* Those interested in measuring and evaluating the effectiveness of PR efforts aimed at enhancing the long-term *relationships* that exist between an organization and its key constituents should consult the companion guidebook, *Guidelines for Measuring Relationships in Public Relations.* (www.instituteforpr.com)

SOME GUIDING PRINCIPLES

In focusing on PR measurement and evaluation, here are some guiding principles or key factors to consider at the outset. These guiding principles are discussed in more detail in the main sections of this booklet.

- Establish clear program, activity, strategic and tactical objectives and desired outputs, outtakes and outcomes before you begin, to provide a basis for measurement of results. PR goals should tie directly to the overall goals of the organization.
- Differentiate between measuring PR *outputs*, which are usually short-term and surface (e.g. the amount of press coverage received or exposure of a particular message), PR *outtakes*, which are usually more far-reaching and can have more impact (e.g. determining if those to whom the activity was directed *received*, *paid attention to*, *comprehended* and *retained* particular messages) and PR *outcomes*, (e.g. did the program or activity change opinion and attitude levels, and possibly behavior patterns?).
- Measuring media content, while of great value, needs to be viewed as only a first step in the PR measurement and evaluation process. It can measure possible exposure to PR messages and actual press coverage; however, it cannot, by itself, measure whether target audiences actually saw the messages and responded to them in any way.
- There is no one, simple, all-encompassing research tool, technique or methodology that can be relied on to measure and evaluate PR effectiveness. Usually, a combination of different measurement techniques are needed. Consideration should be given to any one or several of the following: media content analysis . . . cyberspace analysis . . . trade show and event measurement . . . polls and surveys . . . focus groups . . . experimental and quasi-experimental designs . . . and/or ethnographic studies that rely on observation, participation and/or role playing techniques.
- Be wary of attempts to precisely compare PR effectiveness to advertising effectiveness. The two forms of communication are quite different from each other and the fact that placement of advertising messages can be controlled, whereas placement of PR messages usually cannot be controlled, needs to be taken into consideration.
- PR effectiveness can best be measured if an organization's principal messages, key target audience groups, and desired channels of communication are clearly identified and understood in advance.
- The PR measurement and evaluation process should never be carried out in isolation, by focusing only on the PR components. Wherever and whenever possible, it is always important to link what is planned, and accomplished, through PR, to the overall goals, objectives, strategies and tactics of the organization as a whole.

MAJOR PR MEASUREMENT AND EVALUATION COMPONENTS

For any PR evaluation research to be credible, five major components of the process need to be taken into consideration. They are:

1. Setting Specific Measurable PR Goals and Objectives

This has to come first. No one can really measure the effectiveness of anything, unless they first figure out exactly what it is they are measuring that something against. So, to begin, the public relations practitioner, counselor and/or research supplier ought to ask: What are or were the goals or objectives of the specific public relations program, activity, strategy or tactic? What exactly did the program or the activities hope to accomplish—through its public relations component?

This is not always easy to do, since it is often difficult to separate public relations programs and activities (such as publicity efforts, distribution of informational materials, the holding of special events or shows, etc.) from marketing communications (point-of-purchase promotional activities, coupon redemption programs, special contests and give-away activities, etc.) and from advertising (paid print and broadcast messages, cyberspace commercials, etc.).

In setting PR goals and objectives, it is usually important to recognize that measuring PR effectiveness per se—that is, the management of an organization's overall communications activities with its target audience groups or publics—can be quite difficult to do unless the individual elements or components of the program are clearly defined. We suggest that instead of trying to measure PR as a total entity, steps be taken to measure the effectiveness of individual or particular PR activities, such as measuring the effectiveness of specific publicity efforts, or a particular community relations program, or a special event or trade show activity, or a government affairs or lobbying effort, or a speaker's program, or an investor relations activity, and so on.

Additional ideas and suggestions pertaining to the setting of measurable PR goals and objectives can be obtained in the IPR Commission on PR Measurement and Evaluation guidebook, *Guidelines for Setting Measurable Public Relations Objectives.* (www.institute forpr.com).

2. Measuring PR Outputs

Outputs are usually the immediate results of a particular PR program or activity. More often than not, *outputs* represent what is readily apparent to the eye. *Outputs* measure how well an organization presents itself to others, the amount of exposure that the organization receives.

In media or press relations efforts, *outputs* can be the total number of stories, articles, or "placements" that appear in the media . . . the total number of "impressions"—that is, the number of those who might have had the opportunity to be exposed to the story . . . as well as an assessment of the overall content of what has appeared. Media Content Analysis (see page 347) is one of the principal methodologies used to measure media *outputs*.

For other facets of public relations, *outputs* can be white papers, speaking engagements, the number of times a spokesperson is quoted, specific messages communicated, or specific positioning on an important issue or any number of quantifiable items that are generated as a result of the effort. *Outputs* also might be assessment of a specific event, a direct mail campaign, the number of people who participated in a given activity, how a CEO handles himself or herself at a press conference, or the appearance and contents of a given brochure or booklet.

In any event, both the quantity and quality of *outputs* can be measured and evaluated. Media can be evaluated for their content; an event, as to whether the right people were there; a booklet or brochure for its visual appeal and substance; and so on.

3. Measuring PR Outtakes

Although it is obviously important to measure how well an organization presents itself to others and the amount of exposure obtained, it is even more important to measure PR *outtakes*—that is, determining if key target audience groups actually *received* the messages directed at them, *paid attention to them*, *understood* and/or *comprehended* the messages, and whether they *retained* the messages and can *recall* them in any shape or form.

When a PR program is launched or when given PR activities or events are initiated—such as the distribution of a brochure or a booklet, the placement of announcements on websites, or the delivering of a speech—it is important to assess what, if anything, did the intended recipients "take away" from this effort.

The first unit of *outtake* measurement could very well be that of favorability. Was the PR program or effort favorably received? Were the creative design elements or "packaging" received favorably? Was the "language" received favorably? Was the "ease of use" of the PR effort favorably received?

The second unit of *outtake* measurement relates to understanding and comprehension. Did the messages that were being disseminated make sense to the intended recipients? Were those to whom the messages were targeted able to decipher them and put them into appropriate context?

The third unit of measurement at the *outtake* level is message recall and retention. It measures whether the messages we craft for inclusion in our brochures, booklets and related PR programs and activities make enough of an impression on the intended recipients, that they become memorable. Can the intended recipients recall the embedded messages and can they retain them for any length of time?

The final unit of measurement at the *outtake* level is that of attention and possible immediate response. Did the receiver respond positively to the receipt of the messages? Did he or she do something with the information now in hand, for example, by passing on materials or messages to friends or colleagues? Did the recipient request more information, for example, by going to a website?

It is possible to compare the *outtake* measures of one particular PR program or activity to one or more others.

4. Measuring PR Outcomes

As important as it might be to measure PR *outputs* and *outtakes*, it is far more important to measure PR *outcomes*.

These measure whether the communications materials and messages which were disseminated have resulted in any *opinion*, *attitude* and/or *behavior* changes on the part of those targeted audiences to whom the messages were directed.

It is usually much more difficult and, generally, more expensive, to measure *PR outcomes*, and to some extent *PR outtakes*, than it is to measure *PR outputs*. This is because more sophisticated data-gathering research tools and techniques are required. Measuring *PR outputs* is usually a question of counting, tracking and observing, while for *PR outtakes* and *PR outcomes*, it is a matter of asking and carrying out extensive review and analysis of what was said and what was done.

Research techniques often used to measure *PR outtakes* and *PR outcomes* include quantitative surveys (in-person, by telephone, by mail, via fax, via e-mail, via the Internet, in malls, etc.) . . . focus groups . . . qualitative depth attitude surveys of elite audience groups . . . pre-test/posttest studies (e.g. before-and-after polls) . . . ethnographic studies (relying on observation, participation, and/or role-playing techniques) . . . experimental and quasi-experimental research projects . . . and multi-variate studies that rely on advanced statistical applications such as correlation and regression analyses, Q-sorts, and factor and cluster analysis studies.

5. Measuring Business and/or Organizational Outcomes

Whatever steps PR practitioners take to measure the effectiveness of what they, themselves, do in PR, it is imperative that they also take steps to seek to link their public relations accomplishments to the ultimate goals, objectives, and accomplishments of the organization as a whole.

What we are talking about here is seeking to relate PR *outcomes* to such desired business and/or organizational *outcomes* as increasing market penetration, market share, sales, and, ultimately, increasing an organization's profitability. It needs to be recognized that this is not easy to do. It requires a careful delineation of what the PR program seeks to accomplish in concert with what the organization as a whole seeks to accomplish. It also requires a good understanding of how and why the two processes are supposed to work together. When one has a good understanding of the impacts that are desired, as well as a good understanding of how the process is supposed to work, there are then many research design tools that can be employed to reliably and validly measure that impact.

For example, the subject of tying PR to sales is frequently discussed. Some trade publications offer response cards after specific articles have appeared in print. These offer very valuable "lead-generation" tools. With an effective "lead generation" system, those leads can frequently be tracked through to sales. However, it must be remembered that while PR may have generated the lead, the closure was, of course, heavily influenced by such items as the individual's need for or interest in that product in the first place, the quality of the products and services that are offered, the distribution channel, the availability of the product or service, the price, etc. All of these items, or variables, need to be taken into consideration when seeking to measure the effectiveness of what occurred.

Most organizations, be they business for profit, public sector governmental or non-profit groups and associations, nowadays take the position that PR objectives really do not have value, unless they further the goals of the total organization, or of its business units or sectors. It is most important, therefore, to integrate an organization's PR programs and goals with the strategies and objectives of the organization as a whole. Further, this requires that the practitioner understand what is critical to the organization overall and to its specific business strategies and plans.

Our communication objectives must be tied to business unit or central function operational objectives. These operational objectives are, or should be, behavioral. They should state who will change (customers, employees, suppliers, stakeholders, investors, management, etc.) in what way, by how much and when. In a results-based organization, the only result that matters is a change in behavior (market segment x bought more widgets; employee segment y became more productive; stakeholder segment z supported our environmental policy, etc.).

In a results-based organization, the business unit objective of behavioral change is stated as a Key Result. An achieved communication effectiveness outcome is one indicator of performance towards that result. Our communication program planning objective becomes a Performance Indicator statement in the business line document. We restate the same outcome as a measurable objective in our communication plan. Our objectives are then tied directly to business or organizational objectives.

GETTING SPECIFIC: STANDARDS FOR MEASURING PR OUTPUTS

There are many possible tools and techniques that PR practitioners can utilize to begin to measure PR *outputs*, but these are the four that are most frequently relied on to measure PR impact at the *output* level: Media Content Analysis . . . Cyberspace Analysis . . . Trade Show and Event Measurement . . . and Public Opinion Polls.

1. Media Content Analysis

This is the process of studying and tracking what has been written and broadcast, translating this qualitative material into quantitative form through some type of counting approach that involves coding and classifying of specific messages.

Some researchers and PR practitioners in the U.S. refer to this as "Media Measurement" and/or "Publicity Tracking" research. In the United Kingdom, the technique is often referred to as "Media Evaluation"; and in Germany as "Media Resonance." Whatever the terminology used to describe this particular technique, more often than not its prime function is to determine whether the key messages, concepts and themes that an organization might be interested in disseminating to others via the media do, indeed, receive some measure of exposure as a result of a particular public relations effort or activity.

The coding, classifying and analysis that is done can be relatively limited or far-reaching, depending on the needs and interests of the organization commissioning the research. More often than not, Media Content Analysis studies take into consideration variables such as these:

Media Vehicle Variables, such as date of publication or broadcast . . . frequency of publication or broadcast of the media vehicle . . . media vehicle or type (that is, whether the item appeared in a newspaper, magazine, a newsletter, on radio, or on television) . . . and geographic reach (that is, region, state, city, or ADI markets in which the item appeared).

Placement or News Item Variables, such as source of the story (that is, a press release, a press conference, a special event, or whether the media initiated the item on their own) . . . story form or type (a news story, feature article, editorial, column, or letter to the editor) . . . degree of exposure (that is, column inches or number of paragraphs if the item appeared in print, number of seconds or minutes of air time if the item was broadcast) . . . and the story's author (that is, the byline or name of the broadcaster).

Audience or 'Reach' Variables. The focus here usually is on total number of placements, media impressions and/or circulation or potential overall audience reached (that is, total readers of a newspaper or magazine, total viewers and listeners to a radio or television broadcast). The term "impression" or "opportunity to see" usually refers to the total audited circulation of a publication. For example, if *The Wall Street Journal* has an audited circulation of 1.5 million, one article in that newspaper might be said to generate 1.5 million impressions or opportunities to see the story. Two articles would generate 3 million impressions, and so on. Often more important than impressions is the issue of whether a story reached an organization's target audience group, by specific demographic segments. These data often can be obtained from the U.S. Census Bureau or from various commercial organizations, such as Standard Rate and Data Services. In addition to considering a publication's actual circulation figures, researchers often also take into consideration how many other individuals might possibly be exposed to a given media vehicle, because that publication has been routed or passed on to others.

Subject or Topic Variables, such as who was mentioned and in what context . . . how prominently were key organizations and/or their competitors referred to or featured in the press coverage (that is, were companies cited in the headline, in the body copy only, in both, etc.) . . . who was quoted and how frequently . . . how much coverage, or "share of voice" did an organization receive in comparison to its competitors . . . what issues and messages were covered and to what extent . . . how were different individuals and groups positioned—as leaders, as followers, or another way?

Judgment or Subjective Variables. The focus here usually is on the stance or tone of the item, as that item pertains to a given organization and/or its competitors. Usually tone implies some assessment as to whether or not the item is positive, negative or neutral; favorable, unfavorable or balanced. It is extremely important to recognize that measuring stance or tone is usually a highly subjective measure, open to a possibly different interpretation by others. Clearly-defined criteria or ground rules for assessing positives and negatives—and from whose perspective—need to be established beforehand, in order for stance or tone measures to have any credibility as part of Media Content Analysis.

"Advertising Equivalency" is often an issue that is raised in connection with Media Content Analysis studies. Basically, advertising equivalency is a means of converting editorial space into advertising costs, by measuring the amount of editorial coverage and then calculating what it would have cost to buy that space, if it had been advertising.

Most reputable researchers contend that "advertising equivalency" computations are of questionable validity. In many cases, it may not even be possible to assign an advertising equivalency score to a given amount of editorial coverage (for example, many newspapers and/or magazines do not sell advertising space on their front pages or their front covers; thus, if an article were to appear in that space, it would be impossible to calculate an appropriate advertising equivalency cost, since advertising could never ever appear there).

Some organizations artificially multiply the estimated value of a "possible" editorial placement in comparison to advertising by a factor of 2, 3, 5, 8 or whatever other inflated number they might wish to come up with, to take into account their own perception that editorial space is always of more value than is advertising space. Most reputable researchers view such arbitrary "weighting" schemes aimed at enhancing the alleged value of editorial coverage as unethical, dishonest, and not at all supported by the research literature. Although some studies have, at times, shown that editorial coverage is sometimes more credible or believable than is advertising coverage, other studies have shown the direct opposite, and there is, as yet, no clearly established consensus in the communications field regarding which is truly more effective: publicity or advertising. In reality, it depends on an endless number of factors.

Sometimes, when doing Media Content Analysis, organizations may apply weights to given messages that are being disseminated, simply because they regard some of their messages as more important than others, or give greater credence (or weight) to an article that not only appears in the form of text, but also is accompanied by a photo or a graphic treatment. Given that the future is visuals, organizations are more and more beginning to measure not only words, but also pictures.

It should be noted that whatever ground rules, criteria and variables are built into a Media Content Analysis, whatever "counting" approaches are utilized to turn qualitative information into quantitative form, it is important that all of the elements and components involved be clearly defined and explained upfront by whoever is doing the study. The particular system of media analysis that is applied and utilized by one researcher should—if a second researcher were called in and given the same brief and the same basic criteria pertaining to the aims of the study— result in broadly similar research findings and conclusions.

2. Cyberspace Analysis

Increasingly, a key measure of an organization's image or reputation and of how that organization might be positioned is the chatter and discussion about that organization in cyberspace— specifically in chat rooms, forums and new groups on the World Wide Web. The same criteria used in analyzing print and broadcast articles can be applied when analyzing postings on the Internet.

What appears in print is frequently commented about and editorialized about on the Web. Therefore, one component of *PR output* measurement ought to be a review and analysis of Web postings.

In addition, a second *output* measure of cyberspace might be a review and analysis of website traffic patterns. For example, some of the variables that ought to be considered when designing and carrying out Cyberspace Analysis might include deconstructing "hits" (that is, examining the requests for a file of visitors to the Internet) . . . a review of click-throughs and/or flash-click streams . . . an assessment of home page visits . . . domain tracking and analysis . . . an assessment of bytes transferred . . . a review of time spent per page . . . traffic times . . . browsers used . . . and the number of people filling out and returning feed-back forms.

Best practices for this type of research are covered in *Measures of Success in Cyberspace*, a paper authored by Katharine Delahaye Paine that is available from the IPR Commission on PR Measurement and Evaluation, www.instituteforpr.com; *Getting Started On Interactive Media Measurement*, available from the Advertising Research Foundation, 641 Lexington Avenue, New York, NY 10022, and *Hits Are Not Enough: How to Really Measure Web Site Success*, prepared by *Interactive Marketing News* and available from Phillips Business Information, Inc., 1201 Seven Locks Road, Potomac, MD 20854.

3. Trade Shows and Event Measurement

Frequently, the intent of a public relations program or activity is simply to achieve exposure for an organization, its products or services, through staging trade shows, holding special events and meetings, involvement in speakers' programs and the like.

For shows and events, obviously one possible *output* measure is an assessment of total attendance, not just an actual count of those who showed up, but also an assessment of the types of individuals present, the number of interviews that were generated and conducted in connection with the event, and the number of promotional materials that were distributed. In addition, if the show is used as an opportunity for editorial visits, one can measure the effectiveness of those visits by conducting a content analysis of the resulting articles.

4. Public Opinion Polls

Although most surveys that are designed and carried out are commissioned to measure *PR outtakes* and *PR outcomes* rather than *PR outputs*, public opinion polls are often carried out in an effort to determine whether or not key target audience groups have, indeed, been exposed to particular messages, themes or concepts and to assess the overall effectiveness of a given presentation or promotional effort. For example, conducting a brief survey immediately following a speech or the holding of a special event to assess the short-term impact of that particular activity would constitute a form of *PR output* measurement.

GETTING SPECIFIC: STANDARDS FOR MEASURING PR OUTTAKES

Just as there are many tools and techniques that PR practitioners can utilize to begin to measure PR *outputs*, there also are many that can be used to measure PR *outtakes*. Some of those most frequently relied on include surveys (of all types) . . . focus groups . . . before-and-after polls . . . and ethnographic studies (relying on observation, participation, and/or role playing techniques).

There are many books available that discuss and describe both qualitative and quantitative research techniques. Here are three that specifically discuss such techniques from a public relations perspective: *Using Research In Public Relations*, by Glen M. Broom and David M. Dozier (Englewood Cliffs, NJ: Prentice Hall, 1990) . . . *Primer of Public Relations Research*, by Don W. Stacks (New York: The Guilford Press, 2002) . . . and *Public Relations Research For Planning and Evaluation*, by Walter K. Lindenmann (available from the IPR Commission on PR Measurement and Evaluation, www.instituteforpr.com.).

Ultimately, one intent of public relations is to inform and persuade key target audience groups regarding topics and issues that are of importance to a given organization, with the hope that this will lead those publics to act in a certain way. Usually, this involves two different types of *outtake* measures: Awareness and Comprehension Measurements and Recall and Retention Measurements.

1. Awareness and Comprehension Measurements

The usual starting point for any PR *outtake* measurement is to determine whether target audience groups actually *received* the messages directed at them . . . paid *attention* to them . . . and *understood* the messages.

Obviously, if one is introducing a new product or concept to the marketplace for the first time—one that has never been seen or discussed before—it is reasonable to assume that prior to public relations and/or related communications activities being launched, that familiarity and awareness levels would be at zero. However, many organizations have established some type of "presence" in the marketplace, and thus it is important to obtain benchmark data against which to measure any possible changes in awareness and/or comprehension levels.

Measuring awareness and comprehension levels requires some type of primary research with representatives of key target audience groups.

It is important to keep in mind that Qualitative Research (e.g. focus groups, one-on-one depth interviews, convenience polling) is usually open-ended, free response and unstructured in format . . . generally relies on non-random samples . . . and is rarely "projectable" to larger audiences. Quantitative Research (e.g. telephone, mail, mall, Internet, fax, and e-mail polls), on the other hand, although it may contain some open-ended questions, is far more apt to involve the use of closed-ended, forced choice questions that are highly structured in format . . . generally relies on random samples . . . and usually is "projectable" to larger audiences.

To determine whether there have been any changes at all in audience awareness and comprehension levels, usually requires some type of comparative studies—that is, either a *before* and *after* survey to measure possible change from one period of time to another, or some type of "test" and "control" group study, in which one segment of a target audience group is deliberately exposed to a given message or concept and a second segment is not, with research conducted with both groups to determine if one segment is now better informed regarding the issues than the other.

2. Recall and Retention Measurements

Traditionally, advertising practitioners have paid much more attention to recall and retention measurement, than have those in the public relations field.

It is quite common in advertising, after a series of ads have appeared either in the print or the broadcast media, for research to be fielded to determine whether or not those individuals to whom the ad messages have been targeted actually recall those messages on both an unaided and aided basis. Similarly, several weeks after the ads have run, follow-up studies are often fielded to determine if those in the target audience group have retained any of the key themes, concepts, and messages that were contained in the original advertising copy.

Although recall and retention studies have not been done that frequently by public relations practitioners, they clearly are an important form of *outcome* measurement, that ought to be seriously considered by PR professionals. Various data collection techniques can be used when conducting such studies, including telephone, face-to-face, mail, mall, e-mail, and fax polling.

When conducting such studies, it is extremely important that those individuals fielding the project clearly differentiate between messages that are disseminated via PR techniques (e.g. through stories in the media, by word of mouth, at a special event, through a speech, etc.) from those that are disseminated via paid advertising or through marketing promotional efforts. For example, it is never enough to simply report that someone claims they read, heard or saw a particular item; it is more important to determine whether that individual can determine if the item in question happened to be a news story that appeared in editorial form, or was a paid message that someone placed through advertising. Very often, it is difficult for the "average" consumer to differentiate between the two.

GETTING SPECIFIC: STANDARDS FOR MEASURING PR OUTCOMES

Some of the same tools and techniques that PR practitioners can utilize to begin to measure *PR Outtakes*—surveys, focus groups, before-and-after polls and ethnographic studies—also can be used to measure *PR Outcomes*. In addition, researchers designing and carrying out projects aimed at measuring changes in people's opinions, attitudes and behavior patterns also often rely on experimental and quasi-experimental designs, on multi-variate analysis projects, and on model building.

In addition to those works previously cited, two useful resources for qualitative and quantitative research techniques that can be used at the *PR Outcome* level are the Advertising Research Foundation's two documents: "Guidelines for the Public Use of Market and Opinion

Research" and the *ARF Guidelines Handbook: A Compendium of Guidelines to Good Advertising, Marketing and Media Research Practice.* Both are available from the Advertising Research Foundation, 641 Lexington Avenue, New York, NY 10022.

Two different types of research are usually called for, when conducting public relations measurement and evaluation research at the *outcome* level: Attitude and Preference Measurements and Behavior Measurements.

1. Attitude and Preference Measurements

When it comes to seeking to measure the overall impact or effectiveness of a particular public relations program or activity, assessing individuals' opinions, attitudes, and preferences become extremely important measures of possible *outcomes*.

It needs to be kept in mind that "opinion research" generally measures what people say about something; that is, their verbal expressions or spoken or written points of view. "Attitude research," on the other hand, is far deeper and more complex. Usually, "attitude research" measures not only what people say about something, but also what they know and think (their mental or cognitive predispositions), what they feel (their emotions), and how they're inclined to act (their motivational or drive tendencies).

"Opinion research" is easier to do because one can usually obtain the information desired in a very direct fashion just by asking a few questions. "Attitude research," however, is far harder and, often more expensive to carry out, because the information desired often has to be collected in an indirect fashion. For example, one can easily measure people's stated positions on racial and/or ethnic prejudice, by simply asking one or several direct questions. However, actually determining whether someone is in actual fact racially and/or ethnically prejudiced, usually would necessitate asking a series of indirect questions aimed at obtaining a better understanding of people's cognitions, feelings, and motivational or drive tendencies regarding that topic or issue.

Preference implies that an individual is or will be making a choice, which means that preference measurement more often than not ought to include some alternatives, either competitive or perceived competitive products or organizations. To determine the impact of public relations preference *outcomes* usually necessitates some type of audience exposure to specific public relations *outputs* (such as an article, a white paper, a speech, or participation in an activity or event), with research then carried out to determine the overall likelihood of people preferring one product, service, or organization to another.

Usually, opinion, attitude and preference measurement projects involve interviews not only with those in the public at large, but also with special target audience groups, such as those in the media, business leaders, academicians, security analysts and portfolio managers, those in the health, medical and scientific community, government officials, and representatives of civic, cultural and service organizations. Opinion, attitude and preference measurement research can be carried out many different ways, through focus groups, through qualitative and quantitative surveys, and even through panels.

2. Behavior Measurements

The ultimate test of effectiveness—the highest *outcome* measure possible—is whether the behavior of the target audience has changed, at least to some degree, as a result of the public relations program or activity.

For most media relations programs, if you have changed the behavior of the editor and/or reporter so that what he or she writes primarily reflects an organization's key messages, then that organization has achieved a measure of behavior change.

However, measuring behavior is hard because it is often difficult to prove cause-and-effect relationships. The more specific the desired *outcome* and the more focused the PR program or activity that relates to that hoped-for end result, the easier it is to measure PR behavior change. For example, if the intent of a public relations program or activity is to raise more funds for a non-profit institution and if one can show after the campaign has been concluded that there has, indeed, been increased funding, then one can begin to surmise that the PR activity had a role to play in the behavior change. Or, to give another example: for measuring the effectiveness of a public affairs or government relations program targeted at legislators or regulators, the desired *outcome*—more often than not—would not only be to get legislators or regulators to change their views, but more importantly to have those legislators and regulators either pass or implement a new set of laws or regulations that reflect the aims of the campaign. Behavior change requires someone to act differently than they have in the past.

More often than not, measuring behavior change requires a broad array of data collection tools and techniques, among them before-and-after surveys . . . research utilizing ethnographic techniques (e.g. observation, participation, and role playing) . . . the utilization of experimental and quasi-experimental research designs . . . and studies that rely on multi-variate analyses and sophisticated statistical applications and processes.

What is crucial to bear in mind in connection with PR *outcome* behavior measurement studies is that measuring correlations—that is, the associations or relationships that might exist between two variables—is relatively easy. Measuring causation—that is, seeking to prove that X was the reason that Y happened—is extremely difficult. Often, there are too many intervening variables that need to be taken into consideration.

Those doing PR *outcome* behavior measurement studies need to keep in mind these three requirements that need to exist in order to support or document that some activity or event caused something to happen: 1) Cause must always precede the effect in time; 2) there needs to be a relationship between the two variables under study; and 3) the observed relationship between the two variables cannot be explained away as being due to the influence of some third variable that possibly caused both of them.

The key to effective behavior measurement is a sound, well thought-out, reliable and valid research concept and design. Researchers doing such studies need to make sure that study or test conditions or responses are relevant to the situation to which the findings are supposed to relate, and also clearly demonstrate that the analysis and conclusions that are reached are indeed supported and documented by the field work and data collection that was carried out.

QUESTIONS THAT NEED TO BE PUT TO THOSE ORGANIZATIONS THAT COMMISSION PR MEASUREMENT AND EVALUATION STUDIES

Here are some of the key questions that those who commission PR measurement evaluation studies ought to ask themselves before they begin, and also the types of questions that those who actually carry out the assignment ought to ask their clients to answer before the project is launched:

- What are, or were, the specific goals and/or objectives of the public relations, public affairs, and/or marketing communications program, and can these be at all stated in a quantitative or measurable fashion? (e.g. To double the number of inquiries received from one year to the next? . . . To increase media coverage by achieving greater "share of voice in one year than in a previous year? . . . To have certain legislation passed? . . . To enhance or improve brand, product, or corporate image or reputation?)
- Who are, or were, the principal individuals serving as spokespersons for the organization during the communications effort?
- What are, or were, the principal themes, concepts, and messages that the organization was interested in disseminating?
- Who were the principal target audience groups to whom these messages were directed?
- Which channels of communication were used and/or deemed most important to use in disseminating the messages? (e.g. the media . . . word-of-mouth . . . direct mail . . . special events?)
- What specific public relations strategies and tactics were used to carry out the program? What were the specific components or elements of the campaign?
- What is, or was, the timeline for the overall public relations program or project?
- What is, or were, the desired or hoped-for outputs, outtakes, and/or outcomes of the public relations effort? If those particular hoped-for outputs, outtakes, and/or outcomes could, for some reason, not be met, what alternative outputs, outtakes, and/or outcomes would the organization be willing to accept?
- How does what is or has happened in connection with the organization's public relations effort relate to what is or has happened in connection with related activities or programs in other areas of the company, such as advertising, marketing, and internal communications?
- Who are the organization's principal competitors? Who are their spokespersons? What are their key themes, concepts, and messages that they are seeking to disseminate? Who are their key target audience groups? What channels of communications are they most frequently utilizing?
- Which media vehicles are, or were, most important to reach for the particular public relations and/or marketing communications activities that were undertaken?
- What were the specific public relations materials and resources utilized as part of the effort? Would it be possible to obtain and review copies of any relevant press releases, brochures, speeches, promotional materials that were produced and distributed as part of the program?
- What information is already available to the organization that can be utilized by those carrying out the evaluative research assignment to avoid reinventing the wheel and to build on what is already known?
- If part of the project involves an assessment of media coverage, who will be responsible for collecting the clips or copies of broadcast materials that will have been generated? What are the groundrules and/or parameters for clip and/or broadcast material assessment?
- What major issues or topics pertaining to the public relations undertaking are, or have been, of greatest importance to the organization commissioning the evaluation research project?

- What is the timeline for the PR Measurement and Evaluation Research effort? What are the budgetary parameters and/or limitations for the assignment? Do priorities have to be set?
- Who will be the ultimate recipients of the research findings?
- How will whatever information that is collected be used by the organization that is commissioning the research?

QUESTIONS THAT NEED TO BE PUT TO THOSE RESEARCH SUPPLIERS, AGENCIES AND CONSULTING FIRMS THAT ACTUALLY CONDUCT PR MEASUREMENT AND EVALUATION STUDIES

Here are some of the key questions that ought to be put to those who actually are asked to carry out a PR measurement and evaluation research project, before the assignment is launched:

- What is, or will be, the actual research design or plan for the PR measurement and evaluation project? Is there, or will there be, a full description in non-technical language of what is to be measured, how the data are to be collected, tabulated, analyzed and reported?
- Will the research design be consistent with the state purpose of the PR measurement and evaluation study that is to be conducted? Is there, or will there be, a precise statement of the universe or population to be studied? Does, or will, the sampling source or frame fairly represent the total universe or population under study?
- Who will actually be supervising and/or carrying out the PR measurement and evaluation project? What is, or are, their backgrounds and experience levels? Have they ever done research like this before? Can they give references?
- Who will actually be doing the field work? If the assignment includes media content analysis, who actually will be reading the clips or viewing and/or listening to the broadcast video/audio tapes? If the assignments involve focus groups, who will be moderating the sessions? If the involves conducting interviews, who will be doing those and how will they be trained, briefed, and monitored?
- What quality control mechanisms have been built into the study to assure that all "readers," "moderators," and "interviewers" adhere to the research design and study parameters?
- Who will be preparing any of the data collection instruments, including tally sheets or forms for media content analysis studies, topic guides for focus group projects, and/or questionnaires for telephone, face-to-face, or mail survey research projects? What role will the organization commissioning the PR measurement and evaluation assignment be asked, or be permitted, to play in the final review and approval of these data collection instruments?
- Will there be a written set of instructions and guidelines for the "readers," the "moderators" and the "interviewers"?
- Will the coding rules and procedures be available for review?
- If the data are weighted, will the range of the weights be reported? Will the basis for the weights be described and evaluated? Will the effect of the weights on the reliability of the final estimates be reported?

- Will the sample that is eventually drawn be large enough to provide stable findings? Will sampling error limits be shown, if they can be computed? Will the sample's reliability be discussed in language that can clearly be understood without a technical knowledge of statistics?
- How projectable will the research findings be to the total universe or population under study? Will it be clear which respondents or which media vehicles are underrepresented, or not represented at all, as part of the research undertaking?
- How will the data processing be handled? Who will be responsible for preparing a tab plan for the project? Which analytical and demographic variables will be included as part of the analysis and interpretation?
- How will the research findings and implications be reported? If there are findings based on the data that were collected, but the implications and/or recommendations stemming from the study go far beyond the actual data that were collected, will there be some effort made to separate the conclusions and observations that are specifically based on the data and those that are not?
- Will there be a statement on the limitations of the research and possible misinterpretations of the findings?
- How will the project be budgeted? Can budget parameters be laid out prior to the actual launch of the assignment? What contingencies can be built into the budget to prevent any unexpected surprises or changes once the project is in the field or is approaching the completion stage?

DEFINITIONS OF SELECTED TERMS USED IN PR MEASUREMENT AND EVALUATION

Advertising Equivalency: A means of converting editorial space in the media into advertising costs, by measuring the amount of editorial coverage and then calculating what it would have cost to buy that space, if it had been advertising. Most reputable researchers contend that advertising equivalency computations are of questionable validity, since in many cases the opportunity to "buy" advertising in space that has been specifically allocated to editorial coverage simply does not exist.

Attitude Research: Consists of measuring and interpreting the full range of views, sentiments, feelings, opinions and beliefs which segments of the public may hold toward given people, products, organizations and/or issues. More specifically, attitude research measures what people say (their verbal expressions), what they know and think (their mental or cognitive predispositions), what they feel (their emotions), and how they're inclined to act (their motivational or drive tendencies).

Bivariate Analysis: Examination of the relationship between two variables.

Causal Relationship: A theoretical notion that change in one variable forces, produces, or brings about a change in another.

Circulation: Refers to the number of copies sold of a given edition of a publication, at a given time or as averaged over a period of time.

Communications Audit: A systematic review and analysis—using accepted research techniques and methodologies—of how well an organization communicates with all of its major internal and external target audience groups.

Confidence Interval: In a survey based on a random sample, the range of values within which a population parameter is estimated to fall. For example, in a survey in which a representative sample of 1,000 individuals is interviewed, if 55% express a preference for a given item, we might say that in the population as a whole, in 95 out of 100 cases, the true proportion expressing such a preference probably would fall between 52% and 58%. The plus or minus 3% range is called the confidence interval. The fact that we are using 95 out of 100 cases as our guide (or 95%) is our confidence level.

Content Analysis: The process of studying and tracking what has been written and broadcast and translating this qualitative material into quantitative form through some type of counting approach that involves coding and classifying of specific messages.

Correlation: Any association or relationship between two variables.

Correlation Coefficient: A measure of association (symbolized as *r*) that describes the direction and strength of a linear relationship between two variables, measured at the interval or ratio level (e.g. Pearson's Correlation Coefficient).

Cost Per Thousand (CPM):   The cost of advertising for each 1,000 homes reached by radio or television, for each 1,000 copies of a publication, or for each 1,000 potential viewers of an outdoor advertisement.

Cross-Sectional Study: A study based on observations representing a single point in time.

Demographic Analysis: Consists of looking at the population in terms of special social, political, economic, and geographic subgroups, such as a person's age, sex, income-level, race, education-level, place of residence, or occupation.

Ethnographic Research: Relies on the tools and techniques of cultural anthropologists and sociologists to obtain a better understanding of how individuals and groups function in their natural settings. Usually, this type of research is carried out by a team of impartial, trained researchers who "immerse" themselves into the daily routine of a neighborhood or community, using a mix of observation, participation, and role-playing techniques, in an effort to try to assess what is really happening from a "cultural" perspective.

Evaluation: Determines the *value* or importance of a public relations program or effort, usually through appraisal or comparison with a predetermined set of organization goals and objectives. PR Evaluation is somewhat more subjective in nature, or softer, than PR Measurement, involving a greater amount of interpretation and judgment calls.

Experiment: Any controlled arrangement and manipulation of conditions to systematically observe specific occurrences, with the intention of defining those criteria that might possibly be affecting those occurrences. An experimental, or quasi-experimental, research design usually involves two groups—a "test" group which is exposed to given criteria, and a "control" group, which is not exposed. Comparisons are then made to determine what effect, if any, exposures to the criteria have had on those in the "test" group.

Factor Analysis: A complex algebraic procedure that seeks to group or combine items or variables in a questionnaire based on how they naturally relate to each other, or "hang together," as general descriptors (or "factors").

Focus Group: An exploratory technique in which a group of somewhere between 8 and 12 individuals—under the guidance of a trained moderator—are encouraged, as a group, to discuss freely any and all of their feelings, concerns, problems and frustrations relating to specific topics under discussion. Focus groups are ideal for brainstorming, idea-gathering, and concept testing.

Frequency: The number of advertisements, broadcasts, or exposures of given programming or messaging during a particular period of time.

Gross Rating Point: A unit of measurement of broadcast or outdoor advertising audience size, equal to 1% of the total potential audience universe; used to measure the exposure of one or more programs or commercials, without regard to multiple exposure of the same advertising to individuals. A GRP is the product of media reach times exposure frequency.

A *gross-rating-point buy* is the number of advertisements necessary to obtain the desired percentage of exposure of the message. In outdoor advertising, GRPs, often used as a synonym for showing, generally refer to the daily effective circulation generated by poster panels, divided by market population. The *cost per gross rating point* (CPGRP) is a measure of broadcast media exposure comparable to the *cost per thousand* (CPM) measure of print media.

Hypothesis: An expectation about the nature of things derived from theory.

Hypothesis-Testing: Determining whether the expectations that a hypothesis represents are, indeed, found in the real world.

Impressions: The number of those who might have had the opportunity to be exposed to a story that has appeared in the media. Sometimes referred to as "opportunity to see." An "impression" usually refers to the total audited circulation of a publication or the audience reach of a broadcast vehicle.

Incidence: The frequency with which a condition or event occurs within a given time and population.

Inquiry Study: A systematic review and analysis, using content analysis or sometimes telephone and mail interviewing techniques, to study the range and types of unsolicited inquiries that an organization may receive from customers, prospective customers or other target audience groups.

Inputs: (1) Everything that is involved upfront within the organization in the design, conception, approval, production and distribution of communications materials aimed at targeted audience groups. (2) Also, the research information and data from both internal and external sources that are applied to the initial stage of the communications planning and production process.

Judgmental Sample: A type of non-probability sample in which individuals are deliberately selected for inclusion in the sample by the researcher because they have special knowledge, position, characteristics or represent other relevant dimensions of the population that are deemed important to study. Also known as a "purposive" sample.

Likert Scale: Developed by Rensis Likert, this is a composite measure in which respondents are asked to choose from an ordered series of five responses to indicate their reactions to a sequence of statements (e.g., strongly agree . . . somewhat agree . . . neither agree nor disagree . . . somewhat disagree . . . strongly disagree).

Longitudinal Study: A research design involving the collection of data at different points in time.

Mall Intercept: A special type of in-person interview, in which potential respondents are approached as they stroll through shopping centers or malls. Most mall intercept interviews are based on non-probability sampling.

Market Research: Any systematic study of buying and selling behavior.

Mean: A measure of central tendency which is the arithmetic average of the scores.

Measurement: A way of giving a result a precise dimension, generally by comparison to some standard or baseline, and usually is done in a quantifiable or numerical manner.

Median: A measure of central tendency indicating the midpoint in a series of scores, the point above and below which 50% of the values fall.

Mode: A measure of central tendency which is the most frequently occurring, the most typical, value in a series.

Multivariate Analysis: Examination of the relationship among three or more variables.

Omnibus Survey: An "all-purpose" national consumer poll usually conducted on a regular schedule—once a week or every other week—by major market research firms. Organizations are encouraged to "buy" one or several proprietary questions and have them "added" to the basic questionnaire. Those adding questions are usually charged on a per-question basis. Also, sometimes referred to as "piggyback," or "shared-cost" surveys.

Outcomes: A long-term measure of the effectiveness of a particular communications program or activity, by focusing on whether targeted audience groups changed their *opinions*, *attitudes* and/or *behavior patterns* as a result of having been exposed to and become aware of messages directed at them.

Outgrowths: (1) The culminate effect of all communication programs and products on the positioning of an organization in the minds of its stakeholders or publics. (2) For some, the term used to describe the *outtakes* of a communications program activity (see that definition).

Outputs: (1) The short-term or immediate results of a particular communications program or activity, with a prime focus on how well an organization presents itself to others and the amount of exposure it receives. (2) For some, the final stage in the communications production process, resulting in the production and distribution of such items as brochures, media releases, websites, speeches, etc.

Outtakes: (1) A measure of the effectiveness of a particular communications program or activity, by focusing on whether targeted audience groups *received* the messages directed to them . . . paid *attention* to the messages . . . *understood* or comprehended the messages . . . and *retained* and can *recall* the messages in any shape or form. (2) Initial audience reaction to the receipt of communications materials, including whether the audience heeded or responded to a call for information or action within the messages.

Panel Study: (1) A type of longitudinal study in which the same individuals are interviewed more than once over a period of time to investigate the processes of response change, usually in reference to the same topic or issue. (2) Also, a type of study in which a group of individuals are deliberately recruited by a research firm, because of their special demographic characteristics, for the express purpose of being interviewed more than once over a period of time for various clients on a broad array of different topics or subjects.

Probability Sample: A process of random selection, in which each unit in a population has an equal chance of being included in the sample.

Psychographic Analysis: Consists of looking at the population in terms of people's non-demographic traits and characteristics, such as a person's personality type, life-style, social roles, values and beliefs.

Q-Sort: A personality inventory introduced in the 1950's in which respondents are asked to sort opinion statements along a "most-like-me" to "most-unlike-me" continuum. Q-Sorting allows researchers to construct models of individual respondents' belief systems.

Qualitative Research: Usually refers to studies that are somewhat subjective, but nevertheless in-depth, using a probing, open-end, free-response format.

Quantitative Research: Usually refers to studies that are highly objective and projectable, using closed-end, forced-choice questionnaires. These studies tend to rely heavily on statistics and numerical measures.

Quota Sample: A type of non-probability sample in which individuals are selected on the basis of pre-specified characteristics, so that the total sample will have the same general distribution of characteristics as are assumed to exist in the population being studied.

Range: A measure of variability that is computed by subtracting the lowest score in a distribution from the highest score.

Reach: Refers to the range or scope of influence or effect that a given communications vehicle has on targeted audience groups. In broadcasting, it is the net unduplicated radio or TV audience—the number of different individuals or households—for programs or commercials as measured for a specific time period in quarter-hour units over a period of one to four weeks.

Regression Analysis: A statistical technique for studying relationships among variables, measured at the interval or ratio level.

Reliability: The extent to which the results would be consistent, or replicable, if the research were conducted a number of times.

Screener Question: One or several questions usually asked in the beginning of an interview to determine if the potential respondent is eligible to participate in the study.

Secondary Analysis: A technique for extracting from previously conducted studies new knowledge on topics other than those which were the focus of the original studies. It does this through a systematic re-analysis of a vast array of already existing research data.

Situation Analysis: An impartial, often third-party assessment of the public relations and/or public affairs problems, or opportunities, that an organization may be facing at a given point in time.

Standard Deviation: An index of variability of a distribution. More precisely, it is the range from the mean within which approximately 34% of the cases fall, provided the values are distributed in a normal curve.

Statistical Significance: Refers to the unlikeliness that relationships observed in a sample could be attributed to sampling error alone.

Survey: Any systematic collection of data that uses a questionnaire and a recognized sampling method. There are three basic types of surveys: those conducted face-to-face (in-person) . . . those conducted by telephone . . . and those that are self-administered (usually distributed by mail, e-mail, or fax).

Univariate Analysis: The examination of only one variable at a time.

Validity: The extent to which a research project measures what it is intended, or purports, to measure.

Variance: A measure of the extent to which individual scores in a set differ from each other. More precisely, it is the sum of the squared deviations from the mean divided by the frequencies.

References

(2005). 2005 challenge: Proving the value of public relations. *Tactics, 12*, 14.

AAPOR Cell Phone Task Force. (2010). New considerations for survey researchers when planning and conducting RDD telephone surveys in the U.S. with respondents reached via cell phone numbers. Report prepared for the AAPOR Council. Retrieved 11/20/13 from: http://www.aapor.org/AM/Template.cfm?Section=Cell_Phone_Task_Force_Report&Template=/CM/ContentDisplay.cfm&ContentID=3189

Abramovich, G. (2013). 5 brands getting creative with data. Retrieved 11/20/13 from: http://www.digiday.com/brands/5-brands-getting-creative-with-data/

Adams County Public Hospital District #2. (2006). East Adams Rural Hospital. Retrieved 7/20/13 from: http://earh.com/

Adbusters. (2011, Feb 11). 'Joe Chemo' – Billboard. Retrieved 11/21/13 from: https://www.adbusters.org/content/joe-chemo-billboard

Adler, E. S., & Clark, R. (2011). *An invitation to social research: How it's done*. Belmont, CA: Wadsworth.

Adobe Systems, Inc. (2012). U.S. study reveals online marketing is failing with consumers. Retrieved 7/10/13 from: http://www.adobe.com/aboutadobe/pressroom/pressreleases/201210/102412Adobe AdvertisingResearch.html

Ahles, C. B. (2003). Campaign excellence: A survey of Silver Anvil Award winners compares current PR practice with planning, campaign theory. *Public Relations Strategist*, Summer 2003. Online document retrieved 9/15/13 from Public Relations Society of America website: http://www.prsa.org/Intelligence/TheStrategist/Articles/download/6K-030346/102/Campaign_Excellence_A_Survey_of_Silver_Anvil_Award

Alexander, K. (2004, November 15). In the schools: Turning a traditional time to get into a lesson in giving. *New York Times*, p. F6.

Allen, M. (1991). Meta-analysis comparing the persuasiveness of one-sided and two-sided messages. *Western Journal of Speech Communication, 55*, 390–404.

America's Army. (2013). Retrieved 11/18/13 from: http://www.americasarmy.com/

American Association for Public Opinion Research. (2003). Push polls: Not to be confused with legitimate polling. Retrieved from http://www.aapor.org/pdfs/2003/2003pushpollstatement.pdf.

American Association for Public Opinion Research. (2004). Disclosure standards. Retrieved 11/20/13 from: http://www.aapor.org/Disclosure_Standards1.htm#.Uo0hZmzTnt4

American Association for Public Opinion Research. (2011). *Standard definitions: Final dispositions of case codes and outcome rates for surveys*. Retrieved 11/20/13 from: https://www.aapor.org/AM/Template.cfm?Section=Standard_Definitions2&Template=/CM/ContentDisplay.cfm&ContentID=3156

American Association for Public Opinion Research. (n. d.). Resources for researchers. Retrieved 11/20/13 from: http://www.aapor.org/For_Researchers/5850.htm#.Uo0n32zTnt4

American Cancer Society. (1988). *Where there's no smoke.* Video.

American City Business Journals. (2005). 'Gold' out at Marquette; new name up for vote. Retrieved 6/17/13 from The Business Journal Serving Greater Milwaukee website: http://www.bizjournals.com/milwaukee/stories/2005/05/09/daily27.html

American Dairy Association. (1999). *I love cheese what's new.* Retrieved from http://www.ilovecheese.com/survey.html

Andrews, F. M., & Withey, S. B. (1976). *Social indicators of well being.* New York: Plenum.

Ansolabehere S., and Schaffner B. F. (in press). Does survey mode still matter? *Political Analysis.*

Ashland Health Center. (n.d.). About us. Retrieved 7/21/12 from: http://www.ashlandhc.org/about-us

Associated Press. (2004, March 13). Credit card firm tried to soft-pedal bad news: Discover wants to avoid alienating customers. *Spokesman-Review*, p. A9.

Austin, E. W. (1989). *The effective writer's mind set.* Pullman, WA: Washington State University.

Austin, E.W., & Pinkleton, B. E. (2009). Responses to *No Stank You* Anti-Tobacco Advertisements by Spokane and Seattle Youth ages 12–14: A report to the Washington State Department of Health. *Report commissioned by the Washington State Department of Health, Olympia, WA.* Pullman, WA: Edward R. Murrow School of Communication, Washington State University.

Austin E. W., & Pinkleton, B. E. (2012, September). *A Statewide Review of Parents' Recommendations for Food and Nutrition Websites.* A Report to Food$ense Leadership, Washington State Extension. Murrow Center for Media & Health Promotion Research, Washington State University, Pullman, WA.

Austin, E. W., Pinkleton, B. E., & Dixon, A. (2000). Barriers to public relations program research. *Journal of Public Relations Research, 12*(3), 235–253.

Baxter, L. A., & Babbie, E. (2004). *The basics of communication research.* Toronto, Ontario, Canada: Wadsworth/Thompson Learning.

Berelson, B. (1952). *Content analysis in communication research.* New York: Free Press.

Bernays, E. L. (1923). *Crystallizing public opinion.* New York: Liveright Publishing Corporation.

Blair, J., Czaja, R. F., & Blair, E. A. (2014). *Designing surveys: A guide to decisions and procedures* (3rd edn). Los Angeles, CA: Sage.

Boster, F. J., & Mongeau, P. A. (1984). Fear-arousing persuasive messages. In R. N. Bostrom (ed.), *Communication yearbook 8* (pp. 330–375). Beverly Hills, CA: Sage.

Bourland, P. G. (1993). The nature of conflict in firm–client relations: A content analysis of *Public Relations Journal,* 1980–89. *Public Relations Review, 19,* 385–398.

Breaking through the clutter: Color is a major tool, sometimes. (1999, May 31). *PR Reporter, 42,* 1–2.

Broom, G. M., & Dozier, D. M. (1990). *Using research in public relations: Applications to program management.* Englewood Cliffs, NJ: Prentice Hall.

Broom, G. M., & Sha, B. (2013). *Cutlip and Center's effective public relations* (11th edn). Boston: Pearson.

Building customer loyalty: A little can double profits. (1996, June 3). *PR Reporter, 39,* 3.

Business Journal of Milwaukee. (2005, May 11). Retrieved 3/16/06, from http://555milwaukee.bizjournals.com/milwaukee/stories/2005/05/09/daily27.html.

Butterball.com. (2013). Turkey talk-line. Retrieved 11/20/13 from: http://www.butterball.com/turkey-talk-line

Cameron, G. (1998, February 16). Professor: 2-way symmetrical PR doesn't always work. *PR Reporter, 41,* 1–3.

Campbell, B. A. (1981). Race-of-interviewer effects among southern adolescents. *Public Opinion Quarterly, 45,* 231–244.

Campbell, D. T., & Stanley, J. C. (1963). *Experimental and quasi-experimental designs for research.* Boston: Houghton Mifflin.

Can value of corporate reputation be quantified? (1996, April 15). *PR News, 52,* 7.

Capstrat (n.d.). Smart grid can increase the U.S. grid's efficiency by 9% (Infographic.)Retrieved 11/21/13 from Capstrat website: http://www.capstrat.com/elements/downloads/files/smart-grid-infographic.jpg

Carlson, N.(2012). Teens hate Twitter. Retrieved 11/21/13 from: http://www.businessinsider.com/teens-hate-twitter-2012-7

Cato, F. W. (1982, Fall). Procter and Gamble and the devil. *Public Relations Quarterly, 27*, 16–21.

Centre for Substance Abuse Prevention (1990). Avoiding common errors in the production of prevention materials. (1990, June). *Technical assistance bulletin* [Brochure]. Bethesda, MD: Center for Substance Abuse Prevention.

CF2GS. (1995, July 30). "Talking to your kids about alcohol" final report. Department of Social & Health Services, Division of Alcohol & Substance Abuse.

Chaffee, S. H. (1982). Mass media and interpersonal channels: Competitive, convergent, or complementary. In G. Gumpert & R. Cathcart (eds), *Inter/media: Interpersonal communication in a media world* (2nd edn, pp. 57–77). New York: Oxford University Press.

Charles, D. (2012, February 10). How two bitter adversaries hatched a plan to change the egg business. Retrieved 5/20/13 from: http://www.npr.org/blogs/thesalt/2012/02/10/146635596/how-two-bitter-adversaries-hatched-a-plan-to-change-the-egg-business

Chen, S., & Chaiken, S. (1999). The heuristic–systematic model in its broader context. In S. Chaiken & Y. Trope (eds), *Dual-process theories in social psychology* (pp. 73–96). New York: Guilford Press.

Chiagouris, L. (1998, Winter). Confessions of a Silver Anvil judge. *Public Relations Strategist, 4*, 29–31.

Christian, L. M., & Dillman, D. A. (2004). The influence of graphical and symbolic language manipulations on responses to self-administered questions. *Public Opinion Quarterly, 68*, 57–80.

Cingular Wireless announces safe driving milestone in support of wireless safety week. (2005). *PR Newswire.* Retrieved 6/28/05, from http://news.corporate.findlaw.com/prnewswire/20050518/18may2005111124.html.

Citrus Memorial Hospital. (2013). About us. Retrieved 6/15/13 from: http://www.citrusmh.com/about-us/

Cleveland Clinic. (2013). Mission, vision & values. Retrieved 7/15/13 from: http://my.clevelandclinic.org/locations_directions/regional-locations/medina-hospital/about/mission.aspx

Coady, M. (2010, August 25). The case for CSR: The CEO perspective. Retrieved 11/20/13 from: http://cecp.co/component/k2/item/4-the-case-for-csr-the-ceo-perspective.html

Cochran, W. G. (1977). *Sampling techniques.* New York: Wiley.

Cohen, J. (1960). A coefficient of agreement for nominal scales. *Educational and Psychological Measurement, 20*, 37–46.

College for Creative Studies. (2013). Why we used posters to talk to tech-savvy teenagers. Retrieved 6/25/13 from Team Detroit website: http://www.teamdetroit.com/projects/ccs.php

Committee Encouraging Corporate Philanthropy (CECP). (2010) *Shaping the future: Solving social problems through business strategy. Pathways to sustainable value creation in 2020.* Report by the Committee Encouraging Corporate Philanthropy. Retrieved 5/10/13 from: http://cecp.co/pdfs/resources/Shaping-the-Future.pdf

Cone, C. L., & Feldman, M. A. (2004, January 19). CSR no longer a "nice thing" but a "must have." *PR News, 60*, 7.

Converse, J. M. (1987). *Survey research in the United States: Roots and emergence, 1890–1960.* Berkeley, CA: University of California Press.

Cook, G. (2009, August 30). Why don't teens tweet? We asked over 10,000 of them. Retrieved 11/21/13 from TechCrunch website: http://techcrunch.com/2009/08/30/why-dont-teens-tweet-we-asked-over-10000-of-them/

Culling lessons from SwissAir crash: Across-the-board commitment needed. (1998, September 14). *PR News, 54*, 1–7.

Czaja, R., & Blair, J. (1996). *Designing surveys: A guide to decisions and procedures.* Thousand Oaks, CA: Pine Forge Press.

DegreeSearch.org. (2012, July 6). The top 10 most (and least) LGBT friendly colleges. Retrieved 11/15/13 from: http://degreesearch.org/blog/the-top-10-most-and-least-lgbt-friendly-colleges/

Detroit Receiving Hospital. (2013). Mission statement. Retrieved 7/1/13 from: http://www.drhuhc.org/about/mission/

DHL. (2013). Our mission and vision. Retrieved 6/20/13 from: http://www.dhl-usa.com/en/about_us/company_portrait/mission_and_vision.html

Dillman, D. A. (2000). *Mail and Internet surveys: The tailored method design.* New York: Wiley.

Dillman, D. A., Smyth, J. D., & Christian, L. M. (2009*). Internet, mail, and mixed-mode surveys: The tailored design method* (3rd edn). Hoboken, NJ: John Wiley & Sons, Inc.

Dozier, D. M., Grunig, L. A., & Grunig, J. E. (1995). *Manager's guide to excellence in public relations and communication management.* Mahwah, NJ: Lawrence Erlbaum Associates.

Dugan, L. (2011, December 21). Who are the oldest Twitter users? Retrieved 11/21/13 from: http://www.mediabistro.com/alltwitter/who-are-the-oldest-twitter-users_b3584

Economist. (2013). Global livability ranking and report August 2013. Retrieved 10/13/13 from: https://www.eiu.com/public/topical_report.aspx?campaignid=Liveability2013

Edelman. (2012). 2012 Edelman Trust Barometer executive summary. Retrieved 11/20/13 from: http://www.scribd.com/doc/79026497/2012-Edelman-Trust-Barometer-Executive-Summary

Edelman. (2013). 2013 Edelman Trust Barometer executive summary. Retrieved 11/20/13 from: http://www.scribd.com/doc/121501475/Executive-Summary-2013-Edelman-Trust-Barometer

Ehling, W. P. (1985). Application of decision theory in the construction of a theory of public relations management. II. *Public Relations Research and Education, 2,* 1, 4–22.

Exempla Saint Joseph Hospital. (2013). Mission vision and values. Retrieved 7/15/13 from: http://www.exemplasaintjoseph.org/mission#.UoJ18GzTnt4

Farrelly, M. C., Healton, C. G., Davis, K. C., Messari, P., Hersey, J. C., & Haviland, M. L. (2002). Getting to the truth: Evaluating national tobacco countermarketing campaigns. Retrieved from: http://www.comminit.com/evaluations/ eval2005/evaluations-53.html.

Feder, B. J. (2005, September 10). Restoring light at the end of the tunnel. *New York Times,* p. B2.

Feldstein, L. (1992, June 15). Balancing social responsibility with the bottom line. *Tips and Tactics* (supplement of *PR Reporter), 30,* 1–2.

Felton, J. (1998, May 25). The cultural consequences of color. *Tips and Tactics* (supplement of *PR Reporter), 36,* 1–2.

FEMA. (n.d.). About the Ready campaign. Retrieved 6/20/13 from: http://www.ready.gov/about-us

Fitzgerald, K. (1996, December 16). Publicity about toy shortages feeds the frenzy. *Advertising Age, 67,* 12.

Florida Hospital. (2013). Our mission. Retrieved 7/9/13 from: https://www.floridahospital.com/about/mission

Forbes. (2013). Top ten colleges with the best return on your investment. Retrieved 5/25/13 from: http://www.forbes.com/sites/troyonink/2013/02/19/top-ten-colleges-with-the-best-return-on-your-investment/

Fowler, F. J., Jr. (1995). *Improving survey questions: Design and evaluation.* Thousand Oaks, CA: Sage.

Fowler, F. J., Jr., & Mangione, T. W. (1990). *Standardized survey interviewing: Minimizing interviewer-related error.* Newbury Park, CA: Sage.

Freedman, D., Pisani, R., & Purves, R. (1978). *Statistics.* New York: Norton.

Frey, J. H. (1989). *Survey research by telephone* (2nd edn). Newbury Park, CA: Sage.

Fundación ANAR. (2013). 25 de abril: Dia internacional #contraelmaltratoinfanil. Retrieved 11/22/13 from: http://www.anar.org/ContraElMaltratoInfantil/

Gap research: Why and how it does what other methods don't. (1994, July 18). *PR Reporter, 37,* 1.

Gater, D. (2002, Summer). A review of measures used in *U. S. News & World Report*'s "America's Best Colleges." *The Center.* Gainsville, FL: University of Florida.

Geddes, D. (2013). Setting the standards—changing the way we measure public relations success. Retrieved 9/15/13 from: http://prfirms.org/voice/2013/setting-the-standards-changing-the-way-we-measure-public-relations-success

Geistfeld, R. E. (1995, August 17). What's the problem? That's the question. *This Thursday*, 2.

Goldfarb, A. (2008). How Robert Mondavi Winery maintains its original vision. Retrieved 6/12/13 from: http://www.wines.appellationamerica.com/wine-review/538/Robert-Mondavi-wine-vision.html

Grimes, W. (2012, March 17). Talk to me, customer. *New York Times*, B1.

Groves, R. M. (1989). *Survey errors and survey costs.* New York: Wiley.

Groves, R. M. (2006). Nonresponse rates and nonresponse bias in household surveys. *Public Opinion Quarterly*, *70*(5), 646–675.

Grunig, J. E. (1989). Symmetrical presuppositions as a framework for public relations theory. In C. H. Botan & V. Hazleton, Jr. (eds), *Public relations theory* (pp. 17–44). Hillsdale, NJ: Lawrence Erlbaum Associates.

Grunig, J. E., Grunig, L., & Ehling, W. P. (1992). What is an effective organization? In J. E. Grunig (ed.), *Excellence in public relations and communication management: Contributions to effective organizations* (pp. 117–157). Hillsdale, NJ: Lawrence Erlbaum Associates.

Grunig, J. E., & Huang, Y. (2000). From organization effectiveness to relationship indicators: Antecedents of relationships, public relations strategies, and relationship outcomes. In J. A. Ledingham & S. D. Bruning (eds), *Public relations as relationship management: A relational approach to the study and practice of public relations* (pp. 23–53). Hillsdale, NJ: Lawrence Erlbaum Associates.

Grunig, J. E., & Hunt, T. (1984). *Managing public relations.* New York: Holt, Rinehart& Winston.

Grunig, J. E., & Repper, F. C. (1992). Strategic management, publics, and issues. In J. E. Grunig (ed.), *Excellence in public relations and communication management: Contributions to effective organizations* (pp. 117–157). Hillsdale, NJ: Lawrence Erlbaum Associates.

Grunig's paradigm: Superb issue anticipation and planning tool. (1998, October 5). *PR Reporter*, *41*, 3–4.

Hargittai, E. (2007). Whose space? Differences among users and non-users of social network sites. *Journal of Computer-Mediated Communication*, *13*, 1. Retrieved 11/20/13 from Journal of Mediated Communication website: http://jcmc.indiana.edu/vol13/issue1/hargittai.html

Harris, T. L., & Impulse Research (2004). *Thomas L. Harris/Impulse Research 2004 public relations client survey.* Culver City, CA: Impulse Research Corporation.

Harris, W. (2002, June 12). Personals pay off: Advertising section helps bring together would-be pet owners, animals needing a home. *Spokesman-Review*, p. B3.

Harrison, A. G. (2013). Engagement ring: Building connections between employees and strategy. *Public Relations Tactics, 20*, 5, 16.

Hernandez, B. A. (2011, May 5). Explore Twitter's evolution: 2006 to present. Retrieved 11/21/13 from: http://mashable.com/2011/05/05/history-of-twitter/

Hicks, J. J. (2001). The strategy behind Florida's "truth" campaign. Retrieved from: http://www.tobacco freedom.org/msa/articles/truth review.html.

Holsti, O. (1969). *Content analysis for the social sciences and humanities.* Reading, MA: Addison Wesley.

Hubbell, N. (1999, December 29). Personal communication.

Hughes, J. H. (1999, March 2). Dr. Seuss figure caught in crossfire. *Columbian*, p. B2.

Humor backfires. (1999). "Boogerhead" ad seems bone-headed to educators; taste is more important than gaining attention. (1999, October 4). *PR Reporter*, *42*, 39.

In focused philanthropy era, some don't even publicize gifts. (1996, June 10). *PR Reporter*, *39*, 1–2.

IIP Digital. (2013, March 1). Support grows for patients with rare diseases. Retrieved 11/21/13 from: http://iipdigital.usembassy.gov/st/english/article/2013/03/20130301143550.html#axzz2SvUrMMr9

ImaginePittsburgh.com. (2013). Retrieved 4/15/13 from: http://www.imaginepittsburgh.com/LivingHere. asp

Jefferson Healthcare. (2013). Jefferson Healthcare Hospital. Retrieved 7/20/13 from: http://www. jeffersonhealthcare.org/Facilities/Jefferson-Healthcare-Hospital.aspx

Jeffries-Fox, B. (2004, December 15). PR research shouldn't be like digging through the Sahara with a teaspoon. *PR News*, *60*, 2.

Johnson, J. B., & Reynolds, H. T. (2005). *Political science research methods* (5th edn). Washington, DC: CQ Press.

Karnani, A. (2010, August 23). The case against corporate social responsibility. Retrieved 11/20/13 from the Wall Street Journal website: http://online.wsj.com/news/articles/SB10001424052748703338004575230112664504890

Keeter, S., Kennedy, C., Dimock, M., Best, J., & Craighill, P. (2006). Gauging the impact of growing nonresponse on estimates from a national RDD telephone survey. *Public Opinion Quarterly, 70*, 5, 759–779.

Kendall, R. (1996). *Public relations campaign strategies: Planning for implementation* (2nd edn). New York: Harper Collins.

Keppel, G. (1991). *Design and analysis: A researcher's handbook* (3rd edn). Englewood Cliffs, NJ: Prentice–Hall.

Kerlinger, F. N. (1973). *Foundations of behavioral research* (2nd edn). New York: Holt, Rinehart & Winston.

Ketchum. (2012, March). Ketchum leadership communication monitor. Retrieved 11/20/13 from: http://www.ketchum.com/sites/default/files/ketchum_leadership_communication_monitor_0.pdf

Ketchum Global Research & Analytics. (2014). The principles of PR measurement. Retrieved 11/20/13 from: http://www.ketchum.com/sites/default/files/principles_of_pr_measurement_0.pdf

Keys to world class publications. (1998, April 13). *Tips and Tactics* (supplement of *PR Reporter*), *36*, 1, 2.

Kingsbrook Jewish Medical Center. (2013). Our mission & vision and Kingsbrook Jewish Memorial [*sic*] Center. Retrieved 7/9/13 from: http://www.kingsbrook.org/About_Us/Our_Mission_and_Vision.aspx

Kiplinger. (2013, January). Kiplinger's best values in public colleges. Retrieved 5/26/13 from: http://www.kiplinger.com/tool/college/T014-S001-kiplinger-s-best-values-in-public-colleges/index.php

Kish, L. (1965). *Survey sampling.* New York: Wiley.

Konrad, A. (2013). America's 50 best cities. Retrieved 10/13/13 from: http://images.businessweek.com/slideshows/2012–09–26/americas-50-best-cities

Krueger, R. A. (1994). *Focus groups: A practical guide for applied research* (2nd edn). Thousand Oaks, CA: Sage.

Lavrakas, P. J. (1993). *Telephone survey methods: Sampling, selection, and supervision* (2nd edn). Newbury Park, CA: Sage.

(1997, January 6). Look at one solution: Family-responsive programs, A. *PR Reporter, 40*, 4.

(1998, August 24). M&As: Time for business communicators to prove their worth. *PR News, 54*(1), 7.

Manning, A. (2003, June 30). Safety rules drain blood banks: As new diseases arise, the screening process grows, and more donors are turned away. *USA Today,* p. D1–2.

Marrow, A. J. (1969). *The practical theorist: The life and work of Kurt Lewin.* New York: Basic Books.

Martin, D. (2005). Get to the top: Advancing your corporate PR career. *Strategist, 11*, 2.

Mary Free Bed Hospital & Rehabilitation Center. (2012). About us. Retrieved 7/25/13 from: http://www.maryfreebed.com/About-Us

McGuire, W. J. (1989). Theoretical foundations of campaigns. In R. E. Rice & C. K. Atkin (eds), *Public communication campaigns* (2nd edn, pp. 43–65). Newbury Park, CA: Sage.

McLeod, J. M., & Chaffee, S. H. (1972). The construction of social reality. In J. Tedeschi (ed.), *The social influence process* (pp. 50–59). Chicago: Aldine–Atherton.

Measurement. (2003, September 22). *PR News, 59*, 1.

Medical City Hospital. (2011). Mission, vision, and values. Retrieved 6/15/13 from: http://www.kingsbrook.org/About_Us/Our_Mission_and_Vision.aspx

Melamed, B. G., & Siegel, L. J. (1975). Reduction of anxiety in children facing hospitalization and surgery by use of filmed modeling. *Journal of Consulting and Clinical Psychology, 43*, 511–521.

Mendelsohn, H. (1973). Some reasons why information campaigns can succeed. *Public Opinion Quarterly,37*, 50–61.

Miller, B. (2005, February 25). Public relations often suffer as budgets tighten. *Enterprise.* Retrieved 5/25/05 from: http://seattle.bizjournals.com/seattle/ stories/2005/02/28/smallb2.html?t=printable.

Mitchell, A., & Hitlin, P. (2013). Twitter reaction to events often at odds with overall public opinion. Retrieved 11/15/13 from: http://www.pewresearch.org/2013/03/04/twitter-reaction-to-events-often-at-odds-with-overall-public-opinion/

Monahan, J. L. (1995). Thinking positively: Using positive affect when designing health messages. In E. Maibach & R. L. Parrott (eds), *Designing health messages: Approaches from communication theory and public health practice* (pp. 81–98). Thousand Oaks, CA: Sage.

Moran, G. (2013). Hacking the U.S. Census for market research. Retrieved 11/21/13 from: www. entrepreneur.com/article/220412#

Morgan, D. L., & Krueger, R. A. (1998). *The focus group kit.* Thousand Oaks, CA: Sage.

Nachmias, D., & Nachmias, C. (1981). Research methods in the social sciences (2nd edn). New York: St. Martin's Press.

Nager, N. R., & Allen, T. H. (1984). *Public relations: Management by objectives.* Lanham, MD: University Press of America.

National Cancer Institute. (1999). *Making health communication programs work: A planner's guide.* Retrieved from: http://rex.nci.nih.gov/NCI Pub Interface/HCPW/HOME.HTM.

Newcomb, T. (1953). An approach to the study of communicative acts. *Psychological Review, 60,* 393–404.

New York University Langone Medical Center. (n. d.). About us. Retrieved 7/1/13 from: http://www.med. nyu.edu/about-us

Nickols, F. (2000). Distance consulting, strategy: Definitions and meaning. Retrieved from http:// home.att.net/_nickols/strategy_definition.htm.

No Labels. (2013). Who we are. Retrieved 11/21/13 from: http://www.nolabels.org/whoweare

Numbers don't lie: The case for CSR, *PR News, 60*(3), 6.

O'Keefe, D. J. (2002). *Persuasion: Theory and research.* Newbury Park, CA: Sage.

O'Leary, M. B. (2013). Telecommuting can boost productivity and job performance. Retrieved 11/21/13 from: http://www.usnews.com/opinion/articles/2013/03/15/telecommuting-can-boost-productivity-and-job-performance

Palshaw, J. L. (1990). The fixation on focus groups. *Direct Marketing, 53*(22), 58.

Payscale.com. (2013). 2013 college education ROI rankings: Does a degree always pay off? Retrieved 5/26/13 from: http://www.payscale.com/college-education-value

Pearson, C.B., & Eske, A. (2012). Pressure vs persuasion. The overlooked secret to winning your advocacy campaign. Retrieved 7/22/13 from: http://labs.mrss.com/.wordpress/wp-content/uploads/2012/ 12/Pressure-vs-Persuasion.pdf

Perloff, R. M. (2013). *The dynamics of persuasion: Communication and attitudes in the 21st century* (5th edn). New York: Routledge.

Personal competency and guts will prepare the future of PR. (1998, June 1). *PR Reporter, 41,* 1–2.

Petty, J. E., & Cacioppo, J. T. (1986). *Communication and persuasion: Central and peripheral routes to attitude change.* New York: Springer-Verlag.

Pfau, M. (1995). Designing messages for behavioral inoculation. In E. Maibach & R. L. Parrott (eds), *Designing health messages: Approaches from communication theory and public health practice* (pp. 99–113). Thousand Oaks, CA: Sage.

Pinkleton, B. E., Austin, E. W., & Dixon, A. (1999). Orientations in public relations research and campaign evaluation. *Journal of Marketing Communications, 5,* 85–95.

Pinkleton, B. E., Um, N., & Austin, E. W. (2002). An exploration of the effects of negative political advertising on political decision making. *Journal of Advertising, 31,* 13–25.

Plous, S. (1990, January 15). Tips on motivating publics to act: Advice from a psychologist. *Tips and Tactics* (supplement of *PR Reporter*), *28,* 1–2.

Porter, J. (2009, July 8). How do you measure PR? Retrieved 8/15/09 from Journalistics website: http://blog.journalistics.com/2009/how_do_you_measure_pr/

PR and sales leads perception vs. reality. (2005, January 19). *PR News, 61*, 3.

PR measurement now moving at a not-so-glacial pace. (2004, October 20). *PR News, 40*(60), p. 1.

PR pros content with their career choice but think profession is little understood. (1998, December 21). *PR News, 54*, 1–2.

PR Reporter. (1998, Aug 17). How Mondavi uses vision statement to drive company behavior. *PR Reporter, 41*, 2.

Private Jet Services Group. (2013). Mission statement. Retrieved 6/12/13 from: http://www.pjsgroup. com/about-pjs/mission-statement/

PRSA. (1998). Your thyroid: Gland central – Putting thyroid disease on the fast track. Retrieved 5/15/13 from: http://www.prsa.org/SearchResults/download/6BW-9805C10/0/Your_Thyroid_Gland_Central_ Putting_Thyroid_Disease

PRSA. (1999a). Fire prevention week 1998: "Fire drills: The great escape." Retrieved 11/18/13 from: http://www.prsa.org/SearchResults/download/6BW-9903D/0/Fire_Prevention_Week_1998_Fire_ Drills_The_Great_Es

PRSA. (1999b). Grasscycling gives your mower for less. Retrieved 11/18/13 from: http://www.prsa.org/ SearchResults/download/6BW-9904C/0/Grasscycling_Gives_Your_Mower_For_Less

PRSA. (2004a). Coalition for an informed California: Defeat Propositon 54 on the California recall ballott. Retrieved 11/24/13 from: http://www.prsa.org/SearchResults/download/6BW-0406C05/0/Coalition_ for_an_Informed_California_Defeat_Propos

PRSA. (2004b). The heart of diabetes: Understanding insulin resistance. Retrieved 11/24/13 from: http://www.prsa.org/SearchResults/download/6BW-0414B04/0/The_Heart_of_Diabetes_ Understanding_Insulin_Resist

PRSA. (2012a). Inspiring a generation of beautiful minds: Carmichael Lynch Spong and life's DHA, and ingredient brand of nutritional lipids /DSM nutritional products. Retrieved 5/15/13 from PRSA website: http://www.prsa.org/SearchResults/download/6BW-9805C10/0/Your_Thyroid_Gland_ Central_Putting_Thyroid_Disease

PRSA. (2012b). Creating a new vehicle category and brand personality with the all-new 2012 Hyundai Veloster. Retrieved 5/15/12 from: http://www.prsa.org/SearchResults/download/6BW-1207G05/0/ Creating_a_New_Vehicle_Category_And_Brand_Personal

PRSA. (2012c). Chase Sapphire serves up unique foodie experiences to discerning palettes. Retrieved 5/15/13 from: http://www.prsa.org/SearchResults/download/6BW-1208D03/0/Chase_Sapphire_ Serves_Up_Unique_Foodie_Experiences

PRSA. (2012d). IBM stages largest corporate volunteer event in history, reaching communities in 120 countries. Retrieved 5/15/13 from: http://www.prsa.org/SearchResults/download/6BW-1201B04/ 0/IBM_Stages_Largest_Corporate_Volunteer_Event_in_Hi

PRSA. (2012e). IRS free file – A "less taxing" way to prepare and e-file federal taxes. Retrieved 5/15/13 from: http://www.prsa.org/SearchResults/download/6BW-1208E07/0/IRS_Free_File_A_Less_ Taxing_Way_to_Prepare_And_E_F

PRSA. (2012f). Averting a clash between religion and rock 'n roll. Retrieved 5/15/13 from: http://www. prsa.org/SearchResults/download/6BE-1211C01/0/Averting_a_Clash_Between_Religion_and_ Rock_N_Roll

PRSA. (2012g). Operation Mighty Mo: Managing the flood of 2011 through strategic communications. Retrieved 6/15/13 from: http://www.prsa.org/SearchResults/download/6BW-1211B09/0/Operation_ Mighty_Mo_Managing_the_Flood_of_2011_Thr?

PRSA. (2012h). Challenging perceptions and presenting solutions to stop childhood obesity in Georgia. Retrieved 11/21/13 from: http://www.prsa.org/searchresults/view/6be-1216d45/0/challenging_ perceptions_and_presenting_solutions_t

Public Conversations Project. (2013). Who we are. Retrieved 11/31/13 from: http://public conversations.org/who

Public Relations Society of America. (1995, October). *PRSA Research Committee/National Conference questionnaire results.* Paper presented at the annual conference of the Public Relations Society of America, Seattle, WA.

Public Relations Society of America. (1999). *National credibility index*. Retrieved from http://www.prsa.org/nci/nci.html.

Rady Children's Hospital. (2013). Who we are. Retrieved 7/25/13 from: https://www.rchsd.org/aboutus/whoweare/index.htm

Ragan's PR Daily. (2013). Retrieved 11/20/13 from: http://www.prdaily.com/Main/Home.aspx

(1998, Fall). Reflections of an American guru: An afternoon with Peter Drucker. *Public Relations Strategist, 4*, 8–15.

Reputation as a competitive asset. (1994, December). *Inside PR, 5*, 13–20.

Retention Council Report. (n.d.). Online document retrieved 9/15/13 from: http://vpue.wsu.edu/advisingretention/RetentionCouncilReport.pdf

Rhodes, M. (2011, Feb 15). New study: Majority of U.S. employers offer workplace flexibility. Retrieved 11/21/13 from Business Wire website: http://www.businesswire.com/news/home/20110215005587/en/Study-Majority-U.S.-Employers-Offer-Workplace-Flexibility

Rice, R. E., & Atkin, C. K. (1989). *Public communication campaigns*, 2nd edn Newbury Park: Sage Publications.

Richmond, L. B. (1990). Putting the public in public relations. In D. G. Rutherford (ed.), *Hotel management and operations* (pp. 263–269). New York: Van Nostrand Reinhold.

Riffe, D., Lacy, S., & Fico, F. G. (1998). *Analyzing media messages: Using quantitative content analysis in research*. Mahwah, NJ: Lawrence Erlbaum Associates.

Robert Mondavi Winery. (2013). Winemaking. Retrieved 6/10/13 from: http://www.robertmondaviwinery.com/Winemaking/Winemaking

Rockland, D. B. (2013). What Bill Gates and measurement have in common. *Public Relations Tactics, 20, 5*, 7.

Rodriguez, D. (2013, July 5). El anuncio español de maltrato infantil que solo pueden ver niños se hace viral. Translated using Google Translate. Retrieved 11/22/13 from El Huffington Post website: http://www.huffingtonpost.es/2013/05/07/el-anuncio-espanol-de-mal_n_3228422.html

Rogers, E. M. (1983). *Diffusion of innovations* (3rd edn). New York: The Free Press.

Rogers, E. M., & Kincaid, D. L. (1981). *Communication networks: Toward a new paradigm for research*. New York: Free Press.

Rokeach, M. (1973). *The nature of human values*. New York: Free Press.

Ruiz, M. (2000, May). Truth campaign drives smoking attitude change in Florida youth. Sarasota, FL: Florida Public Relations Association.

Salmon, C.T., & Nichols, J. S. (1983). The next-birthday method of respondent selection. *Public Opinion Quarterly, 47*, 270–276.

Schweld, B. (2005, June 12). Secretary of state plays piano at awareness concert: Rice accompanies a Democrat's grandchild who is suffering from pulmonary hypertension. *Spokesman-Review*, p. A7.

Scott, W. A. (1955). Reliability of content analysis: The case for nominal scale coding. *Public Opinion Quarterly, 19*, 321–325.

Selltiz, C., Jahoda, M., Deutsch, M., & Cook, S. W. (1959). *Research methods in social relations*. New York: Holt.

Settles, C. J. (1989a, December). The tease that backfired. *Public Relations Journal, 45*, 40–41.

Settles, C. J. (1989b). My favorite failure. *Public Relations Journal*, December.

Siebert, S., & Ovaitt, F. (2012). Institute for public relations announces broad coalition to drive standards for public relations research and measurement. Retrieved 9/15/13 from: http://www.instituteforpr.org/releases/institute-for-public-relations-announces-broad-coalition-to-drive-standards-for-public-relations-research-and-measurement/

Siegel, R., & Norris, M. (2005, May 12). Interview: Don Walker discusses Marquette University's struggle to settle on a school nickname. Washington, DC: National Public Radio.

Sierra Club. (2013). The top 10: America's coolest schools. Retrieved 5/25/13 from: http://www.sierraclub.org/sierra/201209/coolschools/

Singapore Airlines. (2013). About us. Retrieved 6/14/13 from: http://www.singaporeair.com/en_UK/about-us/

Snopes.com. (2013). Trademark of the devil. Retrieved 11/20/13 from http://www.snopes.com/business/alliance/procter.asp

Solomon, D. S. (1989). A social marketing perspective on communication campaigns. In R. E. Rice & C. K. Atkin (eds), *Public communication campaigns* (2nd edn, pp. 87–104). Newbury Park, CA: Sage.

Southwest Airlines. (2005). Retrieved 11/4/05, from http://www.flysouthwestairlines.com/investor relations/swaar98.pdf.

Southwest Airlines Co. (2013). About Southwest: Mission. Retrieved 6/12/13 from: http://www.southwest.com/html/about-southwest/index.html

Spiegel Online International. (2011). Tee'd off: Right-wing extremists ticked by Trojan shirts. Retrieved 5/15/12 from: http://www.spiegel.de/international/germany/tee-d-off-right-wing-extremists-tricked-by-trojan-shirts-a-779446.html

Spirit Airlines, Inc. (2013). About Spirit. Retrieved 6/12/13 from: http://www.spirit.com/AboutUs.aspx?culture=es-PR

St. Elizabeth's Belleville. (2013). Our mission. Retrieved 7/20/13 from: http://steliz.org/index.cfm?pageID=11

Stafford, L., & Canary, D. J. (1991). Maintenance strategies and romantic relationship type, gender and relational characteristics. *Journal of Social and Personal Relationships, 8*, 217–242.

Stanford University Medical Center. (2011). Code of conduct. Online document retrieved 7/3/13 from: http://stanfordhospital.org/overview/assets/SOM-Code-of-Conduct%2026July11.pdf

Stateman, A., & Weiner, M. (2001, February). Publicity watch. *Tactics*.

Stoddard, K. (n. d.). Social media campaigns for advocacy. Retrieved 11/21/13 from: http://www.slideshare.net/kyrastoddart/social-media-campaigns-for-advocacy

Sudman, S. (1976). *Applied Sampling*. New York: Academic Press.

Sun, L. H. (2012, May 31). Medical students learned on the bodies, now honor the donors. *The Washington Post*. Retrieved 11/18/13 from Commercial-News website: http://www.commercial-news.com/local/x915996293/Medical-students-learned-on-the-bodies-now-honor-the-donors

Survey finds blue is the color of the millennium. (1998, September 7). *PR Reporter, 41*, 3–4.

Swisher, K. (2013, February 22). "Physically together:" Here's the internal Yahoo no-work-from-home memo for remote workers and maybe more. Retrieved 6/1/13 from: http://allthingsd.com/20130222/physically-together-heres-the-internal-yahoo-no-work-from-home-memo-which-extends-beyond-remote-workers/

Terapeak. (2006). The Elmo craze on eBay. Retrieved 8/12/13 from: http://www.ecommercebytes.com/cab/abn/y06/m11/i17/s03

Thieke, D. (2007). Talk to me: Making public relations meaningful to business executives. Retrieved 9/14/08 from: http://www.prsa.org/Intelligence/TheStrategist/Articles/view/6K-020710/102/Talk_to_Me_Making_Public_Relations_Meaningful_to_B

Top Nonprofits. (2012). 30 example vision statements. Retrieved 6/20/13 from: http://topnonprofits.com/examples/vision-statements/

Tsehootsooi Medical Center. (2013). History. Retrieved 7/10/13 from: http://fdihb.org/about_us.php?id=1

U.S. News and World Report. (2013a). Best cities. Retrieved 4/22/13 from: http://www.usnews.com/news/best-cities

U.S. News and World Report. (2013b). The 10 best cities for public transportation. Retrieved 4/22/13 from: http://www.usnews.com/news/slideshows/the-10-best-cities-for-public-transportation

U.S. News and World Report. (2013c). National university rankings. Retrieved 5/26/13 from: http://colleges.usnews.rankingsandreviews.com/best-colleges/rankings/national-universities

United States Department of Veteran Affairs. (2012). Atlanta VA Medical Center. Retrieved 6/15/13 from: http://www.atlanta.va.gov/about/

USC Annenberg Strategic Communication and Public Relations Center. (2011). GAP VII: Seventh communication and public relations Generally Accepted Practices study (Q4 2011 data). Retrieved 5/15/13 from: http://ascjweb.org/gapstudy/full-results-2/

Valeo Online Marketing. (2013). A nonprofit advocacy campaign checklist. (Infographic). Retrieved 11/21/13 from: http://www.valeomarketing.com/blog/infographic-a-nonprofit-advocacy-campaign-checklist

Van Camp, S. (2012). PR myth of the month: 'CPM' does not apply to public relations. Retrieved 11/13/13 from: http://www.prnewsonline.com/water-cooler/2012/12/06/pr-myth-of-the-month-cpm-does-not-apply-to-public-relations/

Vega, T., & McKinley, J. C. (2013, April 12). Social media, pushing Reebok to drop a rapper. The New York Times. Retrieved 8/22/23 from: http://www.nytimes.com/2013/04/13/arts/music/reebok-drops-rick-ross-after-social-media-protest.html?_r=0

Vincenzini, A. (2012). Jackpot! 50 (mostly) free social media tools for brands. Retrieved 3/15/13 from: http://www.prdaily.com/Main/Articles/Jackpot_50_mostly_free_social_media_tools_for_bran_11184.aspx#

Wallack, L., Dorfman, L., Jernigan, D., & Themba, M. (1993). *Media advocacy and public health: Power for prevention.* Newbury Park, CA: Sage.

Warwick, D. P., & Lininger, C. A. (1975). *The sample survey: Theory and practice.* New York: McGraw-Hill.

Washington Monthly. (2013). College guide. Retrieved 5/25/13 from: http://www.washingtonmonthly.com/college_guide/rankings_2012/liberal_arts_rank.php

Washington State Department of Health. (2004). Youth Media Tracking Survey, June–Sept. 2003. Olympia, Washington: Washington State Department of Health.

Washington State Higher Education Coordinating Board. (1997). HECB instructions on accountability. Retrieved 9/15/13 from: http://public.wsu.edu/~aaa/hecbinstructions.htm

Watson, T. (2013). Advertising value equivalence—PR's orphan metric. *Public Relations Review, 39,* 139–146.

Weiner, M., & Bartholomew, D. (2006). Dispelling the myth of PR multipliers and other inflationary audience measures. Retrieved from: http://www.instituteforpr.org/wp-content/uploads/Dispelling_Myth_of_PR_Multiplier.pdf

What trends are shaping public relations as seen by the Dilenschneider Group? (1997, January 20). *Purview* (supplement of *PR Reporter*), *415,* 1–2.

While agencies and their clients often see eye-to-eye. (2004, May 17). *PR News, 60,* 1.

Williams, A. (2012, December 19). Best places to work. Retrieved 11/21/13 from: http://www.seattlemet.com/news-and-profiles/best-places-to-work/articles/best-places-to-work-january-2013

Williams, F. W. (1992). *Reasoning with statistics: How to read quantitative statistics* (4th edn). Fort Worth, TX: Harcourt, Brace, Jovanovich.

Williamson, W. (2011). Crisis communication during the PB oil spill. Retrieved 8/15/12 from: https://ninaflournoy.wordpress.com/2011/01/26/crisis-communication-during-the-bp-oil-spill/

Wimmer, R. D., & Dominick, J. R. (2014). *Mass media research: An introduction* (10th edn). Boston: Wadsworth.

Witte, K. (1992). Putting the fear back into fear appeals: The extended parallel process model. *Communication Monographs, 59,* 329–349.

Woman's Hospital. (n.d.). Mission, vision, values. Retrieved 7/25/13 from: http://www.womans.org/index.cfm?md=pagebuilder&tmp=home&pid=21&pnid=55&nid=60&tid=2

Working Mother. (2012) 2012 Working Mother 100 best companies. Retrieved 5/23/13 from: http://www.workingmother.com/best-companies/2012-working-mother-100-best-companies

Wright, D. K., Gaunt, R., Leggetter, B., Daniels, M., & Zerfass, A. (2009). *Global survey of communications measurement 2009 – Final report.* Retrieved 8/15/12 from: http://amecorg.com/wp-content/uploads/2011/08/Global-Survey-Communications_Measurement-20091.pdf

Yeager, D.S., Krosnick, J., Chang, L-C., Javitz, H., Levendusky, M., Simpser, A. & Wang, R. (2011). Comparing the accuracy of RDD telephone surveys and Internet surveys conducted with probability and non-probability samples. *Public Opinion Quarterly, 75,* 709–747.

Zickuhr, K., & Smith, A. (2013). *Home broadband 2013.* Report for Pew Research Center, August 26, 2013. Retrieved 11/21/13 from: http://pewinternet.org/Reports/2013/Broadband.aspx

Author Index

Subject Index

Page numbers in **bold** refer to figures, page numbers in *italic* refer to tables.

EXPLORE THESE OTHER PUBLIC RELATIONS TITLES FROM ROUTLEDGE

Strategic Planning for Public Relations
4th Edition

by Ronald D. Smith

This innovative and popular text provides a clear pathway to developing public relations campaigns and other types of strategic communication. Implementing the pragmatic, in-depth approach of the previous editions, author Ronald D. Smith presents a step-by-step unfolding of the strategic campaign process used in public relations practice.

As a classroom text or a resource for professional practice, this volume provides a model that can be adapted to fit specific circumstances and used to improve effectiveness and creativity in communication planning. It serves as an accessible and understandable guide to field-tested procedures, offering practical insights that apply to public relations campaigns and case studies coursework.

Access the companion website for additional resources, including useful links, chapter overviews, a sample syllabus, and PowerPoint presentations. You can find the site at www.routledge.com/cw/smith

Applied Public Relations: Cases in Stakeholder Management
3rd Edition

by Kathy Brittain Richardson and Marcie Hinton

Applied Public Relations provides readers with the opportunity to observe and analyze how contemporary businesses and organizations interact with key groups and influences.

Through the presentation of cases covering a wide variety of industries, locations, and settings, authors Kathy Brittain Richardson and Marcie Hinton examine how real organizations develop and maintain their relationships, offering valuable insights into contemporary business and organizational management practices.

- 25 new and current domestic and international case studies specifically chosen for their relevancy and relatability to students;

- New "Professional Insights" commentaries where practitioners respond to a set of questions relating to their work;

- Increased emphasis on ethics and social responsibility;

- Fully enhanced companion website that is connected with the text, including Case Analysis Worksheets and PowerPoint presentations for instructors, and Chapter Recaps and Internet Resources for students. **www.routledge.com/cw/richardson**